DATE DUE

OC 20 '98			
NO 20 '98			
AG 5 '00			

DEMCO 38-296

SEEING RED

CHINA'S UNCOMPROMISING TAKEOVER OF HONG KONG

JAMIE ALLEN

ng Asia,
Pte Ltd.
1 Temasek Avenue
#17-01 Millenia Tower
Singapore 039192

ISBN 981 00 8083 2

Typeset by Indigo Ink, Sydney
Printed by KHL Printing Co, Singapore

For Helen
and
In memory of
John D Young (Yang Yilung)
1949–1996

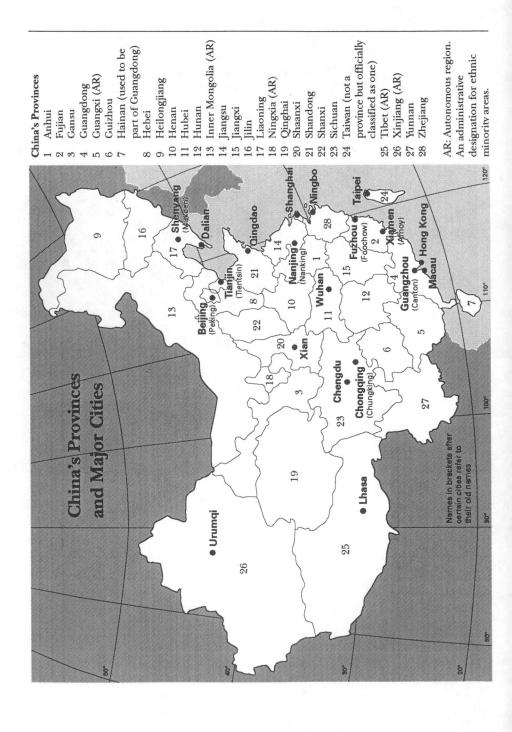

China's Provinces and Major Cities

China's Provinces

1 Anhui
2 Fujian
3 Gansu
4 Guangdong
5 Guangxi (AR)
6 Guizhou
7 Hainan (used to be part of Guangdong)
8 Hebei
9 Heilongjiang
10 Henan
11 Hubei
12 Hunan
13 Inner Mongolia (AR)
14 Jiangsu
15 Jiangxi
16 Jilin
17 Liaoning
18 Ningxia (AR)
19 Qinghai
20 Shaanxi
21 Shandong
22 Shanxi
23 Sichuan
24 Taiwan (not a province but officially classified as one)
25 Tibet (AR)
26 Xinjiang (AR)
27 Yunnan
28 Zhejiang

AR: Autonomous region. An administrative designation for ethnic minority areas.

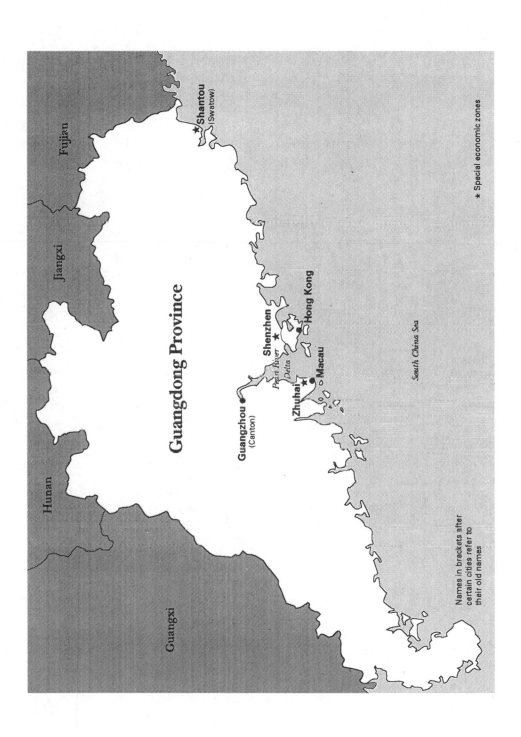

Guangdong Province

Shantou
(Swatow)

Fujian

Jiangxi

Shenzhen

Hong Kong

Macau

Zhuhai

Guangzhou
(Canton)

Pearl River
Delta

South China Sea

Hunan

Guangxi

★ Special economic zones

Names in brackets after
certain cities refer to
their old names

CONTENTS

A Note to the Reader

Some stylistic and structural points about this book require a short explanation.

Endnotes: Although traditional footnotes are not used in this book, a system of endnoting is. All quotations from published material, conferences or press broadcasts, as well as statistical data, are referenced by page number (in the notes section at the back of this book). No marker is put in the text. For example, to find the source of comments by Deng Xiaoping on a particular page in Chapter 2, turn to the notes section, look for the relevant chapter heading, and then for the page number.

This system means that readers who do not want to check a reference can read on uninterrupted by footnote markers; while those who do should have little difficulty checking a source.

Comments made by people interviewed are not referenced.

Figures: Almost all statistics are rounded. The few which are not are kept to one decimal point.

Appendixes: There are two detailed glossaries in this book. The first outlines China's united front and handover-preparation committees (1992–97). These committees are mentioned regularly in Chapters 3–5.

The second glossary gives a concise overview of each significant political party in Hong Kong—their orientation, history, manifestos, and contact details. The names of these parties also appear often in Chapters 3–5.

Acronyms: Because Hong Kong is awash with acronyms, care has been taken to avoid using them as far as possible. But the following do make an appearance:

Political parties and organisations

ADPL: Association for Democracy and People's Livelihood
DAB: Democratic Alliance for the Betterment of Hong Kong
FTU: The Federation of Trade Unions

ICAC: Independent Commission Against Corruption
ICCPR: International Convenant on Civil and Political Rights
MPT: Ministry of Posts and Telecommunications
NGO: Non-governmental organisation
PLA: People's Liberation Army
SAR: Special Administrative Region
TAC: Transport Advisory Committee

Companies

CITIC: China International Trust and Investment Corporation (used only, except in one instance, as a reference to its Hong Kong subsidiary, CITIC Pacific)
CLP: China Light & Power
CNAC: China National Aviation Corporation
HEC: Hong Kong Electric
HSBC: Hong Kong and Shanghai Banking Corporation (used only to refer to HSBC Holdings plc, the international federation of banks of which HongkongBank is a part)
OTB: Overseas Trust Bank

PROLOGUE:
A CHANGING IDENTITY

HONG KONG

After I began working in Hong Kong as a reporter in the late 1980s, I spent a lot of time travelling around the colony on assignment. Some jobs took me to the New Territories, the semi-rural bulge of land located between Kowloon and China. Although always a pleasant experience—the air was fresh and the vistas captivating—one thing always struck me as strange: the local maps I used to find my way around completely disregarded the industrial city of Shenzhen (which sits like a sombrero on top of the northern New Territories). The maps always left its entire area blank.

For China, this zone was a pride and joy—one of its most successful experiments in economic reform and the development of export industries. But Hong Kong stereotypically saw it (and still sees it) as a dusty frontier town with a bad reputation and gold-rush fever: a place that could make the free-wheeling British colony, despite its own insatiable love of money, seem holy and brilliantly governed.

With irreverent hindsight, perhaps the empty space on the map represented something more than disinterest or cost-cutting by tight government cartographers. Maybe it was intended to convey a sense of the colony as a distinct entity from 'all that over there' (ie, China). That is, Hong Kong as predictable, clear, safe and run by a benevolent British administration, and China as the opposite: chaotic, opaque, with an air of danger, and arbitrarily governed by semi-reconstructed communists. Hong Kong represented the future of China (or so everyone hoped). The rest of China still carried the burden of the past.

This *is* the sense of Hong Kong that the British administration most likes to convey. It is a place of responsible government, fiscal prudence, the rule of law, and 'positive non-intervention' (the laissez-faire rallying cry of the colony's economic policy-makers). It is also an international financial centre, one of the world's freest economies (so overseas think-tanks say), and a shipping, aviation and telecommunications hub. Hong Kong is the 'best business address' in Asia—where more than a thousand of the world's biggest multinational corporations have established regional headquarters to oversee their Asian operations. It has an open financial system that has attracted most of the world's largest banks and brokerages. And Hong Kong has a society that is well-educated, whose basic social needs have been taken care of, and which is becoming increasingly sophisticated.

Pictorial images of these developments are displayed again and again in the government's yearbooks. The latest, published in 1996, begins with a review of the past 50 years. Some of the contrasting pairs of photos are predictable, such as a comparison of the central business district skyline in the 1950s with today. Of course there are bound to be more tall buildings! More interesting is a pair illustrating the transformation of the Kowloon waterfront. In 1971 you could still see the original Kowloon–Canton railway terminus (now only the clocktower remains) as well as a line of docks and warehouses. Today on the same spot, in order from west to east, stand the Cultural Centre, the Space Museum, the Museum of Art, the Regent Hotel, and the New World Hotel and Centre. An impressive civic metamorphosis.

But there is, of course, more to Hong Kong ...

HEUNGGONG

Behind the cosmopolitan veil lies the main body of Hong Kong: the 95% of the population who are Chinese. Most can be described as Cantonese, a loose label for those whose parents emigrated from Guangzhou (Canton) or the various counties on either side of the Pearl River Delta to the north and west of Hong Kong (see map). Other pockets of socio-linguistic groups also exist, such as the Chiu Chow (from eastern Guangdong, near the Fujian border), the Hokkien (from Fujian), the Hakka (meaning 'guest people', from different parts of southern China), the Shanghainese, and others from central and northern China. For pragmatic reasons—clan links, safety in numbers and language—these different groups traditionally coalesced in certain districts. Hence, many Shanghainese moved to North Point, while many Chiu Chow went to Sheung Wan and Kennedy Town (all are districts on Hong Kong Island).

It is this 'Chinese-ness' that is most apparent on street level—not any sense of 'Hong Kong the international city'. This is the Hong Kong of cooked-food stalls (*dai pai dongs*), raucous crowds, cheaply built and densely packed buildings, and overworked taxi drivers who utter expletives with machine-gun timing and sound their horn at the slightest provocation. It is a place of mammoth high-rise housing estates built with much engineering pragmatism but little human sensibility; and squatter villages still laying claim to some hillsides (places that are infinitely more human than the estates despite their lack of amenities and rundown appearance).

This is the less rational, but more lovable, side of Hong Kong. It is a culture of superstition (much of which has to do with numbers), ancestor worship (incense at temples, the burning of paper money and objects, and ritual grave sweeping on certain days of the year) and a love of gambling (mahjong, the races, foreign exchange, stocks, Mark Six, the Macau casinos, whatever); a society in which people believe that luck can make a difference, as indeed it has to the Hong Kong economy, and where households wish themselves good fortune and happiness by hanging red and gold signs with the character *fuk* (pronounced 'fook') outside their tiny apartments over Chinese New Year.

Less salubriously, it is a place of triad gangs and entrenched organised crime, old people living in great poverty in 'caged homes' (bunk beds in tiny rooms protected with wire netting), and some perennial urban pollution. That Hong Kong society is as stable as it is, despite the great pressures it is living under, sometimes seems remarkable.

The Cantonese name for Hong Kong is *Heunggong* (pronounced something like 'hurng gong'). It means 'fragrant harbour', a nice name that has become a tired cliché and, unfortunately, an ironic description of the water quality in Victoria Harbour. The origin of this name dates back to well before the arrival of the British in 1841, when incense production was one of Hong Kong's principal agricultural activities, along with salt and pearl diving. The fishing port of Aberdeen on the south side of Hong Kong Island was once called

Heunggong, since it was the point at which the incense was loaded onto ships.

The word also forms the basis of *Heunggong yan,* which translates as 'Hong Kong Belonger' (literally, 'person'). Local identity has strengthened since the 1970s, when Hong Kong society started to become more stable and cohesive after the flux of the 1950s and 1960s (caused by, among other things, the closing of China, the migration of millions into Hong Kong, and the adverse though temporary impact of the Cultural Revolution on the colony). Surveys carried out by local academics typically find that about 50–60% of the population see themselves as Hong Kong Belongers, while another 30% call themselves 'Chinese' (meaning, from China). The rest either consider themselves to be both, or neither.

XIANGGANG

But as the colony prepares to become part of the People's Republic of China, a third element is being added to the mix in this unique corner of Asia—the *Xianggang Tebie Xingzhengqu* , the Mandarin name for the 'Hong Kong Special Administrative Region' (the first word also means 'fragrant harbour' and sounds like 'shee-ung gung'—the 'ung' rhymes with 'hung').

When China promulgated a new state constitution in 1982, it included a clause (Article 31) to allow itself to 'establish special administrative regions when necessary'. The 'systems to be instituted' in these regions would be laid down by new laws which took account of 'specific conditions'; which meant these places could keep their own systems and would not have to implement China's socialist system. (Like most of the fundamental policies developed for reunification with Hong Kong, this clause was originally designed to entice Taiwan back into the fold.)

What effect will this momentous change have on Hong Kong's identity? If 'Hong Kong' represents the international, cosmopolitan and British-influenced side to the colony, and *'Heunggong'* its local character and culture, then *'Xianggang'* represents the determination of the new sovereign to inculcate a sense of nationalism in Hong Kong. The Basic Law, the fundamental law for the new region, intones in its preamble: the resumption of sovereignty over Hong Kong fulfills 'the long-cherished common aspiration of the Chinese people for the recovery of Hong Kong'. The establishment of the region is also intimately related to 'national unity and territorial integrity'.

Signs of this nationalisation have steadily multiplied over the almost 13 years between the Sino–British Joint Declaration (the December 1984 treaty which formed the basis for the transfer of sovereignty) and the handover in July 1997.

First there appeared the organisational signs: the committees preparing for reunification and made up of prominent Hong Kong citizens trusted by Beijing and senior Chinese government officials. These invariably come with long names attached, as Communist Party organs do in China. One recent example was 'The Preliminary Working Committee of the Preparatory Committee for the Hong Kong Special Administrative Region' (usually just called the Preliminary Working Committee). As its name implied, it was to be followed by the Preparatory Committee, whose full name was: 'The Preparatory Committee for the Hong Kong Special Administrative Region under the National People's Congress of the People's Republic of China'. Thus one criticism that cannot be levelled at Beijing over its approach towards Hong Kong is linguistic stinginess!

As reunification edged closer, the symbolic changes became clearer: the removal of British colonial images from the crests and emblems of official bodies, as well as coins and stamps; the dropping of the word 'Royal' from the names of clubs such as the Royal Hong Kong Jockey Club and from institutions such as the Royal Hong Kong Police Force; and the design of a new flag.

Then just before July 1997 came a small advance guard of the People's Liberation Army (the remainder of the garrison came in upon reunification). And there was also the arrival of officials representing certain central government ministries in Beijing, and changes in the titles of some senior Hong Kong civil service posts: the attorney general became the 'secretary for justice', the chief secretary became the 'chief of administration', and the governor was replaced by a 'chief executive'.

The list could go on, but the point is probably clear: Hong Kong is well on the way to becoming closely connected with, if not integrated into, the system of government in China. Not having to implement socialism, as Article 31 implied, was never a promise that government in Hong Kong could remain bureaucratically separate from China.

Xianggang, its process of formation, its near-term future, and its effect on Hong Kong's political and economic identity is what this book is about. The basic ideas on which this book is based follow.

RECOLONISATION, NOT DECOLONISATION

Reunification will not change Hong Kong completely, but its impact will be profound. In politics—the most critical aspect of the whole process for China—there will be a myriad of changes. The new sovereign is changing the political structure to suit itself, including devising a new electoral system, and is repealing or amending laws that it does not like. Many of the latter restrict the political rights which citizens will enjoy as individuals or as members of groups, and which *Xianggang* in general will enjoy in its relationship with China. Politicians who thrived under the colonial system of appointment to the legislature and the Executive Council (the governor's advisory cabinet), but whose careers took a turn for the worse when popular elections were instituted in the 1990s, are being resurrected. And *Xianggang* will be lead by a chief executive (Tung Chee-hwa, a shipping tycoon) who is Shanghainese, not Cantonese, and who has no choice but to follow Beijing's basic priorities.

This is the price which Hong Kong is being asked to pay in return for continued 'prosperity and stability'. Indeed, Beijing links this phrase to its political imperatives so often that its message is unmistakable: if the region resists the reshaping of the political structure too vociferously, then the new sovereign will no longer guarantee economic prosperity (that is, it will not take responsibility for the consequences of any use of force employed to quell disturbances). But if current trends continue, Hong Kong will not sacrifice its economy in order to defend the full integrity of its political system.

The economy and society will be affected in more subtle ways. Although the economic structure will remain largely the same, at least over the next five to ten years, the main dilemma for existing vested interests is the proprietorial interest which mainland Chinese firms are showing in the colony. These firms have brought some good things to the colony, namely business opportunities in China and new listings on the local stock market. But they are state enterprises responsible to economic ministries in Beijing and, with the transfer of sovereignty, will come to wield considerable clout over economic issues. They will also contribute to a blurring of the distinction between the Hong Kong and Chinese economies. In future, the transfer of sovereignty will be seen to have had as much to do with economics as with politics. Today it looks mostly like a political spat.

As for local society, reunification will result in hundreds, if not thousands, of mainland officials and their families moving to *Xianggang*. Many more officials will travel to and through the region on business. In sheer quantitative terms, though, the most noticeable addition will be the arrival over a 10-year period of *at least* another 650,000 immigrants from the mainland. Local population growth over the same time period, in contrast, will be only 350,000.

The figure of 650,000 is based on the 55,000 mainlanders allowed to come in every year on what are called 'one-way permits', plus a conservative estimate of 100,000 children who would be eligible to come because their parents are *already* permanent residents in Hong Kong (this change is allowed for by the Basic Law). No exact figure for the number of children exists, but the government talks of around 40,000–75,000 being eligible almost immediately. Hence, 100,000 over 10 years is extremely conservative. (Note: By the end of 1996 about half a million mainland Chinese had moved to Hong Kong on one-way permits since 1979. This lower figure is due to a smaller number of permits being allowed before 1994–95.)

All of these changes have more in common with a process of colonisation than decolonisation. When Britain annexed Hong Kong, for example, it set up its own political system and imposed its own laws (although it allowed local Chinese customary law to remain). British companies used the colony as a base for their commercial exploits into China and around the region. And expatriates came by the boatload to make new lives. Hong Kong was gradually allowed more and more autonomy over the management of its local affairs, but defence and foreign policy remained in the hands of London.

More specifically, reunification is similar to colonisation because: Hong Kong was never given the choice as to whether it wanted to become part of China again. Yes, it may once have been part of that country, but for 150 years it was administratively and legally separate—and evolved a distinct political, economic and social system. China is not giving Hong Kong self-government, but a form of local autonomy. Beijing will take over responsibility for defence and foreign affairs. Mainland Chinese companies will make full use of their

new political clout to expand their business interests. And new mainland immigrants will make their presence felt within society.

The main difference is that China is not working with as clean a
slate as Britain had in 1841. Hong Kong is a thriving society with an
established rule of law and an advanced economy. None of Britain's
colonies in the nineteenth century had this; which means China is
having to tread much more carefully in Hong Kong than Britain did
when it took over. But none of this changes the essential political
inequity in China's acquisition of Hong Kong.

LOOK AT THE PARTY

Many foreign observers believe that what happens to Hong Kong
after 1997 will depend on who is in power in Beijing (ie, hardliners
or moderates). This is true to a point: when moderate leaders like
Hu Yaobang and Zhao Ziyang were running the Communist Party of
China ('the Party') and the Chinese government in the 1980s, policy
towards Hong Kong was not as harsh as it has been in the 1990s. Hu
was Party general secretary until sacked for his weak handling of student protests in December 1986. Zhao was state premier who took
over as general secretary when Hu left. But he too lost his job for similar reasons soon after the Tiananmen Square student and worker
protests in April–June 1989. Both men had been protégés of Deng
Xiaoping, but ran afoul of hardliners in the Party like Li Peng (and
it was in Deng's nature too to be a hardliner during a political crisis).

But policy towards Hong Kong was softer in the 1980s for a variety
of reasons that were not directly related to Hu and Zhao. One fact
was that reunification was still some way into the future, so Hong
Kong was lower on the agenda. More importantly, the Tiananmen
crisis had yet to occur, which meant the Party felt more secure within
China. Politics in Hong Kong was still largely 'colonial', meaning
direct elections based on universal franchise and real political parties had yet to come into existence. And Beijing had yet to witness the
spontaneous wrath of Hong Kong towards the 4 June 1989 massacre
(an event which many now refer to as an 'incident'). For a brief
period, even Beijing's supporters in the colony disregarded political
correctness and pilloried the Party.

Tougher action was deemed necessary after 1989—and came
quickly. Internal controls over reunification matters within the Chinese government were tightened; and a more conservative director,

Zhou Nan, was sent to head the New China News Agency (to replace his 'liberal' predecessor, Xu Jiatun, who had fled to the United States). A clause on subversion in the Basic Law was made stricter. United front work in Hong Kong was stepped up (see Chapter 3). And the two leading local democratic politicians—Martin Lee, a barrister, and Szeto Wah, a teacher and union leader—were branded as subversives.

The limitations of the individual-leader analysis is apparent from the fact that while Zhao Ziyang did not survive 1989, many of his close colleagues did, including Li Peng, Qiao Shi and Yao Yilin (all members of the Standing Committee of the Politburo, the centre of formal power in the Party). And, of course, so did Deng. So guessing what will happen to Hong Kong based on who holds which formal rank in Beijing begs the question: how widely should you cast the net? Policy was more moderate when Zhao, Li, Qiao and Yao were in charge. Policy became illiberal after Zhao left the scene but Li, Qiao and Yao were still around, plus a few new faces (including the new general secretary, Jiang Zemin).

A more relevant way to understand the general character of China's policies towards Hong Kong would be to emphasise the Party as the unit of analysis, rather than individual leaders. Individuals and factions may help to explain the origin of specific actions, but China's core policies towards Hong Kong are basically a product of both the Party's lingering 'communist' mindset (in the political arena) and its collegiate reactions to external pressures (such as 1989). Despite personality, factional and bureaucratic conflicts within the Chinese government, there is in fact a high degree of coordination and coherency in its Hong Kong policies. This partly stems back to the tightening of internal controls in the early 1990s.

Perhaps the biggest weakness with the leader approach is wishful thinking. In other words, its purveyors often invest too much hope in an individual and give him attributes he may not have; which merely leads to distorted interpretations and disappointment. Thus Qiao Shi, mentioned above, is described in the Western press as a 'liberal'. Yet he chairs a body that has been responsible for overseeing and making a series of decisions which will roll back democracy and civil liberties in Hong Kong (the body is the standing committee of the National People's Congress). Similarly, the 'moderate' foreign minister Qian Qichen has chaired two handover-preparation committees which have done the spade work for the rolling back of democracy and which report to Qiao's standing committee (as will become clear in Chapters 3–4).

READING IN CONTEXT

There is a tendency in Hong Kong to read the Joint Declaration and the Basic Law out of context. That is to say, to apply a reasonable, liberal and foreign interpretation to China's basic promises, namely 'a high degree of autonomy', the enjoyment of 'executive, legislative and independent judicial power', and the safeguarding of 'the rights and freedoms of the residents'. People want to read these promises as if they mean only what the words ostensibly say—that Hong Kong can have the same political system as it had before the handover.

Martin Lee, chairman of the Democratic Party, the colony's largest democratic group, subscribes to this approach—as indeed he has to—and has scored some political coups in the process. For example, on a visit to Washington in April 1997 he impressed upon President Clinton the argument that China's dismantling of Hong Kong's human rights laws contradicts the promises in the Joint Declaration and the Basic Law. After the meeting Clinton made this public statement: 'The agreement made in 1984 by China and Great Britain, which they sought the support of the US on when President Reagan was here, clearly commits China to not only the economic liberties, but also the political and civil liberties of the people of Hong Kong.'

This was good politics on Lee's part, but poor analysis. For if the two documents are read in the context of what senior Chinese leaders have said on the Hong Kong issue over the past 15 years, then it is difficult to come to the conclusion of Messrs Lee and Clinton (though the more one looks at Clinton's statement, the woollier it becomes). Comments by Deng in particular, and which have been echoed by other leaders and Party publications since, indicate quite a different conclusion: that neither of the two documents commits China to upholding the pre-1997 political liberties of the people of Hong Kong in their entirety. This is a sad fact, but I believe a correct interpretation.

Statements of cold fact which describe options being closed off don't go down too well at this particular phase of Hong Kong's history. Understandably, people want signs of hope or practical advice on what to do, not to be told what they can't do for however many more years and why. So there is an aversion, it seems, to looking too deeply into what China's promises to Hong Kong really mean. The fear is that the destination might be depressing, too ennui-producing. Politicians, especially democratic ones, are desperate to convey a sense that they can make a difference—and so launch into programs, action, and demonstration. But how can they make a difference, how can they help to preserve Hong Kong's way of life, if they lack a thorough understanding of the issues? This book contains no practical advice. It is just about the issues.

PART I

THE CHINA CONTEXT

CHAPTER 1

THE PARTY ISN'T OVER (YET)

Of all Mao Zedong's pithy slogans, the unsentimental notion that 'power comes from the barrel of a gun' is one of the most famous. Although concocted within the context of a guerilla war during the ascendancy to power of the Communist Party of China ('the Party'), the phrase has been used by many popular commentators to describe the Party's hard-nosed approach to governing during peace time. In this conventional view, it stays in power through its partnership with the People's Liberation Army (PLA). Deng Xiaoping, also not one to take a soft line in times of crisis, called the army the revolution's 'great wall of steel' and sent it in to crush the pro-democracy, anti-government demonstrations in and around Tiananmen Square, Beijing (and many other cities) in mid-1989. Had the PLA refused to carry out this gruesome task, the Party may well have collapsed.

Few would dispute that the army is, and always has been, a key part of China's power structure. The Party and the Red Army (the forerunner of the PLA) were virtually indistinguishable during the civil war against Chiang Kai-shek in the 1930s and late 1940s, and the war against Japan (1937–45), when the Communists and Chiang entered into an unholy alliance against their common enemy. After the communists won power, the army retained its influence. Even today it makes little sense to draw a sharp distinction between the Party and the PLA. They are in a symbiotic relationship, each providing the other with authority and protection.

Crisis has been good for the army's wallet, if not its image. The reward for its violent role in Tiananmen has been generous budget increases. In 1990 defence expenditure accounted for 8.7% of government spending, but by 1994 the ratio had reached 9.6% (of a larger budget). In local currency (renminbi) terms, the annual increase in 1990 was 15.2%, and in the following four years 12%, 12%, 13.5% and 20%, respectively. These allocations were well ahead of inflation for the first three years, and about equal to inflation in the latter two. They stand in sharp contrast to the period 1980–89, when the army's budget was cut in real terms. The formal budget is not the army's only source of funding: it also receives money from state spending on military industries and research and development, and from arms sales. And from its business interests.

Since 1989, the army has become more involved in affairs of state, domestic as well as foreign. At the first full Party Congress after Tiananmen, in October 1992, a general, Liu Huaqing, became the first military man to be appointed to China's power centre, the Standing Committee of the Politburo, since the Cultural Revolution. Around the same time it was reported that Deng had decided 10 senior generals should attend Politburo meetings as observers and that commanders of military regions could join their respective local Party committees.

Crucial though the army certainly is, force is not the only factor contributing to the Party's survival. Power may come from the barrel of a gun, but China's communists could not have survived for this long if military coercion was their only means of persuasion. Whatever moral stance you take towards the Chinese regime's treatment of its domestic opponents, it is impossible to ignore the way in which it has changed and adapted over the past 20 years. To use a modern term, it has 'reinvented' itself in response to its own past failures, the demands of the Chinese people for better government, and the needs of the market economy. Though it remains conservative, stubborn and autocratic, it has so far been flexible enough not to have become an anachronism.

How much longer the Party can survive is the question that everyone interested in China would like an answer to, especially now that Deng has died. Will a power struggle paralyse the central government in Beijing? Communism collapsed a few years ago in Eastern Europe and the Soviet Union—it must be China's turn soon?

In fact, communism has already collapsed in China, even if its political institutions have not. Most of the social and economic tenets upon which the socialist revolution was built—equality, public rather than private property, communes, nationalised industry, strong central planning, Maoist self-reliance—have been discarded or severely constrained. The Party skillfully dropped unproductive political dogma such as class struggle from its policy priorities, and forged a new and more acceptable version of 'socialism', one which combined economic pragmatism and markets with a reduced role for the central government in Beijing.

But speculating about how much longer the Party can live is a risky business, as even neophyte China-watchers know. During the turmoil and power struggles after Mao's death in 1976, how many observers truly believed that the Communists would still be in power in the late 1990s? When the Tiananmen protests reached their apex in May and June 1989, many foreigners mistakenly thought this could at last be the sounding of the regime's death knell (although the error was understandable given the similar conclusion reached by the beleaguered leadership in Beijing). After the Soviet Union imploded in the early 1990s, there was much discussion in governmental, academic and journalistic circles around the world about the possible break-up of China. To some, this scenario was virtually a certainty: economic reform and trade had vastly increased the wealth and autonomy of the country's coastal provinces at the expense of the 'centre' (ie, Beijing). It could only be a matter of time before the centre withered away.

Yet China of the 1980s and the former Soviet Union were very different, despite their shared ideological heritage. China was relatively richer, having done a much better job with economic reform, and had built its reforms on a more flexible, 'decentralised' economic policy-making foundation to start with (meaning that even under the old centrally-planned economy, the provinces had more input into policy-making than their Soviet counterparts). And the break-up proponents sometimes forget to note that the provinces and Beijing still need each other: for the coordination of infrastructure projects, the resolution of inter-provincial disputes, the development of a national financial system—the list could go on. Clearly, this complex and evolving country does not treat simple predictions kindly.

What this chapter does is to outline some of the main non-coercive ways in which the Party has responded to new political and

economic challenges over the past 20 years—and which have contributed to its survival. It is commonplace to say today that the Party
no longer has the legitimacy it once had as a revolutionary organisation, empowered with the mandate to transform China into a
socialist society. Instead, its weakened authority is based upon,
among other things, its residual coercive power over the population
and the fear among most Chinese of the terrible consequences of
political disintegration. These statements are valid to a point, but
they seem to imply that the regime is essentially stagnant—a distorted view.

Although the Party has failed to resolve some of the worst structural flaws in its current 'communist' hierarchy, such as the lack of a
clear leadership succession process and the absence of real laws governing leadership behaviour, it has not been inactive and inflexible
in its management of the economy (which is arguably the most substantial basis of the popular legitimacy it does have). Even in the
arena of politics, some factions within the Party have tried to promote limited reform (which does not mean Western-style, multi-
party elections, but rather reforms within the institutions of government). Many of the Party's responses to problems may not be
elegant, or even consistent, but the point is that this is an ongoing
process that has yet to reach its conclusion. In contrast to 1989,
therefore, the Party no longer seems in danger of imminent collapse
(that is, within the next few years).

Why is this relevant for Hong Kong? Because the survival of the
Party has a direct bearing on the way in which reunification proceeds. Its strategy for taking control of the British colony draws
heavily upon traditional 'communist' political methods, and the
impulses driving this process flow as much from the Party's need to
strengthen its legitimacy within China as they do from a national
urge to rectify humiliations suffered in the nineteenth century. Were
the Party to fall tomorrow, then communist organisations and networks in Hong Kong would disintegrate immediately. The method
and nature of reunification would be very different.

SHEDDING THE OLD ECONOMY

The economy of China today could hardly have been imagined in
the late 1970s. Rural reforms that started tentatively became wildly
successful in boosting output and productivity, at least in the more

fertile parts of the countryside. Guangdong, because it was near Hong Kong and the ancestral home of many overseas Chinese, won special privileges as the vanguard of national development. Being far away from the rest of the country, unforeseen problems or even complete failures could be contained, and the whole process stopped if necessary. This did not happen and Guangdong now dominates China's manufacturing-for-export sector. It typically accounts for around 40% of the country's total exports. Meanwhile, the rise of new enterprises in townships and villages helped to absorb much of the surplus labour no longer needed on farms. And the political acceptability of private 'individual' enterprises (*getihu*) allowed many people, especially in the countryside, to start their own businesses.

The general fact of China's economic ascent is well-known around the world. Less widely known are the details of the economic restructuring that has taken place. Chinese government numbers state that in 1978 the largest sector of the economy with a 48% share was secondary industry (general industry and construction), followed by primary industry (agriculture) at 28% and, lastly, the tertiary sector (transportation, posts and telecommunications, commerce) at 24%. By 1994 the composition of the economy comprised secondary industry virtually unchanged at 47%, tertiary industry moving up to second place at 32% and primary falling to 21%. Such a shift, particularly the fall in agriculture's share of the economy, was predictable in an industrialising and modernising economy.

More dramatic was the way in which the character of the different sectors themselves changed. In 1980 there were basically three types of companies operating in the general industrial sector. State-owned enterprises operating in urban areas accounted for 76% of the sector's total output, while collectives (state-owned firms in rural areas) were responsible for 23.5% of the output. The remaining half a percent belonged to the 'other' category, which included companies set up by foreign investors. 'Individual' private enterprises were virtually non-existent. But by 1994 the structure of ownership had flipped: collectives accounted for a higher percentage of output in the industrial sector than urban state-owned companies (41% versus 34%), while the shares for 'others' and 'individual' firms were 13.5% and 11.5%, respectively.

Economic growth in China is, to be sure, breeding its own family of problems, jealousies and tensions. Wages have gone up, but so have prices of food, transportation and housing. People resent the privileged access which the children of officials have to money-making opportunities. Rural workers are migrating in their millions to cities as their jobs disappear on the farms (because of increased efficiency in the agricultural sector). The financial rewards produced by growth have been unevenly distributed around the country, between rich coastal provinces and poorer inland ones, and between rich entrepreneurs in the cities and the mass of urban wage earners.

But these negative trends have to be seen in context. They are, for example, forcing the government to improve its management of the economy (one indicator of which is the way that Beijing has brought down the rate of inflation in recent years while maintaining high growth). And they exist within an economic environment that is moving in an overwhelmingly positive direction. Despite the ups and downs which China has experienced since reform began in the late 1970s, most people are much better off than they were 20 years ago.

There are many ways to measure this, both anecdotal and statistical. Compare the clothes people wear today, the food they eat, and the transportation they use with the dour dress, the monotonous fare and the primitive vehicles of the 1970s. Household gadgets such as televisions, refrigerators, hifis and washing machines are ubiquitous in urban areas. Having achieved their initial dreams, city dwellers now want cars, houses and overseas travel. In 1992 China's average intake of food energy per person was more than 2600 kilocalories (kcal) per day, which was only 8% behind Japan and above the Asian mean of just under 2500 kcal per day. India was way behind at only 2200 kcal per day. And China's per capita gross national product (GNP)—the total output of goods and services, plus net national income earned abroad, divided by total population—increased 10 times in nominal terms between 1978 and 1994, or 3.5 times in 'real' terms (taking inflation into account).

The latter statistic is measured in renminbi (Rmb). However, if you look at per capita GNP in United States dollar terms, as the World Bank does in order to compare the wealth of countries, it rises from about US$230 in 1978 to a mere US$438 in 1994. The disparity is due to the fact that China's currency has devalued significantly against the US dollar since reform began, from Rmb1.4 to US$1 in 1978 to Rmb3 in 1985, Rmb4.79 in 1990 and Rmb8.6 in 1994. So although renminbi income had been rising, it was worth less and less in US dollars. The distortions introduced by exchange rates are especially apparent in a comparison of China's per capita income in 1993 and 1994: although the renminbi figure grew in real terms by 10.2% in 1994, it actually fell in US dollar terms from US$508 in 1993 to the abovementioned figure of US$438!

The use of exchange rates is also controversial because they do not take into account what is known as 'purchasing power parity' (PPP). This measurement compares what can be bought with local currency in one country against what can be bought in another. Since the prices of daily goods and 'non-tradeable' goods (like haircuts and many services) are generally lower in China than the United States even after the exchange rate is taken into account, the PPP method argues that the correct way to measure wealth is to look at what Chinese people can buy with their wages, not to think of their income as so many US dollars. This is because per capita income may be much lower in China, but Chinese people are better off than the exchange-rate conversion method implies. In 1993 Vaclav Smil, a Canadian economic geographer, calculated that the purchasing power of the renminbi inside China was 'about equal to that of the dollar in the United States: one renminbi bought roughly as much food in Shanghai as one dollar did in Boston'. Although there is much disagreement over how to measure PPP, and how relevant it is to foreign investors, the method gives a very different picture of wealth. According to the International Monetary Fund, China's 1993 per capita income in these terms was the equivalent of US$2330. This figure may err on the side of exaggeration, but the basic point stands: wealth in China is greater than exchange rates suggest.

THE IDEOLOGICAL BASIS OF PRAGMATISM

One of the most intriguing features of post-Mao politics in China was the way in which Deng and his coalition of allies flexibly reshaped the ideological foundations on which the Communist Party's *raison d'être* rested, thus allowing for the radically different type of economic development just described. The mental gyrations undertaken indicate the dangerous position the Party was in, namely its need to change tack rapidly yet retain continuity with the past. For to discard its core goal of building a communist society would immediately raise the question, 'Why does China need the Communist Party?' Indeed, the Party has not dropped this objective. Its latest constitution (1992) begins with the declaration:

> The Communist Party of China is the vanguard of the Chinese work-
> ing class, the faithful representative of the interests of the people of
> all nationalities in China, and the force at the core leading China's
> cause of socialism. The party's ultimate goal is the creation of a com-
> munist social system.

What Deng and his allies did was to select certain ideas espoused
by Mao or during the Maoist period, and make them the core of an
adapted socialist ideology, one capable of justifying experimentation
with free markets and private production (which China's farmers,
who make up the bulk of the population, had started to push for in
the late 1970s). The issue of experimentation was critical, since it
meant that the planned economy would remain the foundation of
China's economic system, thus mitigating opposition from powerful
vested interests and leftists within the Party. It also implied that the
reforms could be rolled back if they did not work, and something
else put in their place.

The ideas chosen were the pragmatic troika of 'seeking truth from
facts', 'socialism with Chinese characteristics', and the 'four modernisations'. The first two were borrowed from or based on Mao, while
the third was originally a creation of Zhou Enlai, China's state
premier during the Maoist era and number two in the hierarchy.

Whilst building his reform coalition in the late 1970s, soon after
Mao had died, Deng began spreading the concept that to 'seek truth
from facts' was the 'quintessence of Mao's philosophy', as he told the
head of the Ministry of Education in 1977. Then in 1981 when the
Party re-appraised Mao's historical role, the official resolution stated:

> Seeking truth from facts. This means proceeding from reality and
> combining theory and practice, that is, integrating the universal prin-
> ciples of Marxism-Leninism with the concrete practice of the Chinese
> revolution. Comrade Mao Zedong was always against studying Marx-
> ism in isolation from the realities of Chinese society and the Chinese
> revolution.

In basic terms, the principle meant that the practical conditions
of the country should be the basis for economic policy, not inappro-
priate and idealistic dogma. For example, if farmers could increase
productivity by working their own land, and by selling part of their
produce to the state and part in free markets, then such a policy was
a correct one. This led to the erosion of the commune structure in
the countryside and a swift rise in rural incomes, which greatly

boosted the Party's flagging credibility at the time. Later it led to reforms in the urban areas.

How far was Deng stretching the truth? A long way. In Deng's defence, it is correct to say that Mao believed in adapting Marxism to China: the Chinese revolution after all was based upon the peasantry, not the urban working class, which was a very un-Marxist approach to socialism. Indeed, in 1938 Mao said:

> Today's China is an outgrowth of historic China. We are Marxist historicists; we must not mutilate history. From Confucius to Sun Yat-sen we must sum it up critically, and we must constitute ourselves the heirs to this precious legacy. Conversely, the assimilation of this legacy itself becomes a method that aids considerably in guiding the present great movement. A communist is a Marxist internationalist, but Marxism must take on a *national* form before it can be of any practical effect. There is no such thing as abstract Marxism, but only concrete Marxism ... Consequently, the Sinification of Marxism—that is to say, making certain that in all of its manifestations it is imbued *with Chinese characteristics*, using it according to Chinese peculiarities—becomes a problem that must be understood and solved by the whole Party without delay. (italics added)

And from time to time, Mao did adopt a pragmatic position on government policy. In the early 1960s, for example, he made explicit statements supporting the experimental contracting of land to farmers. In March 1961 he told the Party secretary of Anhui Province: 'Try it out! If it doesn't work, you'll do a self-criticism, and that'll be the end of it. If it works, and you can produce an extra 500,000 tons of grain, that will be a great thing.'

But Mao said a lot of things and often changed his mind. At heart he was an ideologue who believed in reshaping society according to his own revolutionary ideas, such as perpetual struggle and the 'mass line' (learning from the masses and then leading them). He was not a practical politician dedicated to responding to specific problems as they arose and having his agenda set by immediate objective reality.

Mao distrusted bureaucrats and professionals because of what he saw as their tendency towards elitism and attempt to entrench their privileged positions through the creation of social stability. And he became increasingly suspicious of motivating people in positions of power with material incentives, convinced by the early 1960s that such rewards were leading to the rise of 'new bourgeois elements', or vested interest groups, in the Party and society. Since the majority of farmers and workers did not enjoy access to similar material benefits, the trend towards inequality was a betrayal of the revolution. Stuart Schram, a veteran Sinologist, has written of this hardening in Mao's attitudes:

> ... whereas Mao had stressed, as late as 1959 and even 1960, the need to combine moral and material incentives, the latter were progressively subordinated to the former, and then condemned altogether as revisionist and immoral.

Hence, the post-open door notion that socialist economic policy was broad enough to allow private production, free markets, and the accumulation of profit by a small number of households, would have been anathema to Mao.

Deng of course knew that he was stretching the truth with his ideological reshuffling, but political expedience demanded that he portray the new pragmatism as a natural progression within Maoist thought. Kenneth Lieberthal, an expert on China's government, has summed up this paradox succinctly in his recent book, *Governing China* : 'By making "seek truth from facts ..." the core idea in Maoist ideology, Deng successfully utilized the Chairman's prestige to release China from the shackles of Mao's political dogmas.'

THE FOUR MODERNISATIONS, the third prominent slogan of the Deng era, referred to the concept of promoting rapid development in four priority areas as the way to carry the national economy forward. The sectors were agriculture, industry, science and technology, and defence.

With uncanny foresight, Zhou Enlai developed the idea as long ago as 1965 and made it the second stage of a two-stage, long-term plan for economic construction. Barry Naughton, a specialist on China's economy, summarised the rationale of the plan:

> During the first stage (1965-80), China would build a self-sufficient industrial base and be relatively autarkic—out of necessity, since it had few export products and little hope of aid from the superpowers. Zhou then envisaged China emerging from isolation around 1980, and beginning a period of accelerated growth and a renewed opening: this he called the four modernisations.

Not surprisingly, the plan was scuppered by the start of the Cultural Revolution in 1966. But Zhou, in what would be one of his last acts in office, relaunched the four modernisations concept in January 1975 at the annual meeting of the National People's Congress, China's quasi-parliament. Since he was too sick with cancer to oversee its implementation, the responsibility passed to Deng, who at the time was a vice-premier and Zhou's chosen successor. Deng incorporated it into a 10-year development initiative that he began orchestrating in early 1975. According to Naughton, this was a 'terrible plan': full of flaws, unrealistic targets and a reliance on the very sector (heavy industry) that was weighing down the planned economy. Perhaps fortuitously, Deng was purged at the instigation of the Party's leftists in April 1976, so his folly was put on hold. He did try to resurrect it after being rehabilitated in 1977, but it never took hold and was quietly dropped.

Ironically, a prominent Maoist also had a stab at making the idea his own, though in a somewhat oblique manner. Hua Guofeng, Mao's hapless successor, told a national conference in late 1975 that China could make a great leap forward in grain production by following the example of Dazhai, a small town in the poor, hilly province of Shanxi in north China. The town became the country's most famous 'model commune' in the 1950s by apparently achieving a huge increase in production through sheer hard work and self-reliance. In 1964 it was immortalised by Mao when he said: 'In agriculture learn from Dazhai.' Having praised Dazhai in his speech, Hua, who at the time was a vice-premier responsible for national agricultural development, claimed that the modernisation of agriculture could 'more effectively push forward and guarantee the modernisation of industry, national defence and science and technology'. Hua's apparent aim in invoking the four modernisations concept was to strike a compromise between Maoist orthodoxy on communes and economic pragmatism, thereby enhancing his claim to the leadership. Such a contradictary strategy was bound to fail, not least because communes were part of the problem (and Dazhai, by the way, was a fraud). Not surprisingly, Hua's time at the top was short-lived. Deng had him pushed aside in 1978.

After a difficult birth and a troubled adolescence, the four modernisations finally reached maturity as a national policy in December 1978. That was the month in which Deng inaugurated the open-door economic reform program, starting with sweeping reforms in agriculture.

THE DENG ERA (1978–97) has transformed the economy and society of China to such an extent that one might think ideology has no serious role to play any more. Pragmatism seems firmly in command, the country seems increasingly open to the West, and economic development is ongoing. If political ideas have any influence, they come not in the form of socialism but nationalism. This can take several forms: anti-Japanese; pro-reunification with Taiwan; or the more abstract concept of 'the new China', a strong and united country regaining its superior position among nations.

Yet ideology remains important to the leadership of the Communist Party. Just as Deng needed to cast himself within the Maoist tradition, so the current 'core leader' and state president, Jiang Zemin, a former Party boss of Shanghai, has seen a need to portray himself as a socialist theoretician on the same level as Mao and Deng. Jiang's much-publicised contribution is the idea that the Party should construct a 'spiritual civilisation' in China, an ideal that promotes a socialism free of corruption, inequality and avaricious leaders. This is his theoretical answer to the many social and economic problems created by 'Dengism'. Indeed, it is a political reaction against the Deng legacy.

Given the entrenchment in China of 'capitalist' ideas like the pursuit of wealth, and the grip which corruption has on the bureaucracy, many view this latest twist in the ideological tale with cynicism. How can Jiang possibly stem the tide? Not only does his theoretical discovery sound similar to the rather hollow campaigns which leftists within the Party launched against 'spiritual pollution' and 'bourgeois liberalisation' in the 1980s, the economic policies which he has endorsed will continue to fuel the fires he is trying to put out.

The point is to not focus on the attainability or veracity of these ideological claims, but to see them as part of a process of ideology negotiation within the Party. Deng was stretching the truth in 1978 when he claimed that the pragmatic notion of 'seeking truth from facts' was the core of Mao Zedong Thought—it wasn't. But what mattered most was Deng's ability to forge a coalition within the Party around his new canon and give 'communism' in China a new lease on life. Similarly, Jiang's ideas may be full of inconsistencies and ironies, but the Party will be stronger if it unites behind them. This is not a given since Jiang still has to emerge triumphant from the 15th National Party Congress in October 1997. If he fails, another leader will have to offer a better reinterpretation of the Party's core ideology. When the day comes that no one can, what then is the value of a communist party to China?

THAT VISION THING

Ideology is one area in which the 'third generation' leadership under Jiang has had to react to the Dengist legacy (the generation of Mao and Zhou was the first, and Deng represented the second). The other major challenge, as the third generation sees it, has been to bring more order (and equity) to actual economic development. Order means more rational policy-making, especially in the management of growth and inflation, with greater participation by the central government and a renewed role for central planning. Equity is an issue because the China left by Deng is increasingly divided between the haves and the have-nots, with inequality creating divisions on a social as well as a provincial level (the coastal provinces are generally much better off than those in the interior). This is of concern to the leadership less because of any inherent egalitarianism on their part, than due to its implications for political stability in China and the survival of the Party. In short, they are trying to bring a more coherent vision to China's industrial development.

What does this vision entail? Conceptually, the biggest change in recent years has been a policy of evening out development across the country. In addition to higher direct subsidies to poor areas and greater investment in agriculture, the approach has entailed downgrading the relative importance of geographic areas such as special economic zones and placing greater policy priority on national 'pillar industries' (machine building, electronics, petrochemicals, motor vehicles, and construction) which can be developed throughout the country. Foreign investment is allowed in these industries, but it is being channelled in ways which suit national economic planners—in contrast to manufacturing, property or service sectors such as retail and fast food, where foreign investors have a much freer hand. The goal of the pillar industry policy is to create a thriving market dominated by domestic companies that have become highly advanced through the use of foreign technology and capital. Since these companies are all owned by the Chinese state, and managed by people who are members of the bureaucracy, a good label for this new industrial structure is 'bureaucratic capitalism'.

In contrast, a central tenet of the Deng-era economic program, shaped at a different period in the country's history, was the belief that Beijing had to detach itself from economic decision-making at the provincial and local level if the productive forces of the country

were to be unleashed. This 'decentralisation' of power comple-
mented a policy of allowing selected parts of the country, including
the special economic zones in southern China and 14 'open coastal
cities', to offer special incentives to foreign investors and to keep a
greater share of their tax revenues for reinvestment locally. In addition to the rationale of containment (if anything went wrong the
damage to the Party's control could be limited), the policy was also
practical (China could not modernise its infrastructure in every part
of the country at once) and catalytic (allowing some areas to 'get rich
first' would trigger change in other areas). Deng also exhorted
coastal cities to turn themselves into 'mini Hong Kongs', meaning
nodes of trade and finance. He placed particular emphasis on the
southern province of Guangdong, just north of Hong Kong, and
Shanghai. While Dengism produced growth, it also resulted in two
especially nasty bouts of inflation (1988–89 and 1993–94) and over-
investment in certain sectors, especially property.

The more cautious tone of economic policy today, and the management style of Jiang and his close conservative cohorts—Li Peng,
state premier since 1988, and Zhu Rongji, senior vice-premier
responsible for the economy—is closer to the statism of Singapore
than to free-wheeling Hong Kong, while the pillar industry policy
follows the early approach to economic development pursued by
Japan and the newly industrialised countries of South Korea and
Taiwan. That is, government-directed economic development, the
promotion of 'national champions' in strategic industries, and
'import substitution' (tough import controls and the rapid development of local production). This may be conservative economics, but
anything less would be politically unacceptable in China today.

The motor vehicle sector offers a good example; indeed it was the
first pillar. Foreign imports have been discouraged through
extremely high duties, starting at more than 100%. Foreign investment is tightly controlled by the central government in Beijing: in
mid-1994 it announced a new car industry policy that included,
among other things, a two-year moratorium on new foreign joint
ventures in assembly plants. And the role envisaged for foreign auto
manufacturers will at best be a supporting one. An exception is
Volkswagen of Germany, which arrived in the early 1980s and produces the country's best-known car, the Santana, and has the largest
market share of any producer. It does all this, of course, through a

joint venture. Other foreign car companies with an established presence, although a much smaller one, include Chrysler and Citroen.

Despite the limitations, all the foreign majors, including the likes of Ford, GM, Mercedes-Benz and Honda, are drawn by the almost frightening potential of the Chinese market. By 2000, China's total production of vehicles (cars, trucks, jeeps, buses and other heavy vehicles) is estimated to have doubled or tripled. But the more interesting statistic is that while the country has a large number of people (1.2 billion), its vehicle population in the mid-1990s was a mere 10 million or so. This suggests a stratospheric upside.

One snag, however, is that few individuals or households can afford to own a car in China. Most motor vehicles are bought by companies, taxi fleets and government agencies. In response, the government is promoting the concept of a national 'family car', a smallish sedan within the price range of the nation's burgeoning middle class.

Another snag, for foreign firms at least, is that the pillar industry policy aims to streamline the chosen strategic sectors by merging the numerous and inefficient state-owned firms within them into fewer but more competitive 'mega firms'. In the car industry, for example, the plan is to remold about 120 producers into just eight.

Yet the pillar industry policy is not uniformly strict, as the telecoms sector shows. Unlike the auto industry, foreigners have been allowed wide scope in the manufacturing and sale of telecoms equipment in China—a policy that has attracted all the major international firms such as AT&T, Alcatel, Ericsson, Nokia and Northern Telecom. But foreign companies are largely forbidden from owning and/or operating telecoms networks, meaning systems for the operation of things like mobile telephones, basic telephones and pagers. Over time, it will be in services where the large profits are made, not equipment manufacture, hence Beijing's determination to keep the sector in local hands.

Out of necessity, however, the ban on foreign ownership and operation has had to be ever so slightly relaxed. Although China made a huge leap forward in telecoms development during the first half of the 1990s, Beijing conceded that the country could do even better with some foreign finance, technology and management expertise. Pressure has also come from within the government: Unicom, China's second national carrier, has been keen to tie up with foreign partners in order to build its business faster and compete more effectively against the country's erstwhile monopoly, the Ministry of Posts and Telecommunications (MPT). Unicom, whose Chinese name means 'United Communications', is owned by an amazing array of government ministries and state enterprises. The basis of its putative national network, and the rationale for its Byzantine ownership structure, are the many 'private' telecoms networks owned by its founders, such as the ministries of railways and power. In contrast to its surfeit of owners, Unicom has a shortage of funds and management expertise.

Resorting to its time-honoured technique of experimentation, therefore, the Chinese government opened the door furtively around April 1995 to limited foreign investment. The deal was not a great one: foreign companies could set up joint ventures with local companies to finance and build 'non-core' networks—mobile phones and pagers, not basic telephone systems—in return for an uncertain revenue-sharing arrangement with a local operator, such as a city posts and telecoms bureau. In other words, the joint venture would lease the network to the operator. From Beijing's point of view, this fuzzy compromise did not alter the ban on foreign ownership and operation, since both would stay firmly in the hands of the Chinese operator. Legal guarantees were weak or non-existent, since foreigners were not being given an equity share in the network in return for their investment and expertise. In case of trouble, they would find it hard to protect their investments.

These grey areas have bothered many prospective foreign telecoms firms, but not Singapore's government-backed telephone company, Singapore Telecom. It signed a deal in 1995 to set up a nationwide paging network with subsidiaries of the MPT in Beijing and the Beijing municipal government. Although subsequently delayed, network construction did go ahead. Another major firm to dip its toe in, although not quite as far, is Hongkong Telecom, the former monopoly provider in Hong Kong owned by Britain's Cable & Wireless.

Unicom, meanwhile, has entered into agreements with foreign firms for the construction of localised mobile phone services. None of these developments, however, seems likely to threaten the MPT's dominance over the country's core telephone system in the foreseeable future. On the contrary, competition or the threat of it, especially from Unicom, has forced the MPT to improve its performance and become stronger—which was one of Beijing's main aims in the first place.

NOT A MONOLITH

By grafting a centralist vision over Dengist decentralisation, the third generation leadership has imposed a greater semblance of structure on top of China's economic transformation. Similarly, it appears to have been able to bring one of the most intractable macroeconomic problems of the 1980s, namely inflation, under some sort of control. Prices went on the rampage in 1993 and 1994, in part due to a tour Deng made to southern China in 1992, when he exhorted leaders to push ahead rapidly with economic reforms. Many feared recession was just around the corner when Zhu Rongji launched an economic austerity program to curb the price rises. On the contrary, inflation came down steadily over the following two years without causing growth to stall. This achievement alone has bolstered the credibility of the current leadership, which in turn can only be good for the Party's political standing among the populace.

But it is important to remember that tough central government policies and one or two practical economic successes do not describe China's total economic reality. In structure, the country is not becoming a monolith, a massive and solidly uniform entity. It is more like a conglomerate, a heterogeneous mass of different pieces held together. Some provinces, like Guangdong, and city governments, like Shanghai, have considerable clout and autonomy within the national political structure. Many central policies are interpreted differently around the country, either because officials do so wilfully and know they can get away with it; or because the policies are not absolutely clear. A byproduct of Dengist decentralisation has been a general decline in Beijing's ability to enforce its will on the provinces through coercion or inspirational leadership, and an increase in negotiation between the provinces and the central government over policy and resource allocation. In fewer words: Beijing no longer 'rules the country' like it did under Mao.

Yet even under Mao, the centre never exercised the same degree of authority over China's economy as it did over the political structure. Susan Shirk, a political scientist who has written on decision-making in China, has compared China's former planned economy with the Soviet Union:

Compared with that of the USSR, the Chinese command economy was cruder, more decentralized, and more dominated by noneconomic, ideological considerations. The differences between the Chinese and Soviet systems had important consequences for their future patterns of reform ...

The Chinese central plan managed a smaller share of economic activity and managed it less effectively than the Soviet plan did. Beginning in 1951, soon after the communist takeover, the Chinese system became a multitiered, regionally based system in which much of the responsibility for planning and coordination devolved to local governments. Large, key enterprises were under the central plan ... Less important enterprises were left to planning and management at the provincial, prefectural, and county levels. According to two prominent Chinese economists, 'strict centralized management of the economy by directives, as under the pure Soviet model, has never existed in China. The "decentralizing movement" which took place in 1958 and has been renewed from time to time ever since has eroded central planning and its power to control'.

In other words, the decentralised character of the economy worked in the Party's favour when it began its economic reforms in 1978. Far from introducing bureaucratic relationships which were completely new, Deng was entrenching and developing old ones. There is a parallel here with Deng's references to Maoist ideology to justify his pragmatic economic program.

A more recent example of the contrast between apparently rigid central policies and flexible local interpretation can be found, again, in the telecoms sector. Despite the ban against foreign ownership and operation of networks, the reality on the ground is far more complicated.

All foreign companies that have put money into networks claim they own a share in the *physical assets* of these networks (the other owner is their Chinese partner). They typically claim that the ownership restrictions refer only to equity in the *operating company*, which *is* wholly Chinese-owned and leases the network from the foreign joint venture. And they steadfastly maintain that they do not participate in operation at all, since this is strictly against the law. Foreign companies will admit to having a contract with the operating company to maintain the network, since having built it they know best how to fix it (but this is a sub-contracting arrangement and, strictly speaking, means they are not involved in management). But even if the line between maintenance and management decision-making is maintained—which in itself would be hard in a developing economy such as China—the claim of foreign investors to enjoy part ownership of the physical network contradicts Beijing's broad ban.

The issue of operation is equally grey. For example, a foreign joint venture which is financing a mobile phone network for Unicom says the two sides will set up a working committee so that they can 'work together on the construction (of the network) and how to operate it'. Even if the joint venture's representatives on this committee come from the Chinese partner, it is inconceivable that the foreign company in question will have no influence over how the network is operated. Moreover, the foreign joint venture intends to set up its own 'finance supervisory committee' to 'monitor and supervise the financial picture of the operating units'. This would again appear to be a clear breach of the rules against foreign operation. A senior manager of the foreign partner says they will do their best to keep an arm's length distance, since the MPT will be watching very closely for any illegal behaviour. Nevertheless, 'Unicom would love us to get (more) involved, because they do not have the expertise and the technology', the manager says ruefully.

Given China's historic decentralised power structure, discrepancies between Beijing's wishes and local commands, and between national policies and specific exceptions, are to be expected and are more a sign of strength than weakness. Without such give and take built into the economy, the system of control created by the Communist Party would surely have collapsed by now—like its erstwhile counterparts in Eastern Europe.

THE DAZED LEADING THE BLIND

While it is fair to conclude that the Party has won for itself another lease on life through its sometimes surprisingly adroit (or lucky?) management of the overall economy, it would be wrong to give the impression that it is close to bringing all problems under control. In the interests of balance, and because it could cause a financial and social crisis in China capable of bringing the Party down, mention must be made of the especially intractable issue of state-enterprise reform.

Most state enterprises in China are inefficient, 70% are losing money, and many churn out useless or substandard goods (a few are efficient and viable, however, such as those which do business with Hong Kong). At least one-third are technically bankrupt. These enterprises are a holdover from the planned economy and are a burden on the state, mainly in terms of the huge 'loans' made by the state banking system to keep them alive (money which is usually not paid back). But they cannot be allowed to go under *en masse* because of the ripple effect that this would have on unemployment and social welfare: these firms are big employers—more than 100 million people in urban areas—and provide their employees with housing, medical care, education and other social services. The prospect of millions of workers losing their jobs, homes, and benefits, and then turning to the central government for assistance or against it in protest, is a terrifying prospect for the Party. It has yet to create welfare systems that could cope with such demands; nor could it use military force to put down unrest without incurring another massive loss of legitimacy similar to the post-Tiananmen days.

There is no quick way to modernise these antiquated factories. New money is needed for investment in machinery and training, but funds are either scarce (because of Zhu Rongji's anti-inflation austerity program) or the companies are not worth investing in. In fact, 'loans' made by the state banks are often limited to working capital, which is money used to run a business on a daily basis (to pay wages, buy raw materials, cover utility bills): in other words, just enough financial support to keep the enterprises afloat. Few loans are extended for the purchase of new equipment or other fixed assets, since this would be 'pouring good money after bad' and would exacerbate inflation. One solution to the state enterprise problem, therefore, is to keep the firms in a perpetual state of financial hunger and hope that they might start to change of their own accord. Obviously easier said than done.

Like a person falling down a hill, Beijing is grasping at anything that might provide a steadying force. There is the motivational tactic: hold out the possibility of a listing on a domestic or international stock market for those firms that have sufficient financial and management capabilities. This approach can be quite effective for the better run and more aggressive state enterprises, since Beijing deliberately keeps the waiting list long by rationing the number of new listings on the Shenzhen and Shanghai stock markets.

There is inspiration: choose a select number of the larger enterprises for special treatment and guide them through the process of change. An example was a plan announced in August 1996 to choose 20 big state firms as leaders in 'technological innovation'. Each would form a special division whose task was to improve their technological capabilities, either through their own devices or by seeking the cooperation of research institutes and universities. Each firm would also develop brandname products over the next 15 years and aim to become competitive internationally.

And there is the merger route: join loss-making state firms with successful ones, but only if there is a good business reason for doing so. The better firm will then, in theory, lift the incompetent one out of the quagmire. As of mid-1996, more than 600 mergers had been announced in Shanghai alone. One was between the country's largest chemical manufacturer, Shanghai Chlor Alkalai Chemical, and Shanghai Tianyuan Chemical Works. But how well these marriages really work, and how much scope there is for more of the same, is the subject of much scepticism.

In essence, Beijing is trying to help the larger state enterprises survive and prosper, while letting the smaller ones go to the wall (although it will not allow too many firms to go bankrupt over a short space of time). And it is counting on rapid growth in other parts of the economy, namely among private enterprises, township and village enterprises, and the ranks of the self-employed, gradually to absorb surplus labour coming out of moribund industries and fill the holes left in industrial output by bankruptcies. As long as China's economy maintains its current growth-with-moderate-inflation path, Beijing may get away with this strategy. Yet the best that can be said about state enterprise reform is that it is moving forward in a muddled and piecemeal manner. A less generous interpretation is that it is in a shambles.

THE SNAIL: POLITICAL EVOLUTION

China is a country strangely split in Western eyes: the door is open to international trade, foreign investment and even some aspects of Western culture, like music and food, but it seems firmly closed to liberal–democratic political principles. The Party remains highly autocratic, does not accept public criticism and discussion of its policies, and imprisons political prisoners. Although there exist some nominal 'patriotic democratic parties', with whom Jiang Zemin and other leaders 'consult' from time to time, the regime is adamantly opposed to the adoption of a Western-style, multi-party system with elections. Village elections do exist, and can include a choice of candidates, but they are limited in scope and effectiveness as a means of political change.

The Party has little time for liberalism, it is true. Deng loathed liberals and their passion for free speech and individual rights. Yet 'democracy' is another matter. In communist theory the Party is democratic because it represents the majority ('the proletariat') and because it operates according to the 'Leninist' concept of 'democratic centralism'. The word democratic refers to higher level officials consulting lower level officials on major decisions, with everyone being allowed to have his or her say without fear of reprisal; the word 'centralism' means that the higher level then makes a decision which all must follow whether or not they agree.

Not surprisingly, this concept has not allowed the sort of 'constructive criticism' that it seems to demand. As early as 1942, Mao defined it as a system 'in which the minority is subject to the majority, the lower level to the higher level, the part to the whole, and the entire membership to the Central Committee (of the Party)'. If the views of the majority and the top leadership always prevailed, what incentive could there be for lower level officials to offer dissenting, minority views? Indeed, Mao often persecuted people for their beliefs. A famous incident in the first decade of the People's Republic was the Hundred Flowers Movement of 1957, when Mao briefly encouraged intellectuals to speak out and give advice to the Party, only to clamp down viciously soon afterwards in response to their largely negative criticisms. The chief organiser of this 'anti-rightist movement' was Deng.

This narrow and hierarchical view of politics in China suggests there has been no political reform at all since economic reform began—a fact apparently confirmed by the violent crackdown on the Tiananmen protests. In terms of Western-style elections and civil rights, such a conclusion may be true. However, if 'politics' is more broadly defined, some new patterns do emerge. The *Oxford Dictionary* defines the word 'political' as 'of or concerning the state or its government', 'relating to, or engaged in politics', 'taking or belonging to a side in politics or controversial matters', and 'relating to or affecting interests of status or authority in an organisation rather than matters of principle'. The first and last of these definitions suggest areas where the public has experienced some political change in China, while the second and third remain out of bounds for the majority of the population. So what does political reform in China mean? And how has it contributed to the Party's survival?

FREEDOMS WITHOUT FREEDOM

At the most basic level, economic change in China has already loosened government restrictions on individuals, groups, enterprises and even parts of the Party itself. People are no longer forced to work in communes. Farmers now effectively own their own land and work for themselves. More people can choose their own jobs, can set up a business, and while there are still restrictions on overseas travel, they are fewer. Religious groups, although still under state supervision, operate in a looser environment. Enterprise managers have greater freedom to make production decisions. The decentralisation that has occurred within government has given lower level officials more decision-making power. And while public freedom of speech is not protected by law, people seem less afraid to express their views in private.

Perhaps the best way to sum up these changes is to say that while 'freedom' remains a tenuous legal and constitutional concept in China, particular 'freedoms' have increased. The examples given all affect the relationship between the governing regime and the people, so can legitimately be called 'political' in the broad sense. Not all are the product of deliberate reforms initiated by the government, but all represent change.

A veteran Hong Kong-based mainland journalist, who fled China after the Cultural Revolution, contends that the Party of today is not the same organisation as that which existed 30 years ago. Its slogans and objectives may be similar, but this has more to do with political survival than reality, since to change the slogans would be to undermine its mandate. While there has been little progress in the area of press freedom, at least the way people live is freer than before, he says, not to mention vastly more comfortable.

Although no fan of the present regime in Beijing, the journalist believes these factors provide a reasonably wide base of public support for the Party. While he does not believe China can maintain a one-party system forever, the organisation should survive into the foreseeable future for five reasons. First, it has already survived for 70 years and has 60 million members. This depth of experience and breadth of membership provides a foundation for its continuation.

Second, China has no 'number two' organisation that has the power
to stage a takeover or the ability to run government once in power.
'People do not like the Communist Party, but they still obey it', he
contends. More importantly, 'the history of China shows that every
change only brings war, suffering and death'. As for people in the
countryside—where he spent 10 years during the Cultural Revolution—they care less about who the 'king' is than that the king should
not change too rapidly. Third, and somewhat controversially, many
intellectuals remain loyal to the Party (despite great suffering within
their ranks in the past). 'People are willing to forgive the Party', he
claims—a view that many foreign observers would find hard to stom-
ach. Fourth, and most importantly in his view, the Party's road is now
'correct'. Relative freedoms have increased and people's quality of
life has improved dramatically. His relatives have bigger houses than
he does—in fact, they have houses, he lives in a small Hong Kong
apartment—and although wages may be lower in China, so are
prices. 'Most of my relatives have a better quality of life than I do!',
he said with mock regret, adding that this was unthinkable 20 years
ago. The fifth reason is simply the army and the public security
forces: the Party would vigorously defend itself against any serious
attack.

The outlook for individual political freedoms and rights, however,
looks pretty bleak in China. Beijing is unlikely to stop targetting
those strong-minded loners who publicly question its authority, nor
will it allow anything like a free press in the near future. Indeed, it is
doubtful whether such liberal rights could ever exist within a one-
party, Leninist state—even a partially reformed one—since they
would surely lead to demands for a multi-party system and real constitutional limitations on the present regime.

But an interesting area of change—although over the medium
term not the short one—could be the social level. China still lacks
independent community organisations and lobby groups (called
'non-governmental organisations' or 'NGOs' in the West) which
check and balance the government's power, provide an input into
the process of government, or perform various welfare functions. All
social organisations in China still have to be linked in some way to
the bureaucracy in order to become established and survive; they all
need the protection of officials. To borrow a phrase from social
science, there is virtually no 'civil society' in China. But over time one
might develop—especially if, paradoxically, the Party centre in

Beijing could turn the change to its own advantage. A useful function of domestic NGOs could be to keep a regular watch on local corruption, or help with the provision of social and medical services to the poorer parts of the population—jobs which the Chinese government cannot manage on its own. Chinese NGOs are never likely to be truly independent from government, but organisations could conceivably be formed which are at least semi-autonomous.

THE POWER TO HIRE AND FIRE

Little known, and rarely written about, are the organisational reforms instituted within the Chinese bureaucracy since the early 1980s—reforms which have facilitated the swing in the balance of power towards the regions (and therefore are justifiably part of the country's political evolution). The main example here is the cadre management system. Through this arcane medium, leaders in Beijing have traditionally wielded considerable power over the appointment of personnel to all the top jobs within the Party, the central and provincial governments, as well as major state corporations, banks, the army, the judiciary, universities, hospitals, and 'mass organisations' such as women's, youth and religious groups. The technical name for this is the *nomenklatura* system, so called because it was borrowed from the former Soviet Union. John Burns, a leading international expert on cadre management in China, wrote in 1987 that this system was 'arguably the major instrument of Communist Party control over contemporary China's political, economic, social, and cultural institutions'. Kenneth Lieberthal, an expert on China's government quoted earlier, has written more recently: 'Through this vehicle the party monopolizes the power to determine who will join—and who will be forced out of—the country's elite in all spheres.'

Central control of this system, although still strong, underwent a significant evolution in the 1980s. As the economy began to grow in both size and complexity, the Party found that it needed to recruit a far higher proportion of technically skilled cadres than ever before. Political loyalty and purity were clearly not appropriate for economic and logistical work. To be efficient, this recruitment process had to take place increasingly at the local level and be conducted by specialist personnel administrators, since neither the central government nor political cadres were in a position to choose people for technical jobs around the country. Local officials were also better placed to decide who should be promoted to particular posts. The decision to reform the cadre management system, therefore, was critical to the expansion and deepening of economic reform. Pressure for this change came from reformers in the centre, as well as provincial leaders, enterprise managers, and educational institutions.

Change began in 1984 when the Party reduced the number of appointments directly controlled by its Central Committee from 13,000 to between 5000–7000 (not including the army). This was achieved by limiting the committee's power of appointment to the most senior positions in central government ministries and provincial governments only. Before 1984 it had the right to choose not only these positions, but also the next level down in the bureaucracy; that is, the heads of 'bureaus' within ministries and 'departments' of provincial governments. As one can imagine, the traditional system did not always work well. Sometimes the Central Committee unwisely overruled recommendations from lower level officials, while at other times the process of appointment was a mere formality. Yet it vested huge power in the centre. Although this power was somewhat diminished after 1984, the Central Committee retained the right to be informed of the appointment of tens of thousands of cadres to secondary positions throughout the government hierarchy.

In 1987 the Party embarked upon an even more radical change—on paper at least. Late in that year the then Party general secretary, Zhao Ziyang, announced further reforms to the system at a landmark National Party Congress meeting (these congresses are convened once every five years and put their stamp to major policy developments). Zhao, a protege of Deng and a radical reformer who was deposed less than two years later because of his 'soft' response to the Tiananmen protests, stated that the principal aim of the new policy was to give government (not Party) personnel agencies greater powers over recruitment and appointment, so as to improve the professionalism and technical competence of government institutions. The reforms also envisaged separating the Party and government in other ways, such as abolishing supervisory Party 'core groups' in certain government departments.

It is necessary here to digress for a moment and define the difference between the Party and the government. So far this book has used the terms interchangeably, which is not unreasonable since the Party effectively is the government of China: all senior positions in the government are held by Party cadres, the Party has committees and cells in every government department to ensure the latter implement its policy, and major policies are decided by the Standing Committee of the Politburo (the seven-member inner sanctum of top leaders headed by Jiang Zemin) before they are refined and implemented by the State Council, China's cabinet. Moreover, the Party holds meetings of its Central Committee a few months prior to the annual gathering of the National People's Congress, China's quasi-parliament. In this way it sets the direction of legislative activity.

In formal terms the Party and the government, although joined at the hip, have separate institutions. At the apex of the Party, as mentioned, is the Politburo and its standing committee; at the top of government is the State Council. In Beijing the Party has a number of departments that fall under its Central Committee, while the State Council oversees 40 commissions, ministries, and agencies. There is much overlap in the work done by the Party and the government, however.

Below the central level, the two bureaucracies duplicate each other almost exactly. Party committees exist in each of the country's 30 provinces or provincial-level units, and at every level of government administration below that: prefecture, county, city, town and village. Party committees outrank government divisions at the same level. Hence, the Party boss of Shanghai stands above the head of the city government, called the mayor.

The logic for this duplicated system, which was copied from the Soviet Union, is control. The Party wanted to ensure that the organs of government did not develop independently of itself, because if they did then it would fail in its revolutionary and political purpose. Mao saw the Party's role as one of penetrating, integrating and unifying all parts and layers of government administration. Once it achieved this, a division of labour could exist between the Party and government without threatening national unity and the socialist movement. Needless to say, this duplication has been enormously wasteful of resources and created bureaucratic inefficiency.

The 1987 *nomenklatura* reforms were therefore an initial attempt to start separating Party and government, and lay the groundwork for more efficient government. Though radical on the surface, they were in fact loaded with so many caveats that their net result could only be mild. When introducing the reforms, for example, Zhao said they would not stop the Party from 'recommending' candidates for

posts in the government bureaucracy. Significantly, 'core groups'
would not be abolished in politically sensitive state ministries, local
people's congresses and mass organisations. In other words, no huge
change in the status quo was intended, just a few small steps forward.
Given the factions and vested interests within the Chinese political
system, this compromise was perhaps the best that could be hoped
for. As it turned out, the reforms were never implemented because
the crisis of 1989 strengthened the hand of hardliners within the
Party and sent the proposals to the deep-freeze—where they have
essentially stayed. The more 'radical' proposals were deleted in 1990
when the Party returned the *nomenklatura* rules to their pre-1987
form.

But what has changed in recent years is the power of central Party
leaders to manipulate the system. As the provinces have become
richer and more powerful, they are bargaining harder with Beijing
over appointments. Especially feisty are the wealthier and more independent provinces, such as Guangdong and Fujian in the south.
Poorer provinces, such as those in the interior, have less leverage.

Meanwhile, the development of markets and a private sector is to
some extent restricting the influence of the system, since more and
more people are looking for work outside the bureaucracy. Its 'scope
is shrinking', says Burns. It is also becoming more difficult for organisation departments in the Party and personnel administration
sections of government to keep control of all cadre files, since
people are moving around more.

With all the changes that have occurred in China in recent years—
decentralisation, expansion of the market economy, and so on—can
the cadre management system still be called the primary instrument
of Communist Party control over China's political, economic, social
and cultural institutions? The answer is basically yes—athough weakened, it remains an enormously powerful tool. There are no exact
figures for the number of cadres recruited, appointed and promoted
under the system by all Party committees nationwide, but Burns estimated that the figure in 1982 was at least eight million. This
calculation was based upon the numbers of 'responsible' people,
that is to say leaders, in all divisions of the Party and the state, as well
as municipalities, communes and enterprises across China. The total
is unlikely to be less today. As long as China has a communist party,
therefore, it will have a far-reaching *nomenklatura* system.

Incidentally, this system does have a human and informal side. Within the Chinese government there are numerous networks of 'patrons' and 'clients'; that is, informal bonds between higher and lower level officials. Higher level officials recruit lower ones as part of the process of building a political constituency, expanding their power, and for support when they want to implement policies. Lower level ones cultivate higher ones for protection and help in securing promotions. These networks may not sound unique to China; indeed, every political system operates around networks of people closely associated with each other and which do not necessarily correspond to the formal power structure.

But a couple of points are worth making with regard to China. In this one-party state where power is often wielded arbitrarily, the protection of a senior leader takes on an especially meaningful function. For example, Deng was sacked from his job during the Cultural Revolution along with many other top leaders. Unlike some of them, however, he was not severely persecuted or killed—because he had the protection of Mao, his main patron. Mao chose not to stop Deng from being disgraced, but he did ensure that his life was spared. (Zhou Enlai, by the way, was also a patron to Deng.) Although China today is not about to be revisited by another Cultural Revolution, the need for protection remains since the country's political system is still potentially unstable—although it may be protection of one's business interests rather than one's life! It should be noted that patrons do not always support their clients. Deng allowed Zhao Ziyang, the former general secretary and one of his main proteges, to be sacked and disgraced following the Tiananmen crackdown. Zhao has remained under house arrest ever since, while some of his advisors were imprisoned.

The other point is that with the weakening of Beijing's power in the post-reform period, and the complex bureaucratic structure of the Chinese state, central leaders have also been forced to bargain over policy and resource usage with provincial leaders to a much greater extent than ever before. A central ministry and a provincial government have the same rank within the bureaucratic structure, so the former cannot simply order the latter what to do. Most policy is therefore the product of huge negotiation and consensus-building between officials at the same or different levels. In such an environment, being able to count on support from a broad spectrum of lower level officials would clearly be of assistance to a senior leader with an agenda to push.

Patron–client networks in China also shape in powerful ways the make-up of the Standing Committee of the Politburo and the central leadership generally, including who gets to move up to Beijing from the provinces. Jiang Zemin, for example, was promoted to the top (by Deng) after his deft handling of the 1989 protests in Shanghai, where he was Party secretary. Since he lacked a constituency in the capital, Jiang began building one. In 1991 Zhu Rongji, former mayor of Shanghai was promoted to senior vice-premier (although by Deng, not Jiang). Zhu became a member of the Standing Committee in 1992. And in 1995, Wu Bangguo, former Shanghai Party secretary, became the vice-premier responsible for industrial development and state-enterprise reform. Jiang has also filled many less senior positions in Beijing with officials from Shanghai, while his protégés have promoted their protégés. Hence references in the media to the rapid growth of a 'Shanghai Faction' within the central leadership in recent years. But Jiang has not been able to elevate as many of his Shanghai 'clients' as he would like, nor have all of his successful choices been warmly received—as the next section shows.

PARLIAMENT GETS A MIND OF ITS OWN

The most public sign of political evolution within the central government in recent years has been the emergence of debate and discussion within the National People's Congress, China's nominal 'legislature'. Always derided as a rubber-stamp parliament, the congress has started to throw a few punches back. At its March annual meeting in 1994, a large minority of delegates abstained or voted against the Budgetary Law, which introduced a new tax-sharing system between Beijing and the provinces. More famously, in 1995 delegates failed to vote unanimously for two new vice-premiers, Wu Bangguo of Shanghai and Jiang Chunyun of Shandong, severely embarrassing the top leadership. Out of the more than 2700 delegates, 210 voted against Wu and 391 against Jiang. While this may seem mild by Western standards, it was a radical departure from the norm in Chinese politics. Jiang now has the dubious honour of gaining the lowest number of votes of any candidate for vice-premier. The votes went against the two largely because delegates from China's inner provinces were fed up with yet more coastal officials being promoted to Beijing; especially those from Shanghai. In the same year, about one-third of delegates voted against a new People's Bank of China Law. And reformist ideas have emerged from the once sleepy congress, such as giving delegates a real choice of candidates when 'electing' senior government leaders (normally there is only one per position) and allowing substantive discussion of policies and laws during its annual meeting.

The person primarily responsible for these developments is the congress's enigmatic and powerful chairman, Qiao Shi, who is also a member of the Standing Committee of the Politburo and is China's former intelligence chief. What such a person is doing reforming the workings of government in China is an intriguing question. Indeed, he has even gained a reputation as a 'liberal' among the foreign media for saying repeatedly that the congress should make greater use of its formal legislative powers and strengthen its supervision of government departments, courts and prosecuting bodies.

As the 'highest organ of state power', the congress has an array of formal powers. The state constitution says that only it can elect or 'decide on' people for the posts of president, vice-president, vice-premiers, ministers, the chairman of the Central Military Commission, and so on. It does not have the crucial power of nomination for these posts—this is vested in the Party—hence its rubber-stamp reputation. But it can vote against a candidate and, on paper, has the right to remove from office any of the senior leaders it nominally puts there.

The congress carries another 'sting'. Its standing committee, made up of the 19 most senior members, is supposed to supervise the work of the highest central government organs such as the State Council—and the Central Military Commission—and can annul rules, regulations and decisions made by the State Council but which contravene the Chinese state constitution (as distinct from the Party constitution).

These powers are, of course, fairly meaningless. It is highly unlikely that a majority of congress delegates would ever independently vote against a candidate for high state office, or seek to remove someone from office, since such action would undoubtedly cause a constitutional crisis and undermine the Party. Delegates owe their positions to the Party machine, so there is an inbuilt correction mechanism to any disobedience.

As for the powers of the congress standing committee, they are hollow because constitutional legality means less in China than real power—and in the Party–government hierarchy, power clearly flows downwards from the Standing Committee of the Politburo to the State Council to the National People's Congress. It is not surprising to find that on average the political seniority of the standing committee's 19 members is below that of the officials they are supervising (with the exception of Qiao, who ranks third in the leadership hierarchy after Jiang Zemin and Li Peng).

So what is Qiao up to? Much speculation among foreign observers falls into the old and worn power-struggle model. This sees just about everything that happens in Beijing as a skirmish in the constant battle of Party faction against Party faction. Hence Qiao-the-moderate is trying to sharpen his spear for the inevitable dual against Jiang-the-conservative in the post-Deng era. By encouraging the congress to be disobedient, Qiao is distancing himself from Jiang and Li Peng. There is no doubt some truth in this, since Qiao's career in intelligence sits oddly with his current image as a liberal. He must have a personal political motive for strengthening the congress, and it is known that he differs from Jiang on questions of ideology and policy. But it does not necessarily follow that Qiao wants Jiang's job. He may want to be the man who pulls the strings while letting others have the titles, just as Deng did.

The other possibility is that Qiao really does want to strengthen China's legislative and policy-making processes, since he seems to understand the importance of predictable laws and regulations for China's continuing economic development. One of his targets may also be corruption, which can only be brought under control in China if checks and balances are put in place. As long as one party holds all the political power, and law is subservient to the ruling regime, bribery and fraud will continue because officials only become accountable for their actions when Beijing decides to launch an anti-corruption drive.

THE NEXT SURPRISE?

The death of Mao in 1976 provided the Party with the opportunity to begin sweeping away counterproductive ideology, hardline leftist leaders, and unproductive economic policies shortly afterwards. The Party really had no choice but to make these changes, since its own legitimacy was at stake and the country was crying out for change. In the 20 years since, China's ruling regime has arguably given the country better government. Many would say it is still not as good as it needs to be—and that is undoubtedly correct. But the government is better than before in the sense that it is more responsive to people's material needs and has improved its management of the economy. This is one way in which it has been able to extend its 'right to rule'. The other ways include the use of force, as in 1989, and the lack of any single organisation that could challenge the Party.

Assuming that no external cataclysm, such as an international financial crisis or a war, knocks China off balance, it is entirely possible that the country will still have a communist party in charge in the early years of next century. But if the Party wants to ensure its longer term survival then it may well need to take another bold step, as it did in the late 1970s under Deng; though this time in the area of political reform. This does not imply the sort of sweeping democratic reforms that many foreigners would like to see, since such reforms do not appear to be at the top of the political agendas of most Chinese at this stage in the country's development (and certainly is not on the Party's agenda—except in small doses, such as harmless village elections). Instead, it means a resolution of endemic problems that affect the average person and the average businessman, namely official corruption and too much bureaucracy.

Resolving these problems will require at least some form of government reform; and almost certainly a separation to some degree of Party and government. For without an effective check-and-balance mechanism built into the system—more powerful than the current one in which the Party tries to police itself—how can corruption be brought under control? And the problems of institutional duplication between Party and government, plus the waste of resources this entails, could only be resolved by reforming their relationship.

The more conservative leaders would, of course, resist any major change in the Party–government structure. But clearly there are some within the Party who believe in experimenting with reform, as the 1987 *nomenklatura* proposals showed. As in the late 1970s, when the leadership was forced by circumstance to institute change, so the same might happen over the next few years. Pressure for more efficient government—perhaps even a neutral 'civil service'—will continue to flow from the demands of an increasingly complex economy; as could pressure for other sorts of reform, such as a loosening of government controls over social organisations. Political reforms of this sort could at some future time be justified within the Party as a necessary component of economic progress, just as the *nomenklatura* reforms in the 1980s were and the National People's Congress reforms of the 1990s have been. Indeed, the 'political' reform which has occurred in China over the past 20 years has had a strong economic rationale. The same will surely be true in future.

A key question is whether the death of Deng in early 1997 has opened up new possibilities for the current third-generation leadership—just as Mao's passing away did for Deng's (second) generation. It surely will, although perhaps not straight away and probably in ways no one can fully appreciate today. The best bet is that it will be a fourth-generation leader, rather than Jiang Zemin, who unveils the Party's next big surprise. Jiang is a conservative, so for him to launch a major political initiative would be highly unusual. Although he may do some small things.

PART II

THE POLITICAL TAKEOVER OF HONG KONG

CHAPTER 2

PAPER TIGER

The Basic Law, Hong Kong's post-reunification constitution, is an eclectic document. Promulgated in April 1990, it begins with the sort of preamble one expects from the Communist Party of China, full of patriotic sentiment and long memory: 'Hong Kong has been part of the territory of China since ancient times …'. It then proceeds to lay down, in nine chapters, three annexes and some additional 'decisions', how China will govern its new Special Administrative Region (the formal administrative label for Hong Kong). One section is copied, almost verbatim, from China's own state constitution. Large swathes show the hand of the country's political commissars. And the part dealing with the economy elaborates on principles identical to those of the 1984 Sino–British Joint Declaration on Hong Kong, which bears the marks of the British officials who helped to draft it. A constitution for all seasons? For China, yes. Not for Hong Kong.

A selective cross-cut reveals the document to be favourable to business, fairly reassuring to religious organisations and, believe it or not, practitioners of traditional Chinese medicine, and alarming with regard to political freedoms. To elaborate briefly, the Basic Law leaves the essence of Hong Kong's capitalist economy in place. Religious groups are allowed to worship without interference as long as they do not get involved in politics. Chinese medicine, largely ignored as a legitimate sector by the British administration until around 1994, is promised equal standing next to Western medicine. And a draft article prohibiting treason and subversion was unilaterally expanded, and sharpened, by the Chinese government after June 1989.

The overwhelming public response to the Basic Law has been either disinterest or disappointment, leading to a low level of public knowledge about what this constitution actually says. Anecdotal evidence suggests that few people have read the document and that this malaise has nothing to do with education or occupation. It is as inscrutable to business consultants, non-political journalists and lawyers, as to housewives, shop-owners and taxi drivers. Hong Kong people are hardly unique on this score. How many citizens of federal systems and republics around the world have read their own country's constitution? Yet in Hong Kong's case this situation is disturbing, given the momentous change upon it.

More surprising is the ignorance shown by some well-intentioned local politicians. To legitimate Hong Kong's nascent democratic development, and to speed its progress, some democratic politicians hold up Article 45 of the Basic Law, which states that the chief executive (the post-1997 equivalent of the governor) will ultimately be elected by universal suffrage. This is only half true, since the clause also says that candidates for election will have to be nominated by a 'broadly representative nominating committee in accordance with democratic procedures'. In Beijing-speak, this means that a loyal, China-appointed committee will suggest names, probably after local 'consultation'. The picture changes colour markedly.

Surveys generally confirm the negative impressions most people have of the Basic Law. One of the more credible is done twice yearly by the Hong Kong Transitions Project at the Baptist University. In 1994, when a bitter argument between China and Britain over democratic development in Hong Kong reached a crescendo, the project asked 636 people the question: 'How much do you trust the PRC [Chinese] government to interpret the Basic Law in the best interest of the Hong Kong people?' Only 4% indicated strong trust, which Michael DeGolyer, director of the project, called a 'nearly invisible' amount. Another 15% had fair trust, while 31% had slight trust and 42% had no trust. Only 8% didn't know, an atypically low figure for this sort of survey.

Yet as 1997 loomed, more and more people, especially politicians, were saying that the Basic Law had to be made to work. The implication was that it was the only post-reunification constitutional foundation Hong Kong had. If it was not implemented, how would Hong Kong be ruled? If no one in Hong Kong treated it with any respect, why should China bother to do so? (Those who have been fairly sure the Basic Law cannot work have emigrated—more than half a million people. The number would probably be higher if more people had the skills or money to enter another country.)

Hong Kong's pro-China politicians, of course, have always been vociferous believers in the Basic Law and China's good intentions. Pro-business groups have increasingly become so. But what is particularly interesting is the way in which members of the democratic lobby have shifted from harsh attack to a more 'constructively critical' position on the eve of reunification. The vice-chairman of the Democratic Party, Anthony Cheung, wrote a patriotic article in early 1996 in which he affirmed the party's recognition of the Basic Law (and the Chinese state constitution for that matter). Quoting from his party's manifesto, Cheung said: 'The party stands firm that Hong Kong is part of China, supports Hong Kong's return to China and opposes any trend of estrangement and separatism.' Hardly the language of a fire-breathing democrat (but then Cheung has always been an ultra-moderate next to his uncompromising fellow leaders, Martin Lee, a barrister, and Szeto Wah, a teachers' union leader). He added that the party wanted to see both constitutions amended to 'achieve safeguards for democracy, freedom, human rights and the rule of law'. This would not be possible in China's case without undermining the current structure of power, which explains Beijing's deep loathing for the Democratic Party. Cheung also declared that his party's way was the cause of 'democratic reintegration', a blend of nationalism and democracy. While one can appreciate the extremely difficult position the Democratic Party is in —trying to love China and oppose its ruling regime at the same time—this awkward compromise is unlikely to make the party any more popular in Beijing. Meanwhile, a few months earlier, Christine Loh, an independent democratic legislator and another one-time critic of the Basic Law, published a booklet in which she stated: 'The Joint Declaration and the Basic Law represent solemn promises made to the people of Hong Kong ... Both China and Hong Kong should put their trust in these documents.' Loh also wants to see the law amended along more democratic lines.

In light of this contradiction between the public and their politicians, how seriously should the Basic Law be taken? Not seriously enough to believe that the Communist Party will follow it to the letter (the Party has already ignored stipulations it does not like) or even in spirit. The law has none of the authority, say, of the United States constitution, which sought to create a democratic society. Not even the Chinese state constitution falls into this class, since it is more a statement justifying the current structure of power in China than a vision of what the country should become. Yet the Basic Law is worth reading carefully because it reveals a great deal about the strategy China is using in its takeover of Hong Kong, how it views its relationship with the colony, and what changes may occur in the future.

THE POWER OF WORDS

One of the first steps in any transfer of sovereignty over a territory must surely be to persuade those affected that the change is in their best interest. Judging by the lack of faith the public have in Beijing's ability to implement the Basic Law, you might think the new sovereign had failed to win over the colony to the idea of reunification. What undermines such a simple conclusion is the paradoxical way in which people want to believe in China's core principles for ruling Hong Kong, despite their inherent suspicions of the Communist Party and their unfamiliarity with the details of the Basic Law. In just about every public discussion or report on 1997 in almost every newspaper, magazine, radio or television show, or academic publication, one or other of the following principles from Hong Kong's future constitution will be repeated, repeated and repeated again. 'One country, two systems.' 'Hong Kong people ruling Hong Kong.' 'No change (in the capitalist system) for 50 years.' And, with somewhat lesser conviction, 'A high degree of autonomy.'

Although reduced to the level of cliché, these slogans have been highly successful in setting the terms of the debate over Hong Kong. When most people talk about 1997 they use the language that China has chosen almost exclusively—even when their better judgment and the evidence before their eyes contradicts it. The four slogans represent powerful ideas that have greatly limited the boundaries of thought. When Donald Tsang, Hong Kong's financial secretary, sat next to Jiang Zemin at a banquet in November 1995 he persuaded China's president to give him a 'letter of guarantee' of Hong Kong's future. Jiang wrote three phrases on a menu and signed it. They were, in order, 'Hong Kong people ruling Hong Kong', 'one country, two systems', and 'maintain stability and prosperity'. Tsang proudly presented this written assurance to the Hong Kong press and the following day it was gladly splashed across the news like a sign from heaven.

Take 'one country, two systems', the most ubiquitous slogan of all. Many people in Hong Kong have doubts about it, yet no contending phrase has emerged within Hong Kong to describe better the post-1997 relationship between the region and its motherland. 'One country, two converging systems' would be a more accurate representation of reality, especially as time passes and China develops. Hong Kong has been reintegrating with southern China for almost 20 years, and more recently with eastern and northern China. Social and economic influences flow both ways across an increasingly porous border. Hong Kong people have been buying property and working in the special economic zone of Shenzhen, just to the north, for years. Within such a fluid economic context, how can China possibly promise that Hong Kong's entire social, economic and political system will be preserved in amber? The notion of two systems, after all, means two distinct systems. Yet the concept has retained credibility because people, understandably, desperately want to believe in it and officials on all sides keep repeating it. And because constant repetition of it crowds out more sensible and deeper discussion.

Likewise the phrases 'Hong Kong people ruling Hong Kong' and 'No change for 50 years', which are chanted over and over in public like Buddhist mantras. The first is supposed to mean that only local people can participate in government. The second that Hong Kong can keep its current way of life for half a century. But under the Basic Law the scope of the 'Hong Kong people' category can broaden over time. It is a far more malleable concept than it appears. Nor should the 50-year promise be taken literally either. No government can possibly promise anything into the distant future; especially not China, which is itself being transformed. In any case, with the market economy rapidly eroding the country's socialist planned economy, the promise not to take Hong Kong down this latter path is surely of little practical value.

Practically, it would be more honest to talk about 'China ruling Hong Kong' and to say 'Change has already started'. Beijing has, for example, been dictating terms to the Hong Kong government on infrastructure development since late 1989, when the colony's new airport and port were first announced. It set up an appointed Provisional Legislature in December 1996 that took over from the previous elected legislature on 1 July 1997. The provisional body will pass laws that create a different sort of political and electoral system from the one Hong Kong had before the handover. Although not specifically provided for in the Basic Law, the Provisional Legislature was been deemed 'legal' by a flexible interpretation of the constitution (this legislature is covered in detail in following chapters). Meanwhile, even if the titular figureheads and the senior civil servants of the future Hong Kong government are local people, it is improbable that Beijing and other provincial governments, especially Guangdong, will not seek to influence policy-making in Hong Kong; Guangdong, for example, is keen to include the Hong Kong economy in its long-term planning process. Whether or not this is politically desirable, there are good economic arguments for the two sides cooperating more closely on cross-border and regional infrastructure development, since the dangers of duplication and poor planning are already apparent. Cooperation has, indeed, already started.

The least convincing of the four slogans is 'a high degree of autonomy'. Unlike the others, which appear to mean one thing only, this principle is open to very wide interpretation from the start. 'Two systems', 'Hong Kong people ruling' and '50 years' all have a numeric or demographic certainty about them. 'A high degree of autonomy' begs the questions—what is a 'high degree' and what is 'autonomy'?

Some mainland legal experts have tried to fill in the gaps by outlining what China means by 'autonomy'. Xiao Weiyun, a member of the group which drafted the Basic Law, listed four things. Autonomy does not mean Hong Kong has the power to get involved in issues concerning national sovereignty or other parts of China. Hong Kong will have 'regional autonomy', which is not the same as national autonomy or the sort of autonomy that federal systems give their states. All the powers of the future Special Administrative Region are conferred by Beijing; the region cannot define its own autonomy. Lastly, the region can only use its powers within its own territory; it cannot interfere with matters outside this geographic area (except in certain limited ways as allowed for by the Basic Law).

Clarifications from Chinese officials on China's policies towards Hong Kong tend to raise as many questions as they answer. If all powers of autonomy are conferred by Beijing, does this mean Beijing can take them back at will? And how can Hong Kong realise regional autonomy without sometimes infringing upon national sovereignty?

For example, Hong Kong has the right to elect its own delegates to the National People's Congress from 1998 onwards. This means Hong Kong will be involved in some national issues.

Political autonomy to people in Hong Kong ideally means something more definite: guaranteed self-government, with the occasional involvement of Beijing in foreign affairs and defence. The sort of autonomy that Hong Kong has been told it will get is qualitatively different from the autonomy that provinces and special economic regions enjoy in China. Hong Kong will remain capitalist. China will remain socialist (which in practice means political control by the Communist Party). China claims it will not send officials to run Hong Kong and has promised that the Special Administrative Region will continue to have an independent judiciary, its own civil service, and a democratically elected legislature.

How can Beijing guarantee this sort of autonomy when no part of China enjoys the clearly defined and constitutionally protected local government of states in a federal system? Many provinces and counties have gained a lot more autonomy as a result of economic reform—some of these powers have been granted formally by Beijing, others were grabbed by the provinces themselves. But these developments are extensions and adaptations of the current system of government in China. They may be the start of a new political economy, but China is still a long way from the formal federal system that Hong Kong would like. The special economic zones, for example, have greater autonomy than most parts of the country, but even they are subject to policies being imposed at Beijing's whim (such as tariff changes on imports and a growing threat to drop the zones' tax privileges). The main point is that China has never worked out a clear and binding division of power between the regions and the capital, and is unlikely to do so in the near future.

But Hong Kong people grew to doubt 'a high degree of autonomy' not because of confusing legalistic arguments, but as a result of the political crisis in 1989 and the Communist Party's subsequent outburst of anger towards alleged subversives in the colony (namely democrats such as Martin Lee and Szeto Wah, and an alliance of democratic groups formed at the time to help dissidents in China). Even the apolitical became worried about the extent of the freedom they would enjoy as citizens of the Special Administrative Region.

Surely of all China's principles this one should have been discarded long ago by those politicians and intellectuals who debate the 1997 issue in Hong Kong and replaced with something like 'limited autonomy', 'autonomy with Chinese characteristics' or 'narrow administrative autonomy'? But it has survived, appearing often in books and articles. Even the colony's democrats lean on the phrase. Martin Lee used it in an interview with a Hong Kong legal magazine in September 1995. In response to a question about whether China would respect Hong Kong's autonomy out of economic self-interest, Lee said (in part):

> If the Chinese leaders feel confident about their own positions then there may well be a 'high degree of autonomy' and sufficient freedom given to Hong Kong. However, if Chinese politicians believe their positions are in jeopardy they will hold Hong Kong tightly in their grip.

Some readers might wonder why the average Hong Kong person shows a tendency to believe in 'one country, two systems' and 'Hong Kong people ruling Hong Kong' while lacking faith in 'a high degree of autonomy'. How can the first two work without the third? They cannot. But it is possible to imagine a scenario in which Hong Kong retains a social and economic system that is quite different from the norm in China, where Hong Kong people hold the top jobs in government and yet in which the Special Administrative Region government is forced to get Beijing's approval before deciding major policies (especially in the area of political reform). In such an environment none of China's promises enshrined in the Basic Law would be fully realised, but Hong Kong might still believe its total system was sufficiently the same. This psychological compromise may well be inevitable—and politically necessary—after 1997.

Why isn't discussion of the four slogans more meaningful and more rooted in original local interpretation? The negative answer is that people intuitively know that China's promises are unattainable, but do not want to say so publicly and do not want to undermine them out of fear that this might make matters even worse, shake confidence, and force a retaliation from China. Upholding the four slogans, or pretending to, at least gives people a standard against which to judge Beijing's actions in future.

The problem with this strategy is that Hong Kong does not have the political power to ensure China keeps its side of the bargain. And however the future turns out, the new sovereign will be sure to say it *is* implementing its promises. All Beijing needs to do is to leave enough of the economy in place so that some continuity is apparent and it will argue that 'one country, two systems' *is* working. Hong Kong is always likely to be different in various ways to most of mainland China, just as the special economic zone of Shenzhen is. Ready evidence of a sort will be there to back up Beijing's claims.

The positive answer to the question above is that while Hong Kong people may not trust Beijing to implement the Basic Law, they harbour an idealistic hope that China's promises will come true if asserted and held high often enough. Particularly since China is changing and the old guard of the Communist Party is dying off. Perhaps the new generation of leaders in Beijing will be kinder to the colony?

It is as if there are two unrelated parts to the Hong Kong mind: the savvy side that sees a need for calculation when dealing with Beijing, and the blind, hopeful side that is willing to be persuaded and led. People seem capable of seeing through actions, but are mesmerised by words.

DOMINATRIX

Language clouds the hierarchical relationship between Hong Kong and China in other ways. In English, both parts of the 'one country, two systems' formula seem to have equal weight. In Chinese the scales shift. The equivalent phrase *yiguo liangzhi* implies that 'one country' (*yiguo*) is the linchpin, because of the connotations that *yiguo* has in Chinese history: a single, united and powerful nation; the 'middle kingdom' (a literal translation of *Zhongguo*, the Mandarin word for China); the centre of the world. The notion in Chinese that 'two systems' (*liangzhi*) could be as important as *yiguo* seems preposterous. Statements from Chinese leaders and certain clauses in the Basic Law make it plain that the Party would never sacrifice the interests of 'one country' in order to preserve 'two systems', and that Hong Kong will always be subordinate to Beijing.

Between 1982 and 1984, Deng Xiaoping outlined with characteristic bluntness how China saw its relationship with Hong Kong. When negotiations with Britain over the Joint Declaration began in Beijing in September 1982, Deng reprimanded Margaret Thatcher, then British prime minister, for earlier claiming that the three 'unequal' treaties over Hong Kong were still valid. These were the agreements that Britain forced China to sign in the nineteenth century, covering the outright cession of Hong Kong Island (1842) and

Kowloon (1860), and the 99-year lease on the New Territories (1898). Although at periodic intervals the Chinese government has said that it would recover Hong Kong eventually, the British government seems never to have quite got the point. In the early 1980s it tried to approach the negotiations over Hong Kong as a bargaining process, one that would hopefully lead to continued British administration of the colony under Chinese sovereignty. This strategy failed, as it was bound to. Deng rebuked Thatcher:

> On the question of sovereignty, China has no room for manoeuvre. To be frank, the question is not open to discussion. The time is ripe for making it unequivocally clear that China will recover Hong Kong in 1997. That is to say, China will recover not only the New Territories but also Hong Kong Island and Kowloon. It must be on that understanding that China and the United Kingdom hold talks on the ways and means of settling the Hong Kong question.

Two years later, in 1984, Deng had a chat with Hong Kong and Macau compatriots attending China's National Day celebrations (October 1) in Beijing. After reassuring them that there would continue to be stability and order in Hong Kong up to and beyond 1997, he warned:

> But we should not think there are no potentially disruptive forces. These forces may come from any direction. If there are disturbances in Hong Kong, the Central Government will intervene.

He then upped the ante by discussing the possible uses of the People's Liberation Army (PLA) after 1997. Referring to discussions he had had with 'some British guests', Deng said rhetorically:

> I said that China had the right to station troops in Hong Kong. I asked what else could demonstrate that China exercised sovereignty over the territory. The Chinese troops in Hong Kong would have another role also—to prevent disturbances. Knowing that there were Chinese troops present, people who intended to incite disturbances would have to think twice about it. And even if there were disturbances, they could be quelled immediately.

It was actually on the issue of Taiwan, for which the 'one country, two systems' formula was originally devised, that Deng was most unequivocal about the need for force if peaceful means did not achieve reunification. In a speech to retired Party leaders in October 1984, he recounted telling 'a foreigner' that China had 'never ruled out the possibility of using non-peaceful means' to take Taiwan back.

(Deng had said much the same thing to a delegation of industrial leaders from Hong Kong in June 1984.) He also reminded the Party leaders of his 1982 talk with Thatcher:

> I told her then that if anything unexpected happened in Hong Kong during the 15-year period of transition—if there were disturbances, for example—and if the Sino–British talks failed, China would reconsider the timing and manner of its recovery of Hong Kong.

Although Deng almost always qualified his harsh statements with assurances that China would prefer to use peaceful means to recover Hong Kong and Taiwan, and that he knew this was the only possible basis for a successful and happy reunification, his commitment to the use of force if necessary was unchanging. Fortunately, this has not been necessary in Hong Kong's case; although the threat to use the PLA to quell unrest remains.

THE BASIC LAW elaborates on this dominant–subordinate relationship between China and Hong Kong. Article 12 states that the Special Administrative Region 'shall enjoy a high degree of autonomy *and come directly under the Central People's Government'* (italics added). This means Hong Kong will report to the central government rather than, say, Guangdong Province, to which Hong Kong is linked geographically. It does not imply that the central government will run the day-to-day operations of Hong Kong, just as it does not directly manage Shanghai or the provinces—that is left up to those governments. Rather, the centre will influence major policies, laws and key personnel appointments in Hong Kong.

The political weakness of Hong Kong comes through louder and more clearly in probably the most controversial clause in the Basic Law, Article 23 on subversion. It is worth quoting in full:

> The Hong Kong Special Administrative Region shall enact laws on its own to prohibit any act of treason, secession, sedition, subversion against the Central People's Government, or theft of state secrets, to prohibit foreign political organizations or bodies from conducting political activities in the Region, and to prohibit political organizations or bodies of the Region from establishing ties with foreign political organizations or bodies.

Hong Kong, not surprisingly, dislikes this clause intensely. While the common law contains sanctions against sedition and treason, it does not recognise subversion (which is specifically a 'counter-revolutionary' crime in a socialist state). How are these things to be defined? The clause says the future Hong Kong legislature will decide this question 'on its own', but one can be sure that Beijing would have a lot to say on the matter. The British team in the Sino–British Joint Liaison Group, a body created by the Joint Declaration to handle the governmental nitty gritty of the transfer of sovereignty, tried to present a draft subversion law for discussion in mid-1996. Beijing told it to back off, saying the matter was something for the future Special Administrative Region to handle.

Article 23 was in fact made more draconian after June 1989, causing local fears to intensify. The first draft of the Basic Law, which was sent out for public consultation in April 1988, merely said:

> The Hong Kong Special Administrative Region (SAR) shall prohibit by law any act designed to undermine national unity or subvert the Central People's Government.

Draft two, in February 1989, started to tighten the screws:

> The Hong Kong SAR shall enact laws on its own to prohibit any act of treason, secession, sedition or theft of state secrets.

The addition of the ban against 'foreign political organisations' came after June 1989 and reflected Beijing's fear that Hong Kong, being an open city, could be used by international pro-democracy and anti-communist groups as a gateway into China. The foreign support given to Chinese dissidents after Tiananmen—many were helped to flee the country—and the creation of an alliance of Hong Kong democratic groups to support their brethren in China, provided the ideal excuse to toughen the provisions against subversion.

THE POLITICAL PECKING order between Beijing and Hong Kong is further defined by Articles 18 and 158. The first vests the standing committee of the National People's Congress, which is the executive committee of China's quasi-parliament, with the power to decide whether or not Hong Kong is in 'a state of emergency'. If it does so, the central government can apply national security laws to the region and take over the system of government for as long as the emergency lasts.

The standing committee, as the previous chapter mentioned, is chaired by the 'moderate' leader Qiao Shi and has a range of formal (but mostly empty) supervisory powers over the Chinese government. It is also vested with far-reaching and real powers over Hong Kong. While the colony is perhaps fortunate in having Qiao running the show, rather than a more hardline leader like state premier Li Peng, the personality dimension needs to be kept in perspective: major policies on Hong Kong are decided by senior leaders and Party elders, not left to Qiao's lower-ranking committee. And China's leadership in the 1990s has become far more collegiate than it ever was under Mao or even Deng. No one leader stands categorically above the others anymore. Nevertheless, the possibility that Li could take over the chairmanship of the National People's Congress when he completes his second five-year term as premier in 1998 is hardly good news for Hong Kong.

Article 158, meanwhile, gives the standing committee of the National People's Congress the right to interpret the Basic Law. Like the constitution of any state, this one is full of holes and grey areas that will have to be filled in or illuminated later. This is typically done by courts or informally through 'constitutional conventions': tacit agreements between different parts of the state as to what the constitution's general clauses mean and how they should be implemented. Constitutions could not work without these additional elements, because they would be too vague and too crude.

The Basic Law envisages that the standing committee will delegate the power of interpretation over matters that relate to Hong Kong's autonomy to the courts of Hong Kong. As the definition of autonomy above outlined, this would cover mainly the operational aspects of local government. Issues relating to defence, foreign policy, a state of emergency or the relationship between Hong Kong and the central government would all fall under the purview of Beijing. It seems reasonable to assume that the interpretative power of the Hong Kong courts will be strongest in areas such as the economy and social structure, and weakest in politics, since the former are less threatening and more clearly within Hong Kong's autonomy than the latter. Almost any political issue, whether to do with rights and duties of citizens or the structure of government, could be viewed by Beijing as an element in its relationship with Hong Kong. If the Hong Kong courts find themselves in the position of adjudicating cases that should fall within the central government's jurisdiction, the Basic Law says they must seek an interpretation from the standing committee—and follow it.

But Article 158's provisions regarding delegation sound almost too reasonable to be true. They probably are, especially with regard to politics. Prior to July 1997, for example, Qiao's committee passed, or oversaw the enactment of, various 'decisions' that will significantly reshape Hong Kong's political system in ways that the Basic Law does not envisage. The most controversial is the Provisional Legislature, which contradicts the Basic Law's letter and spirit. Qiao's team has also greatly expanded the terms of reference of the Preparatory Committee, a body made up of mainland officials and Hong Kong luminaries that is charged with setting up the first post-reunification government (and which reports to the standing committee of the National People's Congress). Indeed, it was the Preparatory Committee which formally decided to set up the Provisional Legislature in Hong Kong. Qiao's committee laid the groundwork for this by deciding that Hong Kong's elected Legislative Council would be disbanded come 1 July 1997. The moral of this is that even under the chairmanship of a relative moderate like Qiao, the standing committee is capable of interpreting the Basic Law in ways foreign and prejudicial to Hong Kong. Not that this should be surprising: even with the best will in the world, officials in Beijing are bound to read the Basic Law differently from people in Hong Kong. How could it be otherwise given the sharply different legal traditions in the two places?

A point of addendum: Article 17 of the Basic Law states that the standing committee also has the power to 'return but not amend' any law enacted by the future Hong Kong legislature that contradicts the Basic Law's provisions on the proper relationship between the colony and the central government. Any law suffering this fate 'shall immediately be invalidated'. This power is constrained slightly by a stipulation that the committee must first consult its own 'Committee for the Basic Law of the Hong Kong Special Administrative Region', a body made up of 12 people, half of whom will come from Hong Kong. But it is unlikely these six people could or would stand up vigorously for Hong Kong, since they are to be nominated jointly by Beijing's most senior local appointees in Hong Kong—the chief executive, the president of the Legislative Council, and the chief justice of the Court of Final Appeal—and then appointed by Beijing. It is significant that the standing committee does not even have to consult the Hong Kong government before objecting to a local law.

HIDDEN MEANINGS

The previous section touches upon an important distinction in China's takeover strategy for Hong Kong—the contrast between political issues and economic/social ones.

The Basic Law does not make this distinction. Its implication is that Hong Kong can keep its own system and way of life almost in its entirety. The colony is to 'enjoy executive, legislative and independent judicial power' and the 'socialist system and policies shall not be practised' there. Articles 18, 23 and 158, therefore, are presented as the exception.

Even machinations by Beijing over the establishment of the first Special Administrative Region government should, say some of China's supporters, be seen merely as an interim measure, the prerogative of the new sovereign. Hence, once the Party has set up its version of democracy in Hong Kong, it will leave the place be.

But statements by Chinese officials, notably again Deng, show that the Party sees the application of 'two systems' to Hong Kong in mostly economic and social terms, not political ones—and that all along it has intended to interfere in politics. This contradictory approach forms the bedrock of China's takeover of Hong Kong, a strategy that involves rearranging the political system to fit in with the Party's imperatives while leaving the structure of the economic system pretty much as it is (though not necessarily the beneficiaries, as will be shown in Part 3 of this book). As in China, the Party is counting on being able to compartmentalise politics separately from economics.

When Deng met that industrial delegation from Hong Kong in June 1984, he started his pep talk by defining 'one country, two systems':

> The Chinese Government is firm in its position, principles and policies on Hong Kong. We have stated on many occasions that after China resumes the exercise of its sovereignty over Hong Kong in 1997, Hong Kong's current *social and economic* systems will remain unchanged, its *legal system* will remain basically unchanged, its way of life and its status as a *free port* and an *international trade and financial centre* will remain unchanged and it can continue to maintain or establish *economic relations* with other countries and regions. We have also stated repeatedly that apart from stationing troops there, Beijing will not assign officials to the government of the Hong Kong Special Administrative Region. This policy too will remain unchanged. We

shall station troops there to safeguard our national security, not to interfere in Hong Kong's internal affairs. Our policies with regard to Hong Kong will remain unchanged for 50 years, and we mean this. (italics added)

Deng studiously avoided saying that Hong Kong's political system, its legislature and its electoral system would remain unchanged. His comment that mainland officials would not be sent to Hong Kong was misleading: it may be true that none will join the Hong Kong government (although even this is open to question), but certain ministries of the central government will set up shop in the colony after reunification, principally the Ministry of Foreign Affairs, and the Communist Party will of course retain its presence there (either behind its traditional front, the New China News Agency, or perhaps in more transparent form). The notion of a 'Chinese wall' between the work of these officials and that of the Hong Kong government is untenable, even if no formal channels of communication have been laid by the Basic Law. Foreign affairs officials will have to deal with numerous levels of the Hong Kong government, including the chief secretary (whose title will become chief of administration), the Constitutional Affairs Branch (on issues relating to the Basic Law and foreign affairs), the Trade and Industry Branch, and the Immigration Department. The Communist Party will certainly liaise regularly with the chief executive and his core group of advisors, the Executive Council.

Deng repeated his definition elsewhere. In a talk with Thatcher in Beijing on 19 December 1984, the day on which the Joint Declaration was signed, the patriarch described China's 'two-systems' formula as an arrangement that would allow Hong Kong to 'retain its capitalist system and its status as a free port and a financial centre'. Again, the political system is not part of the message.

There was one occasion when Deng referred to politics in Hong Kong. During his September 1982 meeting with Thatcher, he said Hong Kong's 'current political and economic systems and even most of its laws can remain in force' after China recovered its lost territory. Yet since this formula was never repeated, it can be safely seen as an aberrant comment, and discarded.

All of this begs the question—didn't Deng accept that capitalism required a specific type of political system, different from socialism? Probably, but he quickly subordinated this to the Party's more pressing political imperative: to restrain the growth of democracy in Hong

Kong. A contradictory stance, but then contradictions are the norm in many 1997 issues.

To elaborate briefly, Deng defined capitalism by contrasting it with socialism. During an 'imperial tour' to southern China in early 1992, he told cadres that the essential difference between the two systems was not the proportion of economic planning to market forces, since markets could exist under socialism and planning was carried out under capitalism: 'The essence of socialism is liberation and development of the productive forces (land, labour and capital), elimination of exploitation and polarization, and the ultimate achievement of prosperity for all.' Capitalism, by contrast, accepted exploitation and inequality.

Deng next commented on the role of the state under socialism, and implied that he saw this system as having a distinct political make-up. The state took a conscious approach to economic development by taking what was good from other systems, by aiming to 'realize common prosperity step by step', and by distributing resources fairly. In other words, big government. By implication, capitalist political systems were less socially conscious, less rational and were characterised by smaller governments.

But Deng never discussed what sort of political system Hong Kong would need in order to maintain its capitalist system and way of life for 50 years. On the contrary, what he did was concentrate on the imperative of 'one country', wherein Hong Kong politics was clearly subordinated to the greater good.

HIDDEN OBLIGATIONS

If there is one area where China's political assumptions have been ignored more than any other in Hong Kong, it is this: What can Hong Kong do for 'one country'? As 1997 drew closer people were beginning to realise that the Communist Party saw 'one country, two systems' as a two-way street. But until 1996 this perspective received little attention in the media or in public discussion. Hong Kong assumed that its economy was, and would continue to be, its contribution to China and focused most of its energies on arguing over whether or not Beijing could preserve the colony's economic success and liberal political environment.

For the Party, the concept of 'two systems' can only operate within the political bounds of 'one country'. If Hong Kong does not meet its political obligations to China, then China will reassess its commitments to Hong Kong. In no uncertain terms, Deng said to Thatcher in 1984:

> I should also like to ask the Prime Minister to make it clear to the people of Hong Kong and of the rest of the world that the concept of 'one country, two systems' includes not only capitalism but also socialism, which will be firmly maintained on the mainland of China, where one billion people live.

Socialism in China increasingly means rule by the Communist Party rather than a serious description of China's economy (although as an economic form it was still very much alive in 1984). Deng went on:

> The fact that one billion people live under socialism is the indispensable precondition that enables us to allow capitalism in these small, limited areas at our side (Taiwan and Hong Kong). We believe the existence of capitalism in limited areas will actually be conducive to the development of socialism.

Whatever one thinks of Deng's understanding of international economics, it is hard to mistake his political message: 'Remember your obligations to the motherland. Do not try to change the socialist system or undermine the dominance of the Communist Party'— clearly a message to Hong Kong's democrats.

Deng's 1984 message has been echoed since by official organs in Beijing. One recent example comes from an April 1997 edition of the *People's Daily*, the Party's main propaganda news-sheet. In a commentary entitled, 'The Legal Guarantees for Safeguarding Hong Kong's Prosperity and Stability', the authors declared:

> Just as we cannot talk only about national unity and sovereignty and ignore Hong Kong's 'high degree of autonomy' and prosperity and stability, so we cannot break away from national unity and sovereignty and talk only of Hong Kong's 'high degree of autonomy' and prosperity and stability. 'One country' is the precondition. To depart from this precondition means we cannot discuss the implementation of 'two systems'.

Window magazine, a now-defunct pro-China current affairs weekly in Hong Kong, ran a cover story on the one-country issue in May 1996. Even it admitted that 'despite the enormous amount of publicity given to Deng Xiaoping's one country, two systems solution ... most of the emphasis so far has been on preserving the 'two systems' and very little on how to foster the sense of 'one country'. The magazine quoted Raymond Wu, a Hong Kong educationalist and member of the China-appointed Preparatory Committee, as saying:

> To build a sense of national belonging would be one of the most important tasks for Hong Kong if the concept of one country, two systems is to be successful ... Nobody is talking about how to reinforce 'one country' but the two halves of 'one country, two systems' have to work hand-in-hand if both are to be successful.

MALLEABLE MEANINGS

The principle of 'Hong Kong people ruling Hong Kong' shows how open the Basic Law is to interpretation in a somewhat different way—in terms of change over time. This apparently straightforward dictum is supposed to mean just what it says: that only local people should be allowed to participate in government. In other words, all the six million Chinese living in Hong Kong *before* the handover and possessing permanent identity cards (of which there are a few different types, depending on whether the holder was born in the colony or emigrated from China). The population includes: around three million Cantonese who were born in Hong Kong; a few hundred thousand Shanghainese and others who fled both the Kuomintang (led by Chiang Kai-shek) and the Communists in the late 1940s and have since become residents, and their descendants; and a couple of million poor immigrants from China's southern and eastern provinces who have fled or migrated since the same period.

Some foreigners and overseas Chinese who have lived in the colony long enough to get residency status (more than seven years) will be allowed to participate in the post-1997 government, but face a variety of restrictions. Those excluded include foreign professionals and overseas Chinese who have lived and worked in Hong Kong for less than seven years, diplomats and other transients. Significantly, Hong Kong Chinese emigrants who decide to return to Hong Kong will also face various restrictions (if they declare their foreign passports).

The reason that the notion of 'Hong Kong people ruling Hong Kong' is open to interpretation boils down to a difference in the wording of the Joint Declaration and the Basic Law. Neither document actually contains the Chinese slogan 'Hong Kong people ruling Hong Kong'; although Chinese officials and Hong Kong people have come to use it in conjunction with the other three slogans. What the Joint Declaration in fact states is that 'the government ... will be composed of *local inhabitants*'. Article 3 of the Basic Law changes this to: 'the executive authorities and legislature ... shall be composed of *permanent residents* of Hong Kong' (italics added). It is this shift to 'permanent residents' from 'local inhabitants' that allows for a different view of political participation than the phrase 'Hong Kong people ruling Hong Kong' seems to imply.

Why is this? Because the term 'Hong Kong people' implies 'local people'. The legal category 'permanent resident' is broader—and could include mainland Chinese businessmen who have lived in Hong Kong for long enough to obtain this status. Mainland Chinese officials, such as those who work for the New China News Agency, are not supposed to apply for permanent residency—even if they meet the criteria—according to internal Party rules.

What all this means is that the Special Administrative Region government could include people who are fairly recently from the mainland and, indeed, still work for the Chinese government. Most mainland businessmen in Hong Kong are employed by Chinese state-owned enterprises, and the more senior ones have close relationships with the central government in Beijing or provincial governments around China. Granted, Hong Kong has always had a cosmopolitan government comprising British, Australian and local Chinese officers, and some foreigners have participated in the Legislative and Executive Councils. So what could be wrong with some mainlanders participating too after the handover? The potential problem is that they would not only have much more political influence than any foreigner, but also that their presence will definitely blur the line around the 'Hong Kong people' category. In this way, Hong Kong's autonomy will be further compromised.

It needs to be explained that mainland Chinese are more likely to be found in the Legislative Council, and possibly Executive Council, in future than in the civil service. They are, in effect, barred from senior civil service jobs. This is because China sought to reassure Hong Kong people that their government would not be deluged by mainlanders come 1997 by erecting an obstacle course for the most senior government jobs. Thus the Basic Law states that:

- The chief executive must be Chinese, at least 40 years of age, a permanent resident with 'no right of abode in any foreign country', and resident in Hong Kong continuously for 20 years (Article 44).

* Principal officials—secretaries and deputy secretaries of branches, the commissioner of police, the director of audit, and so on—must fit the same requirements, except their residency tenure only has to be 15 years (Article 61).

But the door has already opened in the legislature: one member of the Provisional Legislature is a senior manager of China Merchants, one of China's largest commercial enterprises in Hong Kong and a subsidiary of the Ministry of Communications in Beijing. And in future, a seat on Hong Kong's legislature is likely to go to the Hong Kong Chinese Enterprises Association, the chamber of commerce for mainland Chinese enterprises in Hong Kong.

The point is not that the legislature, or the Executive Council for that matter, is about to be inundated with mainland Chinese businessmen. This would be unnecessary in any case since Beijing has plenty of loyal supporters locally willing to cooperate with it. The issue, rather, is that there are cracks in the facade of 'Hong Kong people ruling Hong Kong'—and it does not require too much imagination to see these widening in future.

PLAGIARISM AND UNCERTAINTY

Yet other parts of the Basic Law are, on first glance, open to doubt. 'Extremely liberal' is how one might describe a chapter called 'Fundamental Rights and Duties of the Residents'. Hong Kong people are offered the full gamut of civil liberties, from equality before the law and freedom of speech to the right to vote and freedom of movement. This seems impressive—until you turn to the Chinese state constitution (of 1982) and experience a sense of deja vu.

In a chapter called 'The Fundamental Rights and Duties of Citizens', the Chinese constitution offers people equality before the law and freedom of speech, as well as the right to vote (but not, significantly, the freedom of movement). Its article on free speech says:

> Citizens of the People's Republic of China enjoy freedom of speech, of the press, of assembly, of association, of procession and of demonstration.

Compare this with the Basic Law, which is identical except for a few more rights thrown into the pot:

> Hong Kong residents shall have freedom of speech, of the press and of publication; freedom of association, of assembly, of procession and of demonstration; and the right and freedom to form and join trade unions, and to strike.

Back to the Chinese constitution, this time to two articles on homes and privacy:

> The residences of citizens of the People's Republic of China are inviolable. Unlawful search of, or intrusion into, a citizen's residence is prohibited.

> Freedom and privacy of correspondence of citizens of the People's Republic of China are protected by law. No organisation or individual may, on any ground, infringe upon citizens' freedom and privacy of correspondence, except in cases where, to meet the needs of state security or of criminal investigation, public security or procuratorial organs are permitted to censor correspondence in accordance with procedures prescribed by law.

(Procuratorial organs deal with the prosecution of criminal cases, the investigation of certain criminal cases involving officials, and the supervision of public security organs and courts.)

On these identical issues, the Basic Law says:

> The homes and other premises of Hong Kong residents shall be inviolable. Arbitrary or unlawful search of, or intrusion into, a resident's home or other premises shall be prohibited.

> The freedom and privacy or communication of Hong Kong residents shall be protected by law. No department or individual may, on any grounds, infringe upon the freedom and privacy of communication of residents except that the relevant authorities may inspect communication in accordance with legal procedures to meet the needs of public security or of investigation into criminal offences.

As these comparisons show, the basic civil and political rights offered to Hong Kong people are adapted slightly to local conditions—'homes and other premises' rather than 'residences', and 'communication' rather than 'correspondence'—and are marginally wider in scope. But fundamentally they are the same.

The Basic Law offers a few rights not in the Chinese constitution. Apart from freedom of movement, these include freedom of conscience, freedom of choice of occupation, the right to confidential legal advice, and the right to institute legal proceedings against the government (Chinese citizens merely have the right to complain, criticise and make suggestions to their government). The Basic Law is also supposed to ensure that the provisions of two key United Nations human rights covenants that apply to Hong Kong 'shall remain in force'. And it upholds the traditional rights of the indigenous inhabitants of the rural New Territories. This last issue has been highly controversial in Hong Kong, since it has meant that a small group of people have enjoyed special rights not available to the average resident, such as the right to build property on free village land, and it perpetuated old-fashioned customs, such as a prohibition against daughters inheriting property (this customary law was overturned by the Legislative Council in 1994, causing bitter rural opposition in the process).

Appropriately enough for a socialist state, the Chinese constitution offers a few rights not in the Basic Law. These sometimes double as duties and include the right and duty to work, the right to rest, the right and duty to receive education, and a stipulation that women have the same rights as men.

It would seem, from these comparisons, that the committee charged with drafting this chapter of the Basic Law got off lightly! As for the issue of duties, just one was included:

> Hong Kong residents and other persons in Hong Kong shall have the obligation to abide by the laws in force in the Hong Kong Special Administrative Region.

Compare this to the Chinese constitution, which is top heavy with duties. People must practise family planning, rear and educate their children, help to support their parents (after coming of age), safeguard national unity (and unity between all ethnic groups), observe labour discipline and public order, and respect social ethics. As if this were not enough, citizens must also 'safeguard the security, honour and interests of the motherland', 'defend the motherland and resist aggression' (this is a 'sacred duty') and, somewhat more prosaically, pay taxes.

The broader question to ask is what practical value can the civil rights in the Basic Law have when they are conceived in virtually identical terms to those in the Chinese state constitution? Their value is decidedly mixed.

China's 1982 constitution marked a positive step forward on a formal level in several ways. For example, the protection it offers the individual against unlawful search and invasion of privacy was part of a package 'designed to prevent the recurrence of the gross violations of human rights during the Cultural Revolution', to quote the words of Albert Chen, a Hong Kong expert on Chinese laws. Chen also points out that the introduction in 1982 of the right to equality before the law signified an ideological departure from the 'institutionalised discrimination' practised against millions of 'class enemies' (namely landlords, rich peasants, rightists and counter-revolutionaries) from the early 1950s to 1976, when Mao died and the Cultural Revolution period ended.

However, on a practical political level, people in China have obviously not enjoyed full access to the rights promised in their state constitution. The massacre of June 1989 is only the most blatant example of Party infringement of these rights. Numerous other examples exist, including the incarceration of political dissidents. But in the view of the Party, constitutional rights in China are justifiably limited by 'duties' to the state—and the central duty is to uphold the 'Four Cardinal Principles': the 'Socialist road, the people's democratic dictatorship, leadership of the Communist Party of China, and Marxism–Leninism–Mao Zedong Thought'. In essence this means adhering to the Party's leadership, which the pro-democracy protestors in 1989 clearly did not do.

Should the political situation turn nasty again in China, or should the Party feel nervous about political developments in Hong Kong, then Hong Kong people should not expect the rights in the Basic Law to provide much protection. These rights are, after all, qualifed by the 'duty' to 'abide by the laws in force in the … Special Administrative Region'. One of these laws could be a state of emergency declared by Beijing (as allowed for by Article 18, which could legally strip people of free speech, the right to demonstrate and to hold strikes).

In normal times, the rights offered in the Basic Law will vary in value, since some are clearly more politically charged than others. Thus Beijing is likely to keep a close watch on freedom of speech and demonstration at all times, but may not worry too much about free choice of occupation, freedom to engage in artistic and cultural activities, the right to confidential legal advice (in commercial cases at least), and freedom of marriage.

In between these two extremes fall a number of rights whose sanctity has to be doubted because of China's own closed political and legal environment. They include the freedom to enter or leave the region, freedom of religious belief, the right not to be subject to arbitrary or unlawful arrest, freedom to engage in academic research, and the right to take the government to court.

It is also important to distinguish between the rights of individuals and the rights of groups. While individuals have freedom of religious belief and can 'conduct and participate in religious activities in public', religious organisations themselves are in a trickier position. The Basic Law offers them general protection: the government will not 'interfere in the internal affairs of religious organizations or restrict religious activities which do not contravene the laws of the Region'. But if they become involved in politics, as some are, they may run foul of Article 23, the controversial clause prohibiting subversion against the Chinese government and links between local political organisations and foreign ones.

ONE MORE RULE OF THUMB

Part of the argument in this chapter has turned on the idea that to understand the Party's assumptions underlying the Basic Law one needs to study the pronouncements and comments made by Deng Xiaoping in the early 1980s. As China's patriarch, what he said about Hong Kong had a profound influence on officials below him. One more useful rule of thumb is to look at what lower-ranking Chinese officials with direct responsibility for Hong Kong have been saying about issues of civil and political rights, since their views will represent those of their superiors in Beijing.

The issue of journalistic freedom offers a good example. Zhang Junsheng, a deputy directory of the New China News Agency in Hong Kong and its high-profile spokesman, laid down some pointed guidelines on press freedom to a journalism symposium in November 1995. After praising Hong Kong for creating an international information centre through its characteristic hard work and willingness to accept new ideas, Zhang expounded on the concept of the 'patriotic reporter'. He said that in the field of science and technology, in which he was educated, there was a saying: 'Science has no national boundaries, but scientists have a motherland.' Applying this principle to the news media meant that: 'News has no national boundaries, but journalists have a motherland. To love one's motherland has always been a noble emotion. I think everyone should seriously think about the responsibilities of patriotic reporters at this historic moment.'

One of these responsibilities was to have a better understanding of China's laws relating to news gathering, an area which Zhang believed most local reporters knew little about since they were born and raised in Hong Kong. It was because of this that many reporters worried about being sent to work in China, fearful that they would 'step on a (legal) mine' while doing so. But Zhang advised: 'I think that if only each reporter knew a little more about law in China, was more familiar with relevant mainland rules, and respected China's relevant laws and regulations, then the issue of "stepping on mines" would not happen or would happen a lot less.'

Patriotic reporting also meant understanding that abiding by the law was a fundamental norm of any society. To underline his point, Zhang quoted Tolstoy, the great Russian writer, to the effect that: 'The life of any person should be restrained by definite rules.' And he stressed that freedom, including press freedom, was not absolute.

Turning to the relationship between the Basic Law and Hong Kong, Zhang repeated a common refrain of Chinese officials: 'I believe that the Basic Law already has clear rules for protecting press freedom. After 1997, the press freedom Hong Kong now enjoys will not only not diminish, it will increase.' He did not, however, provide any evidence as to why this should be so.

Local journalists might take particular exception to Zhang's last comment given the restrictions on political liberties in China and a statement made several months later by Lu Ping, head of the Hong Kong and Macau Affairs Office, China's principal central government office managing the process of reunification from Beijing. In August 1996, Lu was reported as saying that while Hong Kong would have press freedom after 1997, there was a sharp distinction between 'objective reporting' and 'advocacy'. *Wen Wei Po*, one of two major pro-China newspapers in Hong Kong, said Lu told a gathering of Hong Kong media professionals in Beijing that he wanted to talk about 'advocacy' because he 'hoped to remind journalists and others in Hong Kong not to have any illusions that after 1997 they could do anything for Taiwan independence or Hong Kong independence, advocate "two Chinas" (that is, one China, one Taiwan), or advocate Tibetan independence. This all constitutes criminal behaviour and is totally different from press freedom.'

Imagine this scenario. A Hong Kong or Hong Kong-based journalist flies to Taiwan and interviews a pro-independence politician. The report is later printed in a Hong Kong newspaper or magazine. The content of the article contains certain inflammatory anti-Beijing and pro-Taiwan-independence statements. Perhaps the Taiwanese interviewee also criticises the transfer of sovereignty over Hong Kong as fundamentally flawed and detrimental to Hong Kong. According to Lu's criteria, such a report would come dangerously close to 'advocacy' in Beijing's eyes—even if the newspaper strenuously avoids any 'comment', say in an editorial. Would the journalist in question, the publication's editor or the publisher, be prosecuted for this 'criminal' act? Presumably a penalty of some sort would have to be meted out, or no one would take the policy against advocacy seriously.

Alternatively, the Party could apply some of the other forms of pressure it has been using in Hong Kong to win over or constrain the media industry in recent years. These include controlling the release of information to favoured publications, and applying economic pressure such as ordering mainland Chinese companies to withdraw advertisements, or persuading a pro-Beijing local businessman to buy out a media organisation. Two other tactics are to 'infiltrate' Hong Kong media companies with mainland journalists, who normally then work on the China beat; and directly castigating individual publications and editors for running negative stories about the Party or China.

A WEAK CONSTITUTION

Hong Kong's ordinary people are ambivalent about their future constitution. A large portion of them, intuition suggests probably more than half, look upon it with wariness or disinterest because it is the product of a state which they inherently distrust and from which many of their families fled in recent decades (this feeling, by the way, is not shared by Hong Kong's business community—but more on this in Part 3 of this book). Another third, it is fair to say, seem to support Hong Kong's pro-Beijing lobby and therefore probably do trust the constitution. The remainder have no opinion.

The paradox is that the vast majority of people have accepted to some degree the core promises which China has decreed as the foundation for reunification and which the Basic Law endorses: 'one country, two systems', 'Hong Kong people ruling Hong Kong', 'No change for 50 years', and 'a high degree of autonomy'. Perhaps because most people have not read the Basic Law they do not always associate these with it. Or it may be that the Basic Law as an abstract document has become the focus of their distrust, while the four slogans have become an avenue for their hopes. Such ambivalence is understandable given Hong Kong's need to maintain optimism and confidence in spite of the inherent weakness and uncertainty of its political position.

No amount of hope, however, can alter the fact that the Basic Law was never intended to maintain Hong Kong entirely as it is. Deng's statements on 'one country' and 'two systems' emphasised that the colony would be allowed to preserve its economy and social system largely intact; he made no similar promise regarding the political system generally or the Legislative Council in particular. Thus in contrast to a liberal reading of 'one country, two systems' and 'Hong Kong people ruling Hong Kong', Hong Kong could neither preserve its late-colonial legislature in its entirety nor decide on its own how political reform should proceed. The implication in Deng's words was always that Beijing would take a close interest in moulding the colony's political structure to its own advantage. The idea—espoused for different reasons by both the pro- and anti-Beijing lobbies—that the Basic Law provides a foundation for the genuine development of democracy in Hong Kong is not credible.

For a recent affirmation of Deng's line of thought, it is worth turning again to the *People's Daily*. In the same April 1997 commentary quoted earlier, called 'The Legal Guarantees for Safeguarding Hong Kong's Prosperity and Stability', the authors discuss what sort of political system would be most appropriate for the colony's 'actual situation'. They conclude:

> In today's world we cannot find any ready-made political structure or model which can be a reference for the Hong Kong Special Administrative Region. Hong Kong's current political system is, in essence, a colonial gubernatorial autocracy. This cannot be retained intact. Nor in future can Hong Kong implement the mainland's socialist system; it cannot take the system of people's congresses and copy them mechanically. But since Hong Kong is not a sovereign nation, neither can it copy the system of separation of powers which exists in Europe and the United States, nor implement a parliamentary or presidential system.

The article then states what sort of system would suit Hong Kong's actual situation and best maintain its prosperity and stability—a 'chief executive system'. This is to be an 'executive-led' system in which the executive and legislature theoretically balance each other and cooperate, and where there is judicial independence—an improved version of Hong Kong's current colonial structure, in other words. But the authors go on to claim that while Hong Kong's future chief executive will not enjoy the 'huge powers' of the governor, and while the Legislative Council will purportedly become a legislative body worthy of its name, they stress that 'the executive powers should not be unduly weakened'. Hence, Beijing has set a tight and conservative framework within which any further political reform could occur in Hong Kong. The fond hope of some that the colony's political structure could, over time, move towards a Western parliamentary model is a non-starter for as long as the Communist Party rules China.

There is a stark dichotomy, therefore, between a liberal reading of the Basic Law and its harsher meaning within the Chinese political and constitutional context. The latter interpretation, unfortunately, will surely be the only one that is relevant to the future sovereign. Beijing might occasionally let up the political pressure on things like freedom of speech and demonstration—if, for example, it believed it had Hong Kong under adequate control—but it seems incapable of ever guaranteeing the type of political non-intervention that most local people want. Indeed, every new official statement or policy on the eve of the handover represented a tightening of the screws, or a new restriction, not a loosening. The practical manner in which Beijing is implementing its takeover of Hong Kong is the subject of the next two chapters.

CHAPTER 3

THE MAGIC WEAPON

The Communist Party of China did not stride to power in 1949 entirely on its own two feet. At critical moments it deployed a strategy known as the 'united front', a way of building alliances and relationships with sympathetic non-communist groups (including the business community) for the purpose of enhancing its power and popular support—and defeating the enemy of the day. In 1951, at a united front conference in south-western China, Deng Xiaoping exhorted: 'So long as there are friends and enemies, we should ally ourselves with our friends in order to isolate and attack the enemy; hence we need united front work.' Although by the time Deng spoke the united front was well on the way to becoming a propaganda frill, it had been a substantive element of Communist strategy. And it is becoming so again: because of the more complex and diverse political economy of China today, front tactics are resurgent. The Communist Party may be autocratic, but it still sees the need to legitimise its position by building a broad network of support throughout Chinese society—especially after the debacle of the Cultural Revolution wiped away its revolutionary credibility.

Employing a similar logic (sans the military part) to that which it used in its takeover of China, the Party built a united front in Hong Kong in preparation for the resumption of sovereignty. The economy and society of pre-1997 Hong Kong is admittedly very different from pre-liberation China, yet there remain some uncanny political similarities. Hong Kong today has a non-communist political and commercial elite willing to cooperate with the new sovereign in return for positions of power after reunification, or to protect and expand its substantial investments. There are groups of workers and intellectuals who, for philosophical or emotional reasons, fall easily into the arms of the front. And a front tactic, that of splitting the enemy, is being assiduously deployed.

It is important to make clear from the outset what the united front is and is not. It is a loosely-knit coalition of groups and individuals who have been persuaded to 'join the team'. Their job is either to do what they can to propagate the Party's messages within their circle— be it a grassroots, professional, or commercial one—and society at large, or at least to be silent supporters, not obstructing the Party's political work. For most people, being in the united front is very much a part-time job. The front is not a formal body. It has no single organisational structure, like a political party with a chairman, formal office holders and an office. In Hong Kong it has a de facto staff: the New China News Agency, the public face of the Party in Hong Kong and the main coordinator of united front work. Although the front comprises a fairly solid cadre of key people at the core, it is far more fluid around the edges—the zone occupied by the less important individuals and community groups. It is, essentially, a cold strategy of divide and rule, one which plays upon existing social and economic divisions for maximum political advantage. Before starting on the story of the united front in Hong Kong, some background on its history in China is necessary.

FIGHTING CONTRADICTIONS

A recurring theme in Chinese communist history was the way in which the Party's enemies were often changing. In the 1920s it was warlords. Next the Kuomintang, the republican party which ruled a fragmented China from the mid-1920s to 1949. Then came the Japanese during the Second World War. After that, the Americans, other 'imperialists', and the Kuomintang again.

For the fledgling Communist Party, fighting different enemies required allying itself with different friends. Against a backdrop of numerous local warlords creating disunity in China after the fall of the Qing Dynasty in 1911, the young Party allied itself with the Kuomintang at the behest of their mutual revolutionary mentor, the Soviet Union, in 1923. Since China was largely a rural society, the Soviets believed that the country had to have a bourgeois (or capitalist) revolution before it could have a socialist one (the correct order in traditional Marxist theory). The Kuomintang, with a support base made up of industrialists and financiers, was the natural group to begin this transformation. Formed in 1912 by Sun Yat-sen, a doctor turned revolutionary, it was also much bigger and more experienced than the Communists, who began life only in 1921 and had a mere 300 members in 1923.

This first united front set up a coalition government in Canton (now called Guangzhou) in the southern province of Guangdong in1923 and a couple of years later launched a successful expedition against warlords to the north. But the alliance fell apart in 1927 after criminal gangs and Kuomintang troops launched a campaign of terror against powerful labour unions in Shanghai. Sun had died by 1925, leaving his party in the hands of Chiang Kai-shek, a young military officer notorious for his brutality against enemies and for his shameless extortion of money from supporters in the business community. Following the split in this first alliance, the Communists and the Kuomintang spent the next 10 years locked in a civil war.

The objectives of the front at this time and later were always the same: strength in numbers, isolation of the enemy, and minimisation of resistance against the Communist cause through education of the population. Although this educational work was partly ideological, it was also driven by practical considerations. The Party around 1930 was still relatively small and had to leverage its power in whatever way it could. Its position became even more precarious after the Long March (1934–35), which it embarked upon to escape the Kuomintang. Deng said in 1951 that when the Communists arrived in northern Shaanxi at the end of the Long March, 'conditions were extremely bad'. They had only about 10,000 men but were facing 100,000 enemy soldiers. 'Thanks to the fact that the Party had sent out some of its finest cadres to do united front work, as well as work in other fields, new prospects for resisting Japan and saving the nation opened up', enthused Deng, with fairly justifiable self-congratulation. And to underline the importance of united front work, he stressed it was one of the three 'decisive factors' that led to the Communists' ultimate victory in the revolution (the other two were armed struggle and Party building). In Communist lore this triad was sanctified as the 'three magic weapons', a label accredited to Mao.

The work done by the 'finest cadres' refers to the negotiations which paved the way for the second alliance with the Kuomintang in 1937. Through delicate diplomacy the two enemies put aside their differences in order to defend China against Japanese invasion and colonisation. Mutual suspicion meant this front was never a tightly knit one, yet it held together until 1945. But once the 'War of Resistance Against Japan' ended, the civil war resumed with a vengeance. For the next four years, the Communists concentrated on ridding China of both the Kuomintang and the foreign 'imperialists'. In addition to the revolution's natural ideological allies—urban workers and poor peasants—the Party at this time was able to win over around six to eight 'middle of the road' democratic parties and a mixed collection of intellectuals, sympathetic business people, and professionals.

The democratic parties make an interesting case study. Originally inspired by Western liberalism, these small left-leaning groups saw themselves as mediators between the two main parties, and played a role in China's coalition government during the Second World War. Several were persecuted by the Kuomintang for being Communist sympathisers and driven out of politics, or underground. Those who were not in fact so predisposed before this harsh treatment, often became so afterwards.

The two largest parties were the China Democratic League and the Kuomintang Revolutionary Committee (a left-wing splinter from the main party). Others included the China Association for Promoting Democracy, the September Third Study Society (Jiusan) and the China National Construction Association. Their lack of national clout is apparent from their combined membership numbers in 1949—a mere 20,000 people. Some were so tiny that they became the butt of derogatory jokes. 'Jiusan', for example, literally means 'nine, three', a reference to September 3rd, the date of the group's inaugural meeting. A cynic at the time said it meant 'nine members and three personnel!'. Although small, the parties were not totally lacking in influence: they had a following among the urban intellectuals and professionals whom the Communists sought to bring onside.

As military victory against the Kuomintang neared in the late 1940s, the Communists started thinking about the demands of civilian administration and the task of rebuilding an economy wrecked by war, civil war, corruption and rampant inflation. As a result, they focused united front work even more sharply on the categories of people whose help was most needed, namely industrialists and educated professionals. But the Party did not want all businessmen: their political value depended on which ideological category they fell into.

At the bottom (in terms of wealth) were the 'petty bourgeoisie', a mostly friendly category that included small companies, craftsmen and intellectuals. Above them were the 'national bourgeoisie', patriotic businessmen whose sympathies stood a good chance of being manipulated. At the top were the 'big bourgeoisie', or comprador capitalists, people who worked as agents for the 'imperialists' and were implacably opposed to the cause of revolution.

While the Party never really trusted businessmen or intellectuals, even those from the petty and national bourgeoisie categories, China needed their money and expertise. Although the Party's suspicions were reciprocated, the new alliance members were won over with a promise that hardcore socialism would not be implemented in China until the economy had recovered. The implication was that any change would be gradual.

Overall, these tactics proved successful. Thousands of businessmen may have fled to Hong Kong and elsewhere around 1949, but a large number stayed, persuading themselves that the Communists could not be as bad as Chiang Kai-shek. Many intellectuals were naturally left-leaning and so sympathised with the revolution. They believed China needed a fresh start and that the Communists were the only political group remotely capable of providing it.

But change turned out to be anything but incremental. The Party froze the assets of foreign businesses in late 1950 and forced most to sell out at heavily discounted prices. The majority of foreigners had left China by 1951. Early the following year came the 'Five Anti' campaign, a mass movement specifically targeted at Chinese capitalists (and one of four major campaigns launched in the early 1950s). The five 'evils' slated for elimination were bribery, tax evasion, theft of state property, cheating on government contracts, and stealing state economic information. Jonathan Spence, an American historian, describes the campaign as 'an act of class war that mirrored in scope, rage, and effectiveness its counterpart in the countryside' (a campaign against rural landlords). Although the 'Five Anti' movement was implemented in all cities throughout China, Shanghai became its most famous battle ground. The next blow came soon after, in 1955, the year in which the government nationalised industry.

If this all sounds fairly deceitful, it was. Yet there did exist a theoretical basis for the brutal twists and turns—Mao's theory of 'contradictions'—which, while not condoning the dishonesty, does at least help to explain what justified it in the minds of the Communist leadership. Influenced by Marxist dialectical materialism, Mao saw historical change as the product of a constant conflict over material resources between opposing social forces. To this he added his idea that in every political situation there were 'major' and 'minor' conflicts, or contradictions. In the words of Kenneth Lieberthal, the American political scientist, it was the role of the Communist Party to identify and resolve 'the major contradiction of an existing situation on terms favorable to the communist cause'. Once this had been achieved, the contradiction ceased being 'major' and the Party had to delineate the next biggest problem to solve. It was only in this way that it could survive and win.

On a practical political level, the relevance of this to the united front was that resolving contradictions necessitated gathering all the supporters the Party could from among non-communist and progressive groups, because it was usually not big enough to handle the matter on its own (as Deng made explicit in his speech in 1951). Thus, in the late 1920s and early 1930s, the major 'contradiction' was the Kuomintang and the Communists drew support from peasants and, to a lesser extent, workers. From 1937 onwards, the Japanese became the major contradiction and the Party allied itself with the Kuomintang. Once the Japanese lost the war, the Kuomintang again became the major enemy and the Communists gathered together as wide a coalition as possible and literally 'surrounded' it. In this highly fluid political environment, enemies could become friends, and friends enemies, depending on the political goal—thus the philosophical ease with which the Party organised a mass campaign against the business sector only a few years after winning them over to its side.

Ironically, united front work seems to have been less persuasive within the Communist camp than outside it. Many strongly left-wing cadres were none too happy rubbing shoulders with former enemies and 'friends' of dubious loyalty. It was for this reason that leaders like Mao and Deng regularly had to remind those below them of the strategic political importance of united front work. In 1941 Mao criticised 'closed-doorism' and urged cadres to 'cooperate democratically and consult with non-Party people'. Deng's speech 10 years later on the subject was entitled, 'The Entire Party Should Attach More Importance to United Front Work' and echoed Mao's statements. Deng particularly chided his listeners by saying many cadres did not understand the front's underlying principles and only got involved in this work 'when pushed'.

In contrast, some of the front's allies displayed a remarkable naivete. A spokesman for the Democratic League, one of the larger democratic parties, said sometime in 1945:

> We quite agree with the Communist Party on China's need for democracy. Since the Communists modified their economic policies on the basis of definite recognition of private property, we agree with them on that subject ... We are also of the conviction that the Communists will not revert to their more radical prewar policies when the war is over. As a matter of fact, although we have no assurances on that point, we believe that after the war the Communist Party may become even more democratic than it already is—providing the Communists are not again attacked by the Kuomintang armies ... The Communists have no ambition of being the sole leaders of the nation. Of this we are convinced, and we know them very well.

On an organisational level, meanwhile, the front was institutionalised by a decision in late 1948 to create a 'consultative' forum, the Chinese People's Political Consultative Conference, and soon after a United Front Work Department within the Party. Needless to say, the conference has never exercised power nor had much influence over government policy (except in the early days when it promulgated a document known as the Common Programme; this served as the new republic's provisional constitution until one was enacted at the first National People's Congress meeting in 1954). The conference exists so that its members can absorb the latest policies and then go forth and propagate them. The work department is, on the other hand, quite powerful. Its responsibilities also extend to ethnic minorities and religious groups.

Both institutions went into eclipse during the Cultural Revolution (1966–76), when left-wing ideologues claimed that alliances perpetuated political differences and impeded socialist construction. As expected, the strategy and its accompanying institutions gained a new lease on life following the demise of hardline leftism and the initiation of economic reforms in the late 1970s. The conference now meets once a year at the same time as the National People's Congress, China's quasi-parliament, while the work department is fully occupied maintaining broad community support for the Party and socialist modernisation.

This latest phase of the united front is called the 'New Era Patriotic United Front'. Its primary strategy is to bring patriots (capitalists of all kinds included) into the fold so as to smooth the process of reunification with Hong Kong, Macau and Taiwan. A mainland Chinese book on the united front published in 1988 stated that this alliance would continue to grow well beyond the realisation of reunification because different social systems and their 'exploiting classes' would remain for a long time in the three places. Lest this reference to 'exploiting' capitalists sound a bit strong, here is a somewhat eyebrow-raising 1984 statement from Deng on the criteria for membership of this new united front:

> What is a patriot? A patriot is one who respects the Chinese nation, sincerely supports the motherland's resumption of sovereignty over Hong Kong and wishes not to impair Hong Kong's prosperity and stability. Those who meet these requirements are patriots, whether they believe in capitalism or feudalism or even slavery.

This resurgence in the importance of united front work is also apparent from the top-level appointments made to the Chinese People's Political Consultative Conference in recent years. The chairman of the conference is Li Ruihuan, a moderate member of the Standing Committee of the Politburo, while among its 26 vice-chairmen are Ye Xuanping, the highly respected and powerful former governor of Guangdong Province, and Wang Zhaoguo, former governor of Fujian Province. Both provinces have been at the forefront of China's opening to the international economy, particularly to Hong Kong and Taiwan. Meanwhile, Wang's heavier hats include head of the United Front Work Department and director of the Central Office for Taiwan Affairs, another unit that falls under the Party organisation (and which effectively doubles as the Taiwan Affairs Office under the State Council). One of Wang's tasks is to drive a wedge between Taiwan businessmen and their government, with a view to pressuring the latter to drop its resistance to direct transport and postal links (and, ultimately, reunification).

THE HONG KONG CONNECTION

Hong Kong-the-place played an indirect role in communist united front work a little before its inhabitants started joining up. First, in the late 1940s several of the Chinese democratic parties, such as the Democratic League and a predecessor of the Kuomintang Revolutionary Committee, retreated to the British colony while being persecuted by Chiang Kai-shek. Second, some of the discussions in 1948 which led to the creation of the Chinese People's Political Consultative Conference took place in Hong Kong. Then delegates were appointed to the first conference held in Beijing in September 1949.

Communist involvement in Hong Kong actually dates back to at least 1925–26, when the Party instigated a huge labour strike lasting 16 months and a boycott against British goods. There were also labour protests in Canton, from where the Party organised the Hong Kong protests. It then expanded its presence in the colony between 1945–49, when its southern command was forced to retreat during the civil war against the Kuomintang. Thus the Hong Kong branch of the New China News Agency came into being in 1947, as well as the China-funded newspaper *Wen Wei Po*, which is still published today. The Communists also began setting up schools and trade unions, many of which have survived and flourished, and gathered a base of local supporters.

There are roughly three periods into which the Party's post-1949 history in Hong Kong falls: 1949–67, 1968–81, and 1982–the present. The first ended with the violent riots sparked by the Cultural Revolution, when Hong Kong security forces suppressed many local trade unions and leftist groups. The middle period was one of quiet rebuilding. The latter began with the announcement of a new unit within the Chinese government to handle reunification matters, the State Council Hong Kong and Macau Affairs Office. Its director was Liao Chengzhi, a specialist on reunification issues. (The office was actually established in 1978, but its existence kept secret—probably to 'avoid provoking speculation in Hong Kong about China's intentions', surmises Robert Cottrell, author of one of the best books on the Sino–British negotiations between 1982–84.) The office is senior to the New China News Agency in the Chinese government hierarchy.

Throughout all three periods, the Communist Party has operated as an underground political organisation in Hong Kong (with the connivance of the British administration, since its position was strictly illegal). Although the New China News Agency is the public face of the Party in the colony, the 'real' power centre is a body called the Hong Kong and Macau Work Committee, chaired by the agency's director and comprising senior mainland business people and officials living in Hong Kong. It has long been Beijing's intention that the Party organisation should remain underground even after the transfer of sovereignty, since to come out into the open could cause local anxiety and might send a (wrong) signal that China wanted to turn its new acquisition into a socialist economy. This policy is credited to Zhou Enlai and was reaffirmed by Liao Chengzhi. However, more recent murmurings suggest that the Party may be considering changing its stance; which must mean it is comfortable with the level of political control it has achieved over Hong Kong so far. Although there are no published figures on the size of the underground organisation, one observer puts it at 6000 people in 1983 and around 11,000 in the mid-1990s. The increase was mainly due to the arrival of mainland companies and new immigrants, although a few would be Hong Kong people.

'But It's Not in the Classics ...'

Most communist activities in Hong Kong prior to the early 1980s were not, strictly speaking, united front work. For until the Joint Declaration negotiations began in 1982, the Hong Kong issue was not high on Beijing's political agenda, and fell well below Taiwan in importance on reunification matters. (It still does, as can be seen above in the heavier institutional structure dedicated to Taiwan issues within the Party and government apparatus.) To use Mao-speak, until the early 1980s Hong Kong was a minor contradiction that could be safely set aside. But once its return to the motherland became an issue requiring the best possible solution (from Beijing's point of view), united front work began in earnest.

Deng set the tone by stating that since the Party's policy on Hong Kong was different from the mainland—that is, the maintenance of capitalism not the creation of socialism—the targets of the united front would have to be different too (though not the methods). Hence his comment that what the Party wanted were patriots, whatever other 'isms' they believed in. His quote above about 'what is a patriot?' goes on to say:

> We don't demand that they be in favour of China's socialist system; we only ask them to love the motherland and Hong Kong.

What this meant in practical terms was that the New China News Agency in Hong Kong should start recruiting supporters from among the local business and political elite in addition to its traditional work with left-wing trade unions, intellectuals, newspapers and schools. In tactical terms it echoed the latter half of the 1940s, when Mao won over 'patriotic businessmen' to help smooth the way for a Communist victory and the return of economic stability. But like Deng's economic reform program, the new united front policy was a significant departure in ideological terms: even in the 1940s, the Communists saw little chance of winning over the 'big bourgeoisie', those comprador capitalists who worked hand-in-glove with foreigners and hated communism. Yet it was precisely this group that was especially thick on the ground in Hong Kong, Taiwan and Macau—for many because their fathers and grandfathers had fled China when Communist victory looked assured.

This shift caused confusion in the minds of some cadres. Xu Jiatun, the director of the New China News Agency during most of the 1980s, is famous for making a droll comment to the effect that he knew of no Marxist–Leninist classic that endorsed the concept of a communist party safeguarding a capitalist system over the long-term! Nevertheless, since Deng himself had once told the Standing Committee of the Politburo that cadres doing united front work in Hong Kong should 'dare to become right-wingers and spies' and 'dare to have social contact and make friends with them (right-wingers)', Xu became 'determined to open up a new vista in the united front', as he writes in an unusual memoir of his time in Hong Kong. Specifically, this entailed getting to know those members of the 'big bourgeoisie' who were friendly with Britain, the United States, and Taiwan.

Xu opened the vistas by holding informal meetings with leading figures in the business community and British political establishment, including Sir S Y Chung, an industrialist who became senior Executive Councillor in the 1980s; Lydia Dunn, a Chinese member of the board of the British company, Swire, and an Executive Councillor at the same time (now Baroness Lydia Dunn); and Lee Quo-wei, the then chairman of Hang Seng Bank, the principal local subsidiary of the HongkongBank. 'I thought that if I could set up regular and direct contact with them, I could understand the ideas of people friendly with the English and also of the Hong Kong British government itself,' says Xu. Ironically, Xu eventually fell foul of his superiors in Beijing for being too 'soft' in his response to the June 4 demonstrations in Hong Kong, and subsequently fled to the

United States. It was there that he wrote his controversial memoirs, published in 1993.

The political acceptance of patriots, whatever their 'ism', into the united front raises an intriguing (if somewhat diversionary) question: Should the national flag of China be modified? The current flag has one big yellow star, which represents the Communist Party, and four smaller stars representing the workers, peasants, petty bourgeoisie, and the national bourgeoisie. It is a symbol of the united front. In this new era, should one more small star be added to represent the big bourgeoisie?

NEW CONVERTS

The Xu years (1983–89) and those of Zhou Nan (1990–today), his rather staid successor as director of the New China News Agency, were and have been extremely productive in winning over the colony's business elite to the united front. It can count, for example, all the leading tycoons as members: Li Ka-shing (of Cheung Kong), Cheng Yu-tung (of New World) and Lee Shau-kee (of Henderson Land)—all property magnates—have appeared prominently on one or more of Beijing's various committees. So have a younger generation of entrepreneurs like Tsui Tsin-tong (China Paint, Citybus, and the New China Hong Kong Group); Walter Kwok (Sun Hung Kai Properties); and Vincent Lo (Shui On).

What were these committees? Two were formed in the latter half of the 1980s to help with the drafting and production of the Basic Law, but it was really in the early 1990s (following Tiananmen Square) that united front work began being consolidated. The first committee was launched in March 1992 and consisted of a group of 44 prominent businessmen, pro-Beijing politicians and professionals, academics and unionists. They were called 'Hong Kong Affairs Advisers', a deliberately neutral term chosen to dampen alarm among the Hong Kong public and government officials that the group would function as a 'second power centre' alongside the colonial administration. The task of these appointees was to advise Beijing on local issues for a two-year period, either when the latter asked for it or when they wanted to convey information. Lu Ping, a former journalist who became director of the Hong Kong and Macau Affairs Office in the 1990s, said the rationale for appointing advisers was to strengthen the mechanism for soliciting Hong Kong people's views in the transition to Chinese rule (Lu had a major hand in selecting the advisors; indeed he was credited with the idea). In keeping with the low-key approach, advisers operated on an individual basis—they were not a formal group with formal terms of reference. Not surprisingly, no Hong Kong democrat was among the 44.

Over the following three years, a further three groups of advisers from similarly diverse backgrounds were appointed—in March 1993, April 1994, and April 1995—taking the total to 186. The significant point about this broad cadre of local leaders was that, along with Hong Kong delegates to the National People's Congress and the Chinese People's Political Consultative Conference, they formed the long list from which Beijing chose the bulk of its appointees to subsequent committees. Equally important was the fact that Beijing went outside the Basic Law to create its Hong Kong Affairs Advisers—as it did when it established its next unilateral body, the Preliminary Working Committee ('the Working Committee').

Formed in July 1993, the Working Committee's task was to examine political, economic, legal, cultural and social/security issues and policies in Hong Kong and decide whether or not they accorded with the Basic Law—then to offer suggestions on what to do if they did not. In essence, its role was to lay the legal and policy groundwork for a more important transitional body—the Preparatory Committee, which was charged under the Basic Law with forming the first government of the Special Administrative Region, and appointed in December 1995.

As its name implied, the Working Committee did a lot of work. It covered a range of transitional matters such as how to set up the first post-reunification government, how to manage the 'tainted' civil service, what the structure of the future electoral system should be, and how China's Nationality Law should be applied to Hong Kong (since China does not allow dual nationality, residency rules have had to change). The committee also examined civil and political rights, legislative amendments that would be necessary to stop Hong Kong laws conflicting with the Basic Law, and a raft of ongoing economic issues. It organised itself into five sub-groups and produced several dozen proposals, many of which became highly controversial because they put Hong Kong's interests firmly below those of Beijing.

Why was there a need for any early work not envisaged in the constitution? Ostensibly because the arrival of a new governor in mid-1992, the British Conservative Party politician Chris Patten, led quickly to proposals for a faster pace of democratic reform in Hong Kong and an about-turn in Britain's traditional policy of allowing China to set the agenda over Hong Kong. Beijing, predictably, was enraged by this unexpected turn of events and decided to go it alone as well—hence the establishment of the Working Committee, designed to leave British and Hong Kong officials out of the loop on key decisions affecting the shape of the Special Administrative Region. Secretive, aggressive and clearly full of a sense of its own self-importance, the Working Committee was deeply unpopular among the general public in Hong Kong. (Whether it was really a *reaction* to Patten's political reforms, or the outward manifestation of a group that would have operated behind the scenes in any case, is considered in the next chapter.)

One more united front institution needs to be mentioned to complete the circle—the Provisional Legislature. Also not prescribed by the Basic Law, this was the body formed by Beijing to replace Hong Kong's last pre-reunification Legislative Council. Since the latter was elected in 1995, it should have gone on to complete its four-year term in 1999. But because it was elected under the new and more democratic voting system championed by Patten, Beijing angrily decided to disband it. The Provisional Legislature was chosen in December 1996 and began preparing for its future role the following month. It will cease to function in mid-1998, when a new two-year Legislative Council will take its place. (This issue is also covered in detail in the following chapter.)

BUSINESS INVOLVEMENT in the united front was not due solely to persuasive officials from Beijing or the New China News Agency. It was a product of this and a range of other factors:

1. The extraordinary transformation of the Chinese economy since the early 1980s, a fact that has given local tycoons a solid and steadily increasing amount of confidence in China and its governing regime (and therefore Hong Kong's commercial future too).

2. A renewed commitment to economic reform on the part of Beijing after a big post-Tiananmen freeze over 1990–91, as well as the growing internationalisation of the country's financial system.

3. The probability that the Party was not about to collapse, as many thought possible in the early 1990s.

4. (Linked to point 3) The increasing certainty that the Party would be in power over the transition period (1997 onwards) and, as a result, the determined lobbying by most local leaders to be on the winning side.

Nevertheless, had Party officials mishandled their dealings with the local elite, the result could have been different. The united front is still the personal face of the Party in the colony and this dimension cannot be underestimated.

BUT THE MOST CONTROVERSIAL of the 'new converts' have been those who were once senior members of the British political establishment. Some were senior civil servants, though most came from outside government and were appointees to high public office. This broad group can be roughly divided into three types: those who went over to the Chinese side noisily, those who slipped over quietly (or tried to), and those who have tried to keep a foot on both sides of the fence.

One of the most vocal prior to 1997 was T S (for Tak-shing) Lo, a solicitor and former member (1980–85) of the governor's advisory body, the Executive Council, who resigned his seat in protest at Britain's handling of the Joint Declaration negotiations. Lo later made his peace with China in a variety of ways, including launching a weekly current affairs magazine, *Window*, which claimed to have 'exclusive China coverage' and promoted a positive view of Beijing's policies on Hong Kong. He also founded a pro-China political party, the New Hong Kong Alliance, in 1989. Although it has made virtually no impression with voters—indeed, Lo himself has never stood for election—the party was given more seats on the Preparatory Committee than any other political group. Even the Democratic Alliance for the Betterment of Hong Kong, a pro-Beijing, grassroots party set up with the help of the New China News Agency, received fewer.

Lo's original hope had been to become the first chief executive (the post-1997 equivalent of the governor) of the Special Administrative Region. But commonsense and opinion polls routinely suggested that he would be an extremely unpopular choice. Snap telephone surveys conducted for the *South China Morning Post* in December 1995 and May 1996 gave him an approval rating of only

1–1.2%. In contrast, Mrs Anson Chan, the then chief secretary (now chief of administration), had a rating of more than 50%.

Lo's problem was image: the public was suspicious of him for brazenly swapping sides and openly courting Beijing's goodwill. He was seen, rightly or wrongly, as someone who would sell out Hong Kong's interests for the purposes of self-aggrandisement. Indeed, Lo has rarely spoken out on behalf of Hong Kong when its interests have been directly threatened. He was quiet during a controversy in late 1995 over China's intention to reinstate several draconian colonial security and media-related laws (which the British administration had amended and softened to fit in with the colony's Bill of Rights, promulgated in 1991 to boost political confidence after June 4). On the contrary, Lo told a conference on Hong Kong's future in June 1996:

> ... I have always believed that to simply confront the Chinese government on disputed issues is non-productive; my basic principle would be to look for the many areas in which both China and its SAR share a coincidence of interests. I strongly believe it is in Hong Kong's best interests to promote stability on the mainland.

To many of Hong Kong's worried citizens, such talk sounds weak and self-defeating. Even if the cause is hopeless, many Hongkongers want their local politicians to stand up to China. This is one reason why the Democratic Party, with its 'anti-Beijing' persona, has consistently performed better than pro-Beijing or business parties in elections to the Legislative Council—it is seen by many to be courageous, a beleaguered defender of civil liberties that sticks to its principles. Yet Lo's exhortations seem naive. Can Hong Kong really work with China on an equal footing, as he appears to suggest? (As it turned out, Lo pulled out of the race for chief executive—and then closed *Window* soon after.)

Two other outspoken changelings have been Rita Fan, a former member of the Executive Council, and Sir S Y Chung, the industrialist mentioned above. Fan sat on the council from 1989 to 1992, when she was dropped by the incoming governor, Chris Patten. Chung was a member from 1972 to 1988, the last eight years of which he was the senior non-government member. Both did long stints as government-appointed members on the Legislative Council as well. And each received British honours: she a CBE and he an OBE, CBE and a knighthood.

Fan, who has had a successful career in education, became an unabashed supporter of China after gaining appointment to the Preliminary Working Committee in 1993. As a sub-group co-convener (co-chair with a mainland official), Fan took a tough pro-China line on many issues. In 1995 she stuck her neck out and publicised a proposal that caused much concern among Hong Kong Chinese who had emigrated in reaction to reunification—at least half a million people by the mid-1990s. The proposal was that they would have to return to Hong Kong by 1 July 1997 if they wanted to guarantee their permanent residency status after reunification. Those who came back after that date would have to live in the colony for another seven years before regaining this status. This caused an uproar at the time, although it later gave way to a more sophisticated policy on the part of Beijing.

Stridency is nothing new to Fan. In the late 1980s, for example, she was among a group of local politicians determined to stop the flow of Vietnamese refugees to Hong Kong. Although her actions were popular with many local people, she angered liberals and social workers in the community with her harsh stance. Fan has been well rewarded for her efforts on behalf of the new sovereign. She went straight from the Working Committee onto the Preparatory Committee, and then was selected to join the Provisional Legislature (of which she became the president). Her role in the first post-reunification government is therefore a powerful one.

Chung, meanwhile, takes a less divisive approach to politics, but is just as capable of dropping bombshells. He made a speech to the Hong Kong Management Association in late 1995 in which he suggested that China would probably need to set up a formal 'shadow government' in Hong Kong around the end of 1996. Chung called it a 'Provisional SAR Government Secretariat' and suggested it would need a few hundred staff. He realised the idea would 'create some concern', but maintained that it was 'inevitable that a shadow government will appear prior to the transfer of power in any government'.

Chung was right in one sense: there certainly was a policy-making shadow government comprising local advisors working with mainland officials—the Working Committee, of which he was a member (though this group was much less formal and smaller staffed than the provisional secretariat he had in mind). Yet his speech was explosive because there were no grounds in any agreement between

Britain and China for a second power centre before the transfer of sovereignty. Lu Ping, director of the State Council Hong Kong and Macau Affairs Office, tried to allay fears by saying that the chief executive-designate and his team would need some support staff, but that they would not be in charge of daily government administration. Chung later claimed he had been misunderstood, but this is difficult to accept, since his speech also referred to the need for a temporary legislature to be in place six months before reunification (to pass bills approving the first budget and creating certain new institutions of government). Like Fan, Chung has been amply recognised for his efforts: he was appointed to the Preparatory Committee in 1996 and was chosen as the senior member of the new chief executive's first Executive Council. This brings Chung, in other words, full circle in his political career.

One other vocal new convert deserves a mention: Sir David Akers-Jones, a former chief secretary of the Hong Kong government in the mid-1980s, acting governor at one point, and one of the few expatriates to be made a Hong Kong Affairs Adviser (in 1993). Having spent most of his working career in Hong Kong, he is as integrated into Chinese society as any British civil servant probably can be (he speaks fluent Cantonese, for example, and has close ties to several local businessmen). A conservative in political outlook, he has gained a reputation as a staunch 'friend of China'. So much so that when he accepted the appointment as an advisor in 1993, he was attacked by some in Britain and Hong Kong for selling out. Akers-Jones defended himself by saying that he wanted to do what he could 'to strengthen cooperation and understanding between Hong Kong and China'. And he added: 'As an "expatriate", perhaps I can play a part by bringing a somewhat different perspective and dimension to the views that are currently being offered to Beijing.'

Although not as vocal as the three politicians just described, Akers-Jones has not been shy to support Beijing publicly. In mid-1996, on a television current affairs program called *Newsline*, he defended China's unilateral decision to replace the elected Legislative Council with the interim Provisional Legislature come July 1997. The decision has been controversial—many say unlawful—because the Basic Law says nothing about such a body. Akers-Jones admitted that the document was 'certainly silent' on this matter, but said the National People's Congress in Beijing had 'filled in the gap'. As the following chapter makes clear, the constitutional foundation of the interim legislature is shaky indeed. The implication of Sir David's remark is that Beijing might unilaterally fill in more gaps in future to suit its own objectives. The Basic Law does not give Hong Kong the constitutional power to block a political imperative—which, of course, is no surprise.

One vocal convert who turned somewhat quieter was Simon Li, a retired judge of the Court of Appeal and a vice-chairman of both the Working Committee and the Preparatory Committee. Li was the co-convener of the Working Committee's legal sub-group, which first proposed the idea for a provisional legislature in September 1994 (shortly after Beijing decided to disband the elected Legislative Council). At the same time, the sub-group mooted the probability that the Special Administrative Region would have to reinstate a tough colonial law on public order and demonstrations (one of the 'draconian' laws which the British Administration had decided to amend in light of the Bill of Rights).

Defending these unpopular proposals, Li said an interim legislature was necessary to bridge any legislative gap after July 1997; and that the tougher public order law was necessary to ensure the police force did not lose its powers to control demonstrations and search suspects. But his remarks also became controversial because he claimed that reinstating the old colonial law was necessary to preserve Hong Kong's stability and prosperity, which was suffering from constant political action. 'We can all see that there is a protest march every three days, and a demonstration every five days. Does this represent a stable social environment?', he asked.

In late 1995 Li had to defend his sub-group's proposal to water down the Bill of Rights (another issue dealt with in the next chapter). Among other criticisms, he charged that Britain was meddling in the affairs of the future Special Administrative Region by enacting the bill. However, with the completion of the Working Committee's role, Li has made fewer public pronouncements and tended to avoid the media spotlight. With one exception: he was a candidate for the post of chief executive in late 1996, but did poorly.

OF THE QUIETER new converts, most are former judges or civil servants. They include Arthur Garcia, a High Court judge who later became the Commissioner for Administrative Complaints (the Ombudsman) and who briefly put his name forward in 1996 as a candidate for chief executive; Li Kwan-ha, a former commissioner of police and close associate of Li Ka-shing; Wilfred Wong, a former deputy secretary in the Civil Service Branch; Nicky Chan, a former secretary for lands and works; and Donald Liao, a former secretary of home affairs.

All these men, except for Liao, were appointed to the Preparatory Committee. Liao, Chan and Wong were also 'Hong Kong Affairs Advisers', while Chan organised a pro-Beijing group called the Former Civil Servants' Association. The association celebrated its first anniversary in September 1995 by inviting around 40 senior civil servants and several New China News Agency officials to a dinner. Each of the 12 tables at the dinner contained one Chinese character which together spelt out three slogans: 'one country, two systems', 'a high degree of autonomy' and 'a stable transition'. Zheng Guoxiong, a deputy director of the agency, praised the association for increasing 'our communication with local civil servants' and enhancing mutual understanding.

One politician in the less vocal category was Maria Tam, a barrister who became an appointed member of the Legislative Council in 1981 and ascended to the Executive Council in 1984. In the latter half of the 1980s her name appeared regularly in the local press as one of Hong Kong's more influential political figures. In 1985 she founded a pressure group, the Progressive Hong Kong Society, and co-founded a conservative political party, the pro-Beijing Liberal Democratic Federation, in November 1990.

But Tam's star steadily dimmed in Hong Kong during the 1990s. Her party has never made much of an impact in Legislative Council elections and she became embroiled in a controversy in 1990 over an apparent conflict of interest between her chairmanship of the government-appointed Transport Advisory Committee (TAC) and her personal investments in a taxi company and close links to a sister company of one of Hong Kong's large bus companies. Tam sold her shares and severed the links, but was widely criticised in the local media nonetheless. She also claimed there was no conflict of interest since the TAC only advised the government on policies regarding buses, taxis and ferries, it did not make decisions. But this did little to quell people's doubts.

Beijing's view of Tam is quite the opposite. In 1992 she was in the first batch of Hong Kong Affairs Advisors. The following year she joined the Chinese People's Political Consultative Conference, China's main united front forum, and the Preliminary Working

Committee. Needless to say, she is also a member of the Preparatory
Committee and the Provisional Legislature.

THE THIRD GROUP of new converts—those who have exhibited
divided loyalties—has been epitomised by the Liberal Party, a pro-
business political group headed by Allen Lee, an industrialist. In
Hong Kong, as in some democracies such as Australia, the word 'liberal' in the names of political parties means 'conservative'. The
Liberal Party's Cantonese name, *Jiyaudong*, literally means 'freedom
party'. The party comprises members of the commercial and industrial establishment, many of whom sat as appointed members on the
Legislative Council in the days before full elections (that is, before
1995). Central to the party's political philosophy is the idea that
Hong Kong's main 'bargaining chip' with China is its economy, and
that the colony should not undermine the status quo by pushing too
hard for democratic development.

True to its Chinese name, the party has not been totally averse to
democracy. It actively contested Hong Kong's first full elections in
1995—in contrast to the minimal showing of candidates from
T S Lo's New Hong Kong Alliance and Maria Tam's Liberal Democratic Federation—and became Hong Kong's second largest party in
the process.

What has made the Liberal Party (or at least some of its members)
slightly unusual has been its willingness to take Hong Kong's side
during periods of conflict with Beijing. For example, during the controversy over the proposal from the Preliminary Working Committee
to dilute the Bill of Rights in late 1995, Allen Lee struck out with this
warning:

> Beijing will have to back off. They don't understand how the common
> people here have accepted the Bill of Rights. There is a perception
> that it protects them from government abuses.

Then, in a Legislative Council motion condemning the proposal
in November of that year, most Liberal Party members joined with
the democratic camp and supported the motion. Only two voted
against it.

Yet this show of defiance did not stop Lee and three other members of the Liberal Party from accepting appointment to the
Preparatory Committee in 1996; nor 10 from being selected to join
the Provisional Legislature in 1997. On other occasions, meanwhile,
Lee has made statements that squarely support China's policies.

After eight democrats flew to Beijing to protest the Provisional Legislature in July 1996, but were prohibited from getting off the plane, Lee was quoted as calling the trip a 'publicity stunt' and said: 'I think before they went they already know (sic) the result.' The Liberal Party itself has made numerous trips to the capital to lobby officials—though always in a non-confrontational manner.

One interpretation of Lee's attitude is that he lets his emotions influence his responses to a greater degree than many of the more self-controlled members of the united front, such as Rita Fan, S Y Chung, and the former government officials mentioned above. At the same time, perhaps Lee realises that Hong Kong people sometimes have to speak out to preserve those elements of their society that are worth protecting—and if this means disagreeing with Beijing, so be it. But it is also a fair bet that the Liberal Party's 'opposition' will be more muted in the Provisional Legislature over 1997–98.

ONE NEW CONVERT to the mainland cause who deserves a category of his own is T K (for Tse-kai) Ann, an industrialist who switched sides much earlier in the game than most—before the ink even reached the Joint Declaration—and subsequently became one of China's closest friends in Hong Kong. Ann was an appointed member of the Legislative Council between 1970–74 and then joined the Executive Council of Governor Murray MacLehose from 1974–79. For his services he was awarded an OBE and later a CBE.

Ann's name started appearing on lists of appointments to mainland political institutions in the early 1980s. He joined the 6th Chinese People's Political Consultative Conference as an ordinary delegate in 1983 and secured reappointment to the 7th in 1988. When the 8th started in 1993, Ann became one of the vice-chairmen.

Between 1985–90 he was a vice-chairman of the Basic Law Drafting Committee and chairman of the Basic Law Consultative Committee. The former body was made up of mainland and Hong Kong members and, as its name suggests, was responsible for drafting the constitution. The second comprised Hong Kong people only and was charged with 'consulting' the community on its views, then passing these on to the Drafting Committee (though much of the time its members argued amongst themselves).

As expected, Ann was in the first batch of Hong Kong Affairs Advisers appointed in March 1992. He became a vice-chairman (one of three) on the Preliminary Working Committee in 1993 and today is the most senior Hong Kong vice-chairman on the Preparatory Committee (in terms of age at least—he is 85). His two senior local colleagues on the Working Committee were Henry Fok, a 74-year-old tycoon, and Simon Li, the former judge referred to above, who is 75. Both Fok and Li also hold vice-chairman positions on the Preparatory Committee, as do two much younger men: Tung Chee-hwa, a shipping magnate and the hot favourite during much of 1996 for the post of first chief executive (he eventually won it by a huge margin), and Leung Chun-ying, a chartered surveyor.

The competitive relationship which exists between Ann and Fok opens a small window to some of the tensions within the united front. Whereas Li has tried to stay above the fray in recent years, the other two raised eyebrows in 1996 by stating their preference for chief executive very early. Ann thought Leung was the best man for the post, while Fok came out for Tung. Critics immediately questioned how the Preparatory Committee could do its job properly if the vice-chairmen took it upon themselves to limit the field from day one.

One interpretation was that these statements were 'test balloons' being flown on behalf of China. That is, Beijing wanted to know whether Hong Kong people would support either Tung or Leung. Others insisted that Ann and Fok were doing battle to stamp their imprint on the post-1997 political structure. But if this was Ann's intention, it backfired: Leung announced fairly quickly that he did not want the top job, while Tung dithered for months over announcing his candidacy. His delay sent some Hong Kong tycoons into a flap. Although many favoured Tung, they were fearful of going public lest he decided not to enter the race and they were left holding worthless betting slips—evidence to the future supremo of who his friends were not. In the end, they needn't have worried.

OLD SOLDIERS AND COMRADES

So who exactly is Henry Fok? Unlike the united front leaders mentioned so far, he has never worked for the British colonial administration, nor picked up any honours in the Queen's Birthday List. (Li Ka-shing of Cheung Kong, in contrast, has a CBE.) Fok is a well-known tycoon, but his company is not especially high-profile—it is Yau Wing, a property and trading concern whose main office is in the Bank of China tower in Hong Kong's central business district.

Most tycoons perch atop a Hang Seng Index constituent company (33 firms make up the index), but Yau Wing is not even listed. Fok is also different in that he first did business with the communists in the early 1950s and has had, therefore, a long personal relationship with the senior leadership (while most other tycoons entered the China market in the 1980s or later). This explains why Fok is arguably the most influential old soldier serving in the united front in Hong Kong.

Of the three Hong Kong vice-chairmen on the Preliminary Working Committee and the five on the Preparatory Committee, Fok is the only one to have, or have had, a seat on all the major mainland political institutions open to Hong Kong Chinese. Unlike Ann, Fok is a member of the National People's Congress (since 1988) as well as a vice-chairman of the Chinese People's Political Consultative Conference—the only Hong Kong person so honoured today. Prior to this latter appointment (in 1993) he had been a member of the conference since the early 1980s. Fok also sat on the Basic Law Drafting Committee and was made a Hong Kong Affairs Adviser in 1992.

Two more old soldiers, although not as important as Fok, are Ng Hong-mun and Lee Lin-sang. Both were delegates to the National People's Congress in 1984 and now sit on the Preparatory Committee. Ng is a former principal of Pui Kiu Middle School, one of Hong Kong's 'leftist' schools, and has been a member of the congress since 1975, which makes him the colony's longest serving current member of this institution. Lee is president of the New Territories Association of Societies, an umbrella association for pro-Beijing groups in that part of Hong Kong.

One member of the Consultative Conference in 1984 who still sits on the body is Gordon Wu, head of property development giant Hopewell Holdings. Although Wu was among the first batch of Hong Kong Affairs Advisers appointed in 1992, he appears to have fallen in Beijing's favour in recent years. He was not, for example, appointed to the Preliminary Working Committee in 1993 or the Preparatory Committee in 1996, although fellow business leaders who were include Li Ka-shing, David Li (who heads the Bank of East Asia), Vincent Lo (of the property group Shui On), Ngai Shiu-kit (an industrialist), Tsang Hin-chi (boss of clothing manufacturer Goldlion), and Tsui Tsin-tong (managing director of Citybus and China Paint).

Conventional wisdom, which is probably close to the mark, is that Wu offended Beijing around 1993 by publicly criticising it for pursuing a restrictive policy on foreign investment in China's power sector. Wu had earlier blazed a trail on infrastructure development in China, starting with his 'super-highway' linking Shenzhen and Guangzhou, and then investing in power plants in Guangdong Province. The rate of return he secured for the latter (around 18%) was unacceptably high in Beijing's view; it subsequently capped the level for all new plants at 12%—a move which naturally went down badly with all potential investors. Wu stuck his neck out and chastised Beijing, saying this was a bad policy because it would deter new foreign investment in power (he was right and Beijing had to relax the policy later). Wu also said he would ignore China in favour of other more reasonable locations, such as India and the Philippines. Such talk reportedly soured his relations with Beijing, though it also showed what a rare bird Wu was among Hong Kong's typically taciturn tycoons.

A MOSTLY YOUNGER BRANCH of the Communist Party's support base is the colony's leftist professionals and unionists. One of the stalwarts here is Tsang Yok-sing, current principal of Pui Kiu Middle School, a moderate, pragmatic Marxist and chairman of the Democratic Alliance for the Betterment of Hong Kong (DAB), the grassroots political party established with the support of the New China News Agency. Despite Beijing's opposition to the Patten democratic reforms announced in 1992, it decided that the agency should help coordinate and promote electioneering by united front candidates to ensure they did as well as possible (and did not run against each other). Other senior members of the DAB include its vice-chairman Cheng Kai-nam, formerly an assistant to Tsang at Pui Kiu, and head of the Hong Kong Federation of Education Workers. Cheng now works for the international public relations firm, Burson Marsteller. And Tam Yiu-chung, former vice-chairman of the DAB (until he was appointed to the first Executive Council of the Special Administrative Region) and vice-chairman of the Hong Kong Federation of Trade Unions, the colony's primary left-wing umbrella trade union. The Federation has more than 200,000 members, which in theory makes it the largest single component of the united front. Its chairman is Cheng Yiu-tong, who is also a delegate to the National People's Congress.

A significant element of the professional left is the media. Tsang Yok-sing's brother, Tsang Tak-sing, is the editor of *Ta Kung Pao,* one of the principal China-financed broadsheet newspapers in Hong Kong (the other is *Wen Wei Po*). T S Tsang is also a delegate to the National People's Congress.

As for magazines, the main pro-Beijing publication is *Mirror,* whose publisher, Xu Simin, is 83 years old and the godfather of the united front media segment. Xu is a member of the Chinese People's Political Consultative Conference.

The New China News Agency supervises and supplies editorials to both *Ta Kung Pao* and *Wen Wei Po.* It publishes its own magazine— *Bauhinia,* the name of the flower that will be the Special Administrative Region's official symbol. And it is closely linked to Sino United Publishing, which publishes, distributes and imports books and related items through companies such as Commercial Press and Joint Publishing. Sino United is a holding company with around 10 subsidiaries. Its chairman is Lee Cho-jat, who sits on the Consultative Conference.

Many of these professionals were assigned to the Preliminary Working Committee (Tsang Yok-sing, Tam Yiu-chung, Xu Simin) and then appointed to the Preparatory Committee (Tsang, Tam, Xu, Cheng Yiu-tong, Lee Cho-jat). Tsang, Tam and Cheng were also selected for the Provisional Legislature.

Intellectuals, meanwhile, are given a role in the front through the One-Country, Two-Systems Research Centre. This is a private think-tank funded by T K Ann and Leung Chun-ying (the vice-chairmen of the Preparatory Committee). The centre has around 30 staff and publishes papers and books on a range of topics relevant to transitional issues. It is headed by Shiu Sin-por, an American-educated labour specialist and publisher who served as deputy secretary general of the Basic Law Consultative Committee and now runs the Hong Kong secretariat of the Preparatory Committee.

GROOMING THE NEW ELITE

As the discussion of the united front's old soldiers/comrades and new converts indicates, there is a considerable overlap between the people appointed as Hong Kong Affairs Advisers or members of the Chinese People's Political Consultative Conference, or elected to bodies such as the National People's Congress, and those appointed to the Preliminary Working Committee and the Preparatory Committee, or selected for the Provisional Legislature. Of the 94 Hong Kong people on the 150-member Preparatory Committee, for example, only a handful have never served on any China-related body in the past. The same applies to the 60 people on the Provisional Legislature, all of whom are from Hong Kong.

The New China News Agency has, therefore, put considerable effort since the early 1980s into expanding the united front beyond its traditional support base of left-wing professionals and old business associates. It has appointed people to various mainland institutions, tested their loyalty (by seeing how they behave and what they say), and then decided whether or not they should join the Special Administrative Region leadership elite. In the meantime Beijing has maintained and expanded the Party's traditional support base. From only 16 delegates to the National People's Congress in 1984, Hong Kong now sends 28. And from 46 delegates on the Consultative Conference in the same year, Hong Kong now has 91. The overall impression is of a leadership development and selection process that is extremely methodical and leaves nothing to chance (if it can help it).

As China resumes sovereignty over Hong Kong, therefore, it can count among its friends most of the city's leading Chinese business people and a large chunk of its professional sector and union movement. It has also expended much effort to woo community groups and district leaders.

WATERING THE GRASS

A flavour of the front's non-elitist side is reflected in a daily section of *Wen Wei Po* called 'Social Organisations' (*shetuan*). In July 1996, for example, it carried an article about 'youth groups of various circles' (that is, 'from all walks of life') holding a meeting to inaugurate a 'preparatory committee' to organise celebrations marking the 47th anniversary of the People's Republic of China on 1 October 1996 and, later, the reunification with Hong Kong. The meeting attracted 285 representatives from more than 200 youth groups and 'friendly organisations'.

Zhang Junsheng, deputy director of the New China News Agency and its main spokesman, told the gathering that it was 'precisely because of the establishment of the new China (in 1949), as well as the motherland's power and prosperity, and the long struggle of Hong Kong compatriots, that we can now take Hong Kong back on 1 July 1997 and resume the exercise of sovereignty'. Warming to his theme, Zhang said: 'This is an important and happy event for everyone in China, including Hong Kong compatriots, and is also a grand occasion that (overseas) Chinese and all the world will be watching.'

The term 'various circles' is one that recurs constantly in reports of pro-Beijing, left-leaning community groups working in geographic, age and occupational areas. There are umbrella 'associations of various circles' on both Hong Kong Island and in Kowloon, such as the Hong Kong Eastern District Association of Various Circles, the Kowloon Eastern District Association of Various Circles, and the Hong Kong Women's Federation Association of Various Circles. Similar networks exist in the New Territories, of which the most important is the New Territories Association of Societies (mentioned above in connection to its chairman, Lee Linsang).

One task of these groups is to mobilise support for China at the community level and to maintain links between district pro-China groups. Another is to do as the association of youth groups above is doing—organise celebrations to mark National Day on 1 October and the transfer of sovereignty. For example, the 1996 National Day 'preparatory committee' of the Kowloon Eastern District Association of Various Circles held its first meeting on 24 July of that year. A couple of days later, the Kwun Tong Industry and Commerce Federation held a meeting to establish its own preparatory committee to celebrate reunification (Kwun Tong is an industrial district in Kowloon). An official committee was also formed under the Preparatory Committee to coordinate all reunification celebrations in Hong Kong. It was chaired by the indefatigable and ubiquitous Rita Fan.

One of the larger non-leftist grassroots organisations in the united front is the Heung Yee Kuk ('the Kuk'), a powerful political group which represents the indigenous villagers of the New Territories. Although this group has been a minority within that part of Hong Kong for some time—the construction of new towns during the 1980s brought in hundreds of thousands of urban Chinese—the Kuk has traditionally wielded political influence out of all proportion to its size. Its roots reach back to 1898, when the British colonial administration allowed indigenous villagers to continue practising their customary law even after the New Territories became part of the colony under the 99-year lease.

The Kuk's importance in the united front is apparent from the fact that two of its leaders sat on the Preliminary Working Committee and three are members of the Preparatory Committee (one of whom is retired from the Kuk). Its chairman is Lau Wong-fat, the biggest landlord in the New Territories and close associate of some former members of the British administration, including Sir David Akers-Jones, who was once the secretary for district administration and had a lot to do with the New Territories during his career. Lau also has a seat on the Provisional Legislature (though he was voted in wearing another hat—that of Liberal Party member).

The New China News Agency keeps in contact with all these grassroots groups through its three district offices in Hong Kong Island, Kowloon, and the New Territories. Overall management of the front is done by its Coordination Department, which is one of the most important of the 17 departments and offices within its Happy Valley headquarters (ironically situated across the road from Hong Kong's greatest symbol of capitalist decadence, the Happy Valley horse racing track).

ISOLATING THE ENEMY

So much for the task of gathering support, an activity that assumes one is isolating the enemy at the same time. In Hong Kong's case, the enemy is theoretically anyone who does not 'love China and love Hong Kong', to use Deng Xiaoping's words, and does not 'support the Basic Law' (a third criterion added in recent years). In practice this of course refers to the colony's anti-Beijing democratic lobby, with the Democratic Party as its backbone.

The Communist Party has made its dislike of Hong Kong's democrats patently obvious. It branded Democratic Party leaders Martin Lee and Szeto Wah as 'subversives' after June 1989 and has expressed its total antipathy towards the Hong Kong Alliance in Support of the Patriotic Democratic Movement in China, a broad coalition of democratic groups set up to assist dissidents in China (and chaired by Szeto Wah). Although Lee and Wah were Basic Law drafters from 1985 to 1989—when they resigned in protest at the massacre—they have been barred from every China-appointed committee since. So strong is Beijing's distrust of the Democratic Party that it appears to believe it is a British creation—at least, this seems to be the view of the more conservative and hardline cadres in the capital. As one mainland journalist in Hong Kong said: 'According to Communist Party logic, when the British leave they will definitely try to leave their mark behind.' One 'hard' piece of evidence of this alleged skullduggery is supposedly the Democratic Party.

It is worth highlighting that during the 1980s the Communist Party's approach to united front work in Hong Kong was more embracing and flexible. Xu Jiatun's quote on the need to 'dare to become a rightist' implied working with traditional political, as well as economic, opponents. Nor could Deng's criteria of patriotism be used against the Hong Kong democrats, since none were (or are) even remotely anti-patriotic (but they do oppose the Communist Party). In fact, in the early part of that decade some nascent pro-democracy groups which supported Hong Kong's return to China were criticised by others in the colony as being too pro-China! But June 1989 turned day into night, and hardened attitudes as much within Hong Kong's democratic camp as in Beijing.

The term 'rightist' as applied to the Democratic Party may seem strange. Most people in Hong Kong view the party as a strong advocate of democratic political reforms, and moderate to populist on most social and economic issues. The 'right', though not a term used commonly in Hong Kong, would include political conservatives opposed to democratic reform and people with conservative views on social policy. To a Chinese communist, on the other hand, a rightist is traditionally anyone who opposes the cause of revolution and the Communist Party (the 'people's democratic dictatorship'). Hence, Hong Kong democrats fall into the same theoretical category as the 'big capitalists' (before they were won over).

While it is possible that united front work could again become more flexible—in reality, not merely in appearance—this would depend, ironically, on how secure a grip the Communists had on China (since the more stable the political situation there, the more relaxed Beijing can feel towards Hong Kong). Even so, it seems extremely unlikely that the verdict on Martin Lee and Szeto Wah could change easily, if at all. They are too far beyond the pale and will remain a 'major contradiction' for the foreseeable future.

SPLITTING THE ENEMY

In his 1951 speech, Deng made it clear that isolating the enemy was merely step one. Step two was to split it, 'so that some members of the enemy camp will come over to the side of the people'. Deng pronounced this statement within the context of criticising those cadres who thought united front work was *only* about dividing the enemy and, having done that, believed it was not worth forming an alliance with potential sympathisers in the enemy camp.

As reunification loomed closer, this strategy became increasingly apparent. Although no one from the democratic camp was invited to sit on the Preliminary Working Committee in 1993, two were chosen as Hong Kong Advisers in 1994. They were Frederick Fung, leader of the ultra-moderate and grassroots-oriented Association for Democracy and People's Livelihood (ADPL), and Chang Ka-mun, one of Fung's colleagues. Fung and Chang were also appointed to the Preparatory Committee in 1996. Then in December of that year, Fung and three other ADPL members were selected to join the Provisional Legislature.

Prying these politicians away from the democratic camp was not an especially difficult thing to do, since tensions between the ADPL and other democrats go back some years. The group did not join the Democratic Party when the latter was created in 1994 because of conflict between personalities, tactics and political agendas: the ADPL did not want to be smothered by the larger party's confrontational character and hardline political policies.

The ADPL had been part of the Democratic Party's forerunner, a broad coalition called the United Democrats of Hong Kong, formed in April 1990. Things were looking good until the alliance had to choose its representatives for the September 1991 Legislative Council elections. (These were significant because they marked the first time that a portion of the council's 60 seats were to be directly elected on a geographic basis.) The result was a great deal of infighting and bitterness, although the elections themselves went very well for the coalition—it won 12 out of the 18 directly elected seats on offer. One rationale for setting up the single party in 1994, therefore, was to achieve greater uniformity and party discipline.

The ADPL's reward for not joining the Democratic Party was subsequent confirmation of Fung and Chang's appointment as Hong Kong Affairs Advisers in April 1994. But Anthony Cheung, chairman of Meeting Point, which was one of the groups to join the Democrats, saw his invitation to become an adviser rescinded immediately.

These machinations show that moderate democrats can become part of the united front merely by not posing a political threat to Beijing. They are not required to propagate China's line as actively and as uncritically as, for example, the leftist Democratic Alliance for the Betterment of Hong Kong or the pro-Beijing media, have to. The new sovereign's calculation is that once such democrats are brought into the fold, their mild principles will be smothered by its own harder priorities and sheer force of numbers—Fung and Chang are, after all, severely isolated on the Preparatory Committee, as the ADPL is on the Provisional Legislature. Ironically, the ADPL is willing to be compromised by Beijing's institutions but not those of its closer ideological allies.

Until around mid-1996 this was pretty much where China's policy on the democrats stood. It had won over a couple, but remained implacably opposed to the Democratic Party and the few independent legislators allied to it, shutting them all out of the Preparatory Committee and warning that they would also be barred from the Provisional Legislature, the first post-reunification legislature.

But this tactic was beginning to wear a little thin. The Democratic Party had performed exceptionally in the September 1995 elections for the Legislative Council—much to Beijing's embarrassment—and proved it was by far Hong Kong's most popular political party. Beijing could manipulate the business community, the grassroots sector, professionals and unionists, but it could not tell Hong Kong people how to vote. Something different was needed to crack the democratic camp.

A new tactic appeared in late July/early August 1996, when some members of the Democratic Party told the press that they had been approached to join the Selection Committee, the 400-strong body which 'elected' the chief executive and the Provisional Legislature.

A member of the Democratic Party, Albert Chan, told Reuters news agency that he had been contacted by pro-Beijing politicians and invited to join the Selection Committee. 'They say if the Democrats could join, tension between China and Hong Kong pro-democracy groups could be reduced and it would boost the credibility of the Selection Committee', Chan was quoted as saying.

The next development came less than two weeks later, when Qian Qichen, China's foreign minister and chairman of the Preparatory

Committee, made a speech in Beijing in which he appeared to make a conciliatory gesture to the democrats—an invitation to dialogue. He told the closing session of a Preparatory Committee plenum that there were 'some people' in Hong Kong who agree with the transfer of sovereignty but 'have different views on the question of Hong Kong's democratic development and the pace of democratisation'. Without naming the democrats as such, he added:

> Only if there is a common basis that we uphold the motherland resuming the exercise of sovereignty of Hong Kong, and hope to have a smooth transition and prosperity and stability for Hong Kong, should we be able to sit together and discuss Hong Kong affairs to achieve the best result.

> That means we have to take in everything and incorporate things of a diverse nature. We have to be largely identical, but with minor differences.

Qian's comments were widely interpreted in Hong Kong as China offering the democrats a genuine 'olive branch'. This phrase was used *ad nauseam* during the week or two after the announcement, and occasionally since. It was even uttered by some of the democrats themselves when cautiously responding to China's invitation. With a collective sigh of relief, pundits and politicians announced that Beijing really had softened towards its enemy.

But relief was unwarranted. Seen through the logic of the united front, the notion of a genuine olive branch was deeply flawed because Beijing's goal of substantially splitting the democratic camp had not changed. The Democratic Party was still a 'major contradiction', since it had the potential to subvert the Chinese political system with the power of its ideas and international political connections. (Martin Lee has been a regular visitor to the United States, where he lobbies the government and political groups for support; and raises cash from private donations.) The party stands for radical things like real freedom of speech, real protection of human rights—and it wants to see these added to an amended Chinese state constitution. From Beijing's point of view, therefore, the party has to be emasculated, if not destroyed.

What Qian's words reflected, therefore, was not a fundamental change of heart in Beijing about the democrats, but a change of tactics to try to keep the democrats as quiet as possible before and during the handover. The Party's broad strategy remained the same. It was merely following a slightly different path to reach its objective. Why would it genuinely want to mend fences? Over the long-term, bigger things are at stake for the Party than being nice to its opponents in Hong Kong. At best (and even this is being generous), Qian's words represented a fake olive branch, not a real one.

Lest this analysis seem too cynical, consider the following points. One, only moderate democrats were approached by pro-China politicians and offered seats on the Selection Committee. There was no indication that the deal extended to firebrands like Martin Lee, Szeto Wah, Lau Chin-shek (a unionist) and others. If the move was really sincere, surely it should apply to everyone?

Two, Qian laid down some fairly tight ground rules for any future dialogue. 'Only if there is a common basis ... should we be able to sit together ...' How common does this common basis have to be? Does it allow for genuine differences of opinion? Qian answers these questions by saying: 'We have to be largely identical, but with minor differences.' This is hardly a sound basis for dialogue between two opposing ideological camps.

Nor would the rules be relaxed by his assurance that 'we have to take in everything and incorporate things of a diverse nature'. This is basically a formulaic statement similar to those repeated by other Chinese officials when promising to 'take account of' public opinion in Hong Kong. It also contains traces of the concept of 'democratic centralism', discussed in Chapter 1. This is the principle which says the Party's central leadership will listen to all views expressed by officials at lower levels before making a decision on its own. But once the decision is made, it is binding on everyone. Under such a system, it is impossible to know to what extent one's views were listened to, and one has no recourse against the final decision. Economic reform in China may have weakened this system—provincial leaders can ignore central directives to a greater extent than before—but Hong Kong is too small and too politically weak to try to dodge Beijing's imperatives.

Three, a subsequent statement by China's top official in Hong Kong delineated more sharply Beijing's 'new' attitude. Zhou Nan, director of the New China News Agency, announced:

> There are some people who have taken the wrong path for some time and recognise that irrational confrontation is not supported by the public and there is no future for them, and they have indicated their willingness to change. We welcome them if they really change ... not only in words but in deeds.

There could be no clearer statement of Beijing's determination that participation and dialogue could only be on its terms.

As it turned out, the Democratic Party responded to Qian by saying, effectively, 'thanks, but no thanks'. Joining the Selection Committee would mean collaborating in the creation of a body they believed was illegal—the Provisional Legislature. And while they expressed a willingness to talk, they refused to do so unless China indicated its willingness to listen to their arguments against the Provisional Legislature and on various other issues. In other words, the agenda would be set by both sides. It had to be a real dialogue, not merely a 'consultation' exercise. (Meanwhile, independent democratic legislators such as Christine Loh and Margaret Ng stayed away from the Selection Committee for the same reason.)

This response was predictably pilloried by many prominent pro-China politicians and united front democrats such as Frederick Fung. Several opinion poll surveys, including even one conducted by the Democratic Party, revealed that the public thought they should accept the 'olive branch'. Fung praised Qian's words as positive, saying they showed that all people who cared about Hong Kong, whatever their beliefs, would be welcome to join the Selection Committee. Fung thought the other democrats should have put their names forward to join the committee because, 'if Qian Qichen says people of different views can sit down (and talk), we should look at it'. He argued that the Democratic Party should join the committee and simply vote for the chief executive (since that was legal under the Basic Law), not the Provisional Legislature. In this way they would at least have some impact on the process and might get some 'reaction' from China. Fung is a great believer, as his comments show, in getting inside the political process and trying to make a difference that way. This is an honest view, but far too reasonable, it is fair to say, for this period in Hong Kong's political development. Meanwhile, Leung Chun-ying, the vice-chairman of the Preparatory Committee mentioned earlier, warned that the democrats would be failing in their duty to voters if they did not accept the opportunity offered them.

From a strategic and moral point of view, the Democratic Party was right to decline the invitation. Had it agreed to join the Selection Committee, its integrity would have been shattered in the eyes of many liberal-minded people in Hong Kong (whatever some opinion polls said). Had it acquiesced in allowing only a few members' names

to be put forward, it would have contributed to its own eventual division. Appearances aside, it is not a homogenous party: there are
cracks between political moderates and relative radicals, professionals and trade unionists, and between those who want to cooperate
with China and those who do not. Beijing would be sure to play upon
this weakness immediately. And had the party followed Fung's
advice—join up but vote only for the chief executive—it would still
have lent the Provisional Legislature legitimacy through its presence
on the Selection Committee.

A POLICY OF OVERKILL?

It would be fair, though perhaps naive, to ask whether Beijing's use
of such a blatant policy of divide and rule is fundamental to the assertion of its sovereign rights in Hong Kong? Britain, not surprisingly,
agreed to give its colony back to China without a fight, and the possibility of armed local resistance against the Chinese government has
always been nil. Rural resistance in the New Territories? Pitched battles in the crowded streets of Kowloon? Scuba divers mining
mainland ships in Victoria Harbour? Such scenarios are obviously
preposterous. Yet if China is not fighting a civil war in Hong Kong,
why the hard-nosed, quasi-military tactics?

The answer is partly that building united fronts is second nature
to the Communist Party. Its *raison d'être* may have changed from
building socialism to pragmatic economic development, but its political methods have not necessarily changed. Since it is determined to
neuter the Democratic Party, what is the best way to do it? It is quite
logical that it should use the tools it knows best and which have
proved successful in China in years past. Just as it rose to victory by
building a solid support base in the countryside and gradually 'surrounding the cities' and its enemy, the Kuomintang, it is taking over
Hong Kong by gathering as much support as it can and surrounding
the democrats.

Hard-nosed tactics also send a message to other parts of China
about the limits of acceptable political behaviour. Beijing does not
want the provinces to start demanding the same freedoms as Hong
Kong after reunification, hence one reason for rolling back the more
unacceptable parts of the colony's political structure, such as the
democratically elected 1995 legislature.

So, in a sense, Beijing is fighting a quasi-civil war. But one where the weapons are political freedoms and the casualties are people's political careers, not their lives. The main deterrent against massive anti-China opposition in Hong Kong remains Beijing's threat to use real force against the city if a political crisis erupts. Given statements made by leaders like Deng, and the Communists' continuing sense of insecurity in China, there seems little reason not to take this threat seriously. In the meantime, expect the unrelenting logic of the united front to continue.

A DIVIDED FRONT

Ironically, a salient feature of the front in Hong Kong is that it has never been wholly united. This may not be too surprising, given the diverse mix of groups and individuals who make up its broad membership. But it presents a real challenge for Beijing and partly explains the latter's underlying harshness (a means to keep the front together as well as isolating the enemy). People know what will happen to their political careers and perhaps even their China investments if they fall out of favour.

But sometimes things explode and people act spontaneously. The sight of student protesters on hunger strike in Tiananmen Square in May 1989, before the tanks began to roll into the capital, was as upsetting for many in the pro-China camp in Hong Kong as it was for those outside. None other than *Wen Wei Po* came out with an unprecedented anti-Beijing outburst on its front page of 21 May. It published an 'editorial' of just four characters—Tung Sam Jat Sau!—which literally means 'grieving heart, pained head', but is also a four-character phrase meaning 'to hate with very strong feeling'. Two senior editors of the paper and several staff were sacked for this act of rebellion. They went on to start their own current affairs magazine, *Contemporary*, which acted as a sort of self-appointed watchdog of the Communist Party in Hong Kong, publishing exposés of the New China News Agency. The publication ran into financial difficulties, was bought out by a Hong Kong businessman on good terms with Beijing, then closed down for good in 1995.

As the 1990s moved on, with the Party still in power and the transfer of sovereignty an inevitability, such open acts of defiance from within the united front became rarer. Yet divisions within the front will continue, and may even widen in future.

One rather large and obvious fault line lies between workers/ grassroots organisations and business. In the free market economy of Hong Kong, the rights of workers and employees have never been sacrosanct. But there have been clear signs that labour wants a better deal. From the recurrent and bitter row over imported labour brought in to work on projects like the new airport (most of the 25,000 or so workers in this scheme were from China), to increased social welfare spending, battle lines have hardened in recent years. The majority of non-business politicians, whether pro-China, anti-China or independent, support greater public spending on social infrastructure. Many do so because they have been elected and are answerable to their constituents. Others contend it is time for deeper intervention in Hong Kong's laissez-faire economy, and to go further than just large public investments in basic infrastructure or social projects (housing, education, hospitals, the environment, transport infrastructure); more social services are needed, especially for the elderly and disabled.

A large part of the business community, especially Hong Kong Chinese tycoons, deplore these developments and have warned that they could damage the colony's economic success. An extreme version of this view was put by Ronnie Chan, chairman of Hang Lung Development, a Hang Seng constituent property stock. Chan told a conference on 'Hong Kong into the 21st Century' in late 1995 that the colony's politicians had used 'revenge disease' to polarise society. 'Politics is irrational. We may end (up) with a social welfare system that is very difficult to reverse', he warned.

Other businessmen are worried about labour activism. Hu Fa-kuang, a member of the Preparatory Committee, as well as a delegate to the Chinese People's Political Consultative Conference and chairman of the Employers Federation of Hong Kong, wrote in *Window* magazine that employers are nervous about 'Hong Kong's rapidly increasing destructive legislation on labour matters'. Hu was not specific about what regulations he was referring to, although he implied things like equal opportunities, maternity leave pay, and any law that increased costs. Hu warned that tampering with the colony's efficient free market for labour—which 'has made the Hong Kong economy so vibrant'—is 'not only doomed to fail but, in the process, will seriously weaken' Hong Kong's future.

In this polarised environment it will take a lot of cajoling on the part of the New China News Agency to keep these tensions under control at all times. Even the Federation of Trade Unions, a stalwart front member, has what one observer describes as a 'complex' relationship with the New China News Agency—sometimes backing it to the hilt, sometimes taking a stand against the 'more conservative elements of the business community, traditionally backed by ... the New China News Agency'.

Tension bubbled up in mid-1996, when the leader of the Democratic Alliance for the Betterment of Hong Kong (DAB), the main pro-Beijing political party, raised doubts about the wisdom of having someone from the business sector as the first chief executive. Tsang Yok-sing warned that appointing someone who was closely associated with a particular business group would encourage suspicions of favouritism. Tsang was not more specific, but his remarks conflicted with Beijing's assumed preference for Tung Chee-hwa, one of the five Preparatory Committee vice-chairmen and chairman of a shipping group, Orient Overseas Container Lines. Tung's close associate is Li Ka-shing, Hong Kong's pre-eminent tycoon and a man used to getting his way in the colony. (A few months later, in December 1996, Beijing's assumed preference was confirmed when Tung won a landslide 'victory' against other candidates.)

There has also been resentment among grassroots and leftist segments of the united front about Party officials like Zhou Nan and Zhang Junsheng spending a lot of time fraternising with the wealthy business elite and their wives and girlfriends at cocktail parties, balls and private dinners. Zhang has been the agency's main partygoer in Hong Kong in recent years, evidence of which can be found on the social pages of *Hong Kong Tatler,* an English-language journal of local high society. Zhou normally takes a much lower profile with the Gucci brigade, though he has been known to attend an art opening or two. The New China News Agency appears aware of these tensions, judging, for example, by the amount of time Zhang spent over 1996 attending community and educational functions.

A different sort of fault line has appeared between the New China News Agency and local delegates to both the National People's Congress and the Chinese People's Political Consultative Conference. In early 1995 there was a spate of criticism from People's Congress delegates directed at Zhou Nan, their bile having risen at his tendency to ignore them at the quasi-parliament's annual March meeting in Beijing and at his inability to attend meetings to explain China's policies on Hong Kong. They also protested that the agency had not answered numerous letters of complaint which they had passed on from people in Hong Kong. These letters normally dealt with problems such as property disputes and detention of relatives in China. One delegate, Ng Hong-mun, former principal of the leftist Pui Kiu Middle School and one of the united front's old soldiers, reportedly claimed that up to 90% of the complaints had not been answered. The agency responded by more actively seeking the views of delegates, although it defended its record on handling complaints.

Around the same time, delegates to the Consultative Conference were upset because the Preliminary Working Committee (predecessor to the Preparatory Committee) had not consulted them before making important decisions. This was not too surprising, since the conference is not accorded the level of respect that its name implies. Yet the incident did show just how little real weight the views of these delegates are accorded. Some delegates protested that they only heard about the Working Committee's proposals through the media.

Problems of communication are in principle capable of resolution, but a deeper problem within the united front may not be. This is the potential for a zero-sum trade-off between the interests of Hong Kong and Beijing during a political crisis. As the former chapter showed, Hong Kong has tended to see the Party's promises enshrined in the Basic Law as vehicles for preserving the status quo. It is only recently that people have begun to realise they may have obligations to 'one country'. Beijing, in contrast, sees Hong Kong as merely one part of a larger whole. True, it is a special part and will receive different treatment from the rest of China, but its interests will always remain subordinate to those of the nation (and the Party). Although the colony has always been exposed to political storms in China, the British colonial administration sheltered it from the worst. This protection will be gone after 1997. When Beijing acts in a time of crisis to safeguard its own interests, whether in the political, legal, economic or military domain, Hong Kong will lose out.

At times like this, how will the local groups in the united front respond? With much awkwardness. Naturally, all groups want to be loyal to China and Hong Kong at the same time. When they do have to choose sides, they quickly become bogged down. There is no easy answer, as the Democratic Alliance for the Betterment of Hong Kong (DAB) can attest.

In the highly emotional atmosphere after the first full elections for the Legislative Council in September 1995, failed DAB candidates said they would not seek appointment to the Provisional Legislature, although they would sit on the body if they won seats in an election similar to the one just held. 'We must follow the same system as we have participated in (in) these elections', said party leader Tsang Yok-sing. This statement was surprising because it contradicted China's explicit reason for setting up the provisional body: to retaliate against Patten's democratic reforms and to cut the electorally successful Democratic Party out of the political process. Yet only a few months later, DAB leaders accepted appointment to the Preparatory Committee and voted with their colleagues to approve the Provisional Legislature, whose members were later 'elected' by the carefully chosen 400–person Selection Committee. This process hardly equated to the open and fair election of September 1995; yet the DAB was happy to win 10 of the 60 seats available. Sympathetic observers say the DAB really tries to do its best for Hong Kong and is pained by these conflicting loyalties. A blunter view is that it is cynically opportunistic. Could Hong Kong truly rely on such a group in a major showdown with China? Could Beijing rely on the entire front to close ranks behind it? The answer to both questions is no. Complexity and confusion will reign if Beijing does decide to crack down.

ALIENATING FRIENDS

The logic of the united front, as explained by leaders like Mao and Deng, is to gather friends around, isolate the enemy and then split it. The one part of the equation never made explicit, probably for obvious reasons, is the need to discard friends once they are no longer useful—or when they do something contrary to the interests of the Party.

An example of this was the treatment meted out to landlords in China before and after 1945. During the war against Japan, landlords were accepted into the front so long as they acted 'patriotically'. Afterwards, a land reform program was launched, and they were categorised as class enemies and treated harshly. This 'flexibility', writes Kenneth Lieberthal, the American Sinologist, 'produced bitterness and cynicism among many in China who found themselves at some point suddenly outside the united front and a target of its often brutal tactics'.

Will such exclusionary tactics affect members of the united front in Hong Kong? To some extent they already have, although ostracism rather than physical brutality is the means used or threatened. Frederick Fung, the mild democrat who led the way into the united front, was famously castigated by Lu Ping, head of the Hong Kong and Macau Affairs Office, for casting the sole vote against the Provisional Legislature in an early meeting of the Preparatory Committee in 1996. Lu accused Fung of 'responding to Mr Patten's call' and said he would be barred from the Selection Committee and the first post-reunification government.

Lu retracted the statement soon after, saying he was merely making a personal comment—a change of heart that probably meant Lu's seniors, or perhaps Lu himself, realised they needed all the democrats they could get. Once kicked out of the front, these new friends could presumably do far more damage. In any case, Fung did put his name forward for the Selection Committee, saying there was no rule in 'black and white' prohibiting him, and that he wanted to play a part in this historic process. As it turned out, he was selected (and he also made it onto the Provisional Legislature, showing that democrats are as capable of a volte-face as Marxists).

But the most famous loner was the late Dorothy Liu, an old friend of China who turned critic and resigned from the Preliminary Working Committee in 1994. Liu was a Basic Law drafter and became a delegate to the National People's Congress in 1988 (a position she held until her death in March 1997). She was also in the first batch of Hong Kong Affairs Advisers appointed in 1992. An outspoken person with a penchant for the dramatic (some would say melodramatic), Liu burst into tears at the inaugural Working Committee plenary meeting in December 1993 in reaction to the presence of Sir S Y Chung and other former pro-British politicians. Like the cadres whom Deng upbraided in 1951, Liu resented having to accept these new, opportunistic members as equal partners in the united front.

Liu quit the Working Committee over its proposal for the Provisional Legislature, which she believed contradicted the Basic Law. When in Beijing for the National People's Congress meeting in March 1995, she told reporters of her intention to put her opposition to the interim legislature on the record—earlier she had said her intention was to have it abolished completely.

After that the tenor of Liu's criticism sharpened. Of Zhou Nan, she said that it was a waste of time expressing any views to him since he never responded. As for the Preparatory Committee, she lampooned it by charging that there were 'no independent minds who will challenge Beijing' and 'those who do will not be tolerated'—a general yet nevertheless accurate comment. And she came out and stated publicly why Beijing was so determined to limit the rights of Hong Kong people with foreign passports—because it did not want Hong Kong to become an 'international political city'. Little wonder then that Beijing did not appoint her to the Preparatory Committee.

Will the future produce more spurned comrades? Undoubtedly, since it is probable that Beijing will not need all its current friends over the long-term. The external political environment will surely change and this in turn will require a different sort of united front (reunification with Taiwan, for example, would change its character). The current body of friends is there to do a specific job: create wide popular support for China's handling of the transfer of sovereignty and ensure that it is a success by helping to maintain stability and confidence in Hong Kong. There will come a time, probably early next century, when these imperatives are no longer as crucial as they are today—and when the Hong Kong issue has slipped down the international agenda. This in turn must mean that the political value to Beijing of many front members will diminish. But, over the short-term, the front is likely to remain stable because it is needed. Beijing cannot afford to have too many more Dorothy Lius barking at its heels.

HOW DEEP IS THEIR LOVE?

What will future historians say about the success of the united front in Hong Kong? It is a harder question to answer than it first appears.

The argument 'for' would say that the front has succeeded admirably because it has won over the majority of the business community, a crucial linchpin since without it commercial confidence in Hong Kong would quickly wither. Such a strong showing of support from Chinese tycoons also stands as a vote in favour of the Chinese economy and a pat on the back for the transformation achieved. The same could be said for the many former and current civil servants who are either members of the front, or publicly positive about the future. Moving down the money ladder, the front has created a wide body of support among professionals, teachers, unionists, schools, community groups and young people. The impression is of a network that spreads its tentacles through every layer of Hong Kong society and into countless nooks and crannies. Just look at the Federation of Trade Unions—it alone has more than 200,000 members. The New Territories Association of Societies claims 60,000. As one political observer said: 'The Communist Party has people everywhere in Hong Kong.'

But there is one rather large problem with counting in these simple terms: elections. If the Communist Party is so loved, why have its preferred candidates performed so poorly in elections? The United Democrats, as you will remember, won 12 out of the 18 directly elected seats on offer in the 1991 elections. In their revamped version as the Democratic Party in the 1995 full elections, they reaffirmed their popular support by winning a total of 19 seats compared to 10 for the Liberal Party (the pro-business group) and seven combined for the DAB/Federation of Trade Unions. None of the three top leaders of the DAB won seats (Tsang Yok-sing, Cheng Kai-nam, Tam Yiu-chung). Although two of these battles were very close, the result was nevertheless a great disappointment for the pro-China forces. Many commentators and the New China News Agency had expected them to do well given the inevitability of the transfer of sovereignty.

The balanced conclusion is that Beijing has succeeded in winning over a good cross-section of elite and local leaders, but has failed to have a decisive impact on the hearts and minds of the public. In other words, the united front is broad yet shallow. It is full of generals, captains and lieutenants, but is lacking in corporals and privates. This image recurs constantly in stories about the various 'associations of various circles' and other grassroots organisations. Many seem like shells with hollow insides.

Apart from being a crucial element in the Party's takeover of Hong Kong, the united front highlights the extent to which China's strategy is deliberate and logical. As in China, united front work will continue in Hong Kong for as long as the Party exists. Beijing will relentlessly pursue the democrats, doing whatever it can to split them. Should this endeavour prove unsuccessful—which seems unlikely in the current unstable political environment—then Beijing wants to ensure that its opponents in Hong Kong operate in a much reduced political environment.

CHAPTER 4

CHANGING TRAINS

There was once a time when people in Hong Kong hoped to be riding on a constitutional 'through train' come 1 July 1997. Like the express trains which run the 130-kilometre route to Guangzhou (Canton) without stopping at the Hong Kong–Shenzhen border, this policy would have allowed all 60 members of the Legislative Council elected in 1995 to carry on and complete their four-year terms in 1999. It also covered the 80 members of the two municipal councils, the Urban and Regional Councils, and the 346 members of Hong Kong's 18 district boards. Together these parts make up the colony's three-tier system of 'representative' government.

It was a neat idea from Hong Kong's point of view, an affirmation of the continuity promised by 'one country, two systems'. For if Hong Kong was to have its own system, why not at least allow its elected 'representatives' to remain in place? After all, many of the top power-holders in the colonial-style government were going to change (though not necessarily all senior civil servants), so what fundamental harm could the relatively weak Legislative Council, and even weaker municipal councils and district boards, do? The legislature may have become a thorn in the side of the executive in recent years, but that is all it is. The party which wins the most votes does not form the government and choose a prime minister, as in the Westminster system. Nor can it initiate legislation, except as 'private members' bills' (and the cards are stacked against these succeeding). It passes countless motions on public policy, but the government effectively ignores most of them (while it must formally respond to these motions, the government is not obligated to act upon them). After reunification, as before, the centre of power will remain in the 'executive'—the chief executive, the Executive Council, the attorney general (whose title changes to secretary for justice), and the policy branches of government.

The Basic Law ensured a spring cleaning of this upper echelon to suit the new sovereign. Apart from the replacement of the governor with the chief executive, the latter chose a new Executive Council. A new attorney general was also a must, since the last one (Jeremy Matthews) did not meet the future senior civil service job criteria: he was British and had the right of abode overseas. The same would have applied to the former chief justice (Sir T L Yang) had he continued on to reunification, since he also held a British passport. Yang was in fact due to retire in early 1997, but resigned the previous October to join the race for the first chief executive, a move which meant he had to give up the passport (and stop calling himself 'Sir'). Senior civil servants who did not fit the criteria also had to go.

By the mid-1990s, if not earlier, most people had come to accept these changes in the executive as a fait accompli. They were the price exacted by 'political reality'. Though a few once hoped that the first chief executive might be elected through universal suffrage, this notion was a non-starter.

But a similar shakeout in the three-tier system, especially the Legislative Council, was a different matter. It represented the small margin allowed for popular participation in the government of Hong Kong—a watchdog role if nothing else—and so should not be dismantled. If Hong Kong had to compromise over the way in which the chief executive was chosen, why could Beijing not compromise on the legislature? Obviously, a hopelessly naive wish.

One group for whom the 'through train' was definitely a bad idea were those pro-Beijing politicians who had failed in elections (or never fought them) and could only enter the representative bodies through a temporarily reinstated appointment system or a rigged electoral system. Many members of the united front would fall into this category. Indeed, the political parties which gained most seats on the transitional Preparatory Committee have never made much of an impression on local voters. They were T S Lo's New Hong Kong Alliance, the Hong Kong Progressive Alliance (a new party set up in 1994 by a solicitor, Ambrose Lau), and the Liberal Democratic Federation of Maria Tam and Hu Fa-kuang, the businessman mentioned in the previous chapter in connection with labour laws.

But certain members of the united front wanted it both ways. The leftist Democratic Alliance for the Betterment of Hong Kong (DAB) and the business-oriented Liberal Party both sought popular legitimacy by contesting the 1995 Legislative Council elections, even though they knew the 'through train' was dead. Then as members of the Preparatory Committee, the two parties happily voted in March 1996 in favour of the Provisional Legislature, thus helping to abolish the very institution they had fought so keenly to get into. For the Liberal Party, this was a case of wanting not to be out of the political loop. The DAB's action reflected its split loyalty (as mentioned in the previous chapter). And it mirrored that great contradiction of pre-reunification politics in Hong Kong: the strong support given to pro-Beijing candidates by the New China News Agency despite the latter's ridiculing of the Legislative Council as only an 'advisory body' and Beijing's determined opposition to democratic development. The rationale was that the agency wanted to prove there was as much, if not more, popular support for the 'pro-China' camp as for the democrats. It failed.

The Chinese government initially supported the 'through train', but only on certain conditions. When the Basic Law was promulgated in April 1990, it included a supplementary decision from the National People's Congress that laid down the rules for such an arrangement: if the last legislature before reunification conformed with the structure outlined for the first legislature of the Special Administrative Region, then its members could continue to hold their seats as long as they abided by the Basic Law, pledged allegiance to the region, and were confirmed by the Preparatory Committee. This was the notion of 'convergence' and was a product of the 1980s, when Sino–British relations were considerably calmer; and politics in Hong Kong was much simpler (political parties, for example, were not allowed until after 1990, when they formed in preparation for the first open elections to the Legislative Council in 1991).

After Patten announced his decision to implement further democratic reforms in late 1992, without getting or even seeking China's 'consent', it quickly became apparent that convergence meant much more than simply following the bare bones of the Basic Law. For Patten did in fact follow the constitution's precise wording: before sending his electoral package to the Legislative Council in June 1994, the Hong Kong government amended the Letters Patent, the colony's constitution, to entrench the new political reforms. The wording of this amendment replicated exactly one section of the 1990 National People's Congress decision.

But Patten offended severely because convergence meant close cooperation between China and Britain on all matters relating to the handover. It was no good Patten claiming to abide by the letter of the Basic Law, for this was not even half the deal. More importantly, Beijing had to feel comfortable with the direction of political development in Hong Kong, and it had to feel in control (even if only indirectly) otherwise the 'through train' could not work. This was the tacit understanding between the two sides before Patten arrived and the British did an about-turn in their policy towards political reform. At the heart of Beijing's anger after 1992 was a deep suspicion of Britain's motives. Was it not trying to create political havoc in post-1997 Hong Kong, which in turn would harm and embarrass the future sovereign? Was it not trying to subvert the Chinese socialist system? And how could it possibly be sincere about democratic reform when it had been happy to rule Hong Kong as an undemocratic colony for 150 years? (This last charge was disingenuous, since the non-introduction of democracy had as much to do with China's longstanding opposition to the idea as with British colonial paternalism.)

Ignoring China's complaints, Patten concluded he had some room to manoeuvre because even the letter of the law was not cut and dried—the brevity of the National People's Congress decision was such that different ways could be devised to structure the region's first legislature. Patten chose to interpret the decision so as to give the Hong Kong people much greater voting power. In the words of Lo Chi-kin, a local political commentator, Patten's constitutional proposals 'merely exploit the grey area of the Basic Law, maximising the room for popular elections within the boundaries of its provisions'. The Chinese government opposed the detail as much as the fact of his reforms. It liked very much the electoral system formerly in use: a hybrid between government appointees to the legislature and a highly restricted electoral franchise. This was not a system anyone in a Western democracy would recognise, since it was the result of a compromise between a colonial government and conservative commercial interests, with a rather contemptuous nod to public opinion. Norman Miners, a political scientist (now retired) from the University of Hong Kong, had a memorable label for it— 'hideously complicated'. Although a reference to the Legislative

Council's first limited franchise elections in 1985, Miners' phrase remains an apt description to this day. Patten may have widened the franchise significantly, but he did little to simplify the structure of the legislature.

One of China's early responses to the Patten plan was to persuade Britain to discuss it in the Joint Liaison Group, the body created by the Joint Declaration to manage the legal and administrative logistics of the transfer of sovereignty. After 17 rounds of fruitless talks ending in November 1993, Patten decided to go it alone. But China had already revealed its hand in July of the same year with its unilateral creation of the Preliminary Working Committee, its first de facto shadow government charged with laying the legal and policy groundwork for the Preparatory Committee (appointed at the end of 1995). As we saw earlier, the Working Committee was not officially sanctioned by either the Joint Declaration or the Basic Law. It therefore marked Beijing's determination to ignore Britain as much as possible in its preparations for the Special Administrative Region.

But the formal derailment of the 'through train' occurred on 31 August 1994, when the Standing Committee of the National People's Congress, the executive committee of China's quasi-parliament chaired by the 'liberal' Qiao Shi, decided to disband Hong Kong's three-tier system of 'representative' government upon reunification. This was followed less than a week later by the Working Committee's infamous 'suggestion' that a provisional legislature replace the existing elected legislature at the transfer of sovereignty—a quick-fire response that indicated the extent to which the committee's deliberations were orchestrated by Beijing. The Provisional Legislature was formally established by a decision of the Preparatory Committee in March 1996, then reaffirmed (because of doubts over the solidity of its legal basis) by another decision of the same committee in February 1997. This latter decision essentially confirmed that the chief executive and the Provisional Legislature had the legal right to begin preliminary work before 30 June 1997.

Why did Britain break its core agreement with China over political development in Hong Kong? What new things did Patten's reforms give to Hong Kong? What will the 'new train' look like, and where will it go? And what does this mean for China's understanding of the common law?

THE PATTEN ANOMALY

The conventional wisdom concerning Britain's about-turn on Hong Kong was that it stemmed from a post-June 1989 malaise which rapidly undermined the autonomy of the Hong Kong government and earned it the sorry sobriquet of 'lame duck'. One of the measures used by Governor David Wilson (1987–91) to boost flagging public morale at the time was a truly massive plan for a new airport, port, and other related projects, including a long suspension bridge linking Lantau Island to the New Territories for the first time, a new tunnel in the western harbour, and gigantic new reclamations in west and north-west Kowloon. The total price tag then was more than US$15 billion (around HK$120 billion) and it was called the biggest civil engineering project in the world (today's price tag is HK$156 billion). To get a sense of size of one project, the width of the West Kowloon Reclamation, for example, is almost as great as the distance across Victoria Harbour from Kowloon to Hong Kong Island.

While these plans went down well in Hong Kong they hit a wall in Beijing, where the central government began to complain bitterly about not being consulted on infrastructure projects that straddled July 1997. This was new, since previously Beijing had not interfered much in economic policy-making. It now demanded to be briefed on all aspects of these projects, especially financing, being convinced that Britain had devised the port and airport as a way to milk Hong Kong of its fiscal reserves before the handover.

The trough during this period was reached in late 1991, when the then British Prime Minister, John Major, was forced to make a humiliating trip to Beijing to sign a 'Memorandum of Understanding' on the new airport. But this was not a final agreement, merely a starting point for further discussions (which did not end until mid-1995). When Wilson lost his job soon after this episode it was widely believed that Major had lost faith both in him and the traditional policy of appeasing China. What was needed for the sake of British dignity in the final years of colonial rule and local morale, therefore, was a stronger governor with a punchier program. Fortuitously for Major (in one sense at least), Patten unexpectedly lost his seat of Bath in Britain's national elections of 1992 and the perfect gubernatorial replacement became available.

Two other factors may also have played a part in causing Britain's about-turn on Hong Kong. First, the overwhelming success of the democratic camp in the 1991 elections for the Legislative Council which intensified the pressure on the Hong Kong government to speed up the process of democratic development. Second, a more complex problem—the declining support offered to the Hong Kong government by the conservatives in the Legislative Council (a group made up largely of government appointees and representatives of business sectors). Although traditionally loyal to the government, these people started shifting their allegiance to Beijing from the early 1990s onwards (and were accepted into the united front). Some also voted against the government on certain controversial issues, such as a deal stitched up in secret between Britain and China over the Court of Final Appeal (which replaces the Privy Council in London as Hong Kong's highest court after 1997). Lo Chi-kin, the political commentator, argues that by early 1992 'it became obvious to the Hong Kong government that a conservative package for constitutional development in 1995 [the next Legislative Council elections] would not guarantee stability of its rule'. Hence the need for something more open and transparent to garner public support, especially from the educated professional class on which Hong Kong's service economy depended and which tended to favour more democracy.

The important factor often left out of the conventional analysis is Patten himself. While the initial catalyst for the change in policy may have been Major and his advisers (among whom Patten was a key figure), the subsequent driving force was the governor himself. It was he who consulted people in Hong Kong; he who sparred with Beijing, defended the reforms during some fairly bleak periods, and went to London to make sure the British cabinet was onside; and he who resisted pressure from the more radical democrats in Hong Kong for an even greater degree of democracy than his reforms offered. Such was the power of the governor in the colony that had Patten not been 100 per cent behind the reforms there is no way the Executive Council would have supported them or new electoral legislation sent to the legislature.

Patten's beliefs make him a moderate conservative, a believer in democracy and basic political liberties, such as the freedom of speech, association, and the right to vote (though he is less convinced of the need for trendier rights like freedom of information and anti-discrimination rules). What he saw when he arrived in Hong Kong—a sophisticated international city with a stunted and unrepresentative political system—must have galled him. Since he believed implicitly in the link between political stability and economic success, his inclination in the face of growing demands in Hong Kong for greater democracy was to respond favourably. If he had not, as he said on countless occasions, surely political tension would have increased and led to a collapse in economic confidence? His opponents contended the opposite: that by bulldozing his reforms through against China's wishes, Patten intensified political conflict and therefore weakened economic confidence. (Neither argument, by the way, is wholly convincing—though that of Patten's detractors is the weaker given the continuing strength of the Hong Kong economy.)

In any case, Patten's unwavering defence of his own position in the face of unwinnable odds—the demise of the 'through train' was in sight before his reforms were even passed—implied a personal commitment that went beyond merely carrying out orders from London. Only he had the authority in London to keep the British cabinet onside during the intense pressure applied by Beijing between 1992–94. A normal governor, drawn from the diplomatic corps, could not have.

Indeed, Patten was unlike any other recent governor of Hong Kong, such as Murray MacLehose (1971–82), Edward Youde (1982–86) or David Wilson. He was a quick-witted and, at times, pugnacious leader. They were all diplomats, more used to the art of behind-the-scenes negotiation than public sparring. They tried to ensure that policy-making in Hong Kong did not upset Britain's broader relationship with China. Patten saw his role as standing up for Hong Kong in arguments with China (although he stood up for Britain in arguments with Hong Kong just as fiercely).

Intriguingly, Patten's personal stake in political reform in Hong Kong goes back to 1979, when he and one other British member of parliament visited the colony and concluded that it deserved direct elections at the district board level. This idea was then put to the Minister for Foreign and Commonwealth Affairs in London and led to the introduction of such elections in 1981. Since this electoral reform never went as far as the younger Patten had hoped, perhaps his 1992 initiative was an attempt to complete the job.

Unwittingly, however, Patten appeared to the Chinese government as a modern reincarnation of the bullying nineteenth century Western imperialist. He had the audacity to tell China what was good for Hong Kong, a territory it was about to reclaim as its own. He was encouraging the very sort of uncontrollable pluralism in Hong Kong that the Communist Party feared could develop in China; hence, his actions were part of a British plot to destabilise Hong Kong and embarrass China. And, the most xenophobic charge of all, he was an agent provocateur for international forces trying to keep China from developing.

THE ALLEGEDLY ARTIFICIAL ELECTORATE

The significance of Patten's reforms lay in the greatly expanded voting franchise that he created as well as the composition of the Legislative Council. Although his plan followed the simple outline of the Basic Law, the way he filled in the blanks was original.

To start with composition—before the Patten reforms, the legislature had 18 geographic constituency seats, 21 'functional constituency' seats, 18 government-appointed members and three senior government officials. Geographic constituencies are self-explanatory, as are appointed members and officials. Functional constituencies, however, require some explanation. They were first devised for the 1985 elections and mostly represented very narrow commercial, industrial and professional interests (a couple of seats were set aside for labour unions and social welfare organisations).

For the September 1995 elections, the government took the following steps, some of which were quite radical for Hong Kong. It:

- abolished the system of appointing local business and community leaders to the legislature.

- abolished the three reserved seats for officials.

- increased the number of geographic constituencies from nine to 20 and instituted a simplified 'single seat, single vote' system. This meant each district had one candidate and each elector voted for just one candidate. In 1991, each district had two seats and each elector voted for two candidates.

- reshaped the functional constituency system. The most important change was that nine new seats were added that represented broad groups of workers and employees (in theory the combined effect was to give the whole working population of 2.9 million a vote). The other 21 seats continued to represent narrow vested interests, although a previous system whereby companies and organisations had votes was abolished. In 1995 only individuals could vote in the functional constituency elections.

- set aside 10 seats to be elected by an 'election committee' made up of all 346 district board members, who themselves had been elected through universal suffrage district elections in 1994. Another way to construe the committee could have been through election by a limited electoral college of appointed people (China's preference).

The end result was the following structure: 20 geographic constituency seats, 30 functional constituency seats, and 10 election committee seats. Since this was exactly the basic framework laid down in the Basic Law for the first post-reunification legislature, Patten argued he was complying with the document.

Although some of these changes would probably have been made anyway by a different governor to ensure that the last legislature under British rule 'converged' with the Basic Law—such as the abolition of the direct appointment system and seats for officials, and the general restructuring of seat numbers—the particulars are not ordained. To reiterate, Beijing dislikes many of the details of the Patten system and intends to change them; it thinks they are too democratic (more on this later). One point worth mentioning in this context is that the new electoral system also abolished appointed seats for the district boards and municipal councils. Beijing intends to reinstate them after July 1997.

But composition was just one aspect of Patten's reforms. The political impact of his changes becomes clearer when one looks at the way in which the voting franchise changed. In 1991, the number of registered voters for functional constituency seats was a mere 71,000 people. Of these, just under 23,000 bothered to vote. Given there were 21 seats, that made an average of not much more than 1000 voters per seat! Or to look at it another way, only 0.4% of the Hong Kong population of 5.7 million people in 1991 voted for a third of the Legislative Council. It gets even worse when you remember that in that election only 39 of the 60 seats were up for grabs (the remainder being appointees and government officials). If there is one fact that epitomises the enduring colonial legacy in Hong Kong, it would have to be the existence of functional constituencies.

In 1995 there was both big change and no change. On a macro level, the number of registered voters in functional constituencies rose from a minuscule 71,000 to a relatively gigantic 1.1 million people. This was mainly due to the nine new seats. In the end 460,000 voted, a fairly respectable turnout of 40%. But what was startling was that 413,000 of these voted in the nine new constituencies. The 21 old and narrow constituencies attracted just 43,000 voters—an improvement on the 1991 record but still only 0.7% of the Hong Kong population of 6.2 million people. The farcical nature of this component is underlined by the fact that nine of the 21 seats were uncontested. They were in constituencies representing finance and the 'industrial', 'commercial', 'rural' and architectural sectors.

The growth in the franchise for the geographic constituencies was less dramatic, but that was because the number of voters was much higher to start with. In 1991, a total of 1.9 million people registered to vote in this contest. By 1995, this had risen to 2.6 million (out of a total eligible voting population of 4 million). Some of this growth came from the dropping of the voting age from 21 to 18 years old; the rest from the efforts of the Boundary and Election Commission.

Pro-Beijing figures in Hong Kong liked to say that Patten expanded the electorate 'artificially', a favourite refrain of *Window* magazine, among others. They were mainly referring to the changes made to the functional constituency system, which they believed should have remained in the hands of narrow sectoral interests. They also liked to point out that the turnout for the 1995 geographic constituency elections (36%) compared unfavourably with 1991 (39%). The implication was clear: support for democracy was declining in Hong Kong. What they neglected to say, of course, was that the percentage was lower because the total size of the electorate was higher. The actual turnout in 1991 was 750,000 people, rising to 920,000 people in 1995. Not a bad increase for a nascent political society (though hardly brilliant, given that the eligible voting population was 4 million).

But what mattered for Hong Kong was less the biased views of pro-Beijing figures than the attitude of the new sovereign. It found just about every aspect of the Patten democratic reforms unacceptable. The last governor was well on the way to becoming a part of history when his reforms were implemented. While the reforms will leave a lasting impression on the experience of Hong Kong, most are being dismantled. The three-tier system was disbanded on 1 July. The rules of the electoral game are being rewritten.

If the logic of the united front was to build a base of local allies who would work to ensure the transition was a smooth one, the strategy now is to reshape the environment within which politics is allowed to operate (including who can enter the arena). Some of Beijing's policies are a step backwards to the Hong Kong of the early to mid-1980s, a period the new sovereign undoubtedly has far more sympathy for. Some reflect the wide gulf between Beijing's and Hong Kong's interpretation of the Basic Law and other laws. These are all fundamental political questions on which Beijing has shown little inclination for compromise.

THE NEW TRAIN

The critical institutional aspect of this new structure is the Provisional Legislature. As explained already, it is an interim body intended to operate as a fully fledged legislature for one year—from 1 July 1997 to 1 July 1998—after which there will be fresh elections for a two-year council. Since it was chosen in late 1996, it started holding informal meetings early in 1997. But since the British administration considered the body illegal under the Basic Law, these meetings could not be held in Hong Kong. The site chosen instead was nearby Shenzhen, the special economic zone north of the colony. Some sub-committee meetings, significantly, were held in Beijing.

What has not yet been explained is the controversial and bureaucratic way in which the legislature was 'elected'. It was a multi-layered process: in late December 1995 Beijing appointed the Preparatory Committee. In August 1996 this committee called for nominations from the public (more than 5000 names went forward) for a 400-seat 'selection committee', intended to be broadly representative of Hong Kong society. But as this body was subsequently chosen by the Preparatory Committee, and because the line-up was a veritable who's who of the united front, claims that the process and the body were 'very democratic' rang hollow.

According to the Basic Law, the Selection Committee's sole task was to 'elect' the chief executive. But following a pattern established since 1992, Beijing ignored its own law and broadened the powers of the Selection Committee to include 'electing' the Provisional Legislative. Both tasks were carried out in December 1996.

The highly selective franchise for these 'small-circle' elections and the fact that almost none of the delegates were willing to cross Beijing (with the exception of the grassroots democrat Frederick Fung), conveyed an apt sense of the 'controlled democracy' acceptable to Beijing. It claimed the Selection Committee was highly representative because a set number of seats were reserved for different sectors of society: business, the professions and the grassroots/religious sectors each got 100 seats, while 'former political figures' got 40, and the remaining 60 went to local members of the National People's Congress and the Chinese People's Political Consultative Conference.

Beijing considered this arrangement to be more democratic than a simple election because it supposedly ensured that all parts of society were equally represented, not merely those people who vote. But this was untrue: in practice, businessmen (and a few women) won many of the seats reserved for other sectors.

None of this stopped China's foreign minister, Qian Qichen, from claiming that the preparation for the Special Administrative Region government was 'the beginning of real democracy' in Hong Kong, meaning its people had never played a part in choosing the governor. True, but then why not open the election of the first chief executive out to universal franchise?

Although Tung Chee-hwa, the first chief executive, and his new Executive Council will be powerful and important, they could get nowhere in implementing China's new legislative program for Hong Kong without the Provisional Legislature. This is simply because the last Legislative Council before reunification had a powerful democratic bloc that, if left in place, would have resisted major legislative changes after July 1997. A malleable yet powerful legislature is therefore crucial to Beijing's strategy.

It is worth remembering that when it was first conceived in 1994, the Provisional Legislature was sold (not very convincingly) to Hong Kong people as a minimalist body. Tsang Yok-sing, head of the pro-Beijing Democratic Alliance for the Betterment of Hong Kong, claimed that it would only carry out legislative work that was absolutely necessary for the formation of the Special Administrative Region, and implied that it might only operate for a few months. And he added:

To allay fears that this stopgap legislature may pass draconian laws against the wishes of the people, *its powers and functions would have to be clearly delimited.* (italics added)

Tsang then listed what these powers would be, basing his explanation on the Basic Law. The legislature would: examine and approve the government's budget; approve taxation and public expenditure; pass legislation to issue Special Administrative Region passports; enact legislation applying various Chinese national laws to the region, as required by the Basic Law; endorse the appointment of judges on the Court of Final Appeal and the chief judge of the High Court; and elect the Legislative Council's new president. In other words, apparently straightforward, mundane functions.

Tsang admitted there would be a few other areas where the Provisional Legislature might have to enact *new* laws, such as electoral arrangements for the new Legislative Council in 1998, the method for forming the new district boards and municipal councils, and possibly laws dealing with Hong Kong's financial system. But he was at pains to emphasise that the legislature's program 'should not cause any fear or worry for the public'.

But Tsang told less than half the story. When the Preparatory Committee confirmed the formation of the Provisional Legislature in March 1996, it stated that the interim body's first task would be to:

Ascertain, according to the rules of the Basic Law, which laws are indispensable for the functioning of the Hong Kong Special Administrative Region, and *amend or abolish* them according to need. (italics added)

Since the other functions listed were either identical to those on Tsang's list or quite bland, such as listening to and discussing the chief executive's policy addresses, it is the first task that has caused most concern. For it transformed the Provisional Legislature from an institution with minimal powers to one with broad and extensive ones. 'Amending and abolishing' law is qualitatively different from Tsang's positive roster of 'examining, approving and (maybe) enacting'. But Beijing believes that it needs to amend and abolish in order to reshape Hong Kong's political system into a less 'subversive' form.

One other factor worth remembering is that the Provisional Legislature was chosen in late 1996, then began holding meetings in early 1997. Thus by 1 July 1997, it had already spent six months considering and agreeing upon a raft of laws and amendments ready for enactment from day one of the Special Administrative Region.

Assuming the legislature's term ends on 30 June 1998, it will effectively have sat for 18, not 12, months. Its influence will be profound, not minimal.

UNWANTED BAGGAGE

Which laws will be amended or repealed? The most controversial are those governing the relationship between the executive arm of government and the legislature, electoral arrangements, and civil rights. Less famous are a series of laws dealing with British administrative regulations and defence. In total, the Preliminary Working Committee concluded that 38 pieces of legislation contravened the Basic Law and so should be amended or abolished. In February 1997, the Preparatory Committee, after a year's study, suggested to the higher National People's Congress standing committee that 25 laws should be partially or fully repealed by the Special Administrative Region.

One of the more complex areas of legislation set to change is Hong Kong's electoral laws and legislative structure. Within the outline laid down by the Basic Law for the first government of the Special Administrative Region, Beijing will make the following basic changes through the formal channels of the Provisional Legislature:

- resurrect the pre-1995 system of appointment for a portion of seats on district boards and the two municipal councils.

- cut the number of geographic constituencies in the Legislative Council from 20 to between seven and ten, and introduce 'multi-seat' constituencies of two to three seats each (thus retaining 20 geographic seats).

- abolish Patten's brain-child of nine broad worker- and employee-based functional constituencies and put in their place nine narrower ones based on organisations such as chambers of commerce, professional groups, and labour unions. The other 21 will probably be left as is, although the pre-1995 voting system looks likely to be reintroduced (that is, companies and groups will have votes).

- abolish the current district-board-based franchise for the election committee of the Legislative Council and put in its place an appointed electoral college, such as the 400-person Selection Committee. Indeed, many members of the influential Preparatory Committee think it would be a good idea if the present Selection Committee simply became the election committee in the 1998 elections for the new two-year legislature.

In other words, Hong Kong's future legislature will have the same basic 20–30–10 structure as Patten's did, but it will be based on a narrower and more Beijing-friendly electoral franchise.

According to Lau Siu-kai, a sociologist, the Hong Kong spokesman for the Preparatory Committee on this issue and the source for most of the above information, the first post-1997 government will also abolish the current voting system for geographic constituencies of 'single-seat, single-vote' and 'first past the post'. This is a simple majority arrangement whereby the candidate with the most votes in each constituency wins, whether or not that person has received more than 50% of the vote. Hence, in seats where there are three or more candidates, as was the case in several districts in the 1995 elections, then the winner may get a lot less than half the vote.

Politicians who won clear victories in this category in the 1995 election included, for example, the independent democrats Christine Loh and Emily Lau, the reformist democrats Martin Lee, Yeung Sum, Huang Chen-ya, Szeto Wah and Lee Wing-tat, the moderate democrats Frederick Fung and Bruce Liu, and the pro-Beijing politicians Chan Yuen-han and Cheung Hon-chung (though only by 48 votes). Winning candidates who received less than 50% of the vote included the businessman Allen Lee and the independent Andrew Wong (who subsequently became president of the Legislative Council). Interestingly, many of the winners in the nine new functional constituencies also gained less than half the vote (most functional constituencies also used 'first past the post').

The beauty of 'first past the post' is its simplicity. Electors usually just vote for one candidate and counting is straightforward. Critics of the system say it is unfair because the true preference of the electorate may not be reflected if the winning candidate gets less than half the vote. It is also a system that tends to benefit big parties, since they are better organised, have a higher profile and can field more candidates.

Countries which use it include Britain, the United States and India. Those which use the other main voting system—proportional representation, or a variation of it—include Japan, Israel, Italy and New Zealand. In proportional representation, electors vote for parties rather than individuals and seats are allocated to the parties according to the proportion of votes each wins. It is a system that small parties love, since without it many would find it impossible to win any seats at all: hence one reason for the complexity of politics in Israel and Italy! Britain's Liberal Democrats, a small centrist party led by Paddy Ashdown, has been arguing for proportional representation for years.

Most pro-Beijing figures in Hong Kong dislike single-seat constituencies with 'first past the post' counting because it allegedly exaggerates the strength of the Democratic Party and promotes 'one party' dominance. The party won 12 of the 20 geographic constituency seats at the 1995 election, while independent democrats won another two. The pro-Beijing Democratic Alliance for the Betterment of Hong Kong won just two. The pro-business Liberal Party won only one. And the Association for Democracy and People's Livelihood, the grassroots democratic party headed by Frederick Fung, won two. Since geographic constituencies were the only ones 'directly elected' by universal suffrage, the Democratic Party emerged as the overwhelming moral winner in the 1995 election.

Beijing's intention is to introduce either a proportional system or what is called 'multi-seat, single-vote': several candidates per district, but each elector voting for just one. Hence the rationale for cutting the number of geographical constituencies from 20 to around seven to 10. The implicit aim is to benefit smaller parties, hopefully those pro-Beijing groups that have failed to muster much public support in elections. Apart from Tsang Yok-sing's Democratic Alliance for the Betterment of Hong Kong, they include Ambrose Lau's Hong Kong Progressive Alliance, Maria Tam's Liberal Democratic Federation, and T S Lo's New Hong Kong Alliance. But the more important aim is to weaken the party system generally in Hong Kong—to bolster the colony's executive-led government.

Lau Siu-kai argues that it is unnecessary to be cynical about this process. First, the Democratic Party could still do quite well under a different system. If, for example, the majority of people voted for the Democrats under a proportional system, then their party would still win the majority of seats. The outcome, however, would be harder to predict under a 'multi-seat, single-vote' system, since it would depend on how the parties ran their campaigns. If candidates from the same party fought against each other in one constituency, for example, then that party would not do as well as it would if it coordinated its candidates properly. Smaller parties would benefit from disorganisation among larger parties. But the bottom line of Lau's argument is that not more than four or five seats (out of the 20) are likely to change hands from larger parties to smaller ones under either voting system.

Second, the Legislative Council is only a body which monitors the government, raises complaints, and acts as a checking-and-balancing mechanism. It does not form the government of Hong Kong. Hence there is no need for a system such as 'first past the post' which is designed to produce a stable government in a full democracy. So why not design a legislature that 'contains all the major (political) interests in Hong Kong?', Lau asks.

Third, while the Basic Law says the ultimate aim is to elect all members of the Legislative Council by universal suffrage (ie, only geographic constituencies), it only lays down the changes that should take place to the year 2003, when half of the 60 seats will be returned through this method. Lau reckons that unless an electoral system is devised in which everyone has a stake, there could be strong resistance after 2003 to any further increase in directly elected seats. 'What I am talking about is a method which will allow all political parties to co-exist', he says, claiming that he is not talking about 'destroying the Democrats'. He does believe, however, that the larger parties, including the Democrats, do not adequately represent the interests of the grassroots sector of society. Those parties which do represent this sector should have a greater stake in the Legislative Council.

Fourth, Lau thinks that larger geographic constituencies would force candidates to address larger social issues, as opposed to 'petty local' ones. This would produce a 'higher quality of candidate', he claims.

Yet a good dose of cynicism about this whole process is justified. It may not be Lau's goal, but it is Beijing's, to cut the Democratic Party down to size (or even better, to destroy it). Indeed, the value to Beijing of a more fragmented Legislative Council is precisely that it is easier to control through 'divide and rule'. For tactical reasons, Beijing does not appear to want any one party to become dominant, even one that is loyal (for what would happen if it became an enemy?).

The notion of giving more of a stake to the grassroots sector is an honourable one, yet the influence of this segment of society will remain limited as long as the legislature is only a 'watchdog' body and real political influence remains in the hands of the business and professional elite. As for allowing *every* party a stake in the political process, surely that contradicts the consensus of modern societies that parties and individual candidates should earn their place in public life through openly competitive, not government-manipulated, elections? If parties were to win seats on the legislature simply because they existed, then the value of the institution itself would diminish and public cynicism would increase.

Lastly, when Beijing's changes to the functional constituency and election committee categories are factored in, the combined effect will be to increase the conservative/pro-China lobby within the Legislative Council and 'surround' the hostile democrats. In this regard, it is significant that the majority opinion within the Preparatory Committee favours the 'multi-seat, single-vote' option (that is, a system less favourable to the democrats than proportional representation).

THE MOST CONTENTIOUS issue which the Provisional Legislature will deal with is the Bill of Rights Ordinance (abbreviated here as the 'bill' or the 'rights charter') and various politically sensitive laws amended as a result of the bill's enactment. The British administration enacted this charter in mid-1991 as part of a package of measures to boost local confidence after the shock of Tiananmen Square. The package included the port and airport project, an offer of British passports to 50,000 families—a highly selective scheme that backfired as a public relations exercise because it caused resentment among the majority of the population which did not qualify— and some mild policies for a faster pace of democratic reform (the weakest part of the package until Patten arrived).

In terms of international law, the effect of the bill was to incorporate into local law the International Covenant on Civil and Political Rights (ICCPR), one of two principal United Nations human rights treaties (the other is the International Covenant on Economic, Social and Cultural Rights). Formal incorporation is not necessary if the laws and legal systems of signatory states already entrench the covenant's principles. But it does have one important implication: a government's claim to be implementing the treaty can be challenged in local courts.

The ICCPR has applied to Hong Kong since 1976, when Britain ratified it on behalf of itself and its remaining colonies. But Britain has never incorporated the covenant into its own laws through a rights charter because it has always believed that existing British legislation and the common law provided adequate protection. It used an identical argument for Hong Kong until 1989, when it was forced to rethink its approach. Before this time, the British administration in Hong Kong had done little to implement the covenant beyond maintaining the political liberties necessary for a free market economy. For example, it did not bother to amend its hard-nosed colonial security laws to bring them up to date with the changing social context of Hong Kong. Imprisoning pro-communist protesters may have been acceptable to Hong Kong society in 1967, but in the 1990s the existence of such a law is anachronistic.

Hong Kong's colonial constraints were such that numerous laws had to be amended after 1991 to comply with the Bill of Rights. A total of 36 legislative amendments affecting 57 pieces of legislation were passed between May 1992 and August 1996 (some amendments covered two or three related laws). These changes ranged from new restrictions placed on the power of the police and the Independent Commission Against Corruption, to laws dealing with drug enforcement and the prevention of bribery, and to changes in social and economic legislation covering miscellaneous things like pensions, adoption, tax collection and massage parlours. The most famous amendments affected six 'draconian' laws that empowered the government to restrict political activity, free speech and enforce martial law during crises. They were:

- the Societies Ordinance, which strictly controlled the creation and operation of political and other societies.

- the Television Ordinance, which gave the Executive Council the power to suspend a broadcaster's licence on political grounds.

- the Telecommunication Ordinance, which allowed the Executive Council to ban radio programs which it deemed were undermining public order.

- the Broadcasting Authority Ordinance, which empowered the Executive Council to give directives to the Broadcasting Authority on television broadcasts.

- the Public Order Ordinance, which strictly controlled both the right of political groups to hold rallies and the size of them.

- the Emergency Regulations Order, which gave the government wide powers to implement martial law and ban publications during a period of civil unrest (this law was repealed, not amended).

In the face of the mostly positive reception of the Bill of Rights and the amendments in Hong Kong, the Preliminary Working Committee announced in October 1995 that certain powerful sections of the bill and the five amendments all contravened the Basic Law and would have to go. And it threw in two other pieces of legislation for good measure: the Legislative Council Commission Ordinance (1994), which strengthened the independence of the council's secretariat, and the New Territories Land (Exemption) Ordinance (1994), which banned the antiquated practice of barring female members of indigenous families from inheriting ancestral property (without the permission of male relatives).

Of the 38 laws which the Working Committee 'suggested' should be amended or abolished, these were the most prominent. In essence, what the committee wanted was the reinstatement of the old colonial versions of these laws.

With memories of June 1989 still prevalent, the public controversy which ensued was intense and cross-sectoral. Alongside the democrats and the liberal media stood conservatives, civil servants and some business voices. As the previous chapter mentioned, even Allen Lee, leader of the pro-business and pro-Beijing Liberal Party, warned Beijing to 'back off', and most of his party voted for a Legislative Council motion condemning the Working Committee's proposal. The only party which voted against was the grassroots Democratic Alliance for the Betterment of Hong Kong (DAB). But the DAB sidestepped the question of whether the proposal was good or bad, saying it should be up to the post-1997 government to decide.

Since the Working Committee's announcement, the one pleasant surprise came in February 1997 when the Preparatory Committee excluded the New Territories Land (Exemption) Ordinance from its list of 25 laws to be repealed in part or full by the Provisional Legislature—and thus upheld the newly acquired rights of women from indigenous families in the formerly rural New Territories. The vote brought a predictable howl of anguish from the Heung Yee Kuk, the powerful political group representing the (mostly male) interests of indigenous villagers in that part of Hong Kong, and a staunch supporter of the united front. Indeed, the Heung Yee Kuk chairman, Lau Wong-fat, walked out of the meeting in protest, and later issued a statement expressing his 'disappointment and anger'. But this was not necessarily the end of the story for the New Territories law, since the Special Administrative Region government could still repeal or amend it after the handover.

Also interesting was the fact that a relatively large number of committee members opposed the proposal on the 25 laws. One voted against (no prizes for guessing who—Frederick Fung) and 10 abstained (out of 135 people who voted). However, some of the abstentions were not a tacit vote in favour of protecting Hong Kong's existing civil rights and political legislation, but came from enraged New Territories' representatives.

But any celebration among Hong Kong's liberal–democratic lobby was shortlived, since the Preparatory Committee's list did include the Bill of Rights, and the amended ordinances dealing with public order and societies (though not the telecommunications, television and broadcast laws, which were of lesser concern to all sides in any case from a civil liberties point of view). As in late 1995, there was a renewed round of argument, criticism and anger towards the planned tightening of political freedoms in Hong Kong. And public morale fell further in April 1997 when the chief executive-designate's office announced the restrictions that it would build back into the Public Order Ordinance and the Societies Ordinance. Although a final decision on these controls awaited the result of a public consultation exercise, the substance of the policy was unlikely to alter.

BUT IS IT LEGAL?

The Provisional Legislature has become a fixture of political life in Hong Kong, but it is doubtful whether the debate over its legality will ever completely disappear. At the heart of the problem are two conflicting and incompatible interpretations of the Basic Law (and indeed law in general).

A Western-educated, liberal, common-law mind would conclude that the provisional body cannot be legal since there is no explicit allowance for it in either the wording or the spirit of the Basic Law. Nowhere does the document talk about an appointed, interim one-year body. On the contrary, it states quite clearly how the first legislature shall be composed: '20 members returned by geographical constituencies *through direct elections*, 10 members *returned* by an election committee, and 30 members *returned* by functional constituencies' (italics added). In other words, elected members are a must.

The Basic Law is also unequivocal in stating that the term of office of the first legislature will be *two* years. Why two years? Perhaps because the document was written in the late 1980s, when the 'through train' was still a possibility. Hence the term of office of the 1995 legislature would end in 1999, two years after the transfer of sovereignty.

And nowhere does the Basic Law say that the Selection Committee should choose any legislature. The committee's only task is to select the first chief executive.

Constitutional scholars and liberal lawyers in Hong Kong are unimpressed with the imposture legislature. Yash Ghai, professor of public law at the University of Hong Kong and a leading authority in this area, wrote an article for the *Hong Kong Law Journal* in 1995, in which he argued that the body 'violates the letter as well as the spirit of the Sino–British Joint Declaration and the Basic Law'. The Provisional Legislature crushes the spirit of these documents because they promise autonomy to Hong Kong, while it paves the way for Beijing's involvement in local government (through legislative activity). The letter of the law is ignored because of the unelected nature of the legislature. As a result: 'Electoral rights of potential candidates and voters, entrenched in the Basic Law, will be violated.'.

Ghai made the salient point, mentioned by almost nobody else in the heated, on-off debate over this issue, that the Basic Law *requires* the Preparatory Committee to make arrangements for the election of the first legislature if the 'through train' model is deemed unacceptable. That the 'through train' idea is not a must, just a possibility, is indicated by the conditional wording of the Basic Law with regard to this concept. But the requirement for an elected legislature, as the quote on the previous page shows, is unconditional.

Ghai was equally concerned about the political implications of the Provisional Legislature. Noting that the legislature will 'undoubtedly have law-making power', Ghai said it was 'not unlikely that it will pass a great deal of legislation'. His key point was:

> The wider and more significant the scope of its legislation, the more it will intrude upon the autonomy of future HKSAR (sic) legislatures, whose members will find themselves unable to repeal or amend them ...
>
> In the space of a year the interim legislature (under the tutelage of China) could irremediably amend key laws and initiate an HKSAR

with greatly diminished autonomy. This would also involve China extensively in the internal affairs of Hong Kong in a manner incompatible with the Basic Law

Indeed, this is exactly what is happening through the amendment and abolition of laws.

THE CHINA CAMP does not dispute that the Provisional Legislature is not mentioned in the Basic Law. What it says is that its creation is legal because the future sovereign has the political and legal latitude to set it up.

The arguments used to justify the legislature on political grounds are, not surprisingly, confidently self-righteous. There are those who believe that the transfer of sovereignty permits China to do whatever it likes (especially in reaction to the connivances of a 'despicable' colonial power). *Window* magazine, in an indignant tirade against critics of the Preparatory Committee and the Provisional Legislature, had this to say in April 1996:

> History is largely written by the victors; for London to attempt to re-write history while in the process of beating a retreat was ambitious and doomed. British hopes that China would lie down and accept Patten's flawed *fait accompli* have been confounded—as *Window* has been predicting since the electoral changes were first floated back in 1992. There was never a chance that Beijing would stand for the blatant gerrymandering of the 1993 political package.
>
> But the outraged reaction to the current Legislative Council being dissolved could lead an outside observer to believe that this was unexpected. The only surprise would have been Beijing allowing this Legco (Legislative Council) to continue. Political coverage of Hong Kong these days is an Alice in Wonderland experience: curiouser and curiouser. It is time for a reality check.
>
> First, a recap of some essential elements. The Preparatory Committee (PC), under the Basic Law, is charged with preparing the establishment of the first special administrative region government and nominating the first chief executive. *[Author's note: Not strictly true—the Selection Committee did this latter task.]*
>
> For legislators—voted in by less than a third of an artificially inflated electorate—to gnash their teeth and wail that the PC is unelected, is to miss the point. We are dealing here with the return to its rightful sovereign of a colony, stolen by *force majeure* and ruled from London for 150 years. The PC is a body authorised by the future sovereign with safeguarding China's interests, as well as those of the people of Hong Kong, during the transition.

Might therefore is right. The sovereign has the prerogative. One alleged outrage condones another. None of this is very Hong Kong-friendly, except that clause in the last sentence; but even it appears to have been added as an afterthought.

A more complex argument for the interim legislature, based on legal reasoning, is that a 1990 decision of the National People's Congress empowered the Preparatory Committee to 'be responsible for the establishment of the Hong Kong Special Administrative Region *and related matters*, and for prescribing the specific method of formation of the first government and first legislature (in accordance with this decision)' (italics added). Thus, for example, an article in the *People's Daily* newspaper, the main mouthpiece of the Communist Party, explained that while the Basic Law may not have explicitly mentioned the Provisional Legislature, it was a 'related matter' and so had a legal basis. (The 1990 decision is attached to the Basic Law and has been referred to earlier; it was also the section which Yash Ghai was discussing.)

When, in 1994, the National People's Congress resolved to disband Hong Kong's three tiers of representative government, it referred to its 1990 decision and the issue of 'related matters', but did not mention the Provisional Legislature by name (since the Working Committee had yet to make its 'suggestion'). It was not until the Preparatory Committee's own confirmation of the Provisional Legislature in March 1996 that the latter body was formally incorporated.

One difficulty with this explanation is that while the language of all three decisions in Chinese is virtually identical, the official English translation of the Basic Law does not contain the phrase 'related matters'. What it says is that the Preparatory Committee:

> ... shall be responsible for preparing the establishment of the Region and shall prescribe the specific method for forming the first government and the first Legislative Council ...

This sort of discrepancy makes it virtually impossible for non-Chinese speakers to follow the logic of what must seem to them a fictitious legal argument, and no doubt adds to the cynicism many feel towards Beijing's disregard for the rule of law in general. Resolving translation conflicts such as these will not stop the deep and genuine disagreements between China and Hong Kong over what the Basic Law means, but at least it would minimise unnecessary confusion—and give non-Chinese speakers a sharper understanding of what Beijing is talking about.

The *People's Daily* article went on to give a second, and somewhat ironic, legal defence of the Provisional Legislature based on the Western legal concept of 'residual powers'. It claimed this meant that any powers not laid down in the Basic Law or other laws of Hong Kong belonged not to Hong Kong, but to China as the future sovereign. Hence, because the Basic Law does not explicitly say an interim legislature cannot be established, Beijing is well within its rights to use its residual power to set one up! As Sir David Akers-Jones, former chief secretary/acting governor of Hong Kong and leading expatriate united front member, put it more colloquially on television: the Basic Law may be silent about the Provisional Legislature, but the National People's Congress has 'filled in the gap'.

These arguments are all weak. If sovereignty means that China can behave badly because Britain allegedly did so, or because the new sovereign has 'residual legal powers', then logically nothing in the Basic Law or any other Hong Kong law is sacrosanct after 1997. As statements of political fact these points may well be correct, but as a legal defence of the Provisional Legislature they are self-defeating. People in China may be able to subsist within a legal system smothered by the arbitrary use of political power—they are used to it—but a free market, open society like Hong Kong could not. It depends on a much greater amount of political predictability and governmental non-interference than Beijing offers its citizens and business community. Were Beijing, for example, to decide at some future point that a low tax regime in Hong Kong was no longer in the nation's best interests, then the pro-Beijing camp would not get very far by pointing to the letter of the Basic Law and saying, 'But this document promises that the SAR government shall take "the low tax policy previously pursued in Hong Kong as reference"' (Article 108). Having acquiesced in the shoddy treatment of the Basic Law for temporary political gain or protection, the camp has set a precedent that it may come to regret.

'Residual powers' and 'filling in the gaps' also sound suspiciously like the National People's Congress is legislating on behalf of Hong Kong—and this it is not supposed to do, even after 1997, except in the limited areas of defence and foreign affairs, in times of emergency or in 'other matters outside the limits of the autonomy of the Region as specified by this (Basic) Law' (Article 18). The Provisional Legislature clearly does not relate to defence, foreign affairs or emergencies, nor can it be a matter outside Hong Kong's autonomy since the Basic Law says that the region will 'enjoy executive, legislative and independent judicial power' (Article 2) and 'shall be vested with legislative power' (Article 17). What legal right, therefore, did the Preparatory Committee (as a sub-committee of the National People's Congress) have to decide that the Provisional Legislature should be set up? China would claim it was a 'related matter' governed by that 1990 decision annexed to the Basic Law. But if you accept this tenuous argument, then Beijing has not only transgressed against its own law, but it gave the Preparatory Committee certain powers before 1997 that not even the National People's Congress is supposed to enjoy afterwards.

What the congress does have is the power to veto future Hong Kong laws that it thinks conflict with the Basic Law's provisions on the responsibilities of the central government (defence, foreign affairs, etc) or the relationship between Beijing and Hong Kong. But this cannot be used to justify the Provisional Legislature, since such power would not come into force until after July 1997; nor does it seem relevant to the legislature in Hong Kong. (While the congress will be able to veto some laws, it cannot amend them.)

IS IT NECESSARY?

Legality was just one aspect of the argument over the Provisional Legislature. The other was necessity. That is, Beijing claimed such a legislature was the *only* solution to the legal abyss allegedly caused by the Patten administration.

The argument went like this: Beijing had to scrap the last Legislative Council because, as a result of Patten's reforms, the body did not converge with the Joint Declaration or the Basic Law. This created the potential for a 'legal vacuum' immediately after reunification and until the first legislature could be organised. That would have been a bad thing, since various laws had to be passed inaugurating the Special Administrative Region, its first Court of Final Appeal, approving its budget, implementing China's nationality law, new residency rules, and so on. What could be done? The Preparatory Committee could not organise elections for a new council prior to or on 1 July 1997, because that would have required cooperation with the Hong Kong government—a non-option as far as the Chinese were concerned. Conversely, elections could not be held after July

1997 because they would take time to organise and that would have created a 'legal vacuum' of at least three months' duration.

The Preliminary Working Committee came up with four options in late 1994 to resolve this 'problem'. The first was to allow the National People's Congress to legislate on behalf of Hong Kong until the first legislature could be formed through elections. Ironically, in hindsight, this was dropped as too contentious and a violation of the Basic Law. The second option was to let the Preparatory Committee take over the legislative role. This was a non-starter for similar reasons (since the committee was appointed by the congress and formally reports to it). The third was to give the power to the first chief executive. But this was ostensibly seen as a bad idea because it would have blurred the separation of powers between the executive and the legislature (although the real reason may have been that it would have given the chief executive too much power). The fourth was to set up an interim legislature for 'the sole purpose of carrying out legislative work that would be absolutely necessary', to quote Tsang Yok-sing, head of the Democratic Alliance for the Betterment of Hong Kong. This last option was considered the best. In the words of the sociologist Lau Siu-kai, the interim body was a 'necessary evil'.

There was a element of building straw men in all of this. Various formal sovereignty-related legal changes were needed upon the transfer of sovereignty, but was it absolutely crucial that these take place on 1 July or in the immediate aftermath? Surely a gap of three of four months, enough time to organise a new election, would not have caused insuperable problems? There were plenty of existing laws in Hong Kong capable of guiding the civil service, the judiciary, police and public, so the situation would not have become unmanageable. The general public has largely accepted the transfer of sovereignty, so would not have challenged a 'legal vacuum'. While this situation may not have been ideal, it would arguably have been far more acceptable to the public than the Provisional Legislature.

The vacuum issue was therefore partially self-induced. It was Beijing that refused to allow the Preparatory Committee to organise new elections before July 1997. The fact that no one in the China camp trusted the Hong Kong government not to sabotage new elections was not wholly the latter's fault. And it was especially ironic that a country which does not follow the letter of even its own laws should be insisting on strict legality in Hong Kong!

A few groups and individuals tried to offer alternatives to the Provisional Legislature, but not surprisingly none stuck. The grass-roots democratic group, the Association for Democracy and People's Livelihood (ADPL), suggested that a new election could be held for just part of the 1995 Legislative Council. The ADPL believed that both the geographic and functional constituency seats complied with the 1990 decision of the National People's Congress; only the 10 seats chosen through the election committee of district board members did not. Hence a new election could be held for just these 10 seats (with the existing 10 members re-contesting, if they wanted to). The remaining 50 members could ride on a 'through train'. The ADPL stated in a press release: 'It is only by complying with the stipulations of the Basic Law, and by founding the Special Administrative Region's legislative institution on the will of the people, that it will have adequate public recognition and legitimacy, and will assist Hong Kong's smooth transition.' It was an admirable thought, but not one the new sovereign had much time for.

AN UNGOVERNABLE TERRITORY?

The necessity for an interim legislature that could turn back the clock was further justified in the mind of the Chinese government by the conviction that the Patten reforms and the legislative amendments following the Bill of Rights were all deliberate attempts by the British to undermine the traditional 'executive-led' system of government in Hong Kong, make the place ungovernable after 1997, and allow anti-China 'subversives' to flourish.

During the mudslinging over the Preliminary Working Committee's October 1995 proposal to water down the Bill of Rights, the New China News Agency issued a statement questioning Patten's motives for repeatedly 'sloganeering on human rights'. Its answer repeated a well-worn refrain: that his 'ultimate motive' was to 'create obstacles for the rule of the future Special Administrative Region government'. And then:

> (The aim is) to open room for the activities of international anti-Chinese forces and the agents of the British side after 1997.

Such statements seem silly, but have to be treated with some caution. They may have been part political huff and puff, an element in Beijing's ongoing campaign of vitriol against Patten and Britain during the period of transition, and part an attempt to play to the gallery of local supporters in Hong Kong and China. Yet having said that, Beijing's concerns about the bill were real. It did (and does) see Hong Kong as a potentially subversive base. If not, why would it be trying to split the Democratic Party and building a new train?

The controversy over the Bill of Rights has been as significant as that over the Provisional Legislature because it has struck at the core of how Hong Kong should be governed (in the broad sense of the allocation of power between the government, the legislature and the judiciary). How much latitude should government departments, the police and the ICAC have in running Hong Kong and keeping the peace? Should there be strict limits on confrontational political speech (for the sake of 'harmony' in relations with China), the right to hold demonstrations that may disrupt traffic, and the number of people in processions (so that the police can provide enough offic-ers to control the protest)? Is it right for the Legislative Council to haul senior civil servants before public hearings, thus making the executive more accountable to 'the people'? Do prisoners have rights?

Beijing's answers to the above questions would be: 'as much as possible', 'yes', 'no', and 'no', respectively. What is interesting about the Bill of Rights debate is that many conservatives in Hong Kong, not merely diehard pro-Beijing loyalists, would generally agree with these answers. Their case against the bill is that it benefits criminals (it is a 'crook's charter'), undermines traditional social values, and complicates the colony's legal system. Some of the most prominent sceptics are senior judges and conservative barristers.

In 1990, Henry Litton, then a well-known Queen's Counsel, wrote two angry articles for the *South China Morning Post* newspaper attack-ing the draft Bill of Rights, released for public consultation between March and May of that year. Litton began his first article, titled 'Much wrong with the Bill of Rights', by relaying the concerns of the ICAC commissioner at the time, David Jeaffreson, about the bill's curtailment of the anti-corruption watchdog's effectiveness. Litton, now a Court of Appeal Judge, then went on to assert:

> He has every reason to be worried. So should every law-abiding citizen in Hong Kong. The Bill of Rights aims not only at curbing the powers of the ICAC; it will effect every other law-enforcement body in Hong Kong and penetrate every aspect of life in the community.

Litton, who said his concern was that of a 'practical lawyer anxious to see that the legal infrastructure of Hong Kong is kept strong', charged that the bill would 'tear up much of the fabric of Hong Kong law'. His complaints ranged from the way in which judges were supposed to interpret the bill to the probability that the charter would overturn what was known as the 'reverse onus provision' in criminal legislation. This convenient mechanism meant that people arrested for crimes such as possession of drugs, weapons and illegal goods bore the burden of proof. That is, they had to prove their innocence—an arrangement that made life a lot easier for the police and government prosecutors. But this conflicted with Article 11 (1) of the draft bill, which reaffirmed the key common law principle of 'presumption of innocence'. Litton was not against this principle *per se*, but he was against it in this instance. So concerned was he about the implications of this change that he asserted Article 11 (1) would become the 'drug dealer's charter in the future'.

His second article, 'A conflict of interests', developed the theme that the draft bill did not fit Hong Kong's traditional laissez-faire philosophy of government. His logic was:

> ... the Government provides the basic infrastructure, ensures law and order, but intervenes in the life of the community as little as possible, and only when a positive need is shown.

> The draft Bill of Rights seems to turn this philosophy on its head.

The foundation of Litton's argument was that Hong Kong was getting along fine—socially, politically and economically—with the legal system it had. He was not against legal reform in its entirety. Indeed he recognised that some police and ICAC powers were probably too wide. But what really niggled him was the comprehensive and 'proactive' aspect of the Bill of Rights. He would have preferred social and political problems, such as racial and sexual discrimination, to have been dealt with by specific, rather than general, legislation (as in Britain). His ideal was an incremental approach, more in keeping with the common law:

> The common law is built-up slowly, through many generations, by the application of single instances; it never erupted full-grown from a test-tube. But this, I fear, is the social experiment which the Secretary for Constitutional Affairs is threatening to practise on us by his Bill.

Anticipating the comments of many judges since, Litton claimed the rights charter would become 'the port of first asylum for every lawyer whenever a client has a grievance to ventilate', since it 'confers on everyone a right of action for every violation of the Bill'. Returning to where Litton started—the concerns of a 'practical lawyer'—it becomes clear that his purpose was to save the judicial system from being overburdened by a lot of 'silly cases'.

How close to, or far from, the mark was Litton? He certainly raised some valid points, such as the suggestion that there were other ways to protect civil rights than through a broad (yet shallow) rights charter. One strength of specific legislation is its very specificity: it is more detailed, attuned to the local social environment and goes further than any general clause in a charter can. Because Hong Kong's Bill of Rights closely follows the International Covenant on Civil and Political Rights (ICCPR), it is by definition 'internationalised' and general (with the exception of one or two areas that have been adapted for local conditions).

But this incremental approach will only work if a government is sincere in protecting rights and developing legislation. So opting not to go the way of a bill of rights could simply be a cynical attempt to do nothing—even if a country has ratified the ICCPR. Until the Bill of Rights came along in 1991, it should be remembered, the deliberate 'application' of the covenant to Hong Kong had not occurred. The Hong Kong government had not been sincere in developing the colony's package of civil rights beyond those basic ones it already allowed, like freedom of speech, conscience and movement.

Yet the opposite could also be true: that the act of enacting a rights charter could be an equally cynical move on the part of a government to avoid doing too much more on the issue. Although a lot happened in Hong Kong after 1991 in terms of the forced amendment of laws, the government's overall commitment to the concept of civil rights is often decidedly lukewarm. For example, it subsequently opposed an anti-discrimination bill and a freedom of information bill proposed by different members of the Legislative Council. One gets the impression that the Hong Kong government believes it has done enough on the score of human rights, and that it views public demands for it to go further as an unreasonable imposition and excessively idealistic. Idealism is certainly one sin which the Hong Kong government has never committed. Enacting the Bill of Rights was largely an act of pragmatism.

The rights and wrongs of a rights charter is a debate with no clear end. Litton would probably sympathise with a famous conservative comment made in 1985 by Sir Harry Gibbs, a former chief justice of Australia, to a senate committee in Canberra:

> If society is tolerant and rational, it does not need a bill of rights. If it is not, no bill of rights will preserve it.

Litton believes that Hong Kong society and its government are adequately tolerant, thus there is no real need for a charter. But this is where he differs from the vocal majority: there was very strong local support for the bill in the early 1990s following the 1989 massacre in Beijing, and equally vociferous condemnation of the Preliminary Working Committee's 1995 proposal to emasculate it. Although Litton claimed to be speaking on behalf of 'the community', at best he represented a mostly older or more conservative part of it (though Litton himself is quite liberal on other issues, such as environmental policy). His articles showed him to be out of touch on this issue with the 'modern' opinions of Hong Kong's younger and more politically aware professionals, many of whom have been educated overseas. They saw government as insufficiently tolerant—and in some ways intolerant—and as having too many colonial autocratic powers stacked away in its executive closet. Whether or not this group represented an absolute majority of Hong Kong society is not the point: you do not need a majority to create political tension. But the fact that this social force existed was reflected by the Hong Kong government's decision to break character and promote the Bill of Rights; and the strong support for the Democratic Party in the 1991 and 1995 Legislative Council elections.

A BIGGER CRITICISM of the conservative argument is that Hong Kong has not become ungovernable. Walk around the streets, read the newspapers, talk to people. It is hard to find evidence that the Bill of Rights, now in its sixth year, has struck fear into the hearts of the average person. While it has forced new debates about the legal system, the tension has not even come close to ripping the system's fabric. On the contrary, a feature of the bill's first half decade is the determinedly conservative line that the judiciary, especially its most senior members in the Court of Appeal, have taken in adjudicating cases. It is worth noting in this context that Litton himself became a Court of Appeal judge in 1992 (a move that caused him to resign from the first batch of Beijing-appointed Hong Kong Affairs Advisers).

Of the bill's path through the judiciary between June 1991 (when it was enacted) and December 1995, one could say in a nutshell that the number of cases has fallen swiftly from a high in 1991–92, the range of cases has started to broaden recently (criminal cases dominated in the early days), and a defendant's chances of success are not much more than 36%.

There were 247 cases in the four and a half years: 46 cases for the second half of 1991, 77 for the whole of 1992, 56 in 1993, 43 in 1994, and only 25 in 1995. As Litton and other conservatives predicted, the majority of these (almost 75%) were criminal cases. The next largest category was 'administrative', meaning those relating to government departments and statutory bodies such as immigration, inland revenue and town planning. Whereas criminal cases have decreased sharply since 1992, administrative ones were on a small upward trend until 1995. A handful of civil, extradition, and election-related cases have also been fought.

Out of the 247 cases, 202 produced a clear outcome: 73 were successful, and 129 were unsuccessful. The average success rates for the different levels of courts were: magistrates courts (33%), district courts (46%), High Court (38%), and the Court of Appeal, the lowest, with only 29%.

Of the 323 challenges launched against different articles of the bill between mid-1991 and the end of 1995 (one case may include several challenges), about half dealt with Article 11, which outlines the rights of people charged with a criminal offence. Most of these challenges related to Article 11(1)—the presumption of innocence. Yet only 40% of these were successful—a slightly higher figure than the overall average of 36%, but not by much.

These figures do not support the contention that the Bill of Rights is a 'crook's charter'. Some alleged criminals may have benefited, but apparently most have not. The system is still intact and not just because of Hong Kong's conservative senior judiciary: the government's whole approach to the bill has been to strike a balance between civil rights and effective law enforcement. The notion that a government as acutely conscious of security issues as Hong Kong's would 'let it all slide' for the sake of a rights charter is absurd.

Liberal legal academics, keen to raise the standard of local jurisprudence, are highly critical of the judiciary's record on the Bill of Rights. Johannes Chan, a law lecturer at the University of Hong Kong and a strong proponent of human rights, reckons that the low success rate is due to the courts applying a 'low standard of scrutiny' when assessing whether legislation complies with the bill—meaning that vague arguments from barristers without strong supporting evidence are accepted by judges.

Chan, who compiled the statistics above, has written scathingly about the Court of Appeal, charging it with a 'lack of detailed and intellectual analysis of legal arguments, despite the fact that such analysis is characteristic of the judgements of the Supreme Courts of many other jurisdictions'. He concludes that:

> This may partly be explained by the reservations held by a number of appellate [Court of Appeal] judges on the Bill of Rights, and partly by the predominant, and sometimes undue, emphasis on having cases decided expeditiously rather than exploring and developing the law and jurisprudence for the benefit of posterity.

That the Hong Kong judiciary is not absolutely first-rate and is more concerned with efficiency than justice is a common complaint of legal academics and liberal lawyers. Some judges, such as Justice Godfrey of the Court of Appeal, have admitted the first charge to be true. At a legal seminar on the Special Administrative Region Court of Final Appeal in October 1995, Godfrey said there was no possible way that the local judges on this new court could be as good as those on the Privy Council in London (Hong Kong's final appeal court until July 1997). Some might be appalled by this, but Godfrey took a benign view—this was simply the product of the different legal systems and traditions in Hong Kong compared to Britain. The latter has a much longer tradition, was a bigger legal system and was more competitive. Thus those who rose to the top were simply much better. It was unrealistic to expect anything else, said Godfrey. As for the second charge, many judges would no doubt retort, 'This is Hong Kong. Things happen quickly. Many court disputes are of a commercial nature and people expect fast decisions.' These may all be accurate statements, but they are not especially reassuring in this context.

TWO OTHER SENIOR judges to oppose the Bill of Rights deserve a mention. The most celebrated was T L Yang, Hong Kong's former chief justice. Unwittingly, Yang became embroiled in the late 1995 controversy over the Preliminary Working Committee's proposal to emasculate the bill and reinstate the amended security laws. When Yang publicly called for calm, a deputy director of the New China

News Agency, Zhang Junsheng, told the press that he had heard Yang criticise the Bill of Rights at a dinner party. The occasion was a dinner organised by the Hong Kong Federation of Youth Groups, during which Yang allegedly said in conversation with other guests that the bill 'undermined Hong Kong's legal system'. The revelation naturally created an uproar, forcing Yang to make a statement clarifying his views on the rights charter.

Yang had two primary complaints: that the bill effectively gave the judiciary 'legislative power', which ran contrary to the principle of separation of powers; and that it effectively occupied a status above other ordinary legislation, 'so that in reality the Ordinance occupies a position between the Basic Law (as from 1 July 1997) and the ordinary statutes'. His charge, in essence, was that both factors adversely affected Hong Kong's legal system.

Had Yang wanted to intensify his troubles, he could not have done it more efficiently—his statement caused another uproar. On the first point he seemed to misunderstand the workings of the judiciary itself—quite a bizarre position for a chief justice—and on the second he contradicted the government's line that the bill was merely an ordinary piece of legislation (and therefore played straight into Beijing's hand). The drama became heavily politicised, with the attorney general, the Bar Association, many liberal legal academics, democratic politicians and parts of the media all attacking the statement, and Zhang Junsheng coming out in support. Some of the issues Yang raised are dealt with in more detail below. For now, what was striking about the statement was Yang's apparently limited understanding of international human rights law (of which the Bill of Rights is a part) and the fact that he phrased his arguments in largely abstract terms. That is to say, he did not justify his complaints by drawing upon concrete examples of the bill's implementation in Hong Kong—surely necessary if he was trying to prove that it had weakened the legal system.

The other senior judge to come out against the Bill of Rights was Benjamin Liu, a justice on the Court of Appeal. On 16 November 1995 Liu published an article in *Ming Pao*, a local newspaper, in which he asserted that the bill 'had had a great adverse impact on criminal and civil litigation; its impact has particularly been felt in criminal law'. Liu developed this theme, then ended his polemic by saying:

The decision of the Preliminary Working Committee/Preparatory
Committee [to emasculate the bill] ... will not bring any adverse effect
to the laws of Hong Kong.

This article was later handed out at a dinner for the Judges'
Association of the People's Republic of China. Liu, as chairman of
the Local Judges Association, was the host for the evening. (He is, by
the way, the brother of the late Dorothy Liu, the outspoken local
delegate to the National People's Congress and the sole person to
resign from the Preliminary Working Committee.)

For many it is not surprising that the Hong Kong judiciary, known
for its provincialism (as opposed to internationalism), has taken a
conservative, if not obstructionist, approach to the Bill of Rights. But
surely the same thought occurred to the bill's local critics from the
start? It doubtless did, which means they probably knew their complaints were exaggerated. A news story on Henry Litton in 1996
quoted unnamed sources as saying that the judge had privately
admitted he was deliberately scaremongering about the Bill of
Rights in 1990, but that he felt his actions were justified given the
many 'problematic' provisions in the draft ordinance.

THE COMMON LAW CONUNDRUM

The bitter arguments over the Bill of Rights have also been significant because, like the Provisional Legislature issue, they highlight a
real difference between Beijing's interpretation of the Basic Law
(and the Joint Declaration) and Hong Kong's.

Beijing maintained that the Bill of Rights and the amended security laws contradicted the spirit of a core principle (Point 3.3) in the
Joint Declaration which stated:

The laws *currently* in force in Hong Kong will remain *basically
unchanged.* (italics added)

Most people in Hong Kong have read this sentence as providing
broad protection for Hong Kong's capitalist way of life and common
law legal system. Not for a moment would they accept that it meant
that the body of legislation which existed in Hong Kong circa 1984
should remain unchanged. Such a concept would be ridiculous,
since dynamic economies like Hong Kong (and China too) are constantly evolving.

But Beijing disagreed. It contended that the Joint Declaration required Britain not to make major changes to Hong Kong law between 1985 and 1997. In other words, China wanted to resume sovereignty over a mid-1980s version of Hong Kong—not the more self-assured and independent 1990s model.

Beijing's interpretation was decidedly odd from many angles, but perhaps strangest of all was that the Basic Law did not support it. The Basic Law in fact said (Article 8):

> The laws *previously* in force in Hong Kong ... *shall be maintained*, except for any that contravene this Law ... (italics added)

Since the Basic Law was to come into effect on 1 July 1997, the word 'previously' could only mean prior to that date, not prior to 1984 or even 1990, when the constitution was promulgated. Hence it has been reasonable to read this as an instruction to the Special Administrative Region government to maintain as much pre-1997 Hong Kong legislation as possible, including new laws and amendments made in the last few years of British rule.

Beijing twisted out of this dilemma by stating that only the *original* version of laws in force before 1997 could be *maintained*. And new post-1984 laws that changed the legal status quo were not acceptable either. In other words, the Bill of Rights (being a new law) and the amendments (being different to their original selves) contravened Beijing's reading of the Basic Law.

This imaginative interpretation was put down in black and white in the Preliminary Working Committee's October 1995 proposal to water down the Bill of Rights. It merged the language of the Joint Declaration and the Basic Law to drive the point home:

> The British/Hong Kong Government, by introducing ... a series of amendments to the pre-existing laws of Hong Kong to bring them in line with the Hong Kong Bill of Rights Ordinance, has violated the principle under the Joint Declaration and the Basic Law that the laws *previously* in force in Hong Kong shall remain *basically unchanged*. (italics added)

This put a very different twist on the wording and meaning of the Basic Law—one it simply did not have (even in the official Chinese version). It was also a hypocritical stance, since Beijing had no intention of applying this interpretation across the board: the new sovereign was prepared to live with the numerous changes in economic, environmental and social legislation in Hong Kong since the mid-1980s (an issue it never talked about), yet applied a different standard to political laws. The new word order, however, has become entrenched in the language of official statements. Qian Qichen, China's foreign minister and chairman of the Preparatory Committee, gave a talk to a meeting of the latter body in early 1997 in which he said that China's policy was to maintain Hong Kong's 'previous laws basically unchanged', since this was stipulated by the Joint Declaration. And he emphasised that this policy was necessary if Hong Kong's long-term prosperity and stability were to be guaranteed.

THE STATUS OF the Bill of Rights in relation to other laws was another major bone of contention. The British administration insisted that it was an ordinary piece of legislation that did not stand above other laws and could be amended like other pieces of legislation (unlike a constitution, in other words, which was extremely difficult to amend). This was a highly political issue since only the Basic Law should have constitutional supremacy over all laws of Hong Kong.

But the Chinese government insisted with equal vehemence that three particular clauses in the bill did give it a superior status. These governed the purposes of the bill and the way in which the judiciary should interpret it; the repeal of inconsistent existing legislation; and the effect of the bill on legislation enacted after it ('subsequent legislation').

Chinese officials maintained that these clauses conflicted with the letter and spirit of the Basic Law. In particular, they contravened three articles which stated that the laws previously in force should remain (the same as Article 8 above); that no law in Hong Kong could contravene the Basic Law; and that it was up to the future Special Administrative Region government to enact laws to implement the International Covenant on Civil and Political Rights (ICCPR), not the British colonial administration.

The primary basis of the Chinese argument was that, since the Bill of Rights repealed all inconsistent existing legislation and subsequent legislation, it lay categorically above other laws. This was a straightforward contradiction of the Basic Law. As Shao Tianren, the Chinese co-convener of the Preliminary Working Committee's legal sub-group, asserted in late 1995:

> The Bill of Rights overrides all other laws and imposes drastic changes on other laws. It is illegal in itself. We cannot accept anything illegal.

Shao's use of the word 'override' came from the 1990 draft of the Bill of Rights, one section of which was entitled, 'Ordinance to override existing law'. A pillar of Beijing's argument rested upon this one word and it continued to use the word despite its deletion from the final version of the bill enacted in June 1991. Yet Chinese officials believed the replacement words had the same effect.

From a common law perspective, this pillar crumbles fairly easily. It is true that the rights charter forces the repeal of inconsistent existing legislation, but there is nothing unusual about this. This is simply the common law principle which says that new laws override old ones. If they did not, the legal system would be stagnant and/or full of unresolvable conflicts.

As for subsequent legislation, the bill does not say—contrary to Beijing's assertion and a common misconception in Hong Kong— that such laws *must* comply with it. If the bill did say this, then it would override all laws and contravene the Basic Law. What the charter does instead is to encourage courts, as far as possible, to interpret later legislation in line with the ICCPR. Because this is not an imperative, merely guidance, the bill is not strictly speaking superior to other legislation.

This section was added for a fairly good reason: what would be the point of a rights charter that influenced old laws but had no impact on new ones? If this were the case, new laws could conflict with the charter and Hong Kong's legal system would quickly tie itself up in knots. Still, Hong Kong courts are not forced to interpret subsequent legislation as complying with the covenant. In specific cases, they can go against it. Most of the time it is hoped that they would take it into account. It is a subtle point but an important one, since it provides a degree of flexibility to the judiciary and ensures that the constitutional superiority of the Basic Law remains.

Beijing cares little for such subtlety. It has always maintained that the bill is not an ordinary law because it has had such a broad impact on other laws: 36 amendments in four and a half years. Perhaps the Chinese government is half right. While Shao's use of the word 'drastic' may be an exaggeration—Hong Kong has 600 laws, 1000 pieces of subsidiary legislation, and 300 laws imported from Britain—there is definitely something different about the Bill of Rights. What other ordinary laws have had the impact it has had? A senior Hong Kong government law official admitted he knew of none, when asked. And to quote the conclusion of two prominent legal academics already mentioned in this chapter, Johannes Chan and Yash Ghai:

> The effect of the (Bill of Rights) Ordinance is profound.

This statement was made in 1993. Two years later, Ghai described the Bill of Rights as having a 'quasi-superior' status to other laws—not a label which the Hong Kong government will accept (according to the same senior law official quoted above). Ghai's reasoning is based upon a small but powerful change the British government made in mid-1991 (and which has never received the same level of publicity as the bill). It amended the Letters Patent, the colonial constitution of Hong Kong, to entrench the ICCPR. The amendment said, in effect, that no law could be made that 'restricted rights and freedoms of people in Hong Kong in ways that were inconsistent with the covenant, as it had traditionally been applied in the territory'. Since it was the task of the bill to implement the covenant in Hong Kong, the amendment indirectly entrenched the bill in the Hong Kong constitution. Had the government put the words 'Bill of Rights' into the Letters Patent, it would have contradicted the Basic Law by directly entrenching an ordinary law. Ghai called this an 'ingenious solution' to the delicate problem of how to encourage the courts to adjudicate subsequent legislation in line with the Bill of Rights, without actually entrenching it.

So on the one hand it would seem as if the British administration has been somewhat economical with the truth in saying the bill 'has a status no different to that of any other ordinances'. Yet at the same time, Beijing has been exaggerating the issue by claiming that the bill is absolutely, not just partially, superior to other laws. Both sides have clearly had their reasons to play up, or down, the issue.

Many scholars and Hong Kong officials have tried to stop this unending argument-go-round by pointing, they think definitively, to Article 39 of the Basic Law. This says:

> The provisions of the International Covenant on Civil and Political Rights, the International Covenant on Economic, Social and Cultural Rights, and international labour conventions as applied to Hong Kong *shall remain in force* and *shall be implemented through the laws* of the Hong Kong Special Administrative Region. (italics added)
>
> The rights and freedoms enjoyed by Hong Kong residents shall not be restricted unless as prescribed by law. Such restrictions shall not contravene the provisions of the preceding paragraph of this Article.

In other words, not only does the Basic Law entrench the ICCPR, just like the Letters Patent, but it requires Hong Kong to implement the covenant through local laws. Since this is precisely what the Bill of Rights does, there should be no conflict between it and the Basic Law. Case closed.

No so fast, says Beijing. The Bill of Rights does contravene Article 39, since it is the responsibility of the Special Administrative Region government to enact laws implementing the ICCPR *after* July 1997, not the colonial government before that date. Not only has Britain jumped the gun, but it has chosen to enact a certain type of rights charter (the Bill of Rights) which Article 39 does not specify. (There are different ways to implement the ICCPR, as we saw before. A bill of rights is one way, but a series of separate laws is also acceptable.)

Moreover, the Basic Law was promulgated in 1990 and referred to the provisions of the covenants 'as applied to Hong Kong remaining in force'. What this means is that before the Bill of Rights was enacted in 1991, the ICCPR applied to Hong Kong (because of Britain's ratification) but with various reservations and limits—because Hong Kong was a colony and did not have a democratic government. China's argument implies that any ICCPR-related legislation enacted by the Special Administrative Region should take these established reservations into account and should not discard them. Thus, the ICCPR should never be fully incorporated into Hong Kong law.

Is Beijing trying to be difficult? No doubt, but there is a deeper reason for its stubbornness too. Keeping in mind the spirit of Harry Gibbs, if China is really intent on quashing free speech in Hong Kong then the Bill of Rights cannot stop it. But what the charter can do is make it more difficult for the future sovereign to impose political restrictions on its opponents 'legally'. This is not an insubstantial thing, since Beijing tries hard to cover its actions with the cloak of legality. It realises that if it cannot justify its action according to some law, then international investors would lose faith in Hong Kong and serious political instability could result. If this happens, Hong Kong might become exactly the sort of subversive base that Beijing fears.

Witness China's arguments over the Provisional Legislature: this was a necessary response to the *illegality* of the Patten reforms; a proper, *legal* decision was taken by the Preparatory Committee; it was the best option for resolving the *'legal vacuum'* created by the end of the 'through train'. Although the Communist Party of today cares little for the 'rule of law' in the specific common law sense, it is aware of the political and economic value (even in China) of acting according to an objective set of rules. These rules are not strong enough to constrain arbitrary action by an authoritative figure, nor do they envisage a sharing of political power with the Party's opponents. But they do seek to create a 'socialist legal system', which is arguably better than no legal system at all (which was the case under Mao during the Cultural Revolution).

Yet it is also naive to think that there are not other, more subtle means open to Beijing to stifle public debate in Hong Kong. The united front policy of undermining the enemy is one. Putting moral or political pressure on publications—either on the editor, individual journalists, or management—is another. Or more profitably for both sides, doing a deal so that certain stories do not get written in return for favours of some sort: advertising revenue, a public appointment for the newspaper's chairman, and so on.

ELEMENTS OF A STRATEGY

Each of the 'surprise' elements that have gone into the production of the new train—the Preliminary Working Committee, the Provisional Legislature, and the proposed abolition of laws—logically fits into the Communist Party's strategy for asserting its political control over Hong Kong and dovetails with the united front.

Take the Working Committee—contrary to Beijing's claim that this was just a reaction to Patten's reforms, it is more correct to see it as the overt form of an institution that would have operated behind the scenes in any case. It is inconceivable that China, having signed an agreement in late 1984 to take back Hong Kong, would wait for 11 years (the appointment of the Preparatory Committee in late 1995) to start formulating detailed policies for its first Special Administrative Region. Such a delay would ensure that the early days of reunification turned into a shambles—precisely the sort of embarrassment that China has always wanted to avoid. In any case, the organisational mentality of the Communist Party would not have tolerated such a lack of preparation.

Both the Working Committee and the Provisional Legislature have fulfilled at different times another useful role: that of giving Beijing's closest allies in Hong Kong a task to perform. After the Basic Law drafting and consultative committees were disbanded in 1990, pro-Beijing figures who were not on the National People's

Congress or the Chinese People's Political Consultative Conference—in other words, most of them—had no public title. Titles are
not merely empty vessels, they signify that the holder has definite
(not pretend) political connections, is someone to whom you can
address a complaint or petition (against either the Hong Kong or
Chinese governments) and is a fairly important person in the community. Titles provide status, even if not a definite rank. Seen in this
light, the creation of the four groups of Hong Kong Affairs Advisers
was a convenient way of stamping a select group of people with a seal
of authority. The Working Committee and Provisional Legislature
were built on more solid terms of reference.

Numbers are one indicator which suggest that the links between
the united front and the new train have not been haphazardly
drawn. Why did China appoint 186 Hong Kong Affairs Advisers and
537 Hong Kong District Affairs Advisers (the district equivalent of
the Hong Kong advisers)? The appointments were, of course, in
addition to the colony's 28 delegates to the National People's Congress and 91 delegates to the Chinese People's Political Consultative
Conference.

To add these numbers together for a total of 842 is somewhat misleading, since many people served or serve on more than one
committee. Yet the total number of appointees reflected the fact that
Beijing needed a sufficiently large pool of tested allies from whom to
choose the membership of the Working Committee, the Preparatory
Committee, the Selection Committee and the Provisional Legislature—its core reunification institutions—whilst keeping that pool as
manageable and intimate as possible. The total number of Hong
Kong seats on these four institutions was 587 (not reduced for
overlap).

But this idea of an integrated strategy begs the following questions: if the creation of the Working Committee in 1993 was not the
simple *reaction* to the Patten reforms that Beijing said it was, then was
its detailed work program all planned in advance as well? And how
could the 'through train', which Beijing initially supported, possibly
fit into the new sovereign's broader aims, such as ensuring that Hong
Kong's colonial laws remained basically unchanged and that the colony would not become a base for subversion? Any 'through train',
even a partially elected one, would surely have obstructed Beijing's
legislative and political program after 1997.

Although the general scope of the Working Committee's work would have been laid down in advance, many of its specific suggestions were in fact a response to the agenda which Patten set. The committee, for example, would have had less to discuss about future electoral arrangements had the new governor not changed the previous system of appointed members, narrow functional constituencies and double-seat geographic constituencies in his reform bill of 1994. Ditto for the all the laws which were amended as a result of the Bill of Rights—an outcome that took China aback as much as the Patten whirlwind in general.

Patten may have made life difficult for Beijing, but what he also did was to give the new sovereign an excellent excuse to create a formal (rather than underground) shadow government well before the Basic Law said the Preparatory Committee could be set up. His actions therefore allowed China to sever its moral ties to Britain in the preparation of a whole slew of political and legal issues, such as residency law, anti-subversion law, and the adaptation and localisation of legislation. From around 1993 onwards, Chinese officials increasingly said these sorts of issues were 'China's business' and did not need to go through the Joint Liaison Group.

Unwittingly, Patten also handed Beijing a powerful propaganda opportunity: to portray him as a modern reincarnation of the 'ruthless' foreign colonialist, intent on keeping China weak and exploiting it for his own advantage. This sort of xenophobia may sound absurd to a modern Western reader—it does to many Hong Kong Chinese and the more outward-looking members of the mainland population—but historical memory runs especially deep among the country's leaders.

And what of the 'through train'? How did it ever fit into the strategy of reshaping and restraining Hong Kong's political structure? It has to be remembered that this idea was the product of the 1980s, before Tiananmen Square, before Hong Kong began developing political parties in preparation for the 1991 elections, and before the democrats emerged as such a powerful electoral force (in 1991 and again in 1995). One might conclude from this that Beijing did not foresee the extent of the political problem it would face in Hong Kong in the 1990s. Or that it included the 'through train' in the Basic Law, which was promulgated *after* Tiananmen, in order to promote stability and confidence in Hong Kong—a tactical manoeuvre therefore. Or perhaps Beijing felt there was no need to drop the idea since it had considerably strengthened Article 23 of the Basic Law (which dealt with subversion and the ban on foreign political ties) after Tiananmen.

But you also have to take into account that an element of contingency was built into the 'through train' concept from the start. The 1990 decision of the National People's Congress appended to the Basic Law says that members of the last legislature before the handover can join the first legislature afterwards 'upon confirmation by the Preparatory Committee'. Hence, Beijing could in theory have excluded those members it did not trust and ensure itself a compliant legislature. Yet this would have been an extremely messy business and far less effective than building a new train—which is surely what Beijing always wanted.

CHAPTER 5

THE ELASTIC SOCIETY

How will Hong Kong react to Beijing's strategy of repackaging the colony's political institutions and laws into a more suitable form for a Special Administrative Region? Will people resent these changes so bitterly that they unite in mass protest, causing chaos and collapse? Or will they give the new sovereign the benefit of the doubt, conscious that there is no alternative to reunification and hopeful that China's political imperatives will have only a shallow impact? Alternatively, will Hong Kong society fragment into groups, most of which do nothing while some fight China over specific issues, such as the Bill of Rights, hopeful they can at least achieve some positive shift in favour of the colony?

When thinking about these questions, a useful perspective to keep in mind is that Hong Kong society is still developing, both within itself and in its relationship with China. Although some definite things can be said about the colony, there are enough unknowns to keep people guessing (which after all is what makes the place so fascinating). An indisputable fact is the increasingly pluralistic character of Hong Kong's political system over the past 15 years. Something harder to define is the way in which the Hong Kong Chinese will act under a Chinese, rather than British, sovereign. Will they instinctively revert to a more conservative and cautious form of behaviour, such as their parents had to use to survive in old China? For example, will people think twice before writing to the papers to attack the Special Administrative Region government or their new masters in Beijing? Tung Chee-hwa, while still a candidate for chief executive, bluntly repeated Beijing's warning against anyone 'advocating' independence for Tibet and Taiwan. Since few in Hong Kong care much about Tibet, and no major political group has ever openly supported Taiwanese independence, the importance of Tung's words lies more in the general message than in the specific: that Hong Kong people must be more sensitive to Beijing's priorities after July 1997 than they are at present. In telling people what they can and cannot do or think, Tung himself is acting more like a Chinese patriarch than any recent British Hong Kong governor.

A sense of history is also helpful when assessing the impact of Beijing's strategy especially given Hong Kong's propensity to lurch in and out of crisis. Indeed, students of irony would relish the number of events that have, in hindsight, turned out to contain false portents of doom. Fear struck during the 1967 pro-communist riots, as the Sino-British negotiations got underway in 1982, after the 1987 world stock market crash and when the tanks rolled into Beijing in May–June 1989. And negativity has manifested itself on a societal scale through what various writers have called the 'end-game syndrome': as people's expectations of a positive future diminished drastically after 1989, and personal 'horizons' shortened, the rush to secure insurance policies (foreign passports, more money, children in overseas schools) intensified.

Yet Hong Kong has always recovered and flourished on an even grander scale than before, as if uncertainty and fear are as much a part of what makes the Hong Kong economy tick as risk-taking, hard work and a love of money-making. Indeed, as July 1997 neared, economic confidence actually started to strengthen after a steady, then alarming, decline in 1994–95. Political confidence also edged up, though it had never fallen quite as sharply. The main source of non-anecdotal evidence for this comes from surveys done by specialist polling companies or by academics. One of the more reliable is a quarterly assessment of political and economic confidence done by Survey Research Hong Kong (SRH) for the *South China Morning Post* and *Ming Pao*. It found that the economic confidence of more than 1000 randomly chosen people reached a trough in late-1995 before bouncing back and rising for most of 1996. These results accord with both improved macro-economic factors (the better than expected shape of the Chinese economy in 1996, when inflation slowed yet growth remained strong) and a heightened 'feel-good factor' in Hong Kong thanks to slowing inflation, rising property prices (good for some) and a booming stock market.

Hong Kong's record of bouncing back produces in some people an unshakeable optimism and belief in the colony's ability to adapt, an idea espoused most strongly (not surprisingly) by the business sector. Henry Tang, a Liberal Party legislator and chairman of the Federation of Hong Kong Industries, said that the SRH poll results in 1996 showed that people were 'practical and pragmatic' not 'resigned'. And he waxed: 'Closer to 1997, the flexibility of Hong Kong will shine.' Even some of those outside the pro-Beijing camp hold similar sentiments, though tend to express them a little more cautiously. Within the democratic camp, for example, independent legislator Christine Loh tends to be more hopeful about the future than most of her colleagues.

There is truth in these notions of adaptability and flexibility. Historically, workers and employees have accepted lower wage rises in times of economic recession (though this 'social contract' has weakened over the past decade as the economy has become richer, society more rights-conscious, and trade unions more determined). During the late-1980s/early 1990s, people quickly took advantage of the fact that demand exceeded supply in the job market and job-hopped frequently, even within the same year, trading job security for higher wages.

But a better word for describing Hong Kong would be 'elastic': this covers adaptability and flexibility yet also implies that there are limits to these attributes. There are clearly some things that local people, many of whom fled China to reach Hong Kong, would not accept: a loss of economic and social freedom being the main one; political freedom is important but is a far more slippery concept. That is to say, people in Hong Kong value highly the economic and personal freedoms that come with the colony's open market, such as being able to move money overseas without the restrictions of currency controls, to travel without having to ask for permission, and to run businesses without government interference and too much tax (freedoms which do not exist in China). Meanwhile, a vocal, influential and mostly younger minority place great importance on freedom of speech, of association, demonstration and the development of civil rights (this group probably makes up around 20–30% of the population judging from voting patterns and political activism in the 1990s).

Whereas in normal times Hong Kong can look like a society which *largely* puts economic concerns above political ones—and is eminently pragmatic—it does have the ability to burst rapidly, if briefly, into flame during periods of tension, such as a spontaneous crisis in China or when Beijing periodically threatens to roll-back political freedoms in Hong Kong. The various fuels which have fed these different fires in the past have included one or more of the following: the colony's political hardcore; a sense of loyalty among Hong Kong people to the Chinese 'nation' (which is not the same as loyalty to the current socialist 'state'); and a tendency towards emotionalism. This volatile mix was most graphically set alight by the Tiananmen protests during April-June 1989, when the zeitgeist in Hong Kong ranged from hope and joy that political change might at last be coming to China to despair and anger when the massacre took place—an event which brought a million people out onto the streets in protest. Prior to this event, most expert commentators firmly believed that the colony's people were politically apathetic. June 1989 was everyone's coming of age.

Hong Kong's potential to become politically engaged again on a mass scale may well be triggered once or twice in the first few years after 1997 by Beijing's reunification strategy. Yet intuition suggests that these crises will not mark the end of the colony. Hong Kong, for one, has become more adept in recent years at living and flourishing in the shadow of political uncertainty. A more significant reason is that reunification with China will bring about immediate change in only one area: the political structure. Were Beijing to reshape the economy as well, then the end almost certainly would be nigh—since this would bring a much wider and deeper reaction than the loss of certain political freedoms. But by leaving the economy and the local 'way of life' intact, it has ensured that the majority of people— including almost all their politicians, democrats as well as the pro-Beijing or business lobbies—have a stake in something worth preserving and will therefore give the new sovereign the benefit of the doubt (indeed, most of them have no choice). This pragmatic consideration will in turn act as a self-constraint on political action in future. (Most politicians, by the way, come from the educated professional class. At their most radical, they are reformers, not revolutionaries.)

Pragmatic self-restraint is only one aspect of Hong Kong's flexibility. Two other features are the propensity of the Hong Kong Chinese to emigrate and a fairly high degree of confidence (as of 1996–97) in the outlook for the economy. But there is also a political reason why Hong Kong is unlikely to oppose China to the point that chaos becomes entrenched: the fragmented and unstable nature of its political party system. In short, Hong Kong has so many political parties that any action it mounted in its own defence would be far less focused, more splintered and harder to sustain than if it had just one or two really large parties.

The only camp which would organise opposition against Beijing is the broad democratic lobby, and it alone contains nine political parties or related groups of greatly varying size (the Democratic Party, the Hong Kong Alliance in Support of the Patriotic Democratic Movement in China, The Frontier, Association for Democracy and People's Livelihood, the Citizens Party, the Confederation of Trade Unions, 123 Democratic Alliance, the Social Democratic Front, and the United Ants—more on these later). Though these groups might come together at a time of crisis—say another outbreak of anti-government protest in China—during normal times they will not *all* work closely together, because of differences in style, strategy, conflicting personalities, and a feeling of alienation among the smaller parties over what they see as the Democratic Party's often autocratic manner. Yet this fragmentation is only partially a product of the politicians themselves. It was initially thrust upon Hong Kong by the colonial political system and will be encouraged, as we saw in the previous chapter, by the incoming sovereign. Forces both internal and external, therefore, seem determined to keep Hong Kong from pushing *itself* too far off the path of continuity and stability.

That a lasting and debilitating crisis in China could knock Hong Kong off its pedestal is another matter entirely (examples of such an event could include war with Taiwan or civil war in China). All predictions would then be worthless. Nor could any amount of bullish optimism lessen Hong Kong's exposure to danger.

THE REVOLVING DOOR

Emigration is a good point from which to embark on a more detailed description of Hong Kong's elastic society because it predates the 1997 issue by a good century or more.

People have always emigrated from (or through) the colony. From the 1860s to 1939, more than six million Chinese labourers fleeing poverty and political instability in China passed through Hong Kong on their way to places such as the United States, Australia, Singapore, the Malay states, Canada, Panama, the West Indies, Borneo, and the Pacific Islands. Hong Kong was not the only port from which the southern Chinese left. Others included modern-day Shantou (then Swatow) in Guangdong Province, as well as Xiamen (then Amoy) and Fuzhou (Foochow) in Fujian Province. And the popularity of destination countries changed depending on their economic conditions and government policies.

This supply of people did not officially resume after the Second World War because the immigration policies of most industrial countries militated against cheap Asian labour (although various illegal channels were set up to meet 'pent-up demand', says Ronald Skeldon, a geographer at the University of Hong Kong and a specialist on migration issues). The one exception was Britain, which ran an open immigration program for Commonwealth countries until the early 1960s. The typical emigré from Hong Kong between these two periods was a villager from the New Territories who moved to London and worked in a Chinese restaurant. A combination of this and a general shift among farmers' sons into urban jobs in recent decades is the reason for the countless numbers of small villages depleted of young people—or all people—around rural Hong Kong.

Patterns changed again from around 1966–67 onwards, when pro-communist riots inspired by the start of the Cultural Revolution swept Hong Kong, exposing the colony's political vulnerability and frightening the wealthier residents into thinking actively about establishing a foothold elsewhere. Around the same time, fortuitously, the United States, Australia and Canada started to drop their racist immigration policies targeted at Asian people. The dual effect of these 'push' and 'pull' factors led to emigration from Hong Kong becoming a distinctly urban-based phenomenon involving well-educated and better-off people. After an initial burst in the late 1960s and early 1970s, the total number of people emigrating hovered around a stable 20,000 per year from 1977 to 1986. Another turning point, this time related to China's resumption of sovereignty and changes in the policies of destination countries in response to the 1997 issue, came in 1987 when 30,000 people left. This jumped again the following year to almost 46,000, fell back a little in 1989, then reached 62,000 people in 1990. The high point in recent years was 1992, when 66,000 secured visas to leave. In terms of accumulated departures, this means that around 200,000 Hong Kong people left from 1977–86 and another 500,000 or so by the end of 1996—most of them skilled or highly skilled.

Balancing these numbers since the Second World War have been around three million arrivals. These were the people who fled China in what Skeldon describes as 'waves': after the Communist victory in 1949, during the famine of the Great Leap Forward period in the late 1950s, and in the late 1970s when China began to open its economy to the outside world. Most came from southern China (the provinces of Guangdong and to a lesser extent Fujian) and were 'illegal' in that they did not have a valid exit permit and entry visa.

Until 1980, the Hong Kong government generously ran what was called a 'touch-base' policy: if an illegal immigrant—swimming into Hong Kong across one of two very wide bays, scrambling across the hilly border between the New Territories and Shenzhen, or being smuggled in on a fishing boat—could evade capture by border patrols and reach urban Hong Kong, then he or she would not be returned to China. But with so many mainlanders already in Hong Kong, and many of them wanting family members to be allowed in, the government shifted its policy to permitting 75 legal immigrants a day just before dropping the touch-base idea. This was increased to 105 in 1994 and 150 in 1995. This adds up to a total of almost half a million people alone coming in on legal permits since 1980.

This constant cycle of arrival and departure has led many observers to comment that Hong Kong's population is a product of migration. But some observers go a step further and see it in psychological terms as well. The late John D Young (Yang Yilung), a Beijing-born historian who lived most of his life in Hong Kong, described the colony as having a 'moveable culture'. This trait was an essential key to understanding the Hong Kong Cantonese identity, other elements of which included a greater sense of individuality than most other Chinese linguistic sub-groups, a lack of preoccupation with high-Confucian culture, and a high degree of religious eclecticism.

Young believed that the practical importance of this was that Hong Kong Chinese, being largely Cantonese, exhibited a higher preponderance than other Chinese groups for moving to other countries when the opportunity arose or when pressures at home became severe. Rather than fighting political problems, therefore, many people would rather leave for safer pastures. Young saw this not as an act of cowardice, but as a proven and intelligent survival strategy in a highly volatile political environment.

The implication is that modern Cantonese society in the world today has developed on both sides of the Pacific. The same applies, although on a smaller scale, to other linguistic sub-groups from southern China, namely the Chiu Chow, Hakka, and Fujianese (which includes Hokkien speakers). Hence, southern Chinese are linked into a regional and international network through their families and friends. This smooths the path of the would-be emigrant and makes the decision to leave a considerably easier one to make.

Does this mean Hong Kong people are not loyal to the colony? No. Since the early 1970s, a feature of the colony is the development of a local Hong Kong identity. This is the notion of *Heunggong yan*, which literally means 'Hong Kong person' but is normally rendered as Hong Kong Belonger. In the 1980s, surveys asking people whether they thought of themselves as Hong Kong Belongers or 'Chinese' (from China) typically showed that around 60% or more opted for the former. In more recent surveys the percentage falls below this, although in one the extent ranges from negligible to quite significant depending on the respondent's political affiliation (that is, between supporters of the democratic and pro-business parties on the one hand and pro-China parties on the other). One survey from 1991 bucks the trend completely and purports to show that only 18% of people considered themselves to be 'Hongkongers'—a finding that is difficult to accept because local identity appears to have been firming since 1989 and as a result of reunification, not weakening. The pro-Beijing lobby often argues that Hong Kong's identity will dilute once it becomes part of the motherland again. Yet the opposite could in fact occur: Beijing's attempt to inculcate a 'national' identity among local people could be the catalyst for the development of a deeper, stronger notion of what it means to be a *Heunggong yan*.

But this throws up a conundrum. If people feel more attached to Hong Kong than their predecessors did, why don't more stay and defend it? The best answer is probably that those who do choose to defend it will do so with greater vigour as a result of the stronger identity, whereas the urge to escape overseas if one has the option remains the strongest 'pull' for the majority.

Emigration reduces political tension between Hong Kong and China in many ways. It acts as a safety valve for the political system, releasing those who have lost all confidence and have the means to leave. It offers people who want to stay the possibility of an escape if things go badly wrong, thus enhancing their feeling of safety. It brings back some of those who emigrated early, which contributes to stability by raising faith in the future. And it is one factor encouraging the immigration into Hong Kong of Western and Asian professionals, who contribute to the internationalisation of the economy and to growth by expanding the stock of expertise, technology and connections (and who therefore indirectly contribute to stability).

Without emigration, it is hard to imagine how Hong Kong would have coped as well as it has with 1997. Imagine if another few hundred thousand articulate and wealthy professionals and their families had stayed for the whole of the 1987–96 period. While many may not have become politically involved, it is inconceivable to think that their presence would not have sharpened tensions and/or raised the general level of panic. Why? Because the lack of a safety valve alone would have added to the pressures which Hong Kong society was experiencing. And because at least some of these people would have become politically active, thus intensifying the level of conflict within Hong Kong.

THE CLOSED DOOR

What about those people—labourers, low-paid white collar workers and semi-skilled service sector employees—who are not among the happy minority with the money to leave, the skills that destination countries want or the family connections overseas? Or those professionals who choose to stay? How will they cope with the political changes which Beijing intends to impose?

The first, and perhaps most obvious point, is that the vast majority of people in Hong Kong have nowhere else to go, except perhaps back to China (which is an option that some retired people are taking up). So it is in their interest, as much as Beijing's, that Hong Kong remains stable. People may not conceive of the equation in such rational terms, but the vulnerability of their society and their own limited resources will produce caution. They no doubt know intuitively that they would suffer disproportionately if political crisis led to a rapid economic decline.

Focusing on the economy is a second mode of survival. Despite the fascinating development of Hong Kong's political arena over the past 15 years, most of the evidence points to economic and social conditions as being at the centre of the majority of people's attention—which is what you would expect in most societies but especially in the crowded and often run-down urban districts of Hong Kong. Some of the hard evidence follows.

The SRH index, mentioned above, is notable for the different pictures it portrays of economic confidence and political confidence. Both indexes dived together in reaction to Tiananmen Square in June 1989, then rose in tandem over the next year. Preparations for the Gulf War sent the economic index into free-fall again, though the political one remained stable. While the latter fluctuated in a fairly narrow band over the next five years, economic confidence rose higher and fell lower during the same period. All of which suggests that people are more concerned about their livelihood than about politics, however upsetting the mere act of reunification is for many Hong Kong Belongers.

To some extent, therefore, people seem able to detach political problems from economic ones. Contrary to the conventional notion that political instability is bad for the economy, Hong Kong society has pretty much learnt to live with a high degree of 'China-related uncertainty', especially having survived the shock of June 1989. Apart from the disparity between the two SRH indexes during the Gulf War, there was also a divergence in 1993 when political confidence slid and faith in the economy rose. That was the year when China and Britain began fighting bitterly over Patten's democratic reforms, and the year when international confidence in the China market was at its height and the Hong Kong stock market boomed. Although political confidence became quite stable over 1994–95, the economic index suffered a 45 degree slide as the stock boom ended and China instituted tough austerity measures to cool its wildly overheated economy. The moral of the story is that although politics affects people's economic optimism to some degree, other factors, not least the general health of the economy itself, are more important.

A similar contrast is strikingly apparent in an academic survey done by the University of Hong Kong and City University of Hong Kong just before elections for the Legislative Council in September 1995. The survey, which was based on face-to-face interviews with 1900 registered voters, found a definite contradiction between attitudes towards Hong Kong's political future after 1997 and its probable economic situation. Whereas an overwhelming majority of respondents were pessimistic about the scope for freedom of speech, of the press, of demonstration, and judicial independence, a clear majority also believed that the colony's way of life would remain the same, and that the continuation of free trade, low taxation and no foreign exchange controls was 'very likely, quite likely, or likely'.

It should be emphasised that these views were expressed only by voters who 'identified' with one of the four major parties. About half of the respondents (856 people) fell into this category, with more than half of this number (498 people) identifying with the Democratic Party. The next largest contingent supported the pro-business Liberal Party (157 people), followed by the leftist Democratic Alliance for the Betterment of Hong Kong (117 people), and lastly the grassroots democratic Association for Democracy and People's Livelihood (47 people).

There is good reason, however, for believing that the other half of the respondents held similar views: although voter attitudes varied to some extent depending on which party they supported, there was such close broad agreement on the divergence between political and economic futures after 1997 that the results could be taken almost to represent a social consensus. This consensus accords also with the anecdotal impressions one gets from talking with local people, who instinctively know Hong Kong will survive despite Beijing's political machinations. Or as Tony Scott, former director of corruption prevention (now retired) at the Independent Commission Against Corruption, put it: 'The main question (of my Chinese staff) is, "What price do we have to pay to stop China from interfering (in the Hong Kong way of life)"?' This price is assumed to be a political one, involving things like not criticising Beijing's authority and not acting subversively. Scott's staff were less worried about issues such as the Bill of Rights than they were about their livelihood and job security.

An obvious conclusion to draw from this is that the majority of Hong Kong people will grudgingly and fatalistically go along with the transfer of sovereignty as long as the economy remains healthy. Assuming there is not a recession in China or around the world over the next five years, the outlook for the Hong Kong economy is positive. But what could really politicise the bystanders is a steadily worsening economic environment and a sense of declining personal wealth and social conditions. Beijing is fortunate that the transfer is taking place when economic conditions at home and abroad are favourable.

THE FRAGMENTED ARENA

Probably the most complex aspect of Hong Kong's elasticity is the varied and unstable nature of its political party system. This system can be traced back to the 1980s when a variety of pressure groups were formed, including pro-democracy organisations like the Hong Kong Affairs Society, Meeting Point, and the Association for Democracy and People's Livelihood, and conservative associations such as the Progressive Hong Kong Society. But the turning point came in 1989–90 as local community, business and political leaders began coalescing in preparation for the first Legislative Council elections based on universal suffrage in September 1991 (when 18 of the 60 seats were contested through direct election in geographic constituencies).

The main parties or coalitions formed included one which strongly advocated democracy, the United Democrats of Hong Kong, founded by the three democratic pressure groups just mentioned and chaired from the start by Martin Lee; one liberal, small-business-oriented party, the Hong Kong Democratic Foundation; and one conservative pro-business and pro-Beijing group, Maria Tam's Liberal Democratic Federation (whose name bore no relation to its policies). Various smaller groups were also established at that time, including T S Lo's New Hong Kong Alliance, though were insignificant from the electorate's point of view. It was a time of great flux, a feature perhaps best illustrated by the inability of the United Democrats to remain united at election time—while the party put up its own candidates, two of its founding associations also decided to field candidates under their own names (Meeting Point and the Association for Democracy and People's Livelihood).

Some of these nascent parties reformed themselves into firmer organisations with clearer identities in preparation for the first fully elected Legislative Council in 1995. With new parties appearing on the scene as well, the result was a veritable explosion in political pluralism. The United Democrats formally merged with Meeting Point to form the Democratic Party in 1994. The Association for Democracy and People's Livelihood continued to keep its own identity and counsel, arguing that it represented grassroots' interests whereas the Democratic Party was more focused on the 'middle class'.

A new pro-Beijing entity was created in 1992 with the help of the New China News Agency—the Democratic Alliance for the Betterment of Hong Kong (DAB). A more substantial pro-business group was established in 1993—the Liberal Party. The other business party, the Liberal Democratic Federation, remained in force (though never did well in the ballot). And another half dozen small groups on both sides of the political fence joined in as well.

(See Appendix 2 for a summary of each party's history and political affiliation.)

The visible symbols of this pluralism are in abundance on the streets—in the form of colourful political placards attached end-to-end along sidewalk railings (and mostly in Chinese). Some of these are merely party notices giving the name of their local representative(s) and office telephone number, with possibly a brief explanation of its *raison d'etre*. A standard green Democratic Party placard in 1996 bore the following statement of the party's goals and services in a white box along the bottom: 'Building management. Improving the environment. Receiving complaints. Legal consultation.' And a DAB placard claimed to be: 'Focusing Hong Kong people to build a new Hong Kong.' The DAB also said it would 'Welcome advice' and 'Receive complaints', using language almost identical to the Democratic Party.

Another form of placard is the slogan. Around the intersection of Pedder Street and Des Voeux Road in the central business district hung the following messages in late November 1996. Whereas the Democratic Party were urging passersby to 'Oppose the Provisional Legislature. Oppose Democracy's Big Step Backwards', the pro-China Hong Kong Federation of Trade Unions (an ally of the DAB) was calling on them to 'Strongly Demand the Hong Kong government Cooperate with the Preparatory Committee to Ensure Hong Kong's Smooth Transition'. The union also told people that the 'Preparatory Committee is Working for Everybody. Let's Come Together and Support It.'

A casual observer might conclude that all this diversity, activity and political involvement should increase the chances of sustained and widespread confrontation with Beijing after 1997. In fact, the opposite is almost certainly the case: precisely because the political arena is so diverse and fragmented, it precludes the formation of an opposition voice strong enough to command the unquestionable support of the majority of voters—not even the Democratic Party has this, despite its sizeable victories in the 1991 and 1995 elections (as we shall see below). Before looking at how this fragmentation has worsened even since 1995, and how this is weakening the political clout of Hong Kong voters, a detour into history is needed in order to understand why such a system developed in the first place.

FRAGMENTATION WAS assured the moment that elections were first introduced to the Legislative Council, which historically had been composed of political appointees and government officials, as we have seen. The first elections, which took place in 1985, introduced functional constituencies and an 'electoral college' for 24 of its then 57 seats, thus assuring the government a continuation of its commanding majority. The next election in 1988 brought a little bit of tinkering: two more functional constituency seats were added. In 1991 the electoral college was dropped and the first geographic constituencies appeared. That was the also the first time that a majority of the now 60 seats on the council were elected. Electoral complexity increased again in 1995, when appointed and official seats were dropped and a new electoral college and nine new functional seats were added. What this meant from a voting point of view was that everyone had a vote in their geographic district, every working person had another vote in their professional/employment area or sector, and all 346 district board members had a third vote in the electoral college.

Although all seats may have been opened to election in 1995, none of the parties or alliances had a natural constituency in each segment. The Democratic Party dominated the districts, winning 12 out of the 20 geographic seats (or 14 if you count its independent allies as well). The party also won two of the nine new functional constituency seats, which represented broad sectors of white and blue collar workers, but only three of the 21 old functional seats, which mostly represented narrow commercial interests (however, the functional constituency tally rises from five to nine if the party's allies are included). The total number of seats won, including the election committee, was 19 for the Democratic Party—and 26 with its allies.

In contrast, the Liberal Party did pathetically in the geographic constituencies, winning only one district, but it coasted through in the old functional sectors. Indeed, five of its six 'wins' in this segment were uncontested! Another seven seats in this segment were won by independent business candidates.

Meanwhile, neither the leftist Democratic Alliance for the Betterment of Hong Kong (DAB) and its close ally, the pro-China Hong
Kong Federation of Trade Unions (FTU), nor the soft democrats,
the Association for Democracy and People's Livelihood (ADPL),
dominated in any segment.

It was a system tailor-made for Hong Kong's colonial and commercial structure. By creating a fragmented legislature, the government
ensured that none of the parties could get too big and thereby
limited damage to the supremacy of the executive-led system of
government. This pleased China for its own sake (until Patten came
along) and because it restricted the influence of the democrats. And
it catered to the influential business community by guaranteeing
that its members would still have a voice on the legislature. Before
1991, business interests dominated the output of the council, as they
did the decisions of the Executive Council.

To emphasise why the government deemed such a system necessary, it is worth considering some alternative and more democratic
scenarios: Imagine if there had been no functional constituencies in
1995 and all seats had been up for direct election through geographic districts—as some of the more radical reformers like the
journalist-cum-independent politician Emily Lau had earlier fought
for. Assuming the same 'first past the post' voting system was used,
then the Democratic Party alone (without its allies) would have won
a clear mandate of 36 seats (an extrapolation based on the 12 out of
20 geographic seats the party won in 1995). The big loser under this
scenario would have been the business sector—the Liberal Party and
independent business candidates. They won a total of around 20
seats in 1995, but would have gained a paltry three or so in a fully
directly elected legislature. In the words of a Hong Kong political scientist, Louie Kin-sheun: 'It is hard to imagine that once functional
constituency elections disappear, the (Liberal) party can still survive.' Meanwhile, the DAB/FTU would have remained at about the
same level, with seven seats; and the ADPL would have increased its
share from four to six seats. (Note: The Basic Law states that the
ultimate aim is to allow all seats on the legislature to be elected by
universal suffrage; but it lays down no schedule as to when or how
this should occur.)

A reality check of sorts should accompany this simplified scenario.
The Democratic Party may not in fact do quite as well as stated, since
there are doubts as to whether it could field high-quality candidates

for all 60 seats. Indeed, when Emily Lau and other radical democrats were pushing for full universal suffrage prior to the 1995 elections, the Democratic Party was lukewarm in its support for the idea. It stuck to a proposal for only 30 directly elected seats; ostensibly because this was in its platform; though sceptics believed the party was afraid to contest a large directly elected ballot. Although the business sector would not fare well in full universal suffrage, those to gain at the Democratic Party's expense would probably be the DAB, smaller parties and independents—since voters would have more choice. Yet even if the Democratic Party was unable to gain the 36 seats postulated above, it would no doubt do better than 19 seats. Add to this the seats of independent democrats and the result could well top 30 (a majority in the legislature).

Or take a different scenario that is less extreme but still more democratic than the current system, such as the half-half concept (30 geographic constituencies and 30 functional ones). Assume the same percentage result for the former as in 1995 and the actual result for the latter in 1995. The result in this case would have been less favourable to the Democratic Party than under the first scenario, yet the combined total for the party *and its allies* would still have been 30 seats—almost a majority and a better result than the actual 1995 tally of 26. The Liberal Party and other business independents would have gained around 17 seats under this second scenario, the DAB/FTU would again have seven seats, and the ADPL would have fallen back to four. (The total does not add up to 60 since there were some independents in 1995 who were not wholly allied to any one party.)

Interestingly, had a proportional system of voting been used for all 60 seats in 1995, then the result would have been quite a bit better for the Democratic Party. Compared to the 19 seats it won from the three segments (geographic, functional, and the election committee), under this system it would have won 25 seats. This back-of-the-envelope calculation is based on the 385,000 votes it won out of a total of 920,000 ballots cast for geographic seats—or 42% of the total. Had the Democratic Party and its independent allies fought a proportional election as one unit, they would have won 30 seats out of the 60 (based on the 470,000 votes they received, or 51% of the total number cast). In other words, identical to the half-half system.

But the big news is that the relative winner under a proportional system would be the China camp (excluding business). The combined tally of all DAB and other pro-Beijing grassroots candidates in the geographic constituencies was 209,000—or 23% of the total number of votes. This would translate into about 14 seats in the legislature—a big improvement on the seven seats won by the DAB/FTU in 1995. However, to achieve this result the various candidates would have had to form into one or two parties—some of them stood as independents or as representatives of small parties.

As for business, it would do as disastrously under a full proportional system as under a full 'first past the post'. Few business candidates entered the race in the geographic districts, and those that did together gained only about 80,000–100,000 votes—or 10% of the total. This would mean a mere six seats.

These calculations underline why the colonial British administration, for its own sake and under pressure from China and the powerful local business community, could never support the advent of real democracy for the Legislative Council. And also why it chose to tightly control the advance of direct elections based on geographic constituencies.

Even the Patten reforms, conventionally seen as speeding up democracy in Hong Kong, did nothing to change the system's essentially fragmented structure and its business bias. Patten made the system fairer, to be sure, but stopped well short of pandering to the majority. Had he even tried, unlikely in any case, there would have been a business sector revolt.

In this context it will be interesting to see what the future holds, given the Basic Law's promise that all seats on the Legislative Council should one day be elected by universal suffrage. The constitution says that elections in the year 2003 should be 'half-half' (30 geographic seats and 30 functional seats). Many people hope that the following elections in 2007 will bring an increase in the geographic component, but no timetable is set for this, as stated earlier. Lau Siu-kai, the Preparatory Committee spokesman on electoral issues, has noted that there may be resistance to expanding the importance of universal suffrage if some groups in Hong Kong feel that they do not have a stake in the process. If current populist voting patterns persist, then the business community would be one such alienated group. So would the government, since it would not want to face a legislature that has a substantial popular mandate.

In fact, one wonders how the notion of 'universal suffrage for all seats' could possibly be compatible with Beijing's stated aim of maintaining Hong Kong's executive-led system of government or its low-tax, free market economy? To return to Lau, one answer could be that Beijing hopes to weaken the party system to the point where the legislature becomes a compliant body again. Or an even more creative solution—the party system develops in such a way that today's pro-Beijing grassroots parties join forces with pro-business parties to form one or two omnibus political organisations. One thing seems certain—the contradictions in the Basic Law are bound to cause great conflict.

BUT IF FRAGMENTATION was thrust upon Hong Kong, the local political community has done a good job of making it worse. In addition to the four main parties, there was an ant colony of smaller ones contesting the 1995 elections. The China side included three we have met before—the Hong Kong Progressive Alliance, the Liberal Democratic Federation and the New Hong Kong Alliance—and another grassroots group, Civic Force. On the democratic side were 123 Democratic Alliance and the United Ants, whose name implied a 'union of small people' and was also a pun on the United Democrats as well as the Cantonese name of a pro-business support group, the Cooperative Resources Centre (a forerunner of the Liberal Party). Both of the colony's major trade union umbrella groups sponsored candidates as well: the pro-Beijing Federation of Trade Unions and the pro-democracy Confederation of Trade Unions.

There has been no consolidation since the 1995 election. On the contrary, Beijing has been carefully dividing and balancing the political forces on its side—with their cooperation. For example, it has raised the status of a group which contested a mere three seats in that election and won just two—the Hong Kong Progressive Alliance, the new party formed in 1994 by the solicitor Ambrose Lau. Despite its insignificance as a political force among voters, the alliance gained the second largest number of seats of any group on the Selection Committee, the 400-strong body chosen by the Preparatory Committee in 1996 and charged with 'electing' the chief executive and Provisional Legislature. Even the more established DAB, formed in 1992 and a consistent apologist for China's policies on Hong Kong, was given fewer seats. The DAB regained its honour by 'winning' 10 seats on the 60-seat interim legislature; yet the alliance still secured five—a huge improvement on the result it achieved when it faced Hong Kong electors.

Another electorally weak pro-Beijing party which has done well out of the Provisional Legislature is the inaptly named Liberal

Democratic Federation. It contested four seats in the 1995 polls and won one. The party now has three seats on the interim law-making body (one of which was given to Maria Tam, party chairman and not a candidate at the earlier public election).

The Liberal Party, meanwhile, acquired 10 seats on the provisional body—the same number as it won at the 1995 ballot (and with exactly the same line-up of candidates too). The remaining 31 seats went to independents, prominent business leaders and representatives of small parties (27) and the united-front democrats, the ADPL (4).

The democratic camp has also continued to fray. Two independent democrats, Emily Lau and Christine Loh, both began working on creating new political parties in 1996. Lau's group, The Frontier, was unusual in that it included several existing members of the Democratic Party; although not its senior leaders, Martin Lee, Anthony Cheung and Szeto Wah. It portrayed itself as a more radical political reform group than the Democratic Party, but tried hard not to imply any criticism of the latter at its launch in August 1996.

Loh's party, called the Citizens Party (Minchuandang) was launched on 4 May 1997 (a significant date in the history of China's democratic movement). Its rationale for existence is to be more creative and less confrontational than the Democratic Party in seeking democratic reform within the constraints of the Special Administrative Region framework, and to urge the future government to involve the public more in the policy-making process than the British administration did. It will also promote a comprehensive platform covering social, women's and environmental policies.

Towards the end of 1996, the ADPL also suffered a split. A group of 16 members (none of whom were legislators) broke away over the party's decision to put candidates forward for the Provisional Legislature in December of that year. The latter decision was ironic since the ADPL's chairman, Frederick Fung, had voted against the interim legislature in March of that year (as a member of the Preparatory Committee)—and had incurred the wrath of China for doing so. The only other party member on the Preparatory Committee, Chang Ka-mun, voted for it. But the futility of Fung's position was such that even he later changed his mind and decided, along with several of his colleagues, to put his name forward for a seat on the interim body (hence, the four seats the party secured, one of which went to Fung). A further irony was that at the same time an old ADPL placard left hanging in Pedder Street, Central, proclaimed, among other things: 'There is no need to set up the Provisional Legislature.' (Meanwhile, the breakaway group from the ADPL launched its own political alliance, the Social Democratic Front—also on 4 May 1997.)

One result of all this fragmentation is that voters will face a dizzying array of choices when choosing the first two-year Legislative Council, due to take over from its provisional predecessor no later than June 1998. There will be around four large and small democratic parties outside the united front, one in the united front, and around six pro-Beijing parties, including the pro-business groups. That makes a total of 11 political parties (not counting the trade unions), which is rather excessive for a city of just six million people—a party for every 550,000 people.

But the bigger issue is that this self-induced fragmentation has stunted the institutional power of the democratic forces in Hong Kong. Their inability to form into one or two larger parties prior to 1997 not only raises Beijing's chances of success when playing its united front game of befriend-and-divide, it undermines the camp's overall bargaining power with Beijing and the new executive-led government of Tung Chee-hwa. This in turn must weaken each individual party's value to its supporters, since the power of every organisation will range from limited to extremely limited.

This is not to suggest that one large democratic party could achieve all it wanted to. The fact of the transfer of sovereignty and Beijing's reshaping of the political structure means that new limits are being imposed that will restrict what any group can do (remember Lau Siu-kai's point about the new post-1997 electoral system being aimed at weakening the party system across the board). Yet greater unity within the democratic camp would bring about a consolidation of finances, electoral support, and a coordination of policies and strategies. This would arguably produce an institution more effective in articulating the demands of the 51% of electors who voted for democratic politicians in 1995. Given the momentous nature of the changes upon Hong Kong, surely strength and unity is called for if Hong Kong's way of life (meaning its political freedoms as much as its economic culture) is to be preserved.

RETURNING TO THE THEME of this chapter, the evolution and nature of the party system in Hong Kong mitigates against massive and organised resistance to Beijing after 1997. Partly self-induced, the fragmentation of the system has also been imposed. Had the

Democratic Party won a convincing majority in the legislature under a Western-style electoral system, then Beijing would have had far more difficulty cutting the party out of the political process, for this would have meant ignoring the wishes of a clear majority of voters— which in turn would have undermined the goal of a smooth transition. As it was, the complete absence of the party's members from the Preparatory Committee and every other China-appointed body organising the handover has caused resentment but no crisis.

Indeed, in the difficult years immediately after the handover, many democratic organisations will simply be trying to survive. Even that would be an achievement for the Democratic Party, since once July 1997 has receded into the past and a smooth transition has been achieved, there is no reason to believe that the Chinese government will not try to undermine the party with even greater vigour. The stubbornness of Szeto Wah, the 'principled' leadership of Martin Lee and, paradoxically, constant pressure from Beijing acting as a bonding mechanism, has so far kept the party from splitting. Yet quite a few observers think that the more moderate members of the Democratic Party—those who have always believed in a conciliatory approach towards China, of which there are many—will eventually quit politics or cooperate with Beijing. One outside sceptic, Harold Ko, convener of the United Ants, reckons that more than half of the party's legislators actually want to work with the new sovereign now, yet cannot be seen to break ranks. The Democratic Party, of course, remains defiant.

The attitude among independent democratic legislators towards working with China is equally mixed. At one extreme is Emily Lau, who rails against the new sovereign with a predictability and passion that none equals (she also happens to be Hong Kong's most popular politician, securing more votes than even Martin Lee in the 1995 election). At the other is Christine Loh, a sharp critic of China at times but also keen to find ways to work within the post-1997 political structure.

Loh's view is that there should be a middle-ground between unimaginatively opposing the new sovereign and submissively kowtowing. She also feels that liberal politicians need to put their case on issues of concern to them to the Chinese government, because if they do not, no one else will. It is a position that confuses many people, for the simple reason that it does not fit easily into either the pro- or anti-Beijing stereotype—and in the highly emotional political environment of present day Hong Kong, it is dangerous not to be one or the other. Thus people who try to build bridges are quickly attacked as 'collaborators' or 'turncoats'—or even worse, they are 'naive'.

When Loh sought a meeting with the New China News Agency in mid-1996 for the purpose of securing an invitation to Beijing to put forward her concerns to the central government, the initial reaction of many was that this was a ruse on her part to join the united front. For example, *The Nineties*, an anti-Beijing current affairs monthly, noted that the leftist press in Hong Kong immediately used her meeting with the New China News Agency as evidence that China did not, as many claimed, 'reject different ideas' and that the door to communication with the democrats was not closed. Pro-China newspapers also praised her willingness to 'change her attitude' towards China and 'adopt a reasonable style of consultation and discussion'. Although Loh was not trying to join the united front, the episode revealed the importance that the democratic lobby attached to appearances on the eve of reunification. Whether this 'form' can be sustained is doubtful.

THE BENEFICENT SOVEREIGN

The other side to this equation of crisis or stability is what does Beijing intend to do to win the 'hearts and minds' of people. Having put so much effort into getting and keeping the business community onside during the 1980s and early 1990s—to the extent of upsetting some of its traditional leftist and labour supporters—Beijing has failed to win over the broader community. Though hardly a day goes by without some Chinese official attending a community function, sports day, celebratory dinner, and so on, most of this is selective activity involving the converted.

What Beijing needs to keep the peace—and it appears to realise this—is a more significant economic package that would address such popular concerns as housing (it is extremely expensive and in short supply), urban renewal (some parts of Hong Kong are Dickensian dumps), a more comprehensive social welfare scheme (including more for the elderly), and better transportation networks (especially between Kowloon and some new towns in the New Territories).

Although Hong Kong's gross domestic product (GDP) per capita in 1995 of just under US$23,000 (HK$180,000) topped by a healthy margin, for example, Australia's figure of US$19,000, no one would suggest real living standards in Hong Kong were higher. Typical apartment sizes in public and private housing estates range from 400–700 square feet (37–65 square metres). Noise and dust from traffic and incessant construction are chronic problems, resulting in the need to keep airconditioners on and windows closed most of the day. And many people earn a lot less than the monthly share US$1900 (HK$15,000) of the GDP per capita. In fact, the average household, not individual, monthly income is around US $1800 (HK$14,000). Very often both husband and wife must work. (Note: GDP per capita in 1996 was US$24,500 or HK$191,000.)

The British administration may have belied its laissez-faire philosophy by being highly interventionist in building or subsidising 'social infrastructure' such as housing, hospitals, educational institutes and transportation, but there is a marked cross-party consensus that much more could be done. For example, the manifesto of the Democratic Party, passed at its first annual general meeting in October 1994, calls on the government to 'spend more resources to provide more public housing so as to bridge the gap between the rich and poor and hence increase social stability'. It also urges the government to 'take measures to regulate the prices of private properties so as to eliminate their chaotic fluctuation'. None of the other major parties, except the Liberal Party, would disagree with this. The manifesto makes a similar statement about social services, argues that improvements could be made in transportation, and says a central medical insurance scheme should be set up.

Exactly the same consensus on social policy is apparent among the supporters of all the major political parties, including those identifying with the Liberal Party. For example, the University of Hong Kong/City University survey of registered voters in 1995 found a definite majority of those who identified with particular parties agreed with the statement that 'government should control property prices'. The percentage figures for supporters of the Democratic Alliance for the Betterment of Hong Kong (DAB), the Democratic Party, and the Liberal Party all fell between 58 and 64%, while the figure for the Association for Democracy and People's Livelihood (ADPL) supporters was 70%.

Other major findings were:

- Support for increasing the tax rate on people earning 'high salaries' was even greater, with percentages ranging from 68% (ADPL supporters) to 78% (DAB supporters).

- Agreement with the statement that 'government has the responsibility to provide the basic needs of every citizen', was higher still: the lowest proportion was 81% (ADPL) and the highest a huge 95% (DAB).

- Around three quarters of all party supporters agreed that government should provide retirement protection for citizens aged 65 years or above, and only slightly fewer said they would be willing to 'pay more tax to enable the government to provide free medical service'.

An early indication that Beijing would try to act upon some of these concerns in order to raise its level of public support came from the social and security (law and order) sub-group of the Preliminary Working Committee (the predecessor of the Preparatory Committee). Various committee members visited housing estates in mid-1995, including Wang Shuwen, the Chinese co-convenor of the sub group; Rita Fan, the Hong Kong co-convenor; and Tian Qiyu, the Chinese vice-minister for public security. The sub-group's housing panel later held a three-day public consultation exercise. The main conclusions of these visits and meetings were that public housing was insufficient to meet demand, that people forced to live in 'temporary housing areas' (regimented camps with row upon row of corrugated-iron terraces) had to wait too long for a flat in a public housing estate, and that new housing was urgently needed for the tens of thousands of relatively poor mainlanders expected to arrive after reunification. The sub-group's fear was that inadequate housing could quickly lead to social instability in the early years of the Special Administrative Region.

More recent signs of awareness came in the policy platforms of the three second-round chief executive candidates. Tung Chee-hwa, the businessman who went on to receive the post, promised to ensure the sale of public housing to existing tenants at 'affordable prices' and to supply more land for housing construction. T L Yang, the former chief justice, said he would build more centres for old people and new public housing for the poor. Peter Woo, another businessman and chairman of the Wharf Group, put forward by far the most specific proposals: to make the construction of public housing more efficient; to cut the wait for public housing from seven to four years; to build an average of 50,000 new flats a year; and to ensure the 'cut-price sale' of public housing to tenants.

These proposals should be seen in context: they were partially a response to meetings the three candidates had held with grassroots and labour organisations after announcing their candidacy, and the considerable criticism each had received in the local media for their ignorance of these matters. At the same time, none of the candidates, especially Tung since he was the most closely connected to the leadership in Beijing, would have put forward such ideas had they not had the tacit acceptance of the new sovereign.

It was significant that Tung's proposals were not only the most vague, but they would probably have the least impact on government expenditure. As the new chief executive, he will have to tread a fine line between improving social infrastructure and keeping the people happy on the one hand, and maintaining the government's traditionally firm grip on the growth in public expenditure on the other. Hong Kong may have large and growing fiscal reserves—an estimated US$24 billion (HK$190 billion) built up from budgetary surpluses by March 1998 and US$22 billion in the Land Fund, a kitty set up by the Joint Declaration to ensure the future Special Administrative Region began life with a financial buffer—but Tung cannot simply go on a spending spree. If the economy is not in recession, then any rapid expansion of social services and infrastructure could have an inflationary impact. Indeed, inflation is forecast to rise in 1997 to 7%, from 6% in 1996 (government estimates). And any excessive spending would incur the wrath of the business community, which is ever fearful of an explosion in 'social welfarism'.

Yet Tung is keenly searching for some new initiatives to unveil. In the six months to July 1997 one of his favourite themes was that 'livelihood' issues were far more important to Hong Kong society than political liberty. In March he told the American television broadcaster, CNN, that the primary concerns of people were housing, spiralling home prices, scarcity of land, as well as issues like education and care for the elderly. 'These are the problems that we have to deal with. These are the *real* problems that people care about,' Tung said. Then three weeks later, he set up three taskforces to formulate policies on housing, education and care for the elderly. Each was headed by one of his new Executive Councillors. A property surveyor was put in charge of housing (Leung Chun-ying, who is also a vice-chairman of the Preparatory Committee). A banker was given education (Antony Leung of Chase Manhattan). And a trade unionist was handed elderly policy (Tam Yiu-chung of the Federation of Trade Unions and former vice-chairman of the DAB).

These taskforces suggest that the general scope of livelihood policy under the first chief executive, whose term runs for five years, may be more narrow than the public would hope for. Assigning a property surveyor to advise on housing is a conservative move, since any good property surveyor (as Leung is) has a stake in the status quo. It would be out of character for him to produce a radical program that, say, aimed to cut prices by hugely increasing the supply of land, forcing developers to sell flats once they were completed (rather than holding on to them and waiting for prices to rise), and breaking the grip which a half dozen large developers have on the mass market. More could come from the education taskforce, but that is a much less controversial area. And it is significant that the elderly are the focus of the social welfare initiative, not the wider community—another politically cautious move. Tung, indeed, is a cautious man.

When he gives his first policy speech as chief executive to the legislature in October 1997, Tung will produce a list of social and economic 'initiatives' like the governors before him have done. At least a few of these will have to be fresh and 'bold' if he is to build a reputation as a leader with the interests of all Hong Kong at heart. As for the business community, Tung will sell these initiatives to them as a necessary component of Hong Kong's economic competitiveness and social stability. Much talk of social policy in Hong Kong falls under the heading of the people 'enjoying the fruits of the economy's success', which puts the emphasis on distributing wealth already created. Tung is quite consciously turning this around and stressing that the creation of future wealth depends on sound social policies, such as education and decent living conditions at affordable prices (while caring for the elderly is a moral issue). 'I want to take Hong Kong into the 21st century, to remain stable, harmonious, free and vibrant. To do this, we must accord high priority to livelihood issues,' he said when announcing his new taskforces.

WHERE A LINE MAY BE DRAWN

One issue on which Hong Kong society may not be quite so elastic is an annual June 4 rally in Victoria Park to commemorate the protesters killed in Beijing in 1989 and the fate of the event's organiser, the Hong Kong Alliance in Support of the Patriotic Democratic Movement in China (whose leader, Szeto Wah, is also a senior member of the Democratic Party, as are many other leading Alliance figures).

The Alliance was formed in response to Tiananmen and comprises a coalition of democratic politicians and groups. It also organises ad hoc demonstrations and marches in support of China's democrats. The Chinese government considers this a subversive organisation, because it has helped dissidents in China in a range of financial and practical ways. Beijing has said repeatedly that it will not tolerate subversion and has often attacked the Alliance publicly. For example, in February 1991 an unrepentant Deng Xiaoping declared: 'The opposition party which organised the alliance in support of democracy has to be kicked out of the political establishment. It is impossible for them to take up key posts in the Special Administrative Region government because they burned the Chinese constitution and the Basic Law (in 1990). If they create turbulence, the Hong Kong government should interfere. If there is a major rebellion the central government has to send in troops.' Later, Qian Qichen, China's foreign minister, strongly implied in an interview with the *Asian Wall Street Journal* in October 1996 that the rally would not be permitted because it constituted interference in the affairs of China.

The whole issue is a highly symbolic and emotional one in Hong Kong: people fear that what happened to the students and workers in Beijing might happen to them in future. Whereas the issue of democratic reform is somewhat abstract to most people, the June 4 violence was real. Beijing may well be able to get away with altering Hong Kong's electoral system, legislature and various contentious laws, but an outright ban against the Alliance or the rally would provoke deepseated fears and could produce mass unrest. This comment is based on the fact that in contrast to rallies protesting Beijing's new curbs on political freedoms in Hong Kong, which only tend to attract between a few hundred and a thousand people, demonstrations against the Chinese government can involve several thousand people. The annual June 4 rally has had an attendance of between 10,000–20,000 people in recent years.

The choice for Beijing is whether it moves swiftly to ban the Alliance and chooses to live with short-term unrest in Hong Kong; or whether it opts for a slower, covert form of pressure. It is in Beijing's interests to see the Alliance implode, not be shut down, since there are considerations of international condemnation and a potential split in the local united front (much of which departed, though only temporarily, from the China camp after Tiananmen Square) to worry about. Yet having elevated the Alliance to the position of public enemy of the Chinese state, Beijing can hardly wait forever to act—nor could it be seen to back down.

The answer to this question could well lie in the statements of Deng, Qian, and other Chinese officials. Deng did not actually say the Alliance should be banned simply because it existed and was offensive to the Chinese government. Instead, he stressed that the Special Administrative Region government would have to 'interfere' if the group 'created turbulence'. Qian's October 1996 comments focused on the rally, not the Alliance. And a few months earlier, on a trip to Japan, Lu Ping, director of the Hong Kong and Macau Affairs Office, said that the Chinese government would have to take steps to prevent demonstrations in Hong Kong from endangering China.

The definition of turbulence is obviously wide open to interpretation. A June 4 rally which became emotional and included attacks on the Beijing leadership, as they all do, could constitute turbulence. Which is why Tung Chee-hwa has often warned Hong Kong people that it will be unlawful in future to make slanderous and derogatory remarks about China's leaders—a piece of advice that has been repeated by Chinese officials on numerous occasions. Or the very act of holding the June 4 rally could be branded as turbulent because it constituted interference in the affairs of China.

Beijing seems ready to wait until the Alliance transgresses the law of the Special Administrative Region (namely Article 23 of the Basic Law on subversion) before it moves against the organisation. The new sovereign needs to sanctify its actions with 'legality', since even a hint of arbitrary action would rapidly undermine confidence in Hong Kong and in the Basic Law. It would also, incidentally, contradict the Communist Party's increasing emphasis on the need for a legal system, albeit a socialist one, in China. Since Beijing cannot act on 4 June 1997, it will have to wait until 1998—or whenever the Alliance holds a rally in the meantime. With the writing on the wall, perhaps the smartest thing for the Alliance to do would be nothing for a while.

The only way in which the subversive label could be removed from the Alliance is if Beijing reversed its verdict on Tiananmen from 'counter-revolutionary rebellion' to something like 'patriotic democratic movement'. But there seems little chance of this happening under the current leadership of Jiang Zemin and Li Peng, both of whom played central roles in the crackdown (though Jiang was in Shanghai not Beijing). Even if the future brought an unexpected and sweeping change at the top—say the return of moderates like Zhao Ziyang, the sacked premier and Party general secretary—the Party would still tread warily over any reassessment, because it has more to lose than gain. In pure political terms, Tiananmen was not the Cultural Revolution. The Party had to admit the latter was a mistake as an atonement to the Chinese people and to justify its subsequent about-turn on economic policy. But China is obviously thriving despite the counter-revolutionary label still attached to Tiananmen. To the strategists in Beijing, this looks very much like they were right after all.

PART III

THE REDDENING OF HONG KONG'S ECONOMY

CHAPTER 6

A BUSINESS DEAL

The difference between China's approach to the Hong Kong economy and its strategy in the political arena is that the latter is based on traditional 'communist' tactics, while the former is ostensibly modelled on local conditions. Whereas the Basic Law promises to uphold the integrity of the Hong Kong political system, it is in fact vague enough to allow Beijing to reshape the system in ways not envisaged by the letter or spirit of the constitution. But in the area of economics, the Basic Law goes out of its way—or so it seems—to preserve the status quo. And it does so with a crispness and lack of qualification that is at odds with the grey haze engulfing much of the document.

Assuming all goes well, the Hong Kong economy in two, five or even 10 years will have the same basic structure as it does today: no tariffs (except on certain luxury items), no currency controls, and low taxes; a separate currency and finances; the continuation of private property and the international financial centre; a separate customs territory, meaning the Special Administrative Region will be able to make its own trade deals with other countries and participate in international arrangements like the World Trade Organisation under the banner 'Hong Kong, China'; the maintenance of its own shipping register as well as previous systems of shipping management and regulation. And in aviation, one of the most sensitive areas given its strategic importance, the Chinese government will give Hong Kong 'specific authorisation' to renew and amend air service agreements between the colony and other parts of the world (excluding those which go through China). What more could Hong Kong business have asked for from a constitution?

The contrast with the political environment is so stark that it is tempting to conclude that the Basic Law, and the Joint Declaration which came before it, are primarily contracts between Beijing and the Hong Kong business community. For it is the latter in whom Beijing is most interested and who can provide real assistance to China in its surge towards economic glory—and, in the process, help the Communist Party to remain in power.

Many worry that the Chinese government may be tempted to damage Hong Kong in order to boost the attractiveness of Shanghai as a financial and trading centre. Putting this issue aside until later, what initially emerges from the text of the Joint Declaration and the Basic Law is that China's leaders have had a reasonable understanding of Hong Kong's economic value to them and their country for some time. They may not have much sympathy for Hong Kong's free-wheeling spirit or the surface anarchy of Cantonese society, but they know what the place represents commercially, how it is useful—at least intuitively. They know that reunification would be a monumental waste of time were the business community not solidly onside. Hence the disproportionate number of seats given to businessmen (and a few women) on every handover-preparation body. Beijing knows it must tend the golden goose for a while since it is a long way from nurturing a bigger and better one for itself. Even when it does eventually get its own, why not have two? Especially if they serve different purposes.

Deng Xiaoping, who claimed never to understand much about economics, emphasised these themes in a famous talk with the then prime minister of Britain, Margaret Thatcher, in late 1984. Deng recounted how a Japanese friend had once asked him why there was a need to 'keep Hong Kong's current capitalist system unchanged for 50 years after 1997?' The patriarch replied that the proposal was based on 'China's realities', namely that the government wanted to quadruple the size of the economy in 20 years (that is, by the year 2000) and should by then have reached a 'level of comparative prosperity'. 'But', Deng stressed,

> ... even then, China will still not be a wealthy or developed country. So that is only our first ambitious goal. It will take another 30 to 50 years after that for China to become a truly developed country, to approach—not surpass—the developed countries ... It is in China's

vital interest to keep Hong Kong prosperous and stable. When we gave a figure of 50 years, we were not speaking casually or on impulse, but in consideration of the realities in China and of our need for development.

Discounting the political gamesmanship of such a statement, and the possibility that China may not be able to live up to its own high ideals, it is nevertheless plausible that Hong Kong stands a better chance of maintaining the integrity of its economic system than any of its other ones. For the incentives to both sides are high: Hong Kong needs China for its cheap labour, plentiful land, natural resources and burgeoning market; China needs Hong Kong as a way to access the international business community, as a trade entrepot, for foreign exchange and financing, and to a lesser extent as a supplier of modern expertise and technology (although Japan, Germany and the United States are kings here). It is a highly interdependent relationship whose bonds will not be severed by the transfer of sovereignty. This chapter outlines the forces pulling the two sides together.

SOUTH HEADING NORTH

Hong Kong surely owes a debt to fortune. Had the Communists not won the civil war against the Kuomintang in 1949, then the rush of Shanghainese industry and money to Hong Kong would probably not have occurred. But it did and the colony began its transformation from a trading port for China into a manufacturing-for-export base in its own right. Had the Communists not turned inward and tried to become economically self-reliant, and had the Korean War not started in the early 1950s (which led to a United Nations trade embargo against China), then Hong Kong would not have had the same impetus to find a replacement for its plummeting China-trade business. And had Shanghai, as a result of all these historical 'discontinuities', not lost its international financial centre status overnight, then Hong Kong might never have taken up its mantle.

Thirty years after the Communist victory, the viability of labour-intensive manufacturing in the colony was declining rapidly. Wages were on the rise. Land costs had risen. And the government was about to drop the 'touch base' policy regarding illegal immigrants from China (that is, those who reached the urban areas could stay, while those caught in the rural New Territories were sent back). This turned off a major source of cheap workers.

But again the historical tide in China was flowing Hong Kong's way. Mao Zedong's death in 1976 allowed the voices of reason in the Communist Party to start an ideological reassessment which led to economic reform and the acceptance of foreign investment a few years later. Although reform was at first limited to the agricultural sector, a few experimental industrial zones were set up as a way to attract foreign money and technology. These were located in the southern Chinese provinces of Guangdong and Fujian, both as a way to contain fallout should they fail and because rich overseas Chinese businessmen mostly came from that area (Deng and other leaders had calculated, correctly, that this group would be more likely to invest early on than other outsiders). The largest of these 'special economic zones' was deliberately situated in Shenzhen, originally a small farming village just north of Hong Kong—yet another lucky break for the colony. Indeed, one could almost say that communism in China (and its demise) has been one of the best things to happen to Hong Kong!

The result of these shifts is that Hong Kong has become by far the largest foreign investor in China. Out of a total of US$403 billion in 'contracted' foreign investment that the country attracted between 1979 and the end of 1995, Hong Kong committed US$237 billion— almost 59%. Contracted investment refers to money that has been promised through signed contracts, but not yet invested or 'utilised'. Most of it is directly invested into Sino-foreign joint ventures of various kinds or wholly foreign-owned businesses. A small amount goes into the 'other' category, which usually means the provision of equipment and perhaps materials to a local producer in China in return for finished products (otherwise called 'compensation trade'). Whereas the foreign partner does not play a part in the management of these arms-length arrangements, in the direct type of investment it does—which is why the latter is more attractive.

Total utilised investment is considerably smaller than the contracted sum since there is usually a time lag between the signing of a contract and payment of capital, or because an investment may be cancelled. Over the same period as above, utilised capital amounted to almost US$138 billion. Of this, Hong Kong supplied US$80 billion or 58%, just one percentage point lower than its share of contracted investment.

It needs to be emphasised immediately that not all this money came from Hong Kong; some of it only went *through* the colony. This is the distinction between Hong Kong as a 'source' of investment and as a 'packager' of other people's money, namely Taiwanese, Japanese, South Korean, South-east Asian Chinese, and American money (although no firm figures are available). Investors from these places sometimes set up Hong Kong-based firms to invest in the mainland, either for the sake of anonymity or for tax purposes. It is also known that some 'Hong Kong' investment is actually mainland Chinese money that was moved out of China and then back in through Hong Kong, thus taking advantage of investment privileges offered to foreign firms. This technique is called 'round tripping'.

While such hidden investment may lessen to some degree the importance of Hong Kong Chinese capital flowing into China, it conversely heightens the colony's role as a conduit between the outside world and the mainland.

The other category of foreign capital is loans, of which there are three sources: foreign governments, international agencies such as the World Bank, and 'other' (mainly commercial banks, although the Chinese government includes bonds and shares in this category as well). Loans once formed the majority of foreign capital used in China, but since the early 1990s the coin has flipped in favour of direct investment, which in recent years has been about three times larger.

Hong Kong does not make official loans to China, but it is the world centre for China-bound syndicated loans (where risk is spread among several commercial banks). Quite how large the volume of business is in this area is open to conjecture. Chinese government figures on this score are notoriously unreliable, since they consistently underestimate commercial loans. Even two of the most reputable financial publications—*IFR* (formerly called *International Finance Review*) and *Euromoney* (through a joint venture called Capital DATA Loanware)—publish quite different estimates. *IFR* calculates that the combined value of all commercial loans between 1990 and 1996 was more than US$35 billion. Capital DATA Loanware, using different criteria, puts the total at almost US$50 billion for the same period. Both calculate their numbers by tracking the media and talking to banks. Adding to these figures an estimate for the 1980s as a whole of US$9 billion produces a total commercial loan amount of somewhere between US$44 billion and US$59 billion since 1979.

One can only guess at Hong Kong's share of this. But since most commercial loans are syndicated, and since most syndicated loans are done in Hong Kong, it would be reasonable to say that the colony supplied at least another US$40 billion to China in foreign capital. In other words, about half as much again as its direct investment total of US$80 billion.

BUT ABSTRACT FIGURES, on their own, are somewhat meaningless. To get a sense of what all these numbers mean for the Chinese economy, it is necessary to look at broader trends.

One way is to compare the sum of utilised foreign investment and loans between 1979 and 1995—US$229 billion—with total investment by all government, state enterprise and private-sector units ('gross investment') in China. The result is that foreign capital works out to be equivalent to just over 9% of the US$2.5 trillion in gross investment.

This is not an entirely satisfactory comparison, either, since the US dollar value of China's gross investment figure would be exaggerated by the over-valuation of the renminbi, China's currency, before 1994. In that year the government ceased setting the official rate by administrative fiat and allowed market forces to play a role. The exchange rate then devalued from 5.7 against the dollar to 8.6.

It may be more relevant, therefore, to produce a comparison just for 1994 and 1995. The result is that the contribution of all foreign investment and loans rises to the equivalent of more than 18% of all national investment. Hong Kong's share of this would be about half—somewhat less than its share of direct investment because it does not provide any official loans.

These figures imply that foreign investment and loans have contributed to China's economic progress by playing a catalytic role. Foreign capital may not form the largest quantity of investment, but it does provide valuable foreign exchange and a qualitative boost through the things that tag along with the money; namely, management expertise, new technology, and foreign customers for the export products to be produced.

What these figures do not explain is that foreign capital is not evenly spread throughout the economy. In the 1980s it largely went into industry, especially export manufacturing, because that is what the government encouraged and what the economy could bear. With low levels of income, there was not a significant local market or ability to pay for services. Industry has continued to dominate in the 1990s, with real estate establishing itself firmly in the number two spot. Other sectors which deserve a mention, but still lag well behind, are public utilities, transportation, architecture, catering and retail.

Certain 'strategic' sectors such as banking, insurance, auto and telecoms use relatively little foreign capital; mainly because the government strictly controls it. Beijing wants local companies to control these new growth areas and fears, correctly in some ways, that foreign firms would quickly dominate if allowed in too early or *en masse*. In telecoms there is another reason: foreign capital is not essential since China's central telecoms ministry and the various provincial telecoms administrations make sufficient profit from local services and incoming international calls (which provides them with foreign exchange) to reinvest in system expansion. Indeed, the lack of foreign investment has not stopped China from achieving the world's fastest growing telephone network in recent years.

Accordingly, Hong Kong's contribution to China is predominantly in light industries such as textiles, electronics and toys, as well as property development (including hotels), retail chains, transportation projects and public utilities. Hong Kong-based stockbrokers are busily trying to encourage the development of the country's two stock markets in Shanghai and Shenzhen, but have been held back by the country's conservative regulators. Their counterparts in the banking sector are also on a short leash.

BECAUSE HONG KONG is the dominant foreign investor in the provinces of Guangdong and Fujian, it is sometimes called the 'capital of southern China' (although much 'Hong Kong' money in Fujian would be disguised Taiwanese direct investment). Although this is true in the sense that Hong Kong is the most advanced city in this region, it is misleading for two reasons. First, the strategy of Hong Kong's industrialists, property developers and entrepreneurs is far more ambitious: to diversify into different regions of the country. Ma Guonan, formerly chief economist with Peregrine, a Hong Kong investment bank, and now economist at Bankers Trust, observes that Hong Kong companies 'only need 10% of (China) business and they will do well'. The colony's tycoons clearly do not want to become too dependent on Guangdong, nor can the latter market absorb all the new investment they want to make.

Second, only about half of all Hong Kong's contracted foreign investment in China since 1990 has gone into Guangdong. Sometimes the ratio is a little more; in a couple of years it is quite a bit less. As the following table for 1995 shows, the colony is spreading its investments around:

Contracted foreign direct investment in selected cities and provinces, 1995 Hong Kong's total volume, US$ million (Letters in brackets refer to geographic location)			
City	Hong Kong's total	Province	Hong Kong's total
Guangzhou (S)	5,400	Guangdong (S)	18,200
Shanghai (E)	3,650	Fujian (SE)	4,415
Shenzhen (S)	2,750	Jiangsu (E)	3,300
Beijing (N)	1,100	Zhejiang (E)	1,500
Xiamen (SE)	991	Liaoning (NE)	1,100
Zhuhai (S)	800	Guangxi (S)	540
Shantou (S)	770	Sichuan (W)	450
Tianjin (N)	460	Jilin (NE)	227

Note 1: Figures are rounded.
Note 2: Data refer to 'contracted' investment because that is what is given in the official statistics. However, Tianjin's figure refers to utilised investment.
Note 3: Shenzhen, Shantou and Zhuhai are special economic zones in Guangdong Province, while Xiamen is a special economic zone in Fujian.
Note 4: Data for Jiangsu, Liaoning and Xiamen refer to 'Hong Kong and Macau' combined investment, although the latter accounts for very little of the total.

Sources: Almanac of China's Foreign Economic Relations and Trade 1996/97; Statistical Yearbook of Shanghai '96.

While it is tempting to surmise from this that the size of Hong Kong's investments in China declines the further a place is from the colony, this is not the case from Hong Kong's point of view. Beijing received more money than Xiamen, which is closer, and Liaoning in the far north-east got more than Guangxi in the south. Outside of Guangdong Province as a whole, volume of investment clearly depends on economic stature and development potential rather than proximity to Hong Kong.

How does Hong Kong stand relative to other foreign investors in each of the locations listed above? Since it is the largest among them, one would expect it to dominate the league table in most places. As the following table shows, the colony not only made the largest commitments in 1995, it was ahead by a wide margin in most places (despite the fact that its degree of influence lessened outside southern China):

Contracted foreign direct investment in selected cities and provinces, 1995 Hong Kong's share and the next largest investor (in brackets) (Letters in brackets after place names refer to geographic location)			
City	Hong Kong's share (next)	Province	Hong Kong's share (next)
Guangzhou (S)	80% (Britain: 4%)	Guangdong (S)	73% (Singapore: 5%)
Shenzhen (S)	79% (Japan: 6%)	Guangxi (S)	52% (Singapore: 17%)
Shantou (S)	61% (Taiwan: 10%)	Fujian (SE)	50% (Taiwan: 20%)
Zhuhai (S)	54% (Singapore: 12%)	Zhejiang (E)	46% (Japan: 12%)
Xiamen (SE)	48% (Taiwan: 14%)	Sichuan (W)	37% (Japan: 11%)
Beijing (N)	39% (USA: 14%)	Liaoning (NE)	28% (Japan: 27%)
Shanghai (E)	35% (Japan: 13%)	Jiangsu (E)	27% (Singapore: 16%)
Tianjin (N)	30% (USA: 17%)	Jilin (NE)	26% (USA: 22%)

Note 1: Figures are rounded.
Note 2: Data refer to 'contracted' investment because that is what is given in the official statistics. However, Tianjin's figure refers to utilised investment.
Note 3: Shenzhen, Shantou and Zhuhai are special economic zones in Guangdong Province, while Xiamen is a special economic zone in Fujian.
Note 4: Data for Jiangsu, Liaoning and Xiamen refer to 'Hong Kong and Macau' combined investment, although the latter accounts for very little of the total.

Sources: Almanac of China's Foreign Economic Relations and Trade 1996/97; Statistical Yearbook of Shanghai '96.

There were some interesting regional patterns in 1995 among the countries holding the number two spot in various places. Thus Japan committed itself to provinces that were mostly on China's eastern and north-eastern coasts—areas close to itself. Taiwan, as expected, showed strong interest in Fujian and its special economic zone, Xiamen. The United States focused on northern China (Beijing, Tianjin, and Jilin). And Singapore went to Jiangsu on the east coast (north and west of Shanghai) and the two southern provinces of Guangdong and Guangxi. Singapore's prominence in Jiangsu would be explained by the industrial and commercial zone it has been building in its sister city of Suzhou, one of the province's larger cities and not too far from Shanghai.

Some readers may wonder whether focusing on only one year, only on direct investment to the exclusion of loans, and only on 'contracted' capital distorts the picture in favour of Hong Kong? To some extent the answer is 'yes', but mostly 'no'. According to official statistics of total 'utilised' foreign capital since 1990, there was one year when Japan outranked Hong Kong—1990. Because its loan volume was so much greater in that year, Japan actually invested US$3 billion in China compared to Hong Kong's US$2.4 billion. But this comparison needs to be treated with great care because of the problem of Chinese statistics understating the volume of commercial loans made in Hong Kong for China. For example, whereas the Chinese government says the colony's loans amounted to a mere US$302 million in 1990, *IFR* estimates total commercial loans were US$1.9 billion and Capital DATA Loanware puts the figure at US$2.8 billion. Since most of these loans would have been arranged in Hong Kong, the official Chinese figure must be far too low. So perhaps Japan was not the top supplier of foreign capital in that year.

As for the other years, even Chinese figures give Hong Kong a strong to commanding lead: from 1.5 times greater than Japan in 1991 to 2.6 times in 1992 and 3.8 times in 1993. Rankings changed in 1994 when Taiwan landed second position; yet Hong Kong's total was still 5.8 times higher. Japan came second again in 1995, but again Hong Kong supplied four times as much capital.

LOOKING AT A single city underlines the lead Hong Kong enjoys among foreign investors. Shanghai is a good example because it is a focus of Japan's interest and because it is being groomed as central China's pre-eminent industrial, trading and business centre, and as a national if not international financial centre in its own right.

Out of a total of US$34 billion committed to Shanghai in contracted foreign direct investment in all years to the end of 1995, Hong Kong accounted for almost half. And of all utilised direct investment during the same period—US$11.5 billion—Hong Kong's share was US$5.6 billion. Again almost half.

Where does Japan stand? At less than one fifth of Hong Kong's overall contribution. Indeed, in terms of utilised direct investment, the United States has contributed more to Shanghai than Japan has; although a big commitment in contracted investment in 1995 put Japan slightly ahead of the United States in that category.

As is the case for China as a whole, foreign capital (investment plus loans) flowing into Shanghai accounts for a minority of 'gross investment', as one would expect. But whereas the ratio for China was just 17% in 1995, in Shanghai in the same year it stood at around 28%. Although the city government's statistical yearbook only gives a country breakdown for direct investment, not loans as well, it is safe to assume that both Hong Kong and Japan lent significantly to the city.

These figures also give a general indication of the extent to which Shanghai benefits from foreign capital, and especially from Hong Kong. While the city could survive without such infusions, the quantity and quality of its overall growth would certainly be affected. Returning to an issue mentioned at the beginning of this chapter, these investment trends suggest that any attempt by Beijing to try to boost Shanghai's economy through undermining Hong Kong's would backfire.

Were Beijing, for the sake of the argument, to force its new Special Administrative Region to raise corporate taxes substantially or to impose new fees of some kind on businesses, the result would be less surplus capital in Hong Kong available for investment in its northern neighbour, not more. Even worse, such a move would deeply anger the colony's leading companies, such as Cheung Kong (property and infrastructure), Henderson Land and the HongkongBank, all of whom make a large, or the largest, share of their profits in Hong Kong and are keenly interested in Shanghai. The colony's two wealthiest men—Lee Shau-kee, chairman of Henderson Land, and Li Ka-shing, chairman of Cheung Kong—would hardly thank Beijing for pulling the rug from under their most lucrative market. Since the support of tycoons such as these is as crucial to the success of the reunification process as to the mainland's economic development, it is hard to make a case for irrationality.

Other countries meanwhile would take fright at any vindictive moves on Beijing's part, leading to a fall in confidence and foreign investment across the board. For if the central government could mismanage Hong Kong, why not the rest of the country? China as a whole would therefore suffer, not only Shanghai. In fact the consequences of this negative scenario extend so far that either people's fears are quite unfounded (based perhaps on emotional memories of how the Communists destroyed Shanghai almost 50 years ago?) or the improved reputation which Beijing has earned in recent years in the area of economic management is a facade. Recent developments in China and the close relationships between leaders in Beijing and

Hong Kong's tycoons suggest that the fears are not based on current facts. Why would a government that is getting considerably more sophisticated at running its own economy turn around and, for the sake of petty economic nationalism, shoot itself in the foot and then the abdomen? Such self-destructive behaviour might result from a political decision, say over Taiwan, but surely not an economic policy.

There are domestic obstacles to such irrationality as well. Who in Beijing would have the dogmatic personality to make such a decision? It would have to come from the top, the Standing Committee of the Politburo (the inner sanctum of seven senior leaders with Jiang Zemin at the top). Yet most of these men are technocrats with some sense of how an economy works. They are not idealistic demagogues like Mao was. And none has his authority.

And how would they persuade the powerful economic ministries in the central and provincial governments to support them? Hurting Hong Kong would directly harm the interests of China's largest and most successful state-owned enterprises. Many of these have been operating in Hong Kong for decades, others have come in the last 15 years, and more are on the waiting list. Hong Kong is not only a strategic market for these companies (as a stepping stone to the outside world), it is the place where they earn a good portion of their profits and raise substantial amounts of money. The colony also happens to account for around 80% of all investment overseas by these enterprises. Since many of them report back to a ministry or an office of the State Council, China's cabinet, any blatant attack on Hong Kong's success would raise the ire of the likes of the powerful Ministry of Foreign Trade and Economic Cooperation, the Ministry of Communications, the People's Bank of China, and the Bank of China. The more one looks into the negative scenario, the less sense it makes. As the following section shows, state economic entities in China are busily increasing their involvement in Hong Kong, not preparing to pull away.

NORTH HEADING SOUTH

Another of Deng Xiaoping's famous remarks to Margaret Thatcher in the early 1980s was that he did not wish to be remembered as a modern day Li Hongzhang. 'It would mean that the present Chinese government was just like the government of the late Qing Dynasty and that the present Chinese leaders were just like Li Hongzhang!',

Deng exclaimed. Thatcher may have had little idea what Deng was talking about, but most Chinese would understand. Li was a senior Qing offical famous (or rather infamous) for signing a series of 'unequal treaties' with foreign powers such as Britain, the United States, Japan and France in the late nineteenth century. As Deng explained, if China failed to recover Hong Kong in 1997, the Chinese leadership would be humiliated in the eyes of its people.

Li, who was more of a patriot than Deng made him out to be, was a man of many hats. When not performing humiliating diplomatic tasks, he was busy playing a leading role in a national 'self-strengthening' movement during the last decades of Qing rule. This entailed the building of new infrastructure such as railways and telegraph lines, education reform, and the creation of new commercial enterprises through joint ventures between the imperial government and Chinese merchants. Echoes of this reverberate in China's current 'bureaucratic capitalist' enterprises—state-owned but acting in many respects like private companies.

What does Li have to do with trade and investment between Hong Kong and China? He founded a firm called China Merchants Steamship Navigation Company in Shanghai in 1872. According to the American historian Jonathan Spence, the company was 'designed to stop the domination of China's coastal shipping by foreign powers'.

Or as one of the company's recent brochures puts it rather more lyrically: 'It came into the world in agony by breaking through Western powers' monopoly on Chinese shipping operations.' China Merchants is also, by several decades, the oldest mainland enterprise doing business in Hong Kong.

China Merchants was duly nationalised after 1949 and came under the control of a ministry in Beijing (the Ministry of Communications, which coordinates the country's transport networks). Although trade between China and Hong Kong diminished rapidly in the 1950s, the company stayed in the colony and carried on shipping in basic foodstuffs and commodities—one of the main ways in which China earned foreign exchange over the next 30 years. Trade increased during the 1960s and 1970s, but remained limited.

The increase in trade with the rest of the world since economic reform began has been a boon for China Merchants. Not only was the company given a barren coastal area near Shenzhen to turn into a port, industrial zone and new town (Shekou) in 1979—the same year as the special economic zones were set up—it has developed into a diversified conglomerate with more than 650 subsidiaries, three companies listed on the Hong Kong stock exchange (including China Merchants Hai Hong and the Union Bank), and total fixed assets of US$4.8 billion (HK$38 billion). It is a major shareholder in Modern Terminals, Hong Kong's second largest port terminal operator, and runs the colony's largest ship-repair yard, the Yiu Lian Dockyards. It has expanded from shipping, warehousing and trading to manufacturing, retailing, banking, insurance, engineering, property investment, travel and tourism. Reflecting this rapid modernisation, a company brochure states proudly: 'With her foothold in Hong Kong, her backing from the mainland and her business worldwide, China Merchants is truly a diversified modern enterprise group.'

Elements of this story are replicated in all the major Chinese enterprises in Hong Kong, especially the last part about diversification and modernisation. Take, for example, China Resources, the main commercial arm of the Ministry of Foreign Trade and Economic Cooperation. Originally formed by the Communist Party as a channel for trading mainland food for guns and medicine from Hong Kong, China Resources was formally incorporated in the colony in 1948. For the next 40 years it enjoyed the exclusive right to be the agent for all mainland produce sold to Hong Kong.

Although this sort of trading is not by definition easily visible to the public eye, the company does run the two most famous mainland department stores: the general goods store, China Products, and the more upmarket Chinese Arts & Crafts. Both are icons of the tourist trade and sell gaudy knickknacks redolent of 'old China', as well as more mundane things like shoes and jackets. Ironically, they are the places many harried tourists and expatriates go to when looking for 'something from Hong Kong' for the folks back home.

China Resources started to lose some of its monopoly power to provincial and foreign trading companies in the late 1980s, so expanded aspects of its business such as retail (it owns the CRC supermarket chain, the third largest in Hong Kong) and diversified into new areas such as banking, construction, shipping, travel, property and insurance—a very similar line-up of businesses to those into which China Merchants has moved, not to mention numerous other Chinese firms. Although trading still accounts for around two-thirds of the turnover of China Resources—US$8.3 billion (HK$65 billion)—the firm has thrived and changed along with the Hong

Kong and international economies. One of its new businesses, for example, is in telecoms.

A third old stalwart is the Bank of China, whose origins also date back to the last years of the Qing Dynasty and whose first Hong Kong branch was set up in 1917. When the branch celebrated its 75th anniversary in 1992, it announced that its deposit base had expanded almost 40 times since 1978 and its loans by 57 times. From its traditional business in retail banking and trade finance, the bank has become increasingly involved in merchant banking, participating in syndicated loans to many of Hong Kong's largest infrastructure and industrial projects. It counts among its customers Hong Kong's underground railway system (the Mass Transit Railway or 'MTR') when that was being constructed in the late 1970s and early 1980s), a second vehicle tunnel under Victoria Harbour, container terminal development and housing estates. And in recent years it has built up its presence in the capital and money markets.

Expansion in Hong Kong has facilitated lending back to China, including more than 200 large projects in 20 mainland provinces, cities and regions by the early 1990s. Sectors covered included energy and petrochemical, transport, and iron and steel. One of the Bank of China's largest loans, made between 1979 and 1981, went to the Baoshan Steel works in Shanghai (a pet project of Deng Xiaoping). Although this loan was huge—US$7.5 billion—it was a burden the bank could apparently carry. Yun-wing Sung, an economist at the Chinese University of Hong Kong who specialises in the colony's trade and investment with China, concluded: 'The Bank of China has a huge deposit base in Hong Kong, large enough to finance a loan several times this size.'

Within Hong Kong the bank's influence spreads through the Bank of China Group, an umbrella for 13 member banks (or 14 if Macau is included). In China, the Bank of China has 5000 branches and its headquarters in Beijing. Internationally it is linked to a network of more than 1300 correspondent banks in 150 countries. To give a sense of the bank's size, it was ranked by *Fortune* magazine in 1994 as the 25th largest in the world in terms of revenue. In comparison, the HongkongBank, the colony's largest, came in at 15th.

HOW MANY mainland Chinese enterprises do business in Hong Kong? And how much have they invested? The truth is that no one really knows. Those approved by Beijing can be enumerated, but it is impossible to calculate all those established by mainland interests in Hong Kong. This is because it is easy to set up a business in Hong Kong and hide the ownership of it through a 'nominee' company, meaning a company is named as the majority shareholder rather than an individual. Alternatively, a mainland businessman could disguise his involvement by setting up a private company under the name of a local relative or friend. And what about firms in which mainland companies or individuals take a substantial, yet still minority share? How should they be counted?

The confusion is apparent from the vague and wildly different estimates that try to answer these questions. The New China News Agency, China's de facto embassy in Hong Kong, says that by the end of 1995 there were almost 1800 approved mainland companies (up from around 1000 in the early 1990s) with about US$43 billion in assets. Total investment grew from US$6.5 billion in the mid-1980s to US$10 billion by 1990, then doubled by 1992, and reached US$25 billion in 1995, making China the largest foreign investor in Hong Kong.

Yet as early as 1990 the *Far Eastern Economic Review* magazine reported that there were 4000 mainland firms in Hong Kong. A 'house cleaning' coordinated by the New China News Agency at the time reportedly closed down 400 of them (Beijing had become concerned about an uncontrolled explosion in their numbers). And in 1996, Kim Eng Securities, a Singaporean stockbroker that has studied mainland enterprises, put the figure at 20,000 firms; although many of these would be 'shell' companies such as those described above.

Shi Jiyang, director of business administration at the Hong Kong Chinese Enterprises Association, the local chamber of commerce for mainland firms, admits that it is probably impossible to arrive at an exact total. This is mainly because of the ease with which people can set up companies in Hong Kong and the many ways in which they can hide their involvement. To highlight the vagueness of most estimates, Shi said he once read that there were supposed to be more than 50,000 'underground' mainland firms in the colony!

China's official figure for combined assets—US$43 billion—is also highly suspect. Adding the Bank of China's share—reportedly half or around US$21 billion—to a conservative estimate of the Hong Kong assets of a handful of other large Chinese enterprises equals slightly more than two-thirds of the total (US$29.5 billion). The other enterprises are China Resources, China Merchants, China

Travel (the biggest tourism enterprise) and CITIC Pacific (the Hong Kong arm of Beijing's principal investment holding company, CITIC). They have a combined asset base of about US$17 billion, although only half of this is included in the calculation above as many of their projects are in China. But this would leave the other 1795 'officially approved' companies with combined assets of US$13.5 billion—or an average of just US$7.5 million each. Since there are some very large corporations included in this group, such as Guangdong Enterprises (the commercial arm of the Guangdong provincial government) and Shougang Holdings (the principal Hong Kong subsidiary of China's largest iron and steel producer), this would mean that numerous mainland firms must have almost no assets at all, which is hard to believe. Even trading companies—of which there are many on the list of members of the Hong Kong Chinese Enterprises Association—would have some assets, whether in liquid or concrete form. And what of all those companies not on the official list? Hence the official figure must be on the low side.

The same applies to total investment. The official figure says that approved mainland investment in Hong Kong doubled to US$20 billion over 1991 and 1992, a period when the Chinese economy started to rise again after a recession caused by the government's heavy-handed response to high inflation in 1988–89. This is believable, especially once you factor in the explosive effect of Deng Xiaoping's 'southern tour' in early 1992, the aim of which was to smash the economic conservatism of the central leadership by calling upon provincial officials and the people of China to throw themselves into business. It worked. But then investment in Hong Kong supposedly increased by only another 25% or just US$5 billion over the next three years—a period when economic growth in China averaged almost 12% per year. Admittedly, 1994 and 1995 were years when the Chinese government had actively started to cool its economy after the high inflation produced by Deng's inspirational urgings and various other one-off factors. Its main weapon was tight controls on bank credit to state enterprises. Even so, US$5 billion over three years after US$10 billion over two seems curiously disproportionate given the ongoing diversification of mainland firms in Hong Kong and their active participation in the local stock market since the early 1990s (a subject dealt with in more detail below).

On the basis of information from local chambers of commerce and foreign diplomats in Hong Kong, Kim Eng reckons that total mainland investment probably stands at around US$50 billion to US$60 billion—or about double the official statistic. It says the higher figure includes investment in the local property market and the capitalisation of mainland firms on the stock market (although not all of this money, of course, is invested in Hong Kong).

The discrepancy in investment estimates may well be due to Chinese official figures including only money that is approved by Beijing (as is the case for the total number of firms). That is, the central government may not count (or be able to count) all the funds raised by its state-owned firms in Hong Kong and then reinvested in the colony.

Indeed, a lot of these firms do not want Beijing to know the true size of their assets and investments. Hong Kong in this context plays the role of a Switzerland, a convenient haven for corporate and individual money desiring anonymity. Kim Eng said in a 1996 report entitled 'The Rise of the Red Chips' that, 'Chinese firms probably have ... deposited tens of billions of dollars of undeclared profits or illegal funds in Hong Kong banks to avoid detection by central government investigation teams.' Naturally, this money would not be put in the Bank of China and its 13 sister banks in Hong Kong and Macau, but in local or foreign banks residing in the colony—of which there are several hundred to choose from.

Whatever the true size of mainland investment in Hong Kong, the figures show that it has grown quickly. But what about its relative importance in the local economy? Data on market share in different sectors indicate that it is a force to be reckoned with. The Hong Kong Chinese Enterprises Association gives the following ballpark figures for 1994–95: banking (24%); insurance (20%); tourism to China (60%); and transportation (20%). A 1996 study carried out by Harvard Business School largely replicated these numbers but added one or two more: foreign trade (22%); and construction (12%). Not bad, considering the low base these firms started from in the early 1980s.

THE STOCK MARKET has helped to fuel this aggressive expansion. During 1996, when the local market boomed again, hardly a week went by without news that one or other mainland 'red chip' (an unofficial nickname to contrast them with 'blue chip') was planning to issue shares or spin off a subsidiary. CITIC Pacific, for many the most attractive mainland enterprise in Hong Kong, kicked off that year by issuing 120 million new shares in January. China Resources

Enterprise, the main stock market-listed subsidiary of China Resources, announced mid-year that it would be spinning off its Beijing property division into a new listed company, and probably its brewery operations at a later date. China Travel International Investment, the listed arm of mainland tourism and entertainment giant China Travel Service (Holdings), sold new shares in August. Guangzhou Investment, the main commercial arm of the Guangzhou (Canton) city government, also talked about spinning off one of its divisions into a newly listed vehicle. And later in the year, China Resources Enterprise raised more than US$128 million (HK$1 billion) through a placement of shares.

The rationale for all these moves was largely identical: to raise 'war chests' while the market was buoyant and to fund new acquisitions in Hong Kong and China. CITIC Pacific, which had cash reserves of US$640 million (HK$5 billion) in early 1996, said it planned to spend as much as US$1.3 billion buying stakes in infrastructure projects. Its managing director, Henry Fan, declared triumphantly: 'We can undertake a HK$20 billion project anytime.' A few months later, China Travel International Investment said it had accumulated more than US$250 million in reserve for acquisition purposes. And Zhu Youlan, head of China Resources Enterprise, outlined a long-term plan whose objective was a doubling in the conglomerate's industrial investments by the year 2000.

Two earlier landmark periods in mainland participation in the local stock market are worth mentioning. The first was the early 1990s, when many of China's more established firms in the colony slipped onto the local exchange through the backdoor. This was a fairly common practice at the time and involved an enterprise taking over a locally listed company (often an unexciting one), changing its name and injecting new assets into its corporate body. This was how CITIC Pacific entered in August 1991 and, because of its size, quite quickly became a constituent stock on the Hang Seng Index (a list of the 33 biggest companies that account for 70% of the exchange's total value). The following year, China Resources took over a company called Winland Investment and changed its name to China Resources Enterprise. And Shougang, China's largest steel producer, came in through the takeover of Tung Wing Steel, calling its new company Shougang Concord International. It later bought another four locally listed companies. In early 1993, the Poly Group, the premier commercial entity of the People's Liberation Army, added itself to this select group by buying a shipping company called Continental Mariner Investment Company and began investing, albeit rather slowly, in industrial and property ventures in Hong Kong and China.

The second period dates from mid-1993, when the Stock Exchange of Hong Kong and the Chinese government began to coordinate the listing of a different type of mainland firm: the 'H' share (the letter stands for 'Hong Kong'). First up in July 1993 was Tsingtao Brewery, which produces China's most famous brand of beer from its home base in Shandong Province. It was followed a couple of weeks later by Shanghai Petrochemical, which is China's largest petrochemical works, and then Beiren Printing and Guangzhou Shipyard. The last two 'H' shares for 1993 were Maanshan Iron and Steel, situated in Anhui Province in central China, and Kunming Machine of Yunnan Province in the south-west. Over the next three years, another 17 'H' shares were listed, taking the total to 23 by the end of 1996 and raising almost US$3.7 billion in all. By April 1997 there were 26 'H' shares.

Other than the fact that these firms are raising capital solely for businesses located in China, they differ from their mainland brethren in certain important ways. First, they are not linked to State Council ministries or agencies, unlike the more established 'red chips' such China Resources, China Merchants, China Travel and CITIC Pacific. Second, in contrast to the diversification that is common among the latter, they tend to focus on one business sector only—a fact that is reflected in their names (others are Luoyang Glass, Qingling Motors and Jingwei Textile Machinery). Third, being smaller and less experienced, they tend to have weaker management and a poorer understanding of what international investors expect. Even Tsingtao Brewery, which many assumed would be savvy because it exports China's best-known brand of beer, created a scandal when it misused some of its $114 million listing proceeds. The company made a loan to a business associate in China rather than using all the money in the way its prospectus had outlined. Fourth, because their businesses are solely in China they have been hit hard by high inflation and the austerity program in recent years.

A combination of all these factors has given 'H' shares a poor reputation in Hong Kong, which explains why their share prices have mostly performed pitifully compared to the Hang Seng Index and the more established 'red chips'. For example, Tsingtao's share price in mid-January 1997 of HK$3.25 represented a rise of just 45 cents or

16% over its issue price in July 1993. The Hang Seng Index almost doubled in the same period, from around 7000 points to 13,500 points, albeit with a crash inbetween. And the share price of China Resources Enterprise quadrupled in 1996 alone.

Although the Stock Exchange of Hong Kong is not prepared to say how many mainland firms there are on the local bourse—since there is no official definition of 'red chip'—various stockbrokers have produced estimates. Kim Eng said there were more than 60 by the first quarter of 1996, and that they represented about 4.5% of the stock market's total value at that time.

Lest the use of Hong Kong by mainland firms as a market and a source of capital makes it seem like they are taking more than giving, it is worth pointing out that inflows of money from China have helped to stabilise the local economy at certain times. When Hong Kong suffered a financial crisis around 1983, China was lending more money to Hong Kong than vice-versa. In the mid-1980s, mainland direct investment in the colony was actually greater, for a short time, than Hong Kong investment in China. In 1985, the Bank of China joined with the HongkongBank to bail out the Ka Wah Bank during yet another financial crisis, this time triggered by the insolvency of the Overseas Trust Bank (OTB). Although the Hong Kong government saved OTB, 'several other banks suspected of imprudence once more became the targets of deposit withdrawal', wrote Y C Jao, an historian of banking at the University of Hong Kong. Ka Wah was one of these. It was eventually bought out the following year by CITIC, Beijing's main investment vehicle. Also in 1986, China Merchants took over the troubled Union Bank in a joint venture with an American company.

In more recent years, the involvement of mainland firms in the local property and stock markets has definitely added an extra boost to the overall upward trajectory in prices (good for those who already own homes or shares; not so good for the rest). And as for shares, most investors would much rather buy the safer 'red chips' listed in better regulated Hong Kong than venture into the wild Shanghai and Shenzhen exchanges.

The one area of interdependence left to look at is trade. While much of what is happening in the China–Hong Kong investment field is new, in trade there is a strong sense of history repeating itself.

NORTH AND SOUTH ENTWINED

Hong Kong before 1949 was much smaller than Shanghai and served as an entrepot for China's trade with the outside world. An entrepot is an intermediate port in a trading chain between producer and final consumer, providing services such as trade financing, transshipment, quality control, and often some final processing and packaging. Goods passing through an entrepot are said to be 're-exported' to other destinations. Not all undergo further processing; some are merely trans-shipped, meaning transferring completed goods or raw materials from smaller ships to larger ships (and vice-versa) at a hubbing port, such as Hong Kong. The smaller ships ply the coasts and rivers of China, whereas the larger ones cross the oceans between continents—an arrangement that boosts efficiency.

But this relationship was rapidly severed when Mao piloted China on an isolationist course, the product of his own policy of economic self-reliance, the Communists' fear of being invaded (which shifted the focus of economic development from the old port cities on the east coast to the inland provinces), and a United Nations embargo during the Korean War. Although Hong Kong continued to import basic necessities from China after the Communist victory, these goods accounted for a smaller share of the colony's total imports in the 1950s than in the decade or so before (from about one-third to one-fifth). But it was in exports that the biggest difference occurred: Hong Kong's exports to China as a proportion of all its exports plummeted from 40% in 1946 to 4% just 10 years later. And its total entrepot function suffered: re-exports fell to 20% of all exports in 1952, down from 80% previously.

Paradoxically, these disasters were good for Hong Kong. They forced it to become a manufacturing centre and they brought to the colony a flood of mainland entrepreneurs and industrialists fleeing repression. With their expertise, equipment and money, Hong Kong was better able to adapt and prosper again quickly after a difficult world war (when the colony had been ruled by the Japanese). For the next 30 years, Hong Kong survived through export production and the industries that went with it, especially shipping, banking and trading.

It was not until China re-opened the door to foreign investment after 1978 that its own export industry took off again. This time the catalytic money and equipment went the other way—from Hong Kong-based manufacturers escaping high land and labour costs and moving to Guangdong and Fujian provinces. As production moved across the border, these companies made their Hong Kong operations responsible for 'intermediary' jobs such as product design, regional sourcing of components and raw materials, and international distribution and marketing. The colony steadily resumed its middleman role in China trade and once again became an international entrepot. Whereas re-exports accounted for only 25% of total exports from Hong Kong when economic reform began in China, a little more than a decade later they had leapt to 65% and by 1995 to 83%.

China is, as you would expect, the single largest supplier of goods to Hong Kong. Recent Hong Kong government figures show that between 1993 and 1995 mainland goods accounted for 36–38% of all imports (by value). The second largest supplier was Japan, which hovered around 15–17%, with Taiwan third at around 9%, and the United States just a percentage point behind that. Two suppliers worth around 5% were Singapore and Korea, while Germany, Britain, France and Malaysia accounted for only about 2% each.

But these figures understate the importance of Chinese-made goods to Hong Kong's re-export trade. In the 1990s these goods have, on average, accounted for 58% of total Hong Kong re-exports each year. The corresponding figures for 1980 and 1985 were 28% and 33%, respectively. And since 1990, the annual share has stayed in a tight range of 57–59%. The total value of re-exports, meanwhile, has increased from US$13.5 billion in 1985 to US$53 billion in 1990 and US$152 billion in 1996. In other words, most of what is imported from China is sold on overseas—and the value of the pie has been increasing rapidly.

China is also the biggest destination for Hong Kong's re-exports, accounting for between 33–35% of the total value in the three years from 1993. Second is the United States, which has remained stable at around 21–22%, then Japan at 6%.

It should be pointed out that Hong Kong is now an entrepot with a difference. Its own markets in sectors like retail and property are much more important now than they were in pre-1950 days. People have grown richer and asset values have exploded, thus attracting the interest of investors and salespeople from all over the world, including China. Hong Kong is now an international finance centre with the world's fourth largest stock exchange (and the second largest in Asia) and branches of all major multinational banks—this it did not have in pre-Second World War days. Meanwhile, the combination of its open financial system, shipping and aviation businesses, and geographic location, has made Hong Kong a convenient base for both multinational corporations setting up regional headquarters sites for Asia-Pacific and for overseas Chinese family firms from South-east Asia wanting a base outside their own (often highly regulated) countries. Although not all these factors are linked to Hong Kong's entrepot function, the financial, transport and business centre aspects certainly are.

GUANGDONG PROVINCE, in trade as in investment, is Hong Kong's main link with China. The province stands head and shoulders above every other province in China's trade stakes: it is the source of 40% of all the country's exports (by value), and is the destination for almost as high a share of imports. Hong Kong handles more than 80% of the province's exports, which in 1995 totalled US$59 billion. No other province comes close to Guangdong in terms of the dollar size of its trading relationship with Hong Kong. As the table below shows, Guangdong's exports to Hong Kong are 10 times as big as the next largest supplier (Fujian). The same goes for imports.

The trading relationship between selected provinces and provincial-level units* with Hong Kong, 1995 (US$ million)		
Units with two-way trade greater than or close to US$1 billion (and location)	Exports to Hong Kong	Imports from Hong Kong
Guangdong (S)	48,450	30,347
Fujian (SE)	4,084	2,990
Jiangsu (E)	2,767	932
Shanghai (E)*	2,326	1,195
Zhejiang (E)	1,981	599
Shandong (E)	1,558	266
Guangxi (S)	1,196	229
Hubei (C)	1,081	390
Hunan (C)	1,010	207
Liaoning (NE)	870	310
Sichuan (W)	822	425
Beijing (N)*	708	239
Tianjin (N)*	548	372
Hainan (S)	444	658
Total non-Guangdong	19,395	8,812

Source: Almanac of China's Foreign Economic Relations and Trade 1996/97
* Certain big cities in China have the same status as provinces, hence are commonly referred to as 'provincial-level units'.

But as was the case with investment, it would be misleading to look only at absolute numbers. One of the reasons Guangdong is so far ahead is that it was given a huge headstart on the rest of China in the early 1980s. While other provinces have been working hard to catch up, even Shanghai (the second largest exporting unit) sells only one-fifth as much overseas as Guangdong does. Hence, the size of Hong Kong's trade with these places is bound to be much lower.

If, however, the figures are re-cast as percentages of each area's total exports and imports, it becomes apparent that Hong Kong's trading relationship with China is significantly more varied. The table below divides the provinces into four broad groups (based on the percentage share of their total exports going to Hong Kong). Guangdong, as expected, is in a class of its own. Then there are those who send 40–60% of their exports to Hong Kong and are located in southern, central and eastern provinces close or fairly close by; those who fall into the 20-30% band, yet come from no one region; and those who stand at less than 20% and, with the exception of Shanghai, are mostly in the north or north-east.

What is interesting is that even in the two lower groups, Hong Kong is the number one or number two export destination for most places. This is a very similar pattern to the one found in investment: that Hong Kong's huge margin of lead may fall outside southern China, yet it is still manages to hold down the number one position as a business partner.

But what is not readily apparent from the table is that even in provinces where Hong Kong ranks second or third, the number one and number two countries do not always enjoy a large lead. In Jiangsu, for example, Japan came out on top, but only by a small fraction. And in Liaoning, the United States was just a whisker ahead of Hong Kong at second place (although Japan was well out in front at first place). Interestingly, while Japan and Russia are, respectively, the main export markets for Liaoning's north-eastern neighbours—Jilin and Heilongjiang—Hong Kong was the second largest export market for both provinces. Heilongjiang borders Siberia and, with the exception of the far western region of Xinjiang and certain parts of Tibet, is about as far away from Hong Kong as you can get in China.

Hong Kong's share of exports and imports of selected provinces and provincial-level units, 1995 (Hong Kong's ranking vs other countries in brackets)		
Major provincial trading partners (and location)	Percentage of exports sold to Hong Kong	Percentage of imports bought from Hong Kong
Guangdong (S)	87% (1st)	80% (1st)
Guangxi (S)	53% (1st)	28% (1st)
Hainan (S)	53% (1st)	46% (1st)
Hunan (C)	48% (1st)	25% (1st)
Hubei (C)	46% (1st)	28% (1st)
Fujian (SE)	44% (1st)	55% (1st)
Sichuan (W)	30% (1st)	27% (1st)
Beijing (N)	28% (1st)	13% (3rd)
Jiangsu (E)	23% (2nd)	18% (2nd)
Zhejiang (E)	23% (1st)	19% (2nd)
Shanghai (E)	18% (2nd)	16% (2nd)
Tianjin (N)	18% (= 1st)	10% (4th)
Shandong (E)	16% (3rd)	9% (4th)
Liaoning (NE)	11% (3rd)	11% (= 2nd)

Note: Provinces are ranked according to export shares. If two are equal, the one with the greater volume of trade is ranked higher.

Source: Almanac of China's Foreign Economic Relations and Trade 1996/97

WHERE NEXT?

This chapter has painted a rosy picture of the economic partnership between China and Hong Kong. How could it do otherwise? Both sides have gained tremendously from having the other next door— for Hong Kong, a huge new market in which it has a headstart over its competitors, and for China, an advanced trading and financial centre that has financed and facilitated its economic development. How many advanced economies have an emerging market on their doorstep that is larger by the same order of magnitude as China is over Hong Kong? How many developing countries have one of the world's largest financial centres right beside them and ready to lend, like China has with Hong Kong? India certainly does not, nor does Russia, Africa, most parts of Asia, or South America. The other major financial centres—New York, London and Tokyo—are not attached to and dependent on these places.

Geography may not explain everything—after all, China issues corporate bonds in Europe, Japan and the United States, and shares in London, New York and Singapore—but in the case of the Hong Kong–China nexus it has been crucial. Hong Kong is the largest supplier and packager of foreign investment heading into China. It dominates the business of arranging syndicated loans, which account for most commercial loans (and which exceed the volume of bonds raised overseas by a hefty margin, and shares by a huge margin). And it is China's principal trading entrepot—a prime example of where geography matters a great deal. Indeed, China and Hong Kong share historic, cultural and linguistic bonds that do not exist at all (or to the same extent) between any other emerging country and one of the three other international financial centres.

The forces of necessity binding Hong Kong and China together, and the fact that China is a long way from replicating the 'Hong Kong model' in any of the port cities on its east coast, imply a strong momentum to the relationship that will be hard to break. Certainly, this closeness will continue through the transfer of sovereignty as if 1 July 1997 was merely a date in the calendar. The changing of the guard will not stop ships from plying the coast, airplanes from flying north and south, and banks from lending. The business community has had the best part of 20 years to get used to the idea of reunification and is now linked into webs of relationships with producers, consumers, entrepreneurs, traders and officials throughout China.

So the question is not , 'Will the Hong Kong economy survive?'. Of course it will. It is, rather, 'How will the Hong Kong economy change as a result of the transfer of sovereignty?' Because even though the Joint Declaration and Basic Law leave the structure of the economy in place, a close inspection reveals that there are some rather large areas of fog. One of them is that the future constitution understandably makes no offer to protect all the existing players. For example, while the concept of private property will remain, there is nothing to stop mainland interests from acquiring more and more plum assets. This would not be a problem if the playing field were level. But how can it be when a new sovereign is taking over? The mildest thing that will happen—indeed, already is happening—is that non-mainland firms will have to bring mainland companies into deals in order to strengthen their relationships with powerbrokers in Beijing. The worst is that mainland state enterprises will force themselves into strategic sectors which they covet. This has already occurred in the aviation sector and rumours abound about more of the same in banking and telecoms. Far from deliberately and vindictively undermining Hong Kong, the danger is that China will take an increasingly proprietary attitude towards it and squeeze out existing interests (although the degree to which existing interests will be affected will vary).

The other main area of fog is the cultural impact which an increased mainland commercial presence in Hong Kong will have on the local business environment. This category covers a multitude of sins, from a lack of sympathy for or inadequate understanding of Hong Kong's rule of law to a blurring of the fairly clear distinction that exists at present between the public and the private sectors (and a subsequent tilt in the playing field towards mainland *state-owned* firms). Areas of exposure also include corruption, which reached a 'new high plateau' in Hong Kong in 1993–95 and seems bound to worsen as Hong Kong becomes more fully integrated into the Chinese state; and competition policy, which refers to a recent trend towards liberalising the colony's many monopolistic, oligopolistic or tightly controlled service sectors (the problem here is that the transfer of sovereignty is more likely to slow down, not accelerate, this consumer-friendly process).

The basic theme is that, contrary to the impression given by the Joint Declaration and the Basic Law, not even the Hong Kong economy will survive 1997 in one complete piece. Parts of it will be the same in five years time, other parts will look and feel quite different. It will remain a place where money can be made, certainly, but the line-up of winners seems bound to alter. But what else could be expected from a transfer of sovereignty?

CHAPTER 7

SCALING THE HEIGHTS

In April 1995, Hong Kong's aviation industry was visited by the demon of 'political reality': China National Aviation Corporation (CNAC), the commercial arm of China's aviation regulatory authority in Beijing, applied to launch a new airline in Hong Kong to compete against the entrenched incumbents, Dragonair and Cathay Pacific. The move surprised most market watchers and terrified Swire Pacific, a venerable though aggressive British-owned conglomerate that dominated the local aviation industry (it controlled Cathay and jointly controlled Dragonair). Swire complained that this just wasn't fair: how could it compete against the Chinese government? And, anyway, CNAC wasn't really a Hong Kong company (as regulations stipulated that anyone applying for an 'air operator's certificate' had to be). Swire tried to invoke the letter and the spirit of the Basic Law to similar ends, although predictably with no success. For CNAC had a locally incorporated company, so it was legally in the clear.

Swire responded by trying to buy off CNAC through selling it a small stake in Dragonair, Hong Kong's number two airline. The tactic failed. CNAC wanted a much larger portion. Negotiations fell apart, came together again, then after 12 months resulted in a serious defeat for Swire: it lost Dragonair to the mainland poacher. The unusual twist in the tale, however, was the other loser from this deal: CITIC Pacific (from here on referred to as 'CITIC'), that bluest of red chips and a company whose impeccable political connections in Beijing were supposed to ensure it always won (its boss, Larry Yung, is the son of China's vice-president, Rong Yiren; they spell their surnames differently). Before the deal CITIC owned slightly more of Dragonair than Swire, but left the running of it to the experienced British firm. Apparently on Beijing's instructions, the red chip sold off the best part of half of its stake—a rare instance of one mainland firm in Hong Kong losing out publicly to another (although it appears that Yung and his managers have been amply rewarded since through a lucrative share deal involving their parent company).

The Dragonair episode illustrated the ability of Hong Kong's media and foreign business community to switch mindset quickly. Having largely convinced themselves that China would not meddle in this 'very important economy', commentators, analysts and business leaders suddenly accepted as 'inevitable' some degree of political interference in business. After all, why would, or should, Beijing leave lucrative franchises in the hands of foreigners, and Britons at that, once Hong Kong becomes part of the motherland again? This is a realistic question, since full preservation of the status quo would conflict with China's own economic nationalism and with traditional practice in most industrial countries. Despite the liberalisation that has swept developed economies over the past decade, some things are still unthinkable—like Chinese control of British Airways or Japanese control of AT&T, America's dominant long-distance telephone company.

But the difference in Hong Kong's case was that it was supposed to be somewhat unique. 'One country, two systems' may not offer *unrestricted protection* for existing companies, but the idea that mainland state-owned enterprises would get hold of prime assets in Hong Kong through blatant arm-twisting, and before July 1997, was not part of the original deal. Swire was justified in raising a complaint, as quixotic as its actions seemed at the time. Not surprisingly, no one went to its defence.

Since then the game among market watchers has been to guess which 'commanding height' of the economy (or strategic service sector) would fall next to mainland Chinese business interests. An obvious potential candidate is banking. Its unquestioned leader, the Hong Kong and Shanghai Banking Corporation (which refers to itself as just the 'HongkongBank'), has a British parent despite its oriental name. A second is telecoms, which is still dominated by Hongkong Telecom, an offspring of another creature of the colonial period, Cable & Wireless. A third is power generation. Except for the last sector mentioned, nothing further has happened. Thus on the eve of reunification, firms with British pedigrees were still in control of Hong Kong's largest airline, bank and telephone company. Although all consider themselves to be 'Hong Kong' firms, since they are locally incorporated, their histories and parentage mark them out, at the very least, as non-Chinese—and as British or foreign in the eyes of many people, including Chinese officials.

But the level of dominance these firms enjoy is surely untenable over time. Most of the evidence points to a determined attempt on the part of mainland Chinese enterprises to scale Hong Kong's commanding heights, a process which began well before CNAC made its move on Dragonair. They have the political support of the new sovereign behind them, not to mention something powerful to trade with—the promise of access or greater access to the China market, which all Hong Kong companies badly want (as do other foreign service firms).

This does not mean that mainland enterprises will eventually control *all* of Hong Kong's strategic service sectors to the detriment of existing Hong Kong Chinese and foreign firms. While one or two bastions of power could change hands, the argument of this chapter is that power sharing is the more probable scenario (a conclusion which assumes that Beijing never simply seizes assets for no or low compensation). Here are some of the factors at play:

1. Although the transfer of sovereignty offers mainland companies a unique political opportunity to muscle further into Hong Kong, they will be constrained by things beyond their control. For example, the cost of taking over an incumbent operator (that is, the dominant company or former monopoly) may be reasonable if the sector is moderate in size, or it may be too expensive if the opposite is true. Or the degree of competition in the sector may make investing in the incumbent an unattractive proposition at this stage; as could the openness of the sector to overseas markets or trade forces, which can cause volatility in earnings or change the international 'rules of the game'.

2. Sectors vary in their economic function and, therefore, in their ability to withstand attack. Whereas the takeover of Dragonair was absorbed by the Hong Kong economy with ease—and eventually relief, once the year of uncertainty had ended—the same would not hold for a leading bank. Hong Kong's two top banks are much larger than its airlines and are the heart of the economy. The repercussions of political trouble in their backyards would shake the confidence of business, the stock market, the

international investment community, and small deposit holders. A bank-run would almost certainly occur. China would be
charged with incompetence. And questions would be raised
about that country's ability to run its own economy. Since at
least some powerful officials in Beijing understand the fragility
of finance, and since the Chinese government does want Hong
Kong to remain a financial centre, it is reasonable to conclude
that any mainland expansion within banking would be measured and more circumspect than CNAC's behaviour in the
aviation sector.

3. A gradualist approach would play better in Taiwan than an
   overly aggressive one. A successful economic reunification with
   Hong Kong may not answer all the doubts that Taiwan has about
   rejoining China—since the Kuomintang-controlled island is
   very different from the British colony—but   can be sure that
   its business community will be watching the Hong Kong situation carefully. If property rights remain as the Basic Law
   promises, but ownership changes too rapidly or in a manner
   blatantly unfair to the incumbent operators, a negative message
   will be received in Taiwan.

These points assume that the State Council, China's cabinet, has
the ability to coordinate major decisions of state-owned enterprises
operating in Hong Kong. Many of these enterprises are subsidiaries
of economic ministries in Beijing; and the ministers of these ministries report to the State Council. While the corporations are allowed
to make a range of commercial decisions autonomously, anything
that impinges on local politics, foreign policy or Hong Kong's economic stability would need to be discussed at a higher level first. The
State Council does not know everything of course (one grey area is
the money 'illegally' stashed in local bank accounts). But its knowledge is likely to grow after 1997 on account of the enhanced role of
the Communist Party in Hong Kong (whether above or below
ground) and the arrival of central agencies such as the Ministry of
Foreign Affairs. These same organisations will presumably keep an
eye on the Hong Kong-based subsidiaries of China's provincial and
city governments.

One further assumption: as much as mainland enterprises want
the power and prestige of controlling Hong Kong's commanding
heights, their mountain climbing is equally an exercise in reform
and modernisation. The standard line from the Hong Kong Chinese
Enterprises Association is that its members view Hong Kong as a 'win-

dow' to the outside world (and a window for foreigners looking in at China), and they seek to act as a 'bridge' across which capital, economic information, technology and equipment can move into (and out of) China. A slogan has been coined to sum up the overall strategy: 'One Centre, Two Flanking Sectors'. Typically Communist Party in its numeric symmetry, this phrase is explained as follows:

> By One Centre we mean that the PRC-invested companies in Hong Kong will continue to be based in Hong Kong, take root in Hong Kong and expand as Hong Kong expands. By Two Flanking Sectors we mean that while based in Hong Kong, the PRC-invested companies will extend their business operations to the Mainland (sic) and the Overseas (sic) in active attempts to make use of the internal and external markets so as to turn themselves into *international enterprise groups* with *modern standards* and multifunctions. (italics added)

The point is, therefore, that these firms cannot avoid paying attention to market forces and external developments that may affect the viability of any investment they make *if* they truly want to become advanced, multinational corporations. This in turn demands a measured approach, for to make a move on any commanding height without first considering the terrain would only increase the chance of commercial failure. And Hong Kong is littered with examples of poor commercial decision-making on the part of mainland enterprises over the past 15 years. Such firms find it more costly to borrow money from banks, more difficult to raise funds on the stock market, and do not engender the respect of the international investor. As a consequence, their ability to reform and modernise is constrained.

One factor which will not be holding back mainland expansion in Hong Kong is the repeated assurance from Beijing that Chinese state corporations will not receive special privileges after the transfer of sovereignty (that is, exclusive business licences granted by government). For example, a 1994 publication of the Hong Kong Chinese Enterprises Association quoted Li Lanqing, vice-premier responsible for trade (and more recently a contender to replace Li Peng as premier in 1998), as saying precisely this. Li added that while mainland firms would continue to participate in Hong Kong, whether or not they prospered depended on their own abilities. And they would not seek a leading position in the economy.

The Dragonair deal showed the limits of such assurances. CNAC was able to force an opening by making its intention known and, with the help of powerful backers in the People's Liberation Army and the Chinese government, arm-twisted Swire and CITIC into sell-ing large chunks of their stakes 'willingly'. Since it got what it wanted through negotiation and apparent use of market mechanisms, it did not contravene the 'no special privileges rule'. This clearly has impli-cations for the robustness of the Basic Law as a line of defence or separation.

AVIATION

Until CNAC made its move in 1995, it looked as if CITIC would be the principal mainland group in Hong Kong aviation. The red chip bought a 12.5% stake in Cathay Pacific in 1987 and overtook the HongkongBank as that airline's second largest shareholder (Swire was the largest with 54%). Three years later, CITIC joined with Swire to take over the financially strapped Dragonair, an airline launched in 1985 to fly to regional destinations such as Kota Kinabalu in Bor-neo (its first route) and several cities in China. The founder of the airline was Chao Kuang-piu (K P Chao), a textile magnate. Chao ini-tially owned the airline outright, but soon sold part of it to the late Y K Pao, Hong Kong's most famous shipping tycoon. Pao sold his equity back to Chao in late 1989 (see table on p 226 for a summary of these ownership changes).

The Dragonair purchase consolidated the dominance of Swire and CITIC in the Hong Kong aviation industry. Since the pair owned the colony's only two passenger carriers, the scope for coordinating operations was considerable. Dragonair strengthened its position as a regional airline, with a special focus on China (picking up Cathay's two routes—Beijing and Shanghai) and Cathay continued as the international long-haul carrier, with some short-haul Asian routes as well. The two airlines dovetailed schedules and prices, and shared management.

While the gradual deregulation of the worldwide aviation industry in recent years has forced Cathay and Dragonair to engage in 'con-trolled competition' with new airlines, both still enjoy an effective oligopoly on most of the routes they fly within Asia (and for Cathay, on many of its longer haul routes). This is because the traditional avi-ation agreements between countries restricted the right to run air services to just one airline from each place (the national carrier). This anti-competitive system is starting to break down, but only slowly. For example, whereas the only airlines previously allowed to run non-stop services between Hong Kong and London were BA and Cathay, today the entrepreneurial British group, Virgin, flies the route as well. Typically, however, incumbent operators retain the best departure and arrival slots and continue to account for the bulk of passengers.

Meanwhile, the centre of gravity within Hong Kong aviation had shifted slightly northwards again in 1992, when the HongkongBank sold its remaining 10% of Cathay to CNAC and the mainland's principal travel business in Hong Kong, China Travel Service. Each bought a 5% parcel. This event almost doubled the total mainland share in the airline, but it did not change the pecking order of the two largest shareholders (see table on p 228).

And there the ownership structure stayed until CNAC dropped its bomb in April 1995. It applied for an 'air operator's certificate' in preparation for setting up its own airline, and said it would compete immediately against Dragonair for Chinese and regional routes and later on against Cathay for regional routes. (Although CNAC was the commercial arm of the country's aviation regulator, it did not run an international airline at that time, although it had stakes in several Chinese domestic airlines. China's aviation industry is divided into numerous regions, each having its own airline. Hence, China Eastern, China Southern, China South-western, Zhejiang Airlines, and so on.)

This was particularly worrying for Dragonair. Although by then an extremely profitable concern, the company was experiencing a steady fall in its rate of profit growth, from an extraordinary 90% in 1992 to an exuberant 50% in 1994, a very respectable 25% in 1995 and disappointing single-digit earnings in 1996. The principle cause of the slide was Dragonair's inability after 1993 to negotiate further services to China—a by-product of jealousy within that country at the huge profits the Hong Kong airline was making. With no new routes to the mainland in hand, and with the prospect of a Chinese competitor, Dragonair's future became decidedly more uncertain.

Swire reacted bitterly and territorially to CNAC's application. It asked how a mainland Chinese firm could possibly meet the legal requirement stating that any company wanting to set up an airline had to prove that Hong Kong was its 'principal place of business'? The same stipulation can be found in the Basic Law. But this counter-argument is not as watertight as it looks: local airline regulations contain no nationality restrictions, so anyone with a 'locally incorporated' company in Hong Kong would meet the principal place of business requirement and could apply for an air operator's certificate. Whether they are successful is another matter. CNAC made the application through CNAC (Hong Kong), a locally incorporated company. This may not appear to be fair play, but in fact many mainland firms are legally 'Hong Kong' companies, including China Resources and China Merchants. The latter's headquarters is actually in Hong Kong, while the former has a dual head office arrangement in Hong Kong and Beijing.

Swire's other complaint was more to the point. Rod Eddington, managing director of Cathay at the time, said:

> Our primary concern is that ... CNAC is the commercial arm of the [China's] regulatory authority. How do you compete with somebody who's a body of the regulatory authority?

Thus cornered, a fearful Swire chose to compromise rather than compete. To cut a long and circuitous story short, Dragonair's owners quickly offered CNAC a 10% stake in their airline in return for dropping plans to start its own airline. Talks were going well enough during the summer of 1995 for the *South China Morning Post* to confidently declare: 'CNAC set for stake in Dragonair'. But the newspaper jumped the gun. CNAC wanted much more than 10%, the talks dragged on, and then both CITIC and the Chao family pulled out of the discussions towards the end of that year. When round two began the following year, CNAC demanded and won a controlling stake of just less than 36%. The deal was announced on 29 April 1996. Swire's stake fell by 40%, as did CITIC's. The Chao family sold a fraction of its small stake. A planned floatation on the stock market—yet to take place—will further reduce the shareholdings of Swire and CITIC. A summary of these ownership changes and the exact size of each company's interest is laid out in the following table. Particularly interesting is the last row, which tallies the rapid change from Hong Kong to mainland Chinese ownership.

There is a theory that CNAC never really wanted to set up its own airline, and only went through the motions to scare the incumbents into selling down their joint control of Dragonair. This makes sense, since taking over a going and profitable concern is clearly a lot easier than starting from scratch. And the State Council, China's cabinet, is known not to favour too much competition—meaning uncontrolled competition—between mainland enterprises in Hong Kong, either now or in the future.

On all fronts, CNAC got a sweet deal. Dragonair continued its management cooperation agreement with its big sister, Cathay, leaving its less experienced new owner little to worry about on the operational and technical side. Dragonair's senior management stayed in place for the rest of 1996. When its chief operating officer returned to Cathay in early 1997, he was replaced by the former head of Air Hong Kong, a cargo airline owned by Swire. And the price CNAC paid was a bargain. Estimates differ, but basically the deal was done at a 20–30% discount to the probable market value of Dragonair shares (had they been listed on the stock market). But no one could object because the airline was a private company.

Flying North (Ownership changes in Dragonair, 1985–96)						
	April 1985	November 1985	January 1990	2nd half 1990	June 1996	Floatation (no set date)
Chao family	100%	less than 100%	27%	11%	5%	5%
Y K Pao	0%	N/A	sold out	0%	0%	0%
Swire/ Cathay	0%	0%	35%	43%	25.5%	20%
CITIC	0%	0%	38%	46%	28.5%	25%
CNAC	0%	0%	0%	0%	36%	36%
Others	0%	0%	0%	0%	5%	14%
Level of mainland ownership	0%	0%	38%	46%	64.5%	61%

Note 1: Figures are rounded to nearest 0.5%.
Note 2: Swire holds part of its share in Dragonair through Cathay Pacific.
Note 3: The Chao family sold more of its shares to 'other' private parties before 1996. Its shareholding immediately before the Dragonair deal was 5.57%.
Sources: Company documents, press releases, news reports.

Swire lost out in two ways. Apart from being forced to capitulate over Dragonair, it agreed to sell a larger share of Cathay to its partner CITIC. Its stake in Hong Kong's premier airline thus fell from 53% to 44%—still a controlling position, but not an outright majority (and therefore more vulnerable to any further attack). Swire, in effect, compensated CITIC for the latter's loss on Dragonair and rewarded it for helping to broker a deal that, while far from perfect, ensured that serious competition was avoided. In compromising, it no doubt hoped to be buying adequate political insurance for the early years of the Special Administrative Region.

But CITIC still left the room blushing in embarrassment. Since it has always been portrayed in Hong Kong as the mainland firm that 'can do no wrong', watching it come off second best was a rare event. The company had, during 1995, signalled its intention to concentrate its airline interests in Dragonair, which it hoped to take over one day and actively manage itself. This implied it would decrease, not increase, its shareholding in Cathay. Behind these changes was a general shift in CITIC's business strategy from acting as a passive investment company to one which managed its own projects. Having done business in Hong Kong for more than a decade, the mainland firm not only reckoned it was ready to make such a move, but believed the new approach would bring a greater return on investment. The Dragonair deal forced CITIC to do a sharp about-turn in its aviation strategy.

Neither Swire nor CITIC went away totally empty-handed. Swire, or to be more precise Cathay, gained an unexpected cash injection from the sale of new shares to CITIC and, of course, from the Dragonair parcel. And CITIC bought its larger stake in Cathay at a good price. It paid US$1.40 (HK$11) per share compared to a market price at the time (late April 1996) of around US$1.64 (HK$12.80).

Stock market reaction to the deal was one of relief: Swire still had a future in aviation and the competitive cloud over Cathay had lifted—at least for the time being. Share prices of both companies dutifully rose, although Cathay's later fell back, standing at around US$1.53 (HK$12) in early 1997. CITIC's shares fell slightly after the announcement (but have since risen). These early price movements were predictable, since the deal ended uncertainty among investors and smudged CITIC's reputation (although in both cases only temporarily).

Somewhat surprising was the optimistic tone of much media commentary. Much attention was focused on Cathay, which the *Far Eastern Economic Review* said had scored a 'coup' and the *South China Morning Post* predicted was 'on course to a brighter future'. Newspapers did note that both Swire and CITIC had come off second-best to CNAC, but quoted stock analysts as saying that the result could have been a lot worse for the incumbent operators. The *Post* warned, however, that the deal probably did not mark the end of the struggle for dominance in the aviation sector.

But in general most news organisations readily accepted the constraints of political reality—'it could have been a lot worse ...'. Few questioned whether CNAC had conformed to the spirit of the No Special Privileges Rule or criticised the strong hand of Beijing in the negotiations. And the coverage understated the severity of the situation facing Swire. The company had been cornered. If it had not sold, it would have incurred the wrath of Beijing and faced new competition. It lost joint control of one airline and could well be on the way to losing control of another. However painted, this was a bad result. Swire may have bought itself some breathing space, but its interests in aviation are hardly secure over the longer term. The following table summarises the trends within Cathay's ownership structure and the threat facing Swire.

Halfway to Beijing? (Major changes in ownership of Cathay Pacific, 1986–96)						
	Pre-floatation	1986	1987	1992	December 1995	June 1996
Swire	70%	54%	54%	52%	53%	44%
Hongkong Bank	30%	23%	10%	0%	0%	0%
CITIC	0%	0%	12.5%	12.5%	10%	25%
CNAC	0%	0%	0%	5%	5%	1.5%
China Travel Service	0%	0%	0%	5%	5%	3.5%
Other/ public float	0%	22.5%	23%	26%	27%	24%
Total mainland share	0%	0%	12.5%	22.5%	20%	30%

Note 1: Figures are rounded, hence may not add up to 100%. Also, the exact size of the stakes held by CNAC and China Travel are hard to determine since they are held through nominees and no disclosure is required. However, CNAC is known to have sold most of its stake in Cathay in June 1996 to help pay for its purchase of Dragonair.

Note 2: When Cathay was floated on the stock exchange in 1986, about 7.5% of the company was bought by three Hong Kong companies: Cheung Kong, Hutchison, and Hysan Development.

Note 3: The table does not show a minor fall in Swire's stake to 52% in 1991.

Sources: Company documents, press releases, news reports.

WHAT HAPPENS NEXT? A logical move would be for CNAC to increase its stake in Dragonair to more than 50%. Although it may not need to do this to ensure secure control—since it is hardly likely that Swire or any foreign airline would take on the powerful corporation—it might want to do it for symbolic reasons or for commercial ones. The growth of Dragonair's business to China and other parts of the region should ensure that it remains a profitable business, so why would CNAC not want a larger stake once it could afford it?

Conversely, the value of Dragonair to its former owners is not what it was. After the public floatation (no date set), Swire's share will fall to 20%, having been 43% in early 1996. This could be worth holding onto for the earnings it will bring and perhaps for political reasons (being in partnership with the regulatory arm of China's aviation regulatory authority). But having sold once, Swire will be in a weak position should CNAC wish to raise its shareholding in future. A more powerful partner can be a mixed blessing.

As for CITIC, its hopes of running Dragonair have evaporated in the wind. Like Swire, it may choose to retain a reasonably large stake in the airline as a good investment. But it faces a similar predicament: having been forced to sell once, what can save it from selling again if CNAC applies the pressure? Indeed, CITIC's 25% shareholding will be a useful political bargaining chip next time it finds itself in a three-way fight. In return for selling out to CNAC, it could surely extract some advantage from the State Council in Beijing.

What are the prospects for Cathay? On the basis of recent trends, CNAC's determination to own an international airline, and the strategic nature of the aviation industry, it requires blinkered vision to think that Swire's position is safe. CNAC has expressed a wish to expand Dragonair's regional presence, which would bring it into direct conflict with Cathay and, therefore, the Swire/Cathay representatives on Dragonair's board. While further friendly agreements between the two airlines over route sharing cannot be ruled out, it is unlikely that Cathay would happily accept a continual erosion of its business in favour of Dragonair.

So Swire would once again face a difficult commercial and political choice. As Rod Eddington, Cathay's former managing director, had said, how do you compete with somebody who's a body of the regulatory authority? If it chose to compete, it would incur the wrath of Beijing and face greater uncertainty over Cathay's earnings growth. If it tried to minimise competition by selling a large chunk of Cathay to CNAC, it could retain an interest in a more stable business and might well gain some sort of quid pro quo from Beijing, such as access to lucrative property deals in China. Property is another of Swire's main business areas; and CITIC is one of its partners in this sector as well.

Historical precedent suggests that Swire would compromise. But to what extent? Numerous scenarios suggest themselves, but one possible outcome would be for Swire to sell half of its 44% stake to CNAC, then for the latter to buy around half of CITIC's 25% stake. Since CNAC already owns 1.5% of Cathay, this would give it a total of 36% of the airline. Swire would end up with 22% and CITIC with 12.5%.

Of course, the British conglomerate would vehemently deny the possibility of selling control of Cathay, just as it previously denied that the airline's ownership structure would change (before the Dragonair deal). But some market watchers think this next step is only a matter of time. Declan Magee, regional transportation analyst for HG Asia, a stockbroking firm, sees Swire's reduction in its Cathay stake from 53% to 44% as symbolically important: 'They have already taken the step to start getting out (of Cathay). That was a rear-guard action.' Having made the decision to fall below the magical 50%, the next sale should be quite a bit easier. As Magee concludes that Swire's returns from aviation are bound to be capped 'for political reasons', he reckons the question facing Swire is: 'At what stage do they sell out or come to an agreement?'

An analyst with a similar opinion is Viktor Shvets, a director of Deutsche Morgan Grenfell, a German–Anglo investment bank. Shvets told the *South China Morning Post* that Swire will be forced out of Dragonair at some stage and that the 1996 deal 'put in motion the process to remove Swire as controllers of Cathay Pacific and further down the line have Chinese control of Cathay'. This followed from CNAC's 'burning ambition to operate its own airline' and from the tensions inherent in the current compromise deal. Shvets concluded, rather ominously, that:

> To expect everyone to operate as one big, happy family and all get on with each other and all love one another is a dream. The solution as it stands is untenable. This is the first stage of a multi-stage process.

Such tensions may take time to emerge, however, because an expansion in the size of Hong Kong's aviation pie from 1998 onwards will generate a large amount of additional business for the two carriers. Hong Kong is building a new airport in the western part of the colony—at Chek Lap Kok off Lantau Island—which will greatly enhance its role as an aviation hub for southern China and, indeed, the world. Chek Lap Kok will ultimately have two runways, whereas the current airport at Kai Tak has only one. It will be able to operate around-the-clock, something which Kai Tak cannot do since it is located next to a densely populated urban area. And the deployment of 'super jumbos' capable of carrying up to 800 people will become a reality soon (Airbus, the European consortium, is looking at a double-decker design that could seat 1000 people). Multiply these three factors together and passenger throughput has the capacity to triple from its 1996 level to 87 million people, while cargo tonnage could just about quintuple to nine million. These figures are based on government estimates to the year 2040, so are subject to change depending on broader economic trends. Yet there seems little reason to doubt that the pie will start to grow early on, meaning that CNAC will not need to grab business from Cathay straight away. Apart from anything else, the mainland newcomer may want to consolidate its control of Dragonair, which could take a few years, before it launches another predatory attack.

SEVERAL PERTINENT THEMES arising from the Dragonair deal and generally relevant to other sectors of the economy, and incumbent operators, in future include:

- **Don't expect sympathy or support:** A striking feature of the Dragonair deal was the way in which most people accepted it as a political *fait accompli*. The prevailing attitude was that, given the transfer of sovereignty, Swire had no choice but to do what it did. For some, there seemed to be a sense of justice arising out of all the machinations. That is, since British interests have enjoyed an historic advantage over many of Hong Kong's commanding heights before 1997, so it is only natural that Chinese ones (mainland and local) should have the edge afterwards.

  Such a swing of the pendulum is understandable, but it means further political incursions will be that much easier for mainland corporations to organise in future, which in turn could damage Hong Kong's image as an international business city (whether this damages the colony's economy in actuality is another matter). If the international business community loses faith in Hong Kong as an economy separate from China, its current status as an autonomous, free port will be downgraded.

Even CITIC's boss, Larry Yung, has warned of potential problems from mainland interference in Hong Kong. In a bizarre prelude to the whole drama, Yung complained about possible damage to Hong Kong's autonomy and its rule of law if such interference was not checked—a highly unusual statement from any businessman, let alone a mainland one. Although he did not target specific transgressors, in light of what has since happened it is probable that he had CNAC in mind. Which would mean he was more interested in defending his own company's patch from an unwelcome intruder than Hong Kong as a whole. Even so, Yung's words do have wider application.

- **The limitations of 'relationships':** During the tense negotiations, CITIC made a political decision to distance itself from Swire (an attempt, most believe, to please Beijing). It had been telling the market that it might get out of Cathay altogether— for example, it sold down its stake from 12.5% to 10% in September 1995—and concentrate on Dragonair. Then in late 1995, after it pulled out of the fruitless discussions to sell CNAC a small stake in Dragonair, CITIC's managing director, Henry Fan, publicly attacked Swire's negative attitude towards new competition. Saying that his own company did 'not believe that any monopoly can today continue', Fan warned:

  > Both Cathay Pacific and Dragonair, and for that matter Air Hong Kong (a cargo carrier owned by Swire), will have to wake up to reality and face competition. It is about time.

And to cap it all off, Yung and Fan abruptly quit the board of Cathay in early 1996.

These actions did not make *prima facie* sense. Fan's comments were odd coming from a company that had benefited nicely from oligopoly profits through its aviation investments (and from monopoly profits in telecoms—see below). By apparently humiliating a long-standing business partner, CITIC did something that normally was 'just not done'. It may have been moving away from Cathay, but it was still a partner of Swire's in Dragonair and in a huge property development in Hong Kong—the Festival Walk shopping and office complex in Kowloon. Finally, in helping to broker the Dragonair deal, CITIC put aside its new-found fervour for competition and preserved the current aviation oligopoly in Hong Kong. Yung and Fan subsequently rejoined Cathay's board. And Fan has since become the airline's joint deputy chairman.

CITIC's words and actions only add up if you believe that Swire's bosses were either fully informed of what was about to hit them beforehand, or had enough of an understanding of their partner's political difficulties not to take what Yung and Fan said or did in public too seriously. Most probably, the reality is a mixture of both alternatives. Not only were Swire's bosses keenly aware of political sensitivities—which is, after all, why they brought CITIC into Cathay in the first place—but they made several trips to Beijing with their mainland partner to negotiate the Dragonair deal. It is inconceivable that the Hong Kong–British firm was ignorant of the pressures on Yung and Fan.

Nevertheless, the episode showed that even well-connected mainland partners can never fully protect the interests of foreign companies in Hong Kong, since there are bound to be people or groups in China more powerful than that partner. CITIC's public criticism of Swire, even if it was a charade, has not ensured Swire a stable future in Hong Kong aviation (at best it has bought the British firm some time).

And how much of themselves do powerful foreign companies in Hong Kong have to sell before they feel safe? Swire took on CITIC as a partner in Cathay in 1987, then CNAC and China Travel Service in 1992. The three mainland enterprises owned a combined 22.5% of Cathay. This was quite a big portion, but obviously not enough to stop CNAC from behaving as it did.

- **The specificity of timing:** Why did CNAC make its move in 1995, not the year before or the year after? Its timing was partly dictated by landmark negotiations which Hong Kong was engaged in at that time over the extremely lucrative Hong Kong–Taiwan service. Previously, just one carrier from each side had flown the route: Cathay and China Airlines (Taiwan's national carrier). The new deal allowed in one more Taiwanese carrier—EVA Air—and gave permission to Dragonair to fly to Kaohsiung, the big port city in southern Taiwan.

CNAC's determination to be part of this agreement was widely known. Indeed, had it not bought into Dragonair, then the airline would probably not have been allowed into the revised agreement (because that would have kept the Swire/CITIC position secure and produced no new competition).

Moreover, since the agreement would continue beyond July 1997, Hong Kong and Taiwan had to gain the approval of the Joint Liaison Group, the Sino–British committee coordinating the multitude of legal, political and economic issues involved in the transfer of sovereignty. This gave the Chinese government the leverage to refuse its approval until CNAC won control of Dragonair—which is basically what happened.

Another deciding factor would have been the length of time it takes for a new air operator's certificate to be approved—at least a year—and the lead time involved in starting a new airline. Two years all up is reasonable. So if CNAC wanted to be in the air by July 1997, then early 1995 was about the right time to start the application process.

In short, mainland encroachment on other commanding heights will be determined and shaped as much by unique factors as general ones. Don't expect a mad rush all at once.

BANKING

In contrast to aviation, which has proved relatively easy for mainland interests to attack, the banking sector in Hong Kong offers a considerably more complicated challenge. Banks are the heart of the economy, circulating money and confidence. Aviation may be a lucrative and politically symbolic sector, but it is not the centre around which all else revolves. A hostile takeover of any large locally incorporated bank would reverberate throughout the financial system and probably undermine business confidence. Would the taken-over bank be as well run? Would it engage in politically motivated lending? Would the assets of deposit holders be as secure? In the highly volatile financial market of Hong Kong, it is easy to imagine any number of issues that could send people into a panic. Which of course is the last thing Beijing wants in the early years of reunification.

The other mitigating factor against a hostile takeover is that it is not as necessary as the airline takeover. Hong Kong has just two airlines, but 182 licensed banks (and a few hundred more restricted-licensed banks, deposit-taking companies, representative offices and finance companies). CNAC had to break down the door to get what it wanted. The Bank of China, in contrast, has been conducting business in Hong Kong since 1917. In addition to the 13 banks under its wing, other mainland banks operate in the colony. Three of the newest are the People's Construction Bank of China, the Industrial and Commercial Bank of China, and the Agricultural Bank of China. All three received approval from the Hong Kong Monetary Authority to set up branches in late 1995. Diligent application, not predatory stalking, is the way into Hong Kong's open banking industry.

And the banking sector is different again because buying into a big bank is extremely expensive. CNAC paid US$253 million for a 36% stake in Dragonair and CITIC Pacific paid US$770 million for a further 15% share of Cathay. Say for the sake of the argument that a Chinese bank wanted to buy 35% of the Hang Seng Bank, a subsidiary of the HongkongBank and the colony's second largest after its parent. Since Hang Seng's market capitalisation in early 1997 was US$23 billion, the price would be around US$8 billion—a different equation entirely from buying into an airline. It might cost more if shareholders refused to accept the going market price as the basis of the sale and instead pushed for a premium. The owners of Dragonair, on the other hand, were able to sell down at a large discount because it is a private company. And while on the subject of size, it is worth noting that the market capitalisation of Cathay is US$5.3 billion—or less than a quarter the value of the Hang Seng Bank. There is no comparable figure for the HongkongBank, the colony's largest, since it is subsumed within the figure for its parent, HSBC Holdings plc, which has a market value of US$63 billion, and is listed in Hong Kong and London (where it has its headquarters).

What about a friendly joining of businesses? There is an argument that says this will not happen either, since the primary mainland candidate, the Bank of China, has enough business on its plate. One who apparently subscribes to this view is David Li, chief executive of the Bank of East Asia, the third largest publicly listed bank in Hong Kong. At a finance conference in Sydney in mid-1996, Li started tongues wagging by claiming that the HongkongBank had offered the Bank of China a partnership with the Hang Seng Bank. This was news to people in Hong Kong and, predictably, denied vehemently by both the relevant parties. But Li, who said his information came from one of the banks under the Bank of China umbrella, assured the audience that the Chinese bank 'did not want' such a connection with a British bank, nor did it need one.

But even if an offer was never made, the idea of a share sale or joint venture between the Hang Seng Bank and the Bank of China is worth pondering because it could make commercial sense at some point in the future. The Bank of China would stand to gain a substantially larger asset base in Hong Kong and access to the know-how of one of the colony's best-run banks. This 'technology' could then be transferred to the Bank of China's operations in China and around the world. If the price was acceptable and the stake sufficient, why wouldn't the mainland bank consider it seriously?

The benefit to the HongkongBank, which owns 61.5% of Hang Seng, would be a formal link with China's most important international bank. This in turn might ease the British-owned bank's path into the burgeoning China market. In an ideal world this would not be necessary and, indeed, some argue that unrestricted access for foreign banks in China would not necessarily result in the demise of local banks, as the Chinese government fears. But this fear is unlikely to go away or change soon. If the HongkongBank waits for China's leaders to become less protectionist, it may be waiting a long time. If, on the other hand, it had a formal link with the Bank of China, it would presumably benefit in some way from its partner's clout and wide network of offices and branches in China. The HongkongBank, in contrast, has just 14 offices there. And although the Hongkong-Bank has an edge over most other foreign banks in China—in late 1996/early 1997 it was one of eight to receive a licence to carry out restricted trade in local currency—it will continue to be held back over the medium term.

A drawback to this scenario is that the Bank of China may not be satisfied with a stake in only the second largest local Hong Kong bank. It might instead ask for a portion of the HongkongBank itself, since this would do more to enhance its regional as well as international contacts and knowledge (the British-owned bank operates in 31 countries). But would HSBC Holdings plc want to sell part of the HongkongBank in its current form? Almost certainly not. There is no logic in having a mainland partner outside Hong Kong/China and such an ownership change could damage the HongkongBank's solid reputation (though not necessarily that of HSBC Holdings plc, because it is an international federation of banks in any case). It should also be remembered that the Bank of China is, after all, a state-owned institution, subject to directives from its government, and still a part of an unstable and half-developed banking industry in China.

One inbetween solution may be workable, however. Say the Hong-kongBank hived off its Hong Kong banking business from its Asian and international divisions, and established a separate Hong Kong–China banking arm (either with or without the Hang Seng Bank as a part of the new structure). This new company could sell a sizable portion of itself to the Bank of China and become a major force in Hong Kong and Chinese banking over the next century.

As outrageous as such a proposal would doubtless seem to many employees of the HongkongBank, there is a partial precedent for it within their group. In 1994 the bank set up a legally separate, locally incorporated bank in Malaysia in response to new government rules. This company is wholly owned; it is not a joint venture with a local Malaysian bank. But at least the concept of legal separation for the sake of a political imperative is not new.

HSBC Holdings, meanwhile, would obviously not consider any restructuring of its principal subsidiary unless the returns were truly lucrative. The HongkongBank is the group's most important franchise, typically accounting for around 40% of total international pre-tax profit, which in 1996 amounted to US$7.2 billion. Hong Kong provides the lion's share of these profits. It goes without saying that any corporate reorganisation would be approached with great caution. Yet HSBC has been known to act with boldness in the past when presented with a strategic opportunity or problem. Perhaps the broad opening of China's banking market will depend as much upon foreign institutions taking bold steps as the Chinese government, since the China of today is in no mood to allow foreign interests control of its potentially lucrative strategic sectors.

The foregoing is just one speculative illustration of a possible future. Things may turn out differently. The Bank of China might choose to tie up with a large Hong Kong Chinese bank, such as the Bank of East Asia or the Dao Heng Bank. Or it could choose to do nothing. But would that be in its best interests? While the bank has improved dramatically over the past decade (especially in Hong Kong, where it has more autonomy than in China), it is still several steps behind the HongkongBank in terms of management and services, and a long way behind in market share. The agenda of both banks, the economic priorities of the Chinese government, and the fact that Hong Kong is shedding its colonial past, argues against a bland continuation of the status quo.

At a minimum, the HongkongBank faces the loss of its 'political' leadership in the local banking sector to the Bank of China. A sign of the times was when the latter took over the chairmanship of the Hong Kong Association of Banks for the first time in 1996. And the HongkongBank has now lost its traditional seat on the Executive

Council, the inner sanctum of non-officials who advise the governor (now the chief executive). Until 1995, the chairman of the bank, always a Briton, occupied the seat. In that year it was taken up by the bank's most senior Hong Kong Chinese officer, Vincent Cheng. But Cheng was among the half dozen advisers not reappointed when Tung Chee-hwa, the first chief executive of the Special Administrative Region, announced his new council in January 1997. The reasons for the change, it should be made clear, were political not personal.

What stood out about the new council was not the fact that two former councillors were kept on—and the HongkongBank was not—but that a seat was given to Antony Leung, regional general manager of the Chase Manhattan Bank, an American bank. Leung won his seat because he has close ties to Beijing—he sits on the China-appointed Preparatory Committee responsible for setting up the first post-1997 government—and presumably as a reassurance to the international business community that Hong Kong will remain open.

Echoing the 'no special privileges rule', Bank of China Group officials have publicly stated that none of their banks will act improperly in future. In a rare newspaper interview in late 1995, a senior manager told the London-based *Financial Times* that his bank would not 'grab' market share after the handover. Another official admitted that they could, and should, be more open about their financial status (since it is not listed on the stock exchange, the bank provides only the barest of details about its operations) and that it would continue to abide by regulations laid down by the Hong Kong Monetary Authority. The subtext here is that Bank of China would not in future seek the sort of 'special privileges' once allegedly enjoyed by the HongkongBank.

But this is a red herring. The banking system has progressed in recent years and, as a consequence, the HongkongBank has steadily lost many of the quasi-central-bank jobs it previously had. Until quite recently, for example, it acted as the clearing bank for the entire banking system in Hong Kong. This involved holding other banks' funds for periods of time, but not having to pay interest on them—an arrangement that displeased some banks because of the commercial benefit and confidential information which allegedly accrued to the dominant bank (although officials within the HongkongBank say such allegations are rarely fully explained and point out, justifiably, that running a clearing system carries as much of a burden as any supposed benefit). In any case, this imperfect arrangement was reformed in 1995–97, when the clearing and settlement task was taken over in phases by the Hong Kong Monetary Authority. To give this function to the Bank of China today, therefore, would be a regressive step and bad for business confidence.

Invoking the 'no special privileges rule' disguises a more general point—that commercial advantage can change direction for informal reasons as much as formal ones (as the Dragonair deal highlighted). The Bank of China Group will gain simply from being the principal mainland financier in Hong Kong. Political expedience and the lure of the China market will encourage local and foreign businesses to seek closer ties with it. Ng Leung-sing, executive director of the China and South Sea Bank, which is part of the Bank of China Group, told a local newspaper that the participation of employees of mainland enterprises in Hong Kong politics would be good for their business. Hence mainland banks will not need to 'grab' market share by pleading for *de jure* privileges (those obtained 'by legal right'). The change of sovereignty provides a *de facto* advantage.

These shifting sands may not necessarily result in an immediate loss of market share for the HongkongBank and its subsidiaries, though the colossus must surely lose part of its huge lead over time (even if the absolute size of its business grows). How far out in front is it? The bank claims that three-quarters of all adults in Hong Kong have accounts with it—and this does not even include the Hang Seng Bank. Many people, however, keep accounts at more than one bank. In May 1995 the HongkongBank boasted in a fact sheet that it was also: 'Hong Kong's leading issuer of credit cards'; 'dominant in the domestic money market and the leading provider of a broad range of treasury products'; a 'leading provider of term and working capital finance' to corporations; the 'market leader in trade finance'; and 'Hong Kong's leading custodian and clearing agent for institutional investors' in securities. In contrast, the Bank of China Group accounts for only 25% of all deposits in Hong Kong and just 9% of the total banking market. Clearly, this is a gap that the mainland corporation will do all it can to narrow.

One thing is sure. The HSBC group, having experienced much turbulence in and around China during its 132-year history, is acutely aware of the unpredictable effects of politics upon business and the need for counter-measures. Take the 1940s, for example. It lost its entire banking business in Hong Kong after the Japanese invaded during the Second World War. A few years later it paid dearly for the privilege of getting it back by honouring unlawfully issued wartime cash worth £7.5 million. Next it watched impotently as its main area of business, China, imploded after the Communist victory. All of this in just eight years (1942–49).

For the next 30 years China was an unknown quantity, a dilemma encapsulated in the concluding paragraph of an official history published during the bank's centenary in 1965. Called 'Wayfoong' after the bank's name in Chinese (which means an 'abundance of remittances'), the book ends by saying:

> Communist China is a neighbour whose intentions are incalculable. All one can assert is that the existence of Hong Kong is seen in that quarter at present as a convenience, a door to the capitalist world through which foreign exchange can enter. As long as it remains a convenience one may suppose that it is safe. But the Hong Kong and Shanghai Banking Corporation's future is no longer bound up with it. Even if one day Hong Kong were taken behind the bamboo curtain, the Bank would survive.

The HSBC group was confident it would survive because of a successful expansion program it had engaged in after the war. With no choice but to grow outside China, it turned its attention to Asia, where it reopened branches in Japan and other countries that had been closed during the war, and opened new branches in Borneo and Malaya. The bank also began to acquire subsidiaries. It bought The British Bank of the Middle East and The Mercantile Bank (which operated in India and South-east Asia) in 1959. It saved the Hang Seng Bank from ruin in 1965 during a financial crisis in Hong Kong. And the program has since continued, with a major investment in the United States in 1980 and in Canada the following year. In 1987 HSBC Holdings plc laid the groundwork for a significant expansion into Britain, and the eventual transfer of its global headquarters from Hong Kong to London, by buying a 15% stake in the Midland Bank, a large British bank. The rest of Midland was bought in 1992 and the head office moved in 1993.

As for China, 20 years of economic reform has turned the country from a mystery into an opportunity. But politics has not gone away. At the very least, the socialist threat has been replaced by old-fashioned political unrest (within China) as the main uncertainty facing Hong Kong. Closer to home, there are the political and business implications of the transfer of sovereignty to deal with. Within this dynamic and unprecedented context, it would be surprising if HSBC's strategists had not considered a wide variety of plans for getting the most out of a resurgent China—and for protecting their patch in Hong Kong. Even if it never ties up with the Bank of China, there are many other large banks in China with whom it could develop a close relationship. Numerous foreign service sector companies have engaged in cross-cultural marriages in China as a necessary modus operandum—why not banking?

TELECOMS

Media and market speculation focused on this key sector as a takeover target soon after the Dragonair deal because of superficial similarities with the aviation industry. Telecoms is of 'strategic' importance to the Chinese government for industrial and security reasons. The dominant and erstwhile monopoly operator, Hongkong Telecom, is majority owned by Cable & Wireless, an old British cable laying and telephone multinational. And Hong Kong's high per capita incomes, as well as its status as an international communications hub, make telecoms an extremely lucrative industry. The day after the CNAC coup was announced by the local media on 30 April 1996, the *Financial Times* ran a story entitled 'Deals offer lessons ahead of 1997', with the sub-title: 'Analysts' attention has already focused on Hongkong Telecom'.

Academics raised such a possibility several years earlier. In a special China issue of an international journal called *Telecommunications Policy* in 1994, an American professor noted that Hongkong Telecom was 'an uncomfortable reminder of the colony's colonial past' and suggested that: 'We must at least raise the question whether China will exert pressure on Hongkong Telecom to increase the Chinese share even further ...'. This was a reference to the purchase by the ubiquitous CITIC of a 20% stake in 1990. A Hong Kong university lecturer asserted in another article: 'China has two goals in telecommunications development in Hong Kong: profits and control.'

The widely held assumption is that Hongkong Telecom is just too rich and powerful a company to leave entirely in British hands. It was the largest corporation on the Hong Kong stock market until 1992, when HSBC Holdings' merger with Midland Bank in the United

Kingdom pushed the bank into the top spot. Now at sixth place, Hongkong Telecom's 1995/96 financial year net profit amounted to US$1.3 billion, which was almost five times larger than Cathay Pacific's and a bit more than half that of the HongkongBank's in the same year. It is known as the 'jewel in the crown' of Cable & Wireless because it has consistently supplied two-thirds of its parent company's annual profit (despite the fact that the British multinational operates in more than 50 countries).

Hongkong Telecom achieved this strength through monopoly profits. For 70 years (1925–95), an entity known as the Hong Kong Telephone Company was the only licensed operator of local 'fixed-wire' telephone services (meaning the basic telephone network embedded in the ground and composed of copper wire or, more recently, fibre optic cables). The government allowed competition in the 1980s, but limited it to equipment sale and services such as paging and mobile phones. Since the new services used radio waves to communicate, and were intended to supplement the core telephone system, the company's monopoly remained intact. On the international side, meanwhile, Cable & Wireless had held a monopoly on overseas calls since 1938 (a gift which was extended in 1981 by the Thatcher government until 2006). The British multinational bought the Hong Kong Telephone Company in 1984 and merged the two sides to form Hongkong Telecom in 1987.

Despite increasing competition from, among other things, the loss of its domestic monopoly in 1995, Hongkong Telecom is by far the dominant telephone company in the colony and turns over a huge amount of business. To put it in perspective, the company's 1995/96 turnover of almost US$3.8 billion (HK$29.4 billion) was equal to 32% of China's total revenue from posts and telecoms in 1995 (which amounted to US$11.9 billion or Rmb99 billion)! This says a lot about China's still under-developed telecoms system and Hong Kong's strength as a regional and international communications hub, the result of its development as a business base for Asia, an international financial centre, a shipping and aviation hub, the primary supplier and packager of foreign investment to China, and its re-emergence as China's principal trade entrepot. All these business activities are voracious consumers of telecoms services.

Does all this mean that Hongkong Telecom will suffer the same fate as its aviation counterparts? Not immediately. Although it seems improbable that the firm could remain under majority British ownership forever, various factors mark the telecoms sector as different from the airline industry. These must influence China's calculations over the short-term (even if they do not alter the long-term likelihood of mainland encroachment).

The first is that the telecoms sector is far more open and competitive than the aviation market. A variety of local and international factors forced the Hong Kong government to deregulate telecoms further in the 1990s, including pressure from the business community and competing telecom service providers, the demands of economic development (for lower tariffs, more efficient service and so on), and competition with Singapore to be Asia's communications hub. New paging and digital mobile phone licences were issued in stages as new technology became available, and then the big bang came in July 1995: three local conglomerates were allowed to launch their own domestic fixed-wire telephone services to compete against the monopolist. The core was now under attack.

In this state of flux, mainland Chinese firms have been playing poacher (though CITIC is a gamekeeper of sorts through its stake in Hongkong Telecom). These poachers are mainly in the paging and mobile telephone businesses, normally as part of mixed nationality consortia bidding for new licences. For example, one of four digital mobile phone licences awarded in 1992 went to a consortium which included a subsidiary of the Ministry of Posts and Telecommunications, China's former monopoly and still dominant operator. The consortium was led by Smartone, a local firm, and also included McCaw, an American company. More recently, large red chips like China Resources and China Travel have been members of consortia which won 'PCN' licences in 1996. This is a new generation of mobile phone technology which is capable of offering a more economical service in urban areas than older digital technology.

As in banking, therefore, the scope for mainland participation in telecoms is considerably greater than in aviation and market entry is easier. This does not dismiss Hongkong Telecom as an object of envy, since it still dominates the market, but it probably buys the firm some time.

The second difference is that new competition at home, and a changing international agenda, are causing problems for Hongkong Telecom that are far more unpredictable, and intractable, than the difficulties Dragonair faced. The airline's slowdown in profit growth from 1993 onwards had a lot to do with political considerations:

China's arbitrary decision not to allow it any new routes, a barrier that was later lifted after CNAC bought into the carrier. Hongkong Telecom is suffering from a worsening financial situation that cannot be so easily turned around. Now is not the best time to buy into the company, for the following reasons:

- Growth in turnover has slowed from 13% in 1991/92 to 9% in 1995/96 (with one exception: 1992/93, when it reached 18%). Over the same period the rate of net profit growth has plunged from 31% to 14% (with a temporary rise in 1993/94). The most recent interim financial statement confirmed these trends. Turnover growth was flat at 9% for the six months to 30 September 1996, while the net profit figure declined further to 12%. These are not the sort of figures which stir the hearts of potential partners. But it gets worse:

- Hongkong Telecom depends on its international direct dialing (IDD) business for more than half its total revenue each year. Yet growth in this area for 1995/96 was only 1.3%—or 4.3% if a slightly different accounting principle was used, the company said. The latest interim results stated that growth over the previous year was only 4.8%.

A major impediment here is competition from the three new fixed-wire telephone companies since mid-1995. Although none of these firms is allowed to operate an 'international gateway', they are permitted to deliver calls destined for overseas to Hongkong Telecom's gateway. In return, they receive a share of the revenue generated from the dominant operator. But all three firms quickly moved to grab market share by offering rates that were, to some countries, significantly less than Hongkong Telecom's. This in turn forced the incumbent to cut its tariffs on the most competitive routes, such as to the United States and Canada. Where it once enjoyed a 100% market share in international voice calls, the erstwhile monopolist is now down to less than 80%.

- Another drag on international call revenue has been a slowdown in China-destined business. The China route, which accounts for around 40% of Hongkong Telecom's annual international call revenue, took a direct hit from the economic austerity program that Beijing implemented in 1994 to curb inflation and rampant investment. Whereas revenue growth had reached 25% in 1993, it slowed to 18% in 1994, and was just

6.6% in 1995. However, improving economic stability in China over 1996, and the subsequent lightening of the government's austerity grip, should flow through into faster growth on the China–Hong Kong route over the next couple of years.

- But Hongkong Telecom may not get much cheer from improved China business, since it is about to face even more competition on the international side. Pressure has been building internationally for countries to end finally whatever IDD monopolies they have in place and to open their telecoms markets even more to foreign involvement. The locus of discussion has been the World Trade Organisation (the successor to GATT), since it is committed to reducing anything that impedes the free flow of trade in goods or services (telecoms, finance, legal services and so on). The internationalisation of the world economy means that more and more individuals and companies must make overseas calls on a regular basis, yet IDD monopolies and oligopolies ensure that prices are kept high. This benefits the few (the telecoms multinationals) at the expense of the many.

  The Hong Kong government's response has been to argue for the retention of Hongkong Telecom's international monopoly (on the grounds that it is a legal contract) but to interpret its 'exclusivity' rights as narrowly as possible. This means that Hongkong Telecom remains the sole keeper of an 'international gateway' for *voice* calls until 2006, but competition will be acceptable in other international telecoms services such as fax, data communications, video-conferencing, and 'private networks' within corporations. The WTO struck a new deal in February 1997 which included Hong Kong's offer.

Unfortunately, the bad news does not even end there for Hongkong Telecom. Being the dominant entity in the market means that the government deliberately shuts it out of some sectors to allow smaller competitors to flourish. For example, it was not among the six licensees winning a 'PCN' licence in 1996—much to its chagrin. And even business units that are doing well, such as its mobile phone division, face huge competition. Revenue from this division grew by 57% in 1996, yet market share was flat!

All these negatives have affected CITIC's level of shareholding in the company. Since 1990, the mainland corporation has steadily sold down its 20% share to just 8% (by mid-1996) as better investment opportunities have arisen elsewhere in Hong Kong or China. But this does not mean that CITIC is necessarily distancing itself from Hongkong Telecom. So far it has maintained a close relationship by retaining its original two seats on the telephone company's board. Despite an agreement that says this arrangement shall last for as long as CITIC owns at least a 10% stake, the reduction to 8% has not brought about any change in board representation.

Because it is unlikely that Hongkong Telecom has hit bottom yet, any new mainland Chinese entity (or even CITIC) interested in making a move on Hongkong Telecom would be wise to let the dust settle over the international call monopoly issue and local competition, and then buy in more cheaply—or at least more securely—at a later date.

Whether any mainland entity could afford to buy the company now is another point of doubt. The cost to CITIC of increasing its stake from 8% to, say, 35% at early 1997 prices would be US$5.4 billion (that is, 27% of the telephone company's US$20 billion market value). Assuming it bought the shares from Cable & Wireless, this would leave the latter with a 31.5% interest. In Hong Kong dollar terms the purchase would amount to HK$42 billion—or almost seven times the price which CITIC paid to increase its share of Cathay Pacific from 10% to 25%. This would be a huge commitment on CITIC's part and one that would severely limit its ability to invest in the other infrastructure projects it has been targetting—bridges, tunnels, and power stations—and which should generate better returns.

If any other mainland firm wanted to buy a 35% stake in Hongkong Telecom, it would have to start from scratch and pay US$7 billion (or HK$55 billion or Rmb61 billion). It is unlikely any could do so at this stage. Remember that China's total revenue from posts and telecoms in 1995 was just US$11.9 billion (Rmb99 billion); and this accrues to a variety of entities at the central and provincial levels. Although it is a revenue stream that is growing extremely fast—the 1996 figure was US$15.2 billion and the forecast for 2000 is US$36 billion—it would be a few years before any single state-owned telecoms enterprise grew to a size where it could raise the necessary finance. Beijing does instruct Chinese banks to make low-interest 'policy loans' to key national infrastructure projects, but an investment in Hongkong Telecom would not fit this category. The purchase price of Rmb61 billion could be far more usefully employed in China, either on general infrastructure or on telecoms itself. Indeed, China's total investment in fixed telecommunication assets in 1995 was not much more—Rmb99 billion (the same as its revenue level).

THE LOGICAL APPROACH for China would be to wait until it can spread the financial load between, say, CITIC and a subsidiary of the Ministry of Posts and Telecommunications (MPT) in Beijing. The obvious candidate is China Telecom, which is the ministry's commercial operating arm and runs the nation's long-distance 'backbone' network (that is, the telecom lines linking provinces and major cities). The MPT used to have a monopoly over the country's telephone network, but lost it in 1994 when a second national carrier was allowed. But it remains the country's regulator and by far the dominant operator in this market. China Telecom could not afford to do a CNAC and force itself into a controlling position in Hongkong Telecom overnight, but it could expand its influence in stages over a period of, say, five to ten years. Meanwhile, other potential suitors could include the provincial posts and telecoms administrations (PTAs) of economically significant regions such as Guangdong or Shanghai. These are part of the MPT's national administrative structure, although they enjoy a fair degree of local autonomy and receive some of their funding from provincial governments (as well as from the MPT).

Unlike CNAC, which had a strategic determination to run an airline from Hong Kong since its holdings in China were limited, China's telecoms companies do not actually need the colony at this stage. They have plenty on their plate at home—being part of the world's fastest growing telecoms industry—and they are becoming more professional as a result of domestic competition since 1994. But a large investment in Hong Kong would certainly be beneficial to one or more of them over the long-term. Not only would they gain a central foothold in an international communications hub, they would have access to well-trained people, modern management systems and technology. People and systems are probably more important than technology, since a great deal of the latter can be bought on the open market and Hongkong Telecom does not do much of its own research and development.

Ironically, a company like China Telecom might one day be able to cast itself in the role of a 'white knight', riding in to save Hongkong Telecom from falling market share and slowing profit growth.

With an even more substantial mainland presence on its board, a reshaped Hongkong Telecom could perhaps be allowed into the Chinese market in some significant way, say through an investment in an existing or new network. Like all foreign firms, the company is barred from owning and running any part of China's core telephone network (its national backbone and provincial networks). Various experiments are being allowed which utilise foreign capital and management expertise in supplementary, advanced services such as paging, mobile telephony and data communications; although a tight control is kept on their scope and the legal protection offered investors is minimal. Unless an imminent telecoms law removes these fundamental restrictions (which it probably will not), companies like Hongkong Telecom, BT (British Telecom), AT&T and other multinationals will face an uphill battle in their quest to run networks and offer services in the Chinese market. But if Hongkong Telecom became, in effect, a Chinese company, then at least some restrictions should fall away.

The suggestion here is not that such an arrangement could be implemented smoothly, rather that some change of ownership within Hongkong Telecom seems inevitable over the medium- to long-term and, like the banking sector, this could be to the commercial benefit of Hongkong Telecom as well as to the mainland Chinese enterprise buying in, whether that is China Telecom or a provincial entity.

Implementation of any such deal would definitely face opposition from competing interests. In Hong Kong, this means the three other fixed-wire telephone companies, all of which are owned by powerful local families, including that of Li Ka-shing, chairman of Cheung Kong and Hutchison Whampoa; and in China, the range of other state ministries and agencies involved in the telecoms sector and left out of any Hong Kong deal.

Hong Kong's other telephone companies hope that once the colony becomes part of China again, they will be considered Chinese and therefore allowed to operate in that country's market. Since all three are Hong Kong Chinese firms, they have some grounds for hope (certainly more than an unrestructured Hongkong Telecom, given its British parent). The problem for them is that under the principle of 'one country, two systems', Hong Kong will continue to be a separate customs territory for telecoms purposes. Hence, a call from the colony to any part of China will continue to be classified as 'external' (ie, non domestic). This may seem an anomaly, but it is no different from the separate status which Hong Kong will enjoy in many economic areas, such as aviation, shipping and trade. Most agree that the continuation of Hong Kong's unique status is necessary for the preservation of its economy. But under such a system, no Hong Kong telecoms company could automatically become a 'mainland Chinese' entity from Beijing's point of view. If Hongkong Telecom were to gain an advantage as a result of a share sale, therefore, the other three would protest. Alternatively, they could look for mainland partners themselves—which they will probably do in any case.

In China, any deal that strengthened the already powerful China Telecom—or one of the provincial telecoms authorities—would raise the hackles of the country's nascent second national carrier, Unicom. Launched in 1994, its name is an abbreviation of United Communications, which is a direct English translation of its Chinese name, *Liantong*. Many doubt how united it really is, however, given its Byzantine structure: founding shareholders include three central government ministries and around two dozen state enterprises and other public institutions (including CITIC). Since Unicom is having a hard time competing against the erstwhile monopolist as it is, it would be bound to complain about any deal that tilted the playing field further in China Telecom's favour.

Not surprisingly, Cable & Wireless is adamant that its crown jewel is not for sale. At the 1995/96 results announcement in May 1996, its new non-executive chairman, Brian Smith, reiterated that Hongkong Telecom was its 'most valuable asset' and declared:

> The issue of selling a stake has not arisen and certainly isn't in my immediate plans.

Strictly speaking, Smith may be right. The idea of a share sale may not have been formally discussed with any Chinese state corporation, and it certainly could have been absent from *his* short-term agenda. But it is an unconvincing denial from a broader perspective. Smith only became chairman after the hurried departure of his predecessor, Lord Young, in late 1995. Young and the firm's managing director, James Ross, were both forced out at that time due to a long-standing conflict between the two men over business strategy. Yet the fact that Cable & Wireless brought CITIC into Hongkong Telecom in 1990 indicated that it had begun thinking about political insurance some time ago. And it must surely have discussed the question of a further share sale again since then, either in relation to CITIC as a purchaser or some other mainland entity. Not to have done so would be a staggering omission for a company in such an exposed position.

Cable & Wireless does have a couple of cards up its sleeve. One is the matter of size: that is, the high cost of Hongkong Telecom. The second is that, unlike Swire and Cathay Pacific, it has been facing progressively harder competition within Hong Kong in recent years. Whereas Swire was fearful of competing against a new carrier, especially a mainland-backed one, Hongkong Telecom has already been forced to accustom itself to a new business environment. The threat of competition, used so effectively by CNAC, would have less leverage over Cable & Wireless. Moreover, a foundation for closer cooperation between the British firm and China does already exist: Cable & Wireless has been cooperating with Chinese authorities to upgrade telecoms links between Hong Kong and Guangdong since 1974, and has sponsored training programs for MPT staff in Hong Kong and Britain. Hongkong Telecom, meanwhile, formed a joint venture with the MPT in the mid-1990s to lay a new fibre-optic cable between the colony and Beijing.

Acting stubbornly, the other alternative, would not be in the British corporation's long-term interests. If it mounted an indefinite and uncompromising defence of Hongkong Telecom, it would make few new friends in Beijing. For example, after Swire capitulated in 1996, it received a pat on the back from no less than Qian Qichen, China's foreign minister. Qian told Sir Adrian Swire, chairman of Swire's London-based parent, John Swire and Sons, that China 'appreciated' his company's positive attitude towards Hong Kong. The New China News Agency reported that Qian commented (rather pointedly):

> John Swire and Sons, and other foreign companies, are welcome to remain in Hong Kong and make a fresh contribution to Hong Kong's prosperity.

Cable & Wireless might need to ponder what 'fresh contribution' it can make.

OTHER SECTORS

Fear of mainland encroachment into other strategic and lucrative areas of the economy, such as utilities and construction, is also prevalent.

Hong Kong, for example, has only two electricity companies and they do not compete. Instead, they service different areas of the colony. Sure enough, in early 1997 the indefatigable CITIC announced it would buy a 20% stake in China Light & Power (CLP), the larger of the two electricity producers. From a short-term financial perspective, it did not make a lot of sense. CLP is one of the least exciting blue chip stocks on the Hang Seng Index and, under pressure from government, has agreed to slow down construction of new plant (since it produces too much electricity already). Electricity companies in Hong Kong operate under an antiquated scheme of control that ties profits to capital investment. To raise prices and grow profits, the companies effectively have to build new plant—whether or not there is a demand for more electricity.

From the point of view of Larry Yung, boss of CITIC, however, buying into the power company offered prestige as well as synergy with his China strategy. Yung, who worked for China's Ministry of Electric Power for 14 years, wants his conglomerate to become, among other things, a major force in the mainland's power sector. Hence, a partnership with a modern utility would buy CITIC access to a level of management and technical expertise that is higher than what is available in China.

For China Light and Power, the deal should help to open doors to high quality investments in China. CLP already has an interest in a nuclear power station in Daya Bay north of Hong Kong and, before the CITIC link was finalised, had announced it was looking at further investments in Shandong Province and the Shenzhen special economic zone. It hopes that CITIC will be able to help smooth the way for these deals.

FOREIGN COMPANIES working in the construction industry also expect to feel the impact of political change. Before the early 1980s mainland construction companies were not a feature in this sector. Today there are almost 30 firms with an obvious construction bent listed in the membership directory of the Hong Kong Chinese Enterprises Association, the chamber of commerce for mainland companies. Two of the most prominent contractors are China State

Construction Engineering Corporation, which counts projects related to the new airport and buildings in the central business district among its major works, and China Harbour Engineering Company, one of whose contracts is the roadworks around a new convention and exhibition centre newly built on reclaimed land in Victoria Harbour. China Harbour is a subsidiary of the Ministry of Communications in Beijing, which makes it a sister company to China Merchants, the diversified shipping, property, industrial and financial conglomerate highlighted in the previous chapter. Another firm with a famous parent is China Travel Building Contractors (Hong Kong).

The going estimate is that mainland firms have a 12% share of the Hong Kong construction industry, with the remainder taken up by local Chinese firms and foreign giants such as Gammon (British), Dragages (French), and Leighton (Australian). There seems little to stop the mainland share from increasing, since pressure for contracts from that quarter will be intense and becau: the competence of mainland contractors is rising. Three managers working for an international contractor in Hong Kong had this to say about mainland encroachment:

It will be their market.

It (change) is already starting. The web of influence will be out of China.

They will dominate the market by the year 2005.

And:

We are preparing for the inevitable. Either (we will get) a smaller piece of cake or less profit.

It needs to be pointed out that the industry is facing cyclical as well as political problems. Over the short-term, at least, lower profit will result from a large (or larger) pool of contractors going for a smaller pool of public work. Government infrastructure investment has been unusually high in recent years as a result of the new airport and its related highway, railway, tunnel and reclamation projects. As these are nearing completion—the airport should open in April 1998—so the level of work is bound to decline. Many hope that the slack will be taken up by greater government investment in public housing—a concern of the incoming administration—and a variety of other transportation schemes still pending (new ports, a new railway in the Western New Territories, and so on). Others believe that the growth of private-sector construction, which started to slow in 1994 because of falling demand and political uncertainty, will pick up again. However, there 'must be a period of consolidation' after the airport and related projects are completed, said one of the foreign managers.

An English project manager working for another international group agreed that mainland contractors would increase their share of the market, but also saw local Chinese contractors, such as Hip Hing, Hsin Chong and SFK, winning a greater share of jobs in future. He said this was due to their increasing proficiency and because some of them belonged to property development groups (for whom they worked on the basis of a negotiated contract, not a publicly tendered one). Hip Hing, for example, is a subsidiary of New World, one of Hong Kong's largest property developers.

These trends will not drive foreign firms out of the Hong Kong construction market completely. But as their market share falls, it is imperative for them to look beyond Hong Kong for new work. This is what the first international firm is doing. Its strategy is to radiate out towards other Asian countries with large infrastructure needs, such as Thailand, Vietnam, India, Malaysia and China. But the fact that it still relies on Hong Kong for 80% of its regional revenue adds a certain urgency to its quest.

JOINT COMMAND

The pace and extent of mainland Chinese encroachment on Hong Kong's commanding heights, therefore, depend on several factors: the agenda of specific aggressors, the cost of buying in, economic issues external to Hong Kong that could destabilise a particular sector or incumbent operator, and the nature of competition within Hong Kong. Since these differ from aviation to banking to telecoms, utilities and construction, no single pattern of ascendancy is likely to be replicated across the board. In other words, one has to be careful taking the CNAC example as *the* model for all future forays by mainland enterprises in Hong Kong. It might work in telecoms—once a Chinese company could afford it—but it would ill serve the Bank of China to be so narrow-minded.

Moving from the means and timing to ends, no one should be surprised if in five years time the demographics of Hong Kong's commanding heights looks quite different from today. The colony's economy is one of the prizes which China will win as a result of reunification and, quite rationally, the country's leading state enterprises see it is as a business opportunity. As the representatives of the new sovereign, they are unlikely to be content with playing second fiddle to existing Hong Kong Chinese and foreign-owned firms. The history of mainland involvement in the Hong Kong economy between 1980–1997 shows that they have steadily increased their local presence and market share (as the previous chapter showed). Reunification will add a special impetus to this process—a political boost—that would not have been available had sovereignty remained in British hands.

It is not inevitable that mainland enterprises will dominate every strategic sector in five years time. They have the determination, and almost certainly the means, to do so in aviation (and possibly utilities), though the picture is more complicated in banking, telecoms and construction, either due to factors that no single company can control or because those sectors are significantly more open and competitive already. But power sharing with existing vested interests is entirely probable in these more difficult industries—and that in itself would be a significant change. Politics and to a lesser extent business acumen will drive the process—not specially granted legal privileges.

CHAPTER 8

A LEAKY BORDER

If the broad structure or framework of the Hong Kong economy remains the same into the next millennium but mainland Chinese firms extend their influence over its commanding heights, or even its lower reaches, what effect will this have on business culture (the sum of attitudes, ideas and practices that have made Hong Kong distinct from the motherland)? Probably a profound, and not necessarily productive, one.

It would be surprising if the effect was neutral, since changes in the ownership of key sectors, and the transfer of sovereignty generally, will bring to prominence companies that are intimately linked to economic ministries in Beijing or provincial governments in other parts of China, and whose experience differs from the norm in Hong Kong. To be accurate, it is important not to tar all mainland enterprises with the same brush. A few have been in Hong Kong for years, have absorbed the local culture, and look more and more like modern corporations. The same applies to some of the people managing these firms, several of whom have been in the colony for up to 20 years. But many have not and betray their bureaucratic character.

Since trade and investment flow both ways across the Hong Kong–China border, and since it is widely agreed that Hong Kong investment in China has contributed to the cultural change which the motherland is undergoing, it is logical to conclude that increased mainland presence south of the border will also have a cultural impact. This view is not particularly fashionable among officials and investors on either side of the border, since all profess a hope that the 'one country, two systems' policy will preserve the essential character of Hong Kong. Even if this were true for the first few years after 1997, which may well be the case, it is unlikely to hold over time. Some of the more serious leaks will flow in intangible areas, such as perceptions of the robustness of the rule of law and of the separation between government and business, and tangible ones like the extent of corruption and competition policy.

Can any person or institution stop these changes? None could for very long. It would be too much to expect the Chinese government to do so, since it will be contributing to them. The local and international business communities could take on the task (indeed, they already have in some respects), but they will always face a conflict of interest between standing up for Hong Kong and seeking advantage for themselves (on an individual company basis). The same applies to the media, which are both businesses and, to varying degrees, independent observers. Which only leaves the first chief executive, Tung Chee-hwa, and the civil service. But they will not only lack the power to hold the line—being subordinate to Beijing in the Chinese government hierarchy—they will be too busy coming to terms with China's constitutional role in Hong Kong's defence and foreign affairs (and Beijing's de facto influence over all major political and economic decisions in the colony).

Hong Kong is not, it should be stressed, facing a life or death situation. It will survive because China has no alternative but to keep it going over the next five to ten years, and because local interests will work hard to keep it viable. This is more an issue of the character of the business environment and the way in which it will evolve—or be restrained—as Hong Kong is subsumed within the broader Chinese state. There may well come a point—perhaps around 2002—when these changes coalesce into a clearer picture and a new Hong Kong hybrid emerges from the fuzziness.

THE RULE OF LAW

The issue of law goes to the heart of the differences between Hong Kong and China. Beijing recognises this, which is why the Basic Law says that 'the common law, rules of equity, ordinances, subordinate legislation and (local Chinese) customary law shall be maintained' in its new Special Administrative Region. This seems an extraordinary concession since it means that China, though delighted to be ridding Hong Kong of British colonial government, is willing to allow the fundamental legal precepts of English civilisation to remain behind.

The common law owes its origins to the post-Norman Conquest period of English history (1066 on), when government became more centralised and judges developed a coherent body of legal principles applicable to the whole country—hence the word 'common'—from England's disparate local customary laws. As judges applied these precepts to new cases, a huge body of case law developed and the 'doctrine of precedent' evolved, binding courts in later cases to decisions made in similar earlier cases. Yet the common law could be inflexible and sometimes harsh: justice was done as long as the proper legal processes were followed and the relevant law fully applied, even if the end result seemed unfair and wrong. So there developed another type of law designed to soften the common law and allow for some discretion by judges—the 'rules of equity'.

Over time, the notion of the rule of law emerged. To paraphrase Peter Wesley-Smith, a law professor at the University of Hong Kong, this means that law is the antithesis of arbitrary political power (everybody should obey it, including government officials); everyone is equal before the law; law is impartially administered by independent judges; law is formal and rational (it is made by people whose authority is recognised, and is consistent, predictable and openly published, rather than informally made, applied inconsistently and unclear); and law benefits the individual (who is presumed to be innocent in criminal cases until proven guilty).

As any student of China knows, these principles hardly describe the legal system that has developed over an even longer period there (the earliest surviving system of law, the Tang Code, was promulgated in 624 AD). The primary purpose of written law in traditional China was to protect the interests of the state. Magistrates worked for the government, they were not independent; and they drew upon rules and legal principles contained in comprehensive 'codes' (the Tang Code comprised 12 volumes), not judge-made precedents drawn from case law. Individuals brought before courts were presumed to be guilty (otherwise why would they have been arrested?), and witnesses were often tortured (which helps to explain why most people distrusted the legal system and local disputes were resolved by village leaders according to customary law). With the exception of this last point, many of these notions still underpin the legal system in China today. Hence the popular foreign conception that the country has no rule of law, but is subject to the rule of men—and the corollary, that Hong Kong's system will suffer once it is exposed to this diametrically opposite system, despite the assurances of the Basic Law.

While Hong Kong does face danger, the situation is a lot less straightforward than these simplified descriptions suggest. The common law itself is not entirely consistent: it allows exceptions to some of its principles (the presumption of innocence is reversed in some jurisdictions, including Hong Kong, for certain types of criminal activity). Nor is it perfect: countries which practice it do not always meet the high ideals of the rule of law. But the main complicating factor is the enormous transition which law in China has been undergoing for the past 20 years.

The demands of the market economy have produced a swathe of new economic, civil and administrative laws, while the social and political changes resulting from economic decentralisation have necessitated the enactment of some new political laws, including one allowing village elections (although it should be stressed that this is a very mild political reform). The slogan describing this evolutionary process—'the socialist market economy is a legal system economy'— stands in contrast to the previous notion that formal law had little role to play in managing the Maoist planned economy. Its chief promoter in the 1990s is Qiao Shi, chairman of the country's 'legislature', the National People's Congress, and one of China's most powerful leaders.

A few things are especially striking about these developments. First, the idea that law has to be clear and more open if the market economy is to function. People need to know what the law is. Second, the introduction of 'rights', as in property rights and contractual rights (not political or human rights). In the early 1990s a group of Hong Kong-based legal scholars—Thomas Chiu, Ian Dobinson and Mark Findlay—wrote of this change:

> Prior to the reform movement of 1979, no citizen could individually enforce his or her rights to property relations through the judicial system ... Historically, the notion of property and associated rights in China were dependent more on social status than on legal guarantees. The communists collectivised such concerns. Only recently have individuals and organisations been deemed to possess actionable connections with property and resultant rights.

Another academic, Albert Chen of the University of Hong Kong, has noted that legal scholars within China who stress the importances of 'duties' are losing ground to those who advocate that rights are fundamental to a market economy.

Third, China's willingness after 1979 to borrow legal concepts and actual laws from foreign jurisdictions, namely Western and Eastern Europe and the United States. This was evident from the promulgation in 1986 of the General Principles of the Civil Law, which borrowed heavily from European civil laws and deals with personal contract, tort and damages, among other matters (European civil laws are 'codified', unlike the common law, and therefore have something in common with traditional Chinese law). American legal experts have advised China on joint venture and patent laws. And English scholars had a hand in the more recent amendment to the Law on Criminal Procedure (1996), which incorporates Western ideas on the legal rights of defendants. In doing this, the Communist Party is actually following a twentieth century trend: the Kuomintang under Sun Yat-sen and Chiang Kai-shek borrowed from Japan and Germany between the two world wars, and the Communists themselves took legal ideas from the Soviet Union from the 1930s onwards.

This resumption of openness helps to explain why even the Communist Party was willing to concede Hong Kong its common law system. Since foreign legal ideas were being imported into China proper, there could be nothing conceptually wrong with allowing its new Special Administrative Region to have them as well; albeit on a much wider scale. On a more practical level, Beijing knew that reunification would be a disaster if Hong Kong's legal system was discarded. And it had already institutionalised pockets of legal separation within China itself through the creation of special economic zones in 1979–80.

Yet many critics of Beijing dismiss China's efforts at legal reform as shallow and insufficiently focused on political and civil rights. They argue, with justification, that while the law may look good, it is poorly enforced and acceptance of the new legal precepts will take a very long time. Courts remain subservient to the Party and the government, hence there is no real judicial independence. Indeed, there is no formal notion of 'separation of powers' in the Chinese constitution between the executive, legislature and judiciary—and unlikely to be one any time soon. Judges are poorly trained. The number of lawyers is grossly inadequate. All in all, it is a system in which the rule of men continues to dominate.

What do these contrary trends and tendencies mean for Hong Kong? The standard fear is of arbitrary interference in the legal system from Beijing or its Hong Kong-based Party and government organs. If the future sovereign does want to interfere there are many ways it could do so, such as meddling behind the scenes in the appointment of judges or seeking to influence judgments in individual cases. Although the latter possibility seems almost a certainty in the event of any serious political case—such as the first application of the new anti-subversion clause (Article 23 of the Basic Law)—intuition and logistics suggests it is exaggerated in the context of economic, civil and ordinary criminal cases. Why would Beijing bother to interfere in most court cases in Hong Kong? Surely it is not interested, nor has the time or resources, to micro-manage the colony to that degree. As Part 2 of this book argued, the Party's strategy is to reshape Hong Kong's political–legal framework into a less threatening form and have loyal guardians watch over it. Sadly, these partisans include some of Hong Kong's more conservative and patriotic judges. The economic–legal framework is being left largely as is.

Nevertheless, threats to the Hong Kong economy do exist. But they will appear more in attitudes and instinctive behaviour than in overt interference on a governmental level. That is to say, reunification will result in a seepage of 'Chinese' legal culture into the colony and its business culture. However much mainland enterprises and officials talk about their willingness to respect Hong Kong law and abide by its regulations, there will for a long time be a tension between this and their degree of sympathy for the rule of law, which remains an alien notion despite China's progress in recent years towards rebuilding a predictable, rules-based legal system. The rule of law, as it has been passed to Hong Kong by Britain, took centuries to develop in England and be truly understood and accepted within society. It is still far from taking root in China and certainly will not flower within the next decade, which is putting it generously. How will mainland enterprises defend and nurture it in Hong Kong, or know when to do so? Given their increasing prominence, this is not a trivial question. So the first threat is that the rule of law could suffer from neglect or ignorance.

Tension may also lie in the difference between law as a set of specific rules and law as guidance. Legislation enacted in Hong Kong is intended to mean what it says and people are beholden to follow both the letter and spirit of it. Yet in China, much legislation passed by the National People's Congress is intended to guide behaviour, not strictly state what people can and cannot do. Indeed, a common complaint among foreign investors there is that they do not understand what new laws mean, since rules are often unclear. Even if they are clear, they are not hard and fast: with the right connections and/or bribe money, people can persuade officials to apply the law to them in the way they want. China's tax laws, for example, provide fertile ground for interpretation and 'negotiation' between companies and officials. It does not require too much of a backward leap to see mainland companies in Hong Kong instinctively interpreting legislation in this looser manner. The second threat is therefore a potential loss of sharpness in the rule of law.

Seepage could also affect the court system. The preference in Chinese legal culture is to resolve civil and economic disputes through conciliation and arbitration, not through litigation in court. As the group of Hong Kong legal scholars quoted earlier have also written:

> In the PRC it is considered that all such matters are capable of reconciliation, which can be undertaken by the parties themselves, or under the guidance of the courts or the Reconciliation Committee. Courts are seen as a last resort, to be used where all other alternatives, including arbitration, have failed.

An identical sentiment is to be found in the statement of objectives of the Hong Kong Chinese Enterprises Association, which seeks to 'foster cooperation and communication among its members and to encourage and assist them to resolve commercial disputes by conciliation'.

A couple of quick caveats are required. There is, in fact, a worldwide trend among private companies to resolve disputes through conciliation and arbitration, since it is usually cheaper, quicker and always out of the public eye. Sectors that have particularly taken to it in Hong Kong include shipping and construction. At the same time, it would be wrong to give the impression that mainland enterprises never use the court system in Hong Kong. In February and March 1997, for example, the Kwangtung Provincial Bank, a member of the Bank of China Group, was the plaintiff in a case before the High Court. And in March of the same year, China Resources was a co-defendant in the Court of Appeal.

However, if mainland Chinese firms de-emphasise the court system in Hong Kong as a mechanism for resolving economic disputes, might not courts in general lose some of their influence and prestige over time? Since this would be a gradual process, optimists could of course argue that no change was occurring. Or that mainland firms were merely echoing the approach of large Hong Kong Chinese firms, which also prefer not to air their conflicts in public. Yet this actually brings the issue into sharper relief: with two of the colony's most powerful groups of companies doing their best to stay out of court, the character of the legal system could subtly change. So the third threat is a possible weakening of one of the pillars of the rule of law.

CORRUPTION

Corruption, like the rule of law generally, has received an unremitting amount of attention as a major pressure point in the post-reunification economy and society. It is widely feared that Hong Kong's return to China will unleash a flood of bribery, fraud and graft flowing southward upon a defenceless colony. As commentators have often quipped, what people are worried about is not 'Chinese style socialism' but 'Chinese style capitalism'. Having spent the past 20 years getting the problem under control—a statutory body with wide powers, the Independent Commission Against Corruption (ICAC), was established in 1974—Hong Kong may revert to the bad old days of the 1960s and early 1970s, when police operated 'graft syndicates' and most believed corruption was out of control (much like they do in China today). Such fears are expressed not merely by anti-Beijing political groups and the liberal media, they are high on the worry list of foreign businesses. A Hong Kong lawyer working for an American law firm says, for example, that many of her clients have asked about the potential problem and sought advice on how to respond.

Only the most complacent could discount these fears entirely. The evidence of corruption in China is voluminous, while the special economic zone of Shenzhen, just north of Hong Kong, is a burgeoning city with a rough, frontier-town mentality. Thus, increasing economic integration between Hong Kong and southern China, while lauded as a positive development for both parties, has a definite downside. One indicator of the seriousness of this problem is that the number of complaints from the colony's private sector to the ICAC about China-related corruption rose from 54 in 1992 to 136 in 1994 (with the number of reports capable of being pursued by the commission increasing from 47 to 70). Another indicator is the close ties which the ICAC has developed with its counterparts in Guangdong, resulting in shared information and joint investigations of suspects. Meanwhile, the higher priority placed by the Chinese government on controlling corruption is reflected in a 'qualitative change' in its policies since 1993, says Andrew Wedeman, a political scientist at the University of Nebraska. Prior to that time the government targeted mainly low and mid-level cadres, but later included more higher ranking officials. Accordingly, the number of cases involving 'senior cadres' (those working at the county level or above) rose from 190 in 1989 to 875 in 1990 and 1800 in 1994. The estimate for 1995 was almost 2300.

Like the wider issue of the rule of law, however, there is a danger of painting an overly simplistic picture of this issue. By far the most erroneous notion is that Hong Kong is lily white, hence any expansion of corruption in future will be largely 'China's fault'. Relatively speaking, of course, the colony is much cleaner than China and has gained kudos from other countries for its anti-corruption legislation and enforcement efforts. Australia, for example, chose to take the Hong Kong model as a precedent. Yet the colony is also home to numerous business people willing to bribe officials in China in return for influence, connections and contracts (although the individuals involved are well-known, no one dares to go on the record for obvious reasons). Taking into account the vast wealth of many of these tycoons, and the extensive trade and investment links which Hong Kong maintains throughout China, one could fairly conclude that the colony is a significant contributor to the motherland's problem. Locally, meanwhile, the incidence of corruption increased dramatically among certain segments of society on the eve of 1997.

A more focused assessment of post-1997 corruption is therefore needed. To what extent will it be home-grown rather than imported? Which segments of society will be most affected? Among mainland Chinese enterprises in Hong Kong, where will corruption be worst? And why should it increase?

The answer to these questions lies partly in recent trends. While the future will not necessarily be a replication of the past, ICAC data on corruption reports received from the public between 1974 and

1995 provide at least a basis for making some comments about the post-1997 period. The commission is largely a reactive body in that it relies upon the public to alert it to problems before it investigates (although the commission's Corruption Prevention Department does do ad-hoc audits of government departments if it notices that 'something is creaky', said Tony Scott, the department's former director). The ICAC, by the way, views an increase in the number of reports as an indication that the incidence of corruption is rising (and not merely that the public has suddenly, for whatever reason, decided to make more complaints).

Looking at historic trends, what is significant about the most recent set of data—for the 1993–95 period—is that it signifies a 'new high plateau of reports not seen since the first year of the Commission', according to the ICAC's 1995 annual report. After an initial burst in 1974–75, when there were more than 3000 reports each year, public complaints fell off sharply in the late 1970s before rising again and settling at around 2300 in 1981; after that the total number remained fairly stable until 1992. But the figure shot up in 1993 to 3270, reached 3,600 in 1994, then declined in 1995 to a still high 3230.

The main culprits behind these rises, in relative terms, were the private sector and the police. Complaints about the former rose by 52% in 1993 and 17% in 1994, when they reached a peak of more than 2100 cases. Those against the police increased by 35% in 1993 and 9% in 1994—to 670 cases. (Although reports concerning all 'other government departments' increased substantially in 1993—by 31% to 752 cases—they started falling off (in 1994), before the other two categories.)

This means that business corruption accounted for the largest chunk of the 'new high plateau' (whereas civil service corruption was the primary pillar beneath the old high plateau).

Within the private sector, the nature of the problem has changed over the past decade. Whereas in the 1980s there were a few extremely large financial fraud cases in Hong Kong (such as the Carrian trial), recent years have brought a greater number of smaller scale problems, often in smaller businesses. Real (although anonymous) examples provided by the ICAC include conspiracy among department store employees to defraud their employers, crooked bank officials, factory supervisors soliciting bribes from sub-contractors, sales staff embezzling money from a paging company during a special sales promotion, and a hotel night manager selling information from guest credit cards to a counterfeiting syndicate.

From a broader perspective, a survey into commercial fraud carried out by KPMG Peat Marwick in August 1994 found that 34% of respondents had experienced fraud in the previous 12 months, and 70% believed it would get worse.

Although the majority of reports investigated by the ICAC concern business, and this sector provides overwhelmingly the largest number of convictions, it is the public sector, especially the police, which remains the ICAC's major political concern. This is due to the central role which the civil service plays in society, bad memories of organised corruption within its ranks in the past, and the fact that both the government and the public place a higher priority on weeding out corruption within the public than private sector. According to an annual ICAC survey of public attitudes towards corruption, around 46% of respondents in recent years said they were 'more tolerant' of corruption in the business sector than in the government, whereas just 5% held the opposite view (although a high proportion are 'intolerant' of corruption in both). On their views towards law enforcement, 35% believed that 'battling public sector corruption should have a higher priority', with 13% seeing it the other way around. Bertrand de Speville, former ICAC commissioner, said in the commission's 1994 annual report:

> Although the business sector continued to need our attention, the public sector remained our first priority, in particular the disciplined services where some isolated spots of organized corruption appeared.

De Speville caused a furor in late 1995 when he made public his concerns about a return within the police of graft syndicates (such as prostitution protection rackets) similar to those of the 1960s. Despite emphasising that the size of the problem was not as great, his comments were immediately seized upon by a nervous public and created a mini controversy. The decline in reports against the police in 1995 suggests that the problem may have eased somewhat; however, the total number is still higher than in 1992, when things were more stable.

What factors explain the 'new high plateau' of 1993–95? There is no consensus about the answer. The ICAC does not try to explain what motivates people to act corruptly, which is probably sensible since it is a law enforcement agency not an institute of psychology. However, much of the public debate centres on the transfer of sovereignty as a catalyst. And a public opinion survey commissioned by the ICAC in September 1994 found that more than 70% of respondents thought corruption would become worse in the years prior to 1997.

Why? Because reunification has created a great deal of uncertainty in the community, prompting around half a million people to emigrate since the mid-1980s. Those leaving have an incentive to accumulate as much wealth as possible before moving to the West, where job opportunities and wages have typically been less attractive than in Hong Kong. Among those who cannot leave, there are no doubt many who feel pressured to acquire additional wealth as a safety net for the future.

Interestingly, there has been no agreement within the ICAC as to whether 1997 is a factor or not. Scott, formerly of the Corruption Prevention Department, was one of the doubters. He recognised that there was a 'popular perception' that the handover was a cause, but said he was not convinced it was really contributing to the problem and pointed out that no analysis had been done. For example, police officers prosecuted for corruption were not systematically asked whether they were planning to emigrate or what motivated their criminal actions. Nor were any of the others. Scott said that cross-border business links between Hong Kong and Guangdong Province have been a cause for concern, since the 'reality is that we cannot live that close to that much corruption and not be tarnished by it, because Hong Kong people are involved'. Even some civil servants had business interests across the border that might 'make them susceptible to pressure', such as policemen owning karaoke lounges. (While this may help to explain general corruption, it is not a complete answer for the 1993–95 plateau, most of which occurred within Hong Kong.) Scott also cautioned against exaggerating the cross-border issue.

A counter line of thought was held by Peter Graham, former assistant director (also retired) in charge of the Administration Department:

> Statistically, you could not support the contention that 1997 is having an impact. But I nonetheless feel that it is having an effect, generated by the uncertainty of what the post-1997 era will actually bring. It is the sort of uncertainty which could persuade, and probably has persuaded people who will be looking to ways of making money quickly. 'Let's get in while we can. Then we will be in a better position to see what we can do.'

What does the above portend for post-1997 corruption? First, home-grown corruption, although not out of control as in China, will continue to be a problem and certainly has the potential to get worse. While the general public in Hong Kong will not reverse its strong antipathy towards corruption any time soon, certain groups remain vulnerable to temptation; namely the police and the private sector. Second, since political uncertainty does seem to contribute to unlawful behaviour, the continuation of this state after reunification (as much due to developments in China as in Hong Kong) will presumably prompt some people to take bribes and act fraudulently. Third, since it is agreed that the economic integration of Hong Kong and China is one factor leading to corruption, the ever closer bond between the two economies will logically result in an increase in the opportunities for bribery, fraud, conspiracy and so on.

The incidence of corruption might increase in future as well because of the arrival of new mainland enterprises and individuals in the colony after reunification and the sense of power that some of the latter will feel as the process of China regaining its 'rightful' sovereignty is entrenched. This may seem overly cynical to some, yet is illustrated by the following real-life example. A Hong Kong accounting firm was hired by a mainland enterprise to carry out an audit of its books. The accountant, not surprisingly, discovered that the company had   inventory which it was still counting among its assets. When the accountant refused to sign the audit unless these worthless goods were written off, the mainland firm retorted angrily that he had better sign off otherwise his future business prospects were dim. One of the mainland managers chided the accountant that 'this was how business was done in China'.

Finally, a point about corruption among mainland enterprises in Hong Kong. To the extent that it grows, the problem will probably be more serious among the thousands of smaller, relatively anonymous companies than the larger, more prominent ones, such as China Resources, CITIC and Guangdong Enterprises—hence mimicking the recent pattern within the local private sector. The larger corporations have an image to uphold, if not enhance, and will come under pressure to set an example. Evidence that this has already crossed their minds can be found among the membership list of the advisory committee for the Hong Kong Ethics Development Centre, a body set up by the ICAC's Community Relations Department. The list names the Hong Kong Chinese Enterprises Association as a member alongside the five other main chambers of commerce. The centre grew out of a conference on business ethics organised in 1994 to discuss the problem of worsening private sector corruption. The conference also produced a 'corporate code of conduct' on business ethics, with the aim of encouraging all companies listed on the stock exchange and all large private companies to sign. Mainland-owned firms that endorsed it include CITIC, Shougang Concord, Ka Wah Bank, Union Bank, Yue Xiu Enterprises, Bank of China and the Kwangtung Provincial Bank. Discounting the obvious public relations aspects of this exercise, it nevertheless shows that some mainland firms are aware of the market value of a clean image. As a proportion of all Chinese firms in Hong Kong, however, these prominent entities represent a distinct minority.

BUSINESSMEN VS BUREAUCRATS

All of Hong Kong's tycoons and virtually all the pro-business politicians on the Executive and Legislative Councils have spent their lives running or working for private companies. Some civil servants have gone into business at the end of their careers, although many have done so as consultants rather than managers. Even those who become managers, or have investments in a business, would at least be familiar with the fairly clear division between the public and private sectors in Hong Kong—unlike in China. Yet a new feature of the post-1997 economy will be the political prominence of business people who have spent their careers as managers of Chinese state enterprises or as government officials.

The change in sovereignty is already giving a greater leadership role to mainland enterprises. In 1996, the new chairman of the Hong Kong Association of Banks was Yang Zilin, chief executive of the Bank of China's Hong Kong and Macau Regional Office. Yang came to Hong Kong in 1994 from the bank's head office in Beijing. Later that same year, Yuan Wu, a senior vice president of China Merchants, the shipping and property conglomerate controlled by the Ministry of Communications, was selected to join the 60-person Provisional Legislature, the interim body appointed by Beijing to take over from the elected Legislative Council on 1 July 1997. And it is envisaged that the Hong Kong Chinese Enterprises Association, like the local chambers of commerce, may be allocated a seat in the first proper post-1997 legislature (scheduled to begin sitting in 1998).

The board of directors of the Hong Kong Chinese Enterprises Association highlights the relationship between these firms and the Chinese state. The current chairman, Gu Yongjiang, is also the current chairman of China Resources and formerly a vice-minister in the Ministry of Foreign Trade and Economic Cooperation (MOFTEC). Among the vice-chairmen, there is Yang Zilin of the Bank of China; Li Yinfei, president of China Merchants Holdings (whose chairman, Huang Zhendong, is the Minister of Communications in Beijing); and Zhu Yuening, chairman and general manager of China Travel Service and the former vice-mayor of Shenzhen. Two other vice-chairmen with links to southern China are He Keqin, chairman of Guangdong Enterprises, the commercial arm of the Guangdong provincial government; and Wang Chengming, chairman and general manager of Fujian Enterprises, the same for that province.

Meanwhile, there is the influential Huang Diyan holding the special post of honorary president of the association. Huang came to Hong Kong from Beijing in 1983 and rose to chief executive of the Bank of China's Hong Kong and Macau Regional Office. He retired from this post in 1994, but stayed on at the bank as 'managing director' and adviser to the regional office. He also sits on the bank's board of directors in Beijing; and back in Hong Kong is a member of China's key Preparatory Committee overseeing the formation of the first Special Administrative Region government. (The other Hong Kong-based mainland businessman on the committee is, again, Yuan Wu of China Merchants.)

Most large mainland enterprises in Hong Kong are headed by former bureaucrats or enterprise managers; though, to be fair, many of their senior and middle managers are foreign-educated mainlanders or Hong Kong Chinese. Furthest along the modernisation path is CITIC, whose chairman is a former government official (Larry Yung) but whose board of directors is entirely made up of Hong Kong Chinese, overseas Chinese and foreign professional managers. This latter group includes a past president of the American Chamber of Commerce in Hong Kong and a former partner of Price Waterhouse. All of which helps to explain why CITIC is the darling of the red chips on the local stock market and is well-managed. Yet CITIC is way ahead of other mainland firms and has a distinctly different corporate culture. It looks and feels like a multinational corpora-

corporation, whereas firms like China Resources and China Merchants continue to project a bureaucratic and opaque demeanour.

What effect will this coterie of 'ex-communist' capitalists have on local business culture in future? Some optimists would argue very little. Until now the group has followed Hong Kong's laws and regulations, learned about commerce in the colony, and used it as a place to raise funds and build links to the rest of the world. The optimists would also say that mainland companies are being changed by Hong Kong more than they are changing it (witness the business ethics conference). After all, the ability of Chinese government enterprises to adapt to new economic forms is apparent in other parts of China, notably Shenzhen, Guangdong province, Shanghai, Beijing and other cities along the coast as well as inland. The trend is therefore one of China coming closer to Hong Kong, not vice-versa.

This is very much the sort of impression which the Hong Kong Chinese Enterprises Association wants to give as well. It tries to be seen as fitting in with the local business culture, not rocking the boat, for anything less could destabilise the transition. Moreover, since many of the enterprises still follow outdated business practices shaped by China's former socialist economy, the pressure is on them to transform themselves into modern companies. As an Association booklet exhorts:

> The Chinese companies should be reformed after the rules and requirements for the operation of Hong Kong's economy. This is to say that from the inside out, they should conform to Hong Kong's 'Rules of Games' (sic), to the internationally established practices, and participate in fair competition by means of their own strength. Only in this way can they merge themselves with Hong Kong's economic environment.

Accepting this argument in full requires a certain blinkeredness. The most curious thing about it is that it is logically inconsistent with the proud belief within Hong Kong that the colony is a force for change *within* China. If Hong Kong's involvement in the Chinese economy can have a cultural impact there—helping to transform the motherland into an open, more individualistic, consumption-oriented society—then the reverse should also be true. China is taking back control of Hong Kong from the British, and its better state-owned companies are steadily expanding their economic power there. The notion that this major historic change will have no cultural impact on Hong Kong seems strange indeed. Initially perhaps, say until the year 2000, the influences may not be too noticeable (since China has an incentive to restrain itself in the interests of a smooth transition). But over time there must be changes.

A point that flies in the face of the optimists is the obvious link between mainland enterprises in Hong Kong and economic ministries in Beijing or at the provincial level. Despite efforts within China over the past decade to minimise the direct control of enterprises by government organs (as was the case under the 'plan' economy), and despite some of the larger and more successful ones having a fairly high degree of management autonomy (CITIC for example), most are far from being private companies. The new chairman of China Resources, Gu Yongjiang, arrived in Hong Kong from the central government bureaucracy only in 1996. And CITIC, despite looking more like a private company than any other enterprise, clearly had to take orders from Beijing during the 1995–96 dogfight over Dragonair.

Probably the main general effect which this group will have on the business culture will be to blur the line separating government and the private sector, and change the balance of power between them. Government in Hong Kong regulates the economy with a relatively light touch and invests in a variety of public goods necessary either to facilitate market activity (such as infrastructure development) or strengthen social stability (spending on housing for lower income families, education, health and minimum social welfare for the old or disabled). Government does not engage in productive activity, a role it happily leaves to the private sector. And it only bails out the latter in extreme circumstances, such as the financial assistance it gave the futures market after the crash of 1987.

After 1 July 1997, the role of the Special Administrative Region government will look very similar to this. What will be different, however, is that a large number of commercial enterprises representing the sovereign power will be engaging in economic activity—a competitive situation which the private sector in Hong Kong did not face in terms of the British government. The combination of the Chinese government's direct stake in the Hong Kong economy, its new sovereignty and the colony's administrative subservience to Beijing suggests that the economic role of the wider 'state' will expand, crossing the boundary that exists at present between the public and private sectors, and become quite intrusive over time.

Such intrusion could take several forms, including attempts by Beijing to influence the ownership of property rights (as in the Dragonair episode) or the direction of economic policy, and a greater proclivity to intervene in the economy during times of crisis or hardship. Indeed, in late 1996 there were reports that Beijing may establish a fund to prop up the Hong Kong stock market in the event of a collapse following the transfer of sovereignty.

The irony is that the Hong Kong government has been laying some of the groundwork for a shift in the balance of power between the public and private sectors. Contrary to Hong Kong's famous image as a laissez-faire economy, regulation of the private sector in recent years has increased or is threatened across the board, from the workings of the stock market to fairer labour rules, and from the introduction of a mandatory provident (pension) fund for workers to a new data privacy law (adapted from the British model). Many of these changes are, of course, extremely popular—though not within the business sector (unless the company happens to benefit in some way from them, such as managing pension funds). A common complaint among industrialists and financiers is that the Hong Kong government has been getting more bureaucratic since the late 1980s and is enacting new economic legislation that is not properly thought through. Typically, much of the blame is laid at the feet of Hong Kong's 'populist' politicians—a product of the introduction of elections in the 1990s—who lobby government for more redistribution of wealth and more protection for workers.

Paradoxically, there are some areas where the impact of the transfer of sovereignty might affect the business culture by impeding change, rather than causing it. A case in point is competition policy. Although Hong Kong is a free port for the trade in goods, many of its service sectors have traditionally been characterised by monopolies (in telecoms until recently, power, some bus services), oligopolies (the aviation industry, though this has been a worldwide phenomenon), and closed shops (the legal profession). Complaints from the public, business itself and other countries in recent years have forced the Hong Kong government to liberalise many sectors— which usually results in lower profits and market share for the incumbent operator (as the last chapter showed in the case of telecoms). Since mainland investment interest is often centred upon the incumbents, the danger is that Chinese corporations will use their political clout to arrest the trend towards greater openness and competition.

They will want to operate in Hong Kong like they do in China: in a state of controlled, not unrestricted, competition. This would not be good for the colony.

Competition Policy

For the average person, economic competition may seem a non-issue. Most people do not know, and are not particularly interested in knowing, who owns what in the commercial world. As long as a product or service quality provided by the companies in question remains basically the same, chances are that consumers will not notice a change in ownership. Electricity seems the same no matter who produces it. The same goes for telephone calls. And how many passengers flying Dragonair from Hong Kong to any destination in China feel a tangible difference because the chairman of the company is now Wang Guixiang, who is also the chairman of CNAC (Hong Kong) and therefore an employee of the Chinese government, rather than Chao Kuang-piu, textile magnate, founder of Dragonair, and now honorary chairman?

Yet these are, or should be, issues of concern to the average person since they could have an effect on the prices and choices which consumers are offered. Had CNAC, for example, set up a third airline in Hong Kong as it had originally threatened, a more substantial competitive environment would have eventually opened up against Dragonair and Cathay. For example, Dragonair still shares the China route with mainland airlines, such as China Eastern and China Southwestern, but the latter group are still way behind Dragonair in their general public image, safety record and quality of service (despite improving in recent years). A third Hong Kong-based airline, on the other hand, might have changed the picture considerably by offering more choice and cheaper flights over time. Instead, the China route remains an oligopoly (which is no doubt what CNAC always wanted).

Even if Dragonair starts to encroach upon Cathay's patch in future, which it probably will, the result is more likely to be further cooperation and compromise rather than out-and-out competition. And if CNAC wins control of Cathay eventually, it will then become a full gamekeeper determined to keep out new poachers for as long as possible. On balance, therefore, what has the change in ownership of Dragonair given to the Hong Kong economy? Any new routes to

China that it wins will boost the attractiveness of its stock when the airline is finally listed on the Hong Kong stock market, but the impact on the economy is neutral: had CNAC not taken over Dragonair, then any new routes would surely have gone to CNAC's new airline. Meanwhile, Dragonair is still being run by the same people or same type of people, and CNAC has little to offer in terms of management skills that the airline did not already have.

Expanded mainland involvement in sectors that are already fairly competitive, such as telecoms, or becoming increasingly so, such as banking (an interest cartel existed until 1994), may make little difference to the current momentum of those sectors. Over the longer term it may smother competition to some extent if competitors choose to join forces through formal mergers or try to create new cartel arrangements (some local firms may not want to compete against a mainland enterprise with powerful connections in Beijing). For example, Hong Kong's numerous mobile phone and paging companies may choose to consolidate into a smaller number of larger firms.

Other monopolistic/oligopolistic sectors to watch will be power generation (where two monopolies supply electricity to separate sections of the colony, as we have seen) and property (where developers allegedly help to keep prices from falling by coordinating the supply of new flats to the market; although this is not the only reason for sky-high apartment values). In power, as briefly noted in the previous chapter, an antiquated regulatory arrangement known as the 'scheme of control' has created a severe contradiction between generating capacity (there is far too much of it) and public demand (which has been growing fairly slowly in recent years). This has happened because the scheme links profit growth to investment in hardware such as plant and equipment. If the power companies do not keep building plant, in essence, their profits will stagnate. They get no financial benefit, for example, from encouraging energy efficiency. Since the cost of new investment in capacity can be recouped through tariffs, and with demand flat, the net result has been steadily rising tariffs.

Although the Hong Kong government has been criticised for its management of the power sector for many years, it was only in late 1996 that the issue really came to a head and the government began trying to persuade China Light & Power (CLP), the larger of the two utilities, to postpone further plant expansion. In addition to having an estimated 60% reserve capacity in Hong Kong, CLP buys power from two stations which it partially owns in Guangdong Province (the Daya Bay nuclear facility and the Guangzhou pumped storage station). The other utility, Hong Kong Electric (HEC), has about a 30% reserve capacity and wants not only to expand its existing station but build a whole new one as well! The upshot of this wasteful and costly conundrum is that legislators and the media have been pressuring the government to modify the scheme of control (which comes up for an interim review in October 1997) and allow competition between the two suppliers. This could be done by allowing each supplier 'access to the other's power grid on the basis of a fair access charge', which in turn would 'immediately reduce the need for each company to maintain and increase a separate reserve capacity, and would lower tariffs for all electricity users', according to a paper on the subject by the former independent legislator Christine Loh. One of the most enlightening statistics in this lopsided sector is that CLP's reserve capacity is larger than HEC's entire generating capacity. Hong Kong is clearly awash with potential power.

Naturally, CLP and HEC would not give in without a fight. Their forward planning is based upon the assumption that the scheme of control will continue. Like Hongkong Telecom in relation to the continuation of its international call monopoly until 2006, they will argue that the government cannot simply renege on a longstanding agreement/licence and change the operating environment overnight. And both companies have powerful parents or partners: CLP recently joined in partnership with CITIC (also mentioned in the previous chapter), and HEC is controlled by Li Ka-shing, Hong Kong's most powerful tycoon. While CITIC's 20% acquisition of CLP in early 1997 appeared to be more a 'strategic' play than for any short-term financial gain, it obviously has no interest in seeing the utility's profit margin eroded by too much competition and a radically new scheme of control. For these reasons, and because the power sector is a key part of the Hong Kong economy, Beijing is bound to interfere with and influence any attempt to change the status quo significantly.

In property, the allegation is that Hong Kong's handful of large developers conspire to limit the supply of new apartments to the market, thereby keeping prices to home buyers high. This is not the first stage in the problem, which is land supply. Since the government earns a significant portion of its annual revenue from land sales to private developers, it keeps the supply of land tight so as to maximise returns to the public kitty. Within this constrained environment, developers then ensure that the market is never flooded with a glut of new apartments. Indeed, supply and demand are so out of sync that prospective buyers usually have to enter a ballot to decide who gets the right to buy and who does not. Not surprisingly, places in the queue are traded for large sums of money, bringing huge profit to some (often criminal gangs). Moreover, the extremely high cost of residential land in government land auctions, and a complicated development control process, limit the participation of small developers in the market.

Pressure has been building for an end to the plethora of restrictive trade practices across the Hong Kong economy, of which those already mentioned are just some examples. The Consumer Council, a statutory body, has also received complaints about the following: two 'big' supermarket chains demanding that suppliers deal with them on an exclusive basis only; two 'big' port operators imposing a new gate charge in addition to terminal handling charges; abuse by Hong Kong's sole supplier of piped gas of its dominant position in the gas supply market; identical prices for gasoline and diesel at all petrol stations; price fixing by trade associations protecting the driving instruction industry; and scale fees rather than free competition for property conveyancing carried out by solicitors. The Council is careful to stress that it is not able to verify the truth of all allegations, hence the anonymous references to the companies concerned (although in small Hong Kong most would know who they are). But the list of transgressors goes on and on, producing a very different picture of Hong Kong from the one in economic textbooks and popular mythology.

In a nutshell, the argument of the Consumer Council is that business practices which artificially raise prices to the individual or corporate consumer cannot be good for Hong Kong's already high-cost economy. Rentals, for example, are among the highest in the world. Port charges are way above those in Taiwan and China, and greater than what could be justified by high land costs alone. The colony is in danger of tarnishing its international reputation as a free trader by not addressing these problems (a reputation built, of course, more upon goods than services, the financial sector excepted).

The Council published a report on competition policy in late 1996, arguing that Hong Kong needed a competition law and a competition authority. The Legislative Council liked the report and passed a motion supporting it in mid-January 1997. But it is doubtful whether the new Special Administrative Region government will welcome it with open arms, and implement it *in toto* over the next few years, given the Hong Kong government's traditional reticence to interfere in business and its normally piecemeal approach to problem-solving.

Nor would mainland corporate interests in Hong Kong be overjoyed with the report. Their natural preference would be to enjoy the same privileges as their predecessors (as far as possible). Beijing wants to see the existing body of mainland enterprises in the colony improve their business performance and profitability, not fight a war of attrition with each other and/or local firms. Shi Jiyang, the director of business administration for the Hong Kong Chinese Enterprises Association, said the reason that only a small proportion of China's 500,000 large and medium state-owned enterprises had received permission to operate in Hong Kong was because the Chinese government did not want to cause 'over-competition', which would be bad for mainland firms, local Hong Kong firms and the economy.

IT'S NOT JUST ABOUT QUANTITY

In the early years after reunification, with the economy continuing to steam ahead and the stock market probably buoyant, many in the pro-Beijing camp in Hong Kong will enjoy attacking the leftover party-pooping doubters of Chinese rule over the former British colony. Chinese officials will join the chorus, saying their prediction that Hong Kong would become 'even better' under Chinese sovereignty has come true.

Mainland firms will help to open up more opportunities in China for favoured Hong Kong business associates. One marriage to watch will be CITIC and CLP in the power sector. Another very public one is CITIC and Swire in the property sector. And mainland firms will continue to contribute to the ongoing expansion of the stock market through the listing of new firms and the injection of new assets, such as state-owned infrastructure or industrial facilities, into existing red chips (often at a discount to their real value). Through this partial privatisation of state assets, investors should gain access to a steady supply of new and higher quality China stocks.

The money of Hong Kong's Chinese tycoons is also increasingly China-bound. A 1996 study by a British stockbroker produced some interesting comparisons of the China-related earnings in that year and 2000 of Hong Kong's 40 most liquid publicly listed companies. While the average change over the five years was not that dramatic— from 4% of total 1996 earnings to 11% in 2000—the picture for Hong Kong Chinese property companies was. New World, a property developer-cum-infrastructure conglomerate that is probably Hong Kong's biggest investor in China, should see its China earnings rise from 13% of 1996 profit to 40% in 2000, according to Kleinwort Benson, the brokerage house which produced the report. Likewise, Li Ka-shing's Cheung Kong will go from 5% to 25%, and Lee Shau-kee's Henderson Land from 4% to 30%.

It is interesting to contrast this definite progression with the mixed outlook for Hong Kong-based (but not local Chinese) firms in other sectors. HongkongBank's China-related earnings in the year 2000 will account for only 3% of its total profit, compared with 2% in 1996 (though this would reflect less its nationality than its wider regional and international spread than most Hong Kong companies, as well as the tight restrictions on foreign involvement in China's banking sector). CLP, the power company, could do somewhat better, increasing its share from 1% to 5%. And mainland Chinese conglomerates like CITIC and Guangdong Investment may not see any big change because of the already high contribution of China earnings to their current profits, according to Kleinwort Benson's projections. While these estimates could of course turn out to be wrong, their value is in highlighting the trends in the market.

Emphasising only the quantitative aspects of economic activity, as politically correct argument in future is bound to, fails however to give proper weight to qualitative questions. What will China bring to the economic management of Hong Kong that the colony doesn't already have? It is truly hard to think of anything. Hong Kong's strength as a business base has always had as much to do with its separation from China, as with whatever was happening (or not happening) in China. Thus when productivity in China was suffering under the Maoist yoke, Hong Kong was able to follow a different development path and take over from Shanghai as the pre-eminent financial and trading centre on the China coast. When China began to reform its economy, Hong Kong took advantage of the momentous change and, with its open and distinct financial system, became the largest conduit for foreign direct investment and syndicated loans flowing into China. To argue that the Basic Law promises to maintain this separate status adds nothing to China's score, since the status quo would have been maintained in any case had reunification not been taking place.

But reunion will change the status quo. At the very least, the new sovereign will bring its own values and priorities to the governance of its newly acquired territory (as any new ruler would). This means that the potential for a dilution of Hong Kong's uniqueness will always remain high. There may be no change in the first year or two after 1997, but that will prove little. What matters is whether or not Hong Kong can maintain its special economic identity five, ten years hence *in its entirety*.

The argument of the last two chapters is that it cannot—and that the business environment in the colony will deteriorate as a result. Apart from the basic fact of the change in sovereignty, the ongoing expansion of mainland business interests in Hong Kong after 1997, and the need to deal increasingly with Guangdong province on economic and social issues, is bound to result in the importation of different attitudes towards law, corruption, and government; and conservative notions about economic competition. The net result will not be economic ignominy (there will still be money to be made), rather a commercial hybrid that is noticeably different from today's. Mainland firms and mainlanders have been guests in Hong Kong over the past 20 years and have worked hard to keep a low profile. From 1997 onwards, they will be doing business in an integral part of China. Many will feel like kings of the castle. The more brash will act so. To expect all of this to have no effect on the colony's business culture is asking too much.

EPILOGUE: WORKING WITHIN THE SYSTEM

Three decades after the Second World War Hong Kong still accepted that it could not develop a democratic political system because the People's Republic of China would not allow it. The late Richard Hughes, the famous foreign correspondent, did not mince his words in 1975: 'Hong Kong persists—on borrowed soil and borrowed time—because it *is* China, and because its affects no suicidal pretences of "democracy" or independence.'

Ten years later, Hong Kong did start to experiment with democracy, albeit of a strange colonial sort (the narrowly cast and mostly elitist functional constituency elections). Another six years on and the first open elections were introduced—though only for a portion of seats.

Did these changes prove Hughes wrong? Was China in fact becoming tolerant of political change in Hong Kong? Not at all. Because in 1995 Hong Kong went even further and held elections for all seats on the Legislative Council. Although again only a portion were filled by universal suffrage, the electoral rules were rewritten to broaden considerably the franchise for the other seats. Beijing was not amused and, as we have seen, expressed its displeasure by announcing that it would scrap this last pre-1997 legislature and replace it with a provisional body; which it has done.

Hughes' words are still relevant for another reason. Beijing may accept a quasi-democratic process in Hong Kong—the Provisional Legislature, after all, will be replaced by a newly elected body in 1998—but it shows no intention of allowing Western-style democracy (which seems to be what Hughes had in mind). Nor would it con-done, obviously, independence for Hong Kong.

What Beijing will allow is a new electoral system, functioning according to new rules passed by the Provisional Legislature and aimed at weakening political parties in general, the democratic lobby in particular, and keeping the Legislative Council in its 'right-ful place' (subordinate to the executive).

If Beijing gets away with this—which I think it probably will judg-ing by the way in which the democratic camp continues to fragment and shows signs of wanting to cooperate with the new sovereign—then Hong Kong's existence in future will offer poor support to the liberal tenet that advanced economies can only thrive in genuine democracies.

There are several factors which underpin this conservative prognosis:

Hong Kong will remain an 'executive-led' system for at least the next 10 years, if not longer. Almost all political parties accept this constraint, although they have different ideas about how it should evolve (the democratic ones in particular). All parties support reuni-fication. The Democratic Party, Hong Kong's largest pro-democracy organisation and widely considered to be 'anti-Beijing', outwardly recognises the People's Republic of China and its state constitution (despite the fact that it is a one-party state). And most of the demo-cratic parties want Hong Kong delegates to the National People's Congress, China's quasi or 'rubber stamp' parliament, to be elected by universal suffrage—another sign of their willingness to legitimise the one-party system and to work within it.

At the same time, no one in the anti-Beijing camp is willing to push political principles to the point of causing an economic down-turn. None of Hong Kong's democrats are revolutionaries (it would be quite surprising if they were). Many have a significant stake in the status quo—those who are highly paid professionals. Others want to see the current system reformed, not destroyed—like the grassroots democrats—and are pragmatic enough to realise that a damaged economy would be of little benefit to their constituents. Meanwhile, surveys and commonsense show that a lot of people are quite opti-mistic about the future of the economy *despite* their pessimism over political freedoms. And business is positively buoyant about their prospects, and that of the economy overall, in future.

This is a less exciting description of politics in Hong Kong than the black and white one of popular mythology. It is a story in which the 'heroes' (the democrats) compromise because they have no other choice. They are facing a vastly superior force and are cornered. Discipline in their own ranks is weakening. Some want to fly the white flag, but don't dare to yet lest they be called cowards and turncoats. It is not a story in which every person fights to the last.

Hong Kong is too rich for heroics.

APPENDIX 1: HANDOVER-PREPARATION COMMITTEES

BEIJING'S UNITED FRONT AND HANDOVER-PREPARATION COMMITTEES IN HONG KONG, 1992–97

(Arranged in chronological order, with starting date in brackets)

HONG KONG AFFAIRS ADVISERS (1992)

- Not envisaged by the Basic Law.
- Four groups of advisers totalling 186 people were appointed between March 1992 and April 1995, each with a two-year term.

A mixed group of prominent and pro-Beijing business leaders, politicians, professionals, academics, unionists, former civil servants and community leaders chosen to advise the Chinese government on Hong Kong affairs. The rationale for appointing advisers was to strengthen the mechanism for soliciting Hong Kong people's views during the transition to Chinese rule. To dampen alarm among the Hong Kong public and government that the advisors would become a second power centre alongside the British administration, Beijing kept their tasks deliberately vague. None of the four groups had a formal structure or terms of reference, although they did hold meetings (but with no agenda). Even the term 'advisor' was selected because of its neutrality.

Yet this group did become—along with Hong Kong delegates to the National People's Congress and the Chinese People's Political Consultative Conference—the core from which Beijing chose the bulk of its appointees to subsequent committees, most of which did operate as shadow governments in various ways.

(Note: A further 537 people were appointed by Beijing over the same period as District Affairs Advisers. A lesser order honour, the job of these people was to advise Beijing on community affairs.)

THE PRELIMINARY WORKING COMMITTEE (1993)

- Not envisaged by the Basic Law.
- Formed in July 1993 and wound-up in December 1995.
- 69 members, of which around two thirds were from Hong Kong; the remainder were senior mainland officials.

Ostensibly formed in reaction to Governor Chris Patten's political reforms, the Preliminary Working Committee's task was to examine political, economic, legal, cultural and social/security issues and developments during the final years of British rule, to decide whether or not they complied with the Basic Law and, if they did not, to offer suggestions to Beijing on a course of action. In essence, its role was to lay the legal and policy groundwork for a larger and more important transitional body—the Preparatory Committee (see below).

As its name implied, the Preliminary Working Committee did a lot of work. It covered a range of transitional matters such as how to set up the first post-reunification government, how to manage the 'tainted' civil service, what the structure of the future electoral system should look like, and how China's Nationality Law should be applied to Hong Kong (since China does not allow dual nationality, residency rules had to change). The committee also cast an antagonistic eye over Hong Kong's expanded civil and political rights, legislative amendments that had occurred as a result of the Bill of Rights, and a raft of ongoing economic issues. It produced several dozen proposals, many of which became highly controversial because they put Hong Kong's interests firmly below those of Beijing. Indeed, the committee was highly unpopular in Hong Kong.

Of the 69 members on the committee, 26 were from China and the other 43 represented Hong Kong (although the committee initially had 56 members, with 23 from China and 33 from the colony). As was typical of such a committee, however, a few of the 'Hong Kong' members were actually officials working in the local branch of the New China News Agency.

Most of the mainland Chinese members were officials based in Beijing. The committee was chaired by Qian Qichen, China's foreign minister, and counted among its vice-chairmen people like Lu Ping (director of the State Council Hong Kong and Macau Affairs Office) and Zhou Nan (director of the Hong Kong branch of the New China News Agency).

Other mainland members included more people from the Ministry of Foreign Affairs and the Hong Kong and Macau Affairs Office, as well as senior members of the National People's Congress, the United Front Work Department (which falls under the Party), the Ministry of Foreign Trade and Economic Cooperation, the Ministry of Public Security, the Law Faculty of Beijing University, the People's Bank of China, the Bank of China, and the People's Liberation Army. In other words, a good cross section of the Party and government units which have a stake in Hong Kong.

The most senior Hong Kong members were Henry Fok (entrepreneur and property tycoon) and T. K Ann (retired industrialist), both of whom later played leading roles in the Preparatory Committee (see below).

Other prominent local members included Tsang Yok-sing (chairman of the Democratic Alliance for the Betterment of Hong Kong), Maria Tam (chairman of the Liberal Democratic Federation), Li Ka-shing (chairman of Cheung Kong), David Li (chairman of the Bank of East Asia), Rita Fan (former Executive Councillor under Governor David Wilson who went on to become a vocal proponent of Beijing's views) and T S Lo (solicitor, founder of *Window* magazine and the New Hong Kong Alliance, and a one-time chief executive hopeful).

(Note: Qian Qichen chaired the committee because the Ministry of Foreign Affairs is one of two Chinese central government bodies with primary responsibility for reunification matters. It carries out this work through its Hong Kong and Macau Office.)

The other body has a similar title: the State Council Hong Kong and Macau Affairs Office. Its current director is Lu Ping, a former journalist who was close to Liao Chengzhi, the first director of the office and a specialist on reunification matters.

The difference between the two offices is that the former, logically, looks after foreign affairs issues arising from the transfer of sovereignty, while the latter has broader responsibility for policy-making, coordination of reunification matters (including jointly handling foreign affairs matters with the other office), management of Hong Kong's interaction with units of government in China, and research into political, economic, cultural and social trends in Hong Kong.

Although Lu's office is ranked on the same level as a ministry, he is junior to Qian both in terms of his formal rank and authority status. In addition to being a minister, Qian is also a vice-premier, of which there are only six on the State Council. Other vice-premiers mentioned in this book include Zhu Rongji, Li Lanqing, Wu Bangguo and Jiang Chunyun. The premier is, of course, Li Peng.

(For a more detailed examination of the roles of these two bodies see: John P Burns, 'The Role of the New China News Agency and China's Policy Towards Hong Kong', in *Hong Kong and China in Transition*, Canada and Hong Kong Papers No 3, Joint Centre for Asia Pacific Studies, Toronto, 1994.)

THE PREPARATORY COMMITTEE (1996)

- Envisaged by the Basic Law.

- Membership announced in late December 1995 and officially launched in January 1996.
- No set completion date (will be either the second half of 1997 or mid-1998).
- 150 members.

The Preparatory Committee's role was to prepare the establishment of the first legislature and first government of the Special Administrative Region. Its original terms of reference under the Basic Law were vague and seemingly narrow: its only tasks were to set up the Selection Committee (see below) and to confirm whether or not members of the last Legislative Council before the handover could join the first legislature afterwards (the 'through train' model). The constitution also implied that the Preparatory Committee would oversee the work of the Selection Committee and should organise elections for a new two-year legislature if the 'through train' was not permitted. (These terms were laid down in a decision taken by the National People's Congress in April 1990 and attached to the Basic Law.)

But following the establishment of the Preliminary Working Committee in 1993—and its comprehensive examination of political, economic, legal and social issues—it became apparent that the Preparatory Committee's scope of work would be broad not narrow. Thus between January 1996 and February 1997, for example, the committee met eight times and held 31 sub-committee meetings. It completed the following tasks (with the help of a full-time secretariat based in Hong Kong):

- March 1996: endorsed the Preliminary Working Committee's controversial 1994 suggestion for a provisional legislature.
- August–November 1996: organised the formation of the 400-person Selection Committee. It 'elected' the latter in November 1996.
- December 1996: oversaw the election (by the Selection Committee) of the first chief executive (Tung Chee-hwa) and the Provisional Legislature.
- February 1997: reaffirmed that the chief executive and the Provisional Legislature could legally begin preparatory work for the Special Administrative Region before July 1997.
- Examined Hong Kong's existing laws with a view to seeing which were inconsistent with the Basic Law (basing its work on the proposals of the Preliminary Working Committee). In February 1997 it suggested to the National People's Congress that 25 laws should be repealed or amended. The list included the Bill of Rights (1991), and two laws expanding political freedoms (the Public Order and Societies Ordinances).
- Made suggestions on various economic issues affected by the transfer of sovereignty, including the 1997/98 handover budget.

- Set up a committee to coordinate activities celebrating the transfer of sovereignty.

The legal basis for this expansion of responsibility, according to Beijing, lay in the 1990 National People's Congress decision. This said the Preparatory Committee was 'responsible for preparing the establishment of the Hong Kong Special Administrative Region *and related matters*, and for prescribing the specific method for the formation of the first government and the first legislature (in accordance with this decision)' (italics added). The decision on the Provisional Legislature and the other additional tasks were said to be 'related matters', hence were legal. However, the official English translation did not contain the phrase 'related matters'.

Yet even the English version of the 1990 decision seems to allow for some flexibility in the Preparatory Committee's terms of reference. The clause stating that the committee shall prescribe the 'specific method for the formation of the first government and the first legislature (in accordance with this decision)' could be read to imply a broader scope of work than merely choosing the Selection Committee and managing the 'through train' or new elections. But it would be stretching the point to say it condoned a one-year interim legislature, because the phrase 'in accordance with this decision' meant that the Preparatory Committee should have limited itself to the options before it (ie, the 'through train' or new elections for a two-year legislature).

Of the 150 members on the committee, 94 were from Hong Kong and the remainder from China. Once again, Qian Qichen, China's foreign minister, chaired the body; and Lu Ping and Zhou Nan were among the four Chinese vice-chairmen (see similarities above in the section on the Preliminary Working Committee). But the difference with the mainland membership on this committee was the way in which it expanded beyond Beijing and included a heavier united front representation.

As expected, there were numerous high-ranking officials from the Ministry of Foreign Affairs, the State Council Hong Kong and Macau Affairs Office, and the Joint Liaison Group.

There were also representatives of various economic ministries, agencies or corporations such as: the People's Bank of China; the Bank of China; the State Planning Commission; the State Economic and Trade Commission; the Ministry of Foreign Trade and Economic Cooperation; China Merchants (the shipping and property conglomerate); the State Council Special Economic Zones Office; and the Finance Ministry.

Some security organs: the People's Liberation Army; the Ministry of Public Security; and the Ministry of State Security.

But also national united front bodies: the United Front Work Department of the Communist Party's central committee; the Association for

Relations Across the Taiwan Strait; and the State Council Overseas Chinese Affairs Office.

And some provincial or city leaders from: the Shenzhen Communist Party committee; the Guangdong people's congress; and the Beijing Communist Party committee.

This is an even more comprehensive description of who Hong Kong will be dealing with in the Chinese government after reunification.

Meanwhile, Hong Kong contributed five vice-chairmen: T. K Ann (retired industrialist), Henry Fok (entrepreneur and property tycoon), Simon Li (retired judge), Tung Chee-hwa (shipping tycoon and soon-to-be first chief executive) and Leung Chun-ying (property surveyor).

A large proportion of the other Hong Kong members were businessmen (and a few women); and the rest were professionals, politicians, and representatives of grassroots, religious, social work and rural organisations.

It was a highly predictable line-up, drawn as it was from people previously appointed as Hong Kong Affairs Advisers, Preliminary Working Committee members, or delegates to the National People's Congress and the Chinese People's Political Consultative Conference.

What was most interesting about the Hong Kong group was the preference shown to certain conservative and electorally insignificant pro-Beijing political parties, namely the Hong Kong Progressive Alliance, the Liberal Democratic Federation, and the New Hong Kong Alliance. All received one or two more seats than the more moderate and popular Democratic Alliance for the Betterment of Hong Kong. This was an attempt by Beijing to balance the strength of its forces and set a conservative tone.

The Preparatory Committee will either wind up its work soon after 1 July 1997 or will continue on and oversee the elections for a new two-year legislature in mid-1998 (scheduled to take over from the Provisional Legislature). Although it has long been assumed that the committee would keep meeting until 1998, some members believe that this is unnecessary since the first Special Administrative Region government will undertake the task of drafting new electoral legislation and will organise the next elections in any case (leaving the Preparatory Committee with little to do, in theory).

THE SELECTION COMMITTEE (1996)

- Envisaged by the Basic Law (but tasks expanded).
- Chosen in November 1996 by the Preparatory Committee.
- No set completion date (could continue until 1998).
- 400 members.

According to the Basic Law, the Selection Committee had just one task: to choose the chief executive (which it did on 11 December 1996). But it was given another by Beijing: to choose the Provisional Legislature (it did this on 21 December 1996). And it may get a couple more: to elect the ten-person election committee for the new legislature in mid-1998; and to choose the Hong Kong delegates for the next five-year National People's Congress (the 9th), starting in March 1998. (But no decisions had been taken by the time this book went to press.)

The original logic for the Selection Committee was that a broadly representative body of Hong Kong people should choose the first chief executive. Because these 400 people were to be drawn equally from business, the professions, labour/grassroots, and a category including 'former political figures' and delegates to the National People's Congress or the Chinese People's Political Consultative Conference, Beijing could then argue (as it eventually did) that the process was far more democratic than the way in which the British had chosen its governors.

Many democrats and liberals in Hong Kong begged to differ: they charged that the Selection Committee would be dominated by the pro-Beijing lobby, which in turn would vote for a favoured chief-executive candidate (namely Tung Chee-hwa). To win nomination as a candidate, a person had to secure the backing of 50 members of the committee. But this effectively limited the choice to people who were acceptable to Beijing: no democrat like Martin Lee or Szeto Wah could possibly have gained the requisite 50 names. Which was why the process was often referred to by critics as a 'small-circle election'.

After a first round of voting designed to weed out non-contenders among the requisite eight candidates, three people made it to the second round: Tung Chee-hwa; T L Yang, the former chief justice; and Peter Woo, chairman of Wharf Holdings, a property and services conglomerate. Tung eventually won the post of chief executive with an even greater than expected 320 of the 400 votes—fairly strong confirmation that the process was heavily tilted in his favour after all. Tung has often claimed since that he had to 'win over' the members of the Selection Committee—that it was not merely a foregone conclusion. Though it may be true that some the 320 votes he won were due to his charm and persuasiveness, it was not a coincidence that the man constantly tipped by the press as Beijing's favourite since at least mid-1996 won such a resounding victory.

The Democratic Party and independent democratic legislators also refused to join the Selection Committee because its other task was to choose the Provisional Legislature—a body which they considered to illegal.

How was the Selection Committee itself chosen? First, the Preparatory Committee called for nominations from the public in August–September 1996. This resulted in 5791 names going forward: 3112 from the grassroots sector; 1265 from business and finance; 1176 from the professional sector; and 147 from the 'former politicians' category. Almost 100 people were disqualified because they did not fill in their forms correctly, while a few said they would not vote for the Provisional Legislature (which accounts for a discrepancy between the total number of applications and the sectoral breakdown).

Second, the members of the Preparatory Committee were asked to comment on the long list and choose 340 names each (the other 60 being guaranteed seats for the delegates to the National People's Congress and the Chinese People's Political Consultative Conference). Third, the chairman and vice-chairmen of the Preparatory Committee produced a shortlist of 408 people. Fourth, the full Preparatory Committee then voted on this list to produce a final cast of 340. The whole process was completed by November 1996.

The main point to notice was the powerful role given to the chairman and vice-chairmen in producing the shortlist. This guaranteed that the majority of people on the Selection Committee would be acceptable to Beijing.

THE PROVISIONAL LEGISLATURE (1997)

- Not envisaged by the Basic Law.
- 'Elected' on 21 December 1996 by the Selection Committee.
- Held its first meeting in January 1997. Cannot run beyond mid-1998.
- 60 seats (same as the normal Legislative Council).

Formed by Beijing to replace Hong Kong's last pre-reunification Legislative Council. Since the latter was elected in 1995, it should have gone on to complete its four-year term in 1999. But because it was elected under a new and more democratic voting system championed by Governor Chris Patten, Beijing decided to disband it (as well as the elected municipal councils and district boards). The decision was taken by the standing committee of the National People's Congress on 31 August 1994. A week later a sub-group of the then Preliminary Working Committee suggested, with surprising speed, that an interim legislature be set up around the time of the handover. In March 1996 the Preparatory Committee voted almost unanimously to accept the Working Committee's proposal (the one dissenting vote was from Frederick Fung, chairman of the Association for Democracy and People's Livelihood). The Provisional Legislature was then 'elected' in December 1996 by the Selection Committee.

The arguments for the Provisional Legislature were:

- Hong Kong would suffer a temporary 'legal vacuum' after 1 July 1997 if no legislature was in place. Laws needed to be passed establishing the Special Administrative Region immediately.
- The Preparatory Committee could not organise new elections *before* 1 July because tensions between China and Britain over political reform ruled out cooperation.

- The Preparatory Committee could not wait *until* 1 July to organise elections because that would contribute to the 'legal vacuum' dilemma.
- Other options were ruled out as being in conflict with Hong Kong's promised autonomy and the Basic Law. They included allowing the National People's Congress or the first chief executive to assume legislative responsibility for Hong Kong for a short period.

The arguments against the Provisional Legislature were:

- It was patently illegal under any sensible reading of the Basic Law.
- The 'legal vacuum' argument was an exaggeration: the treaty and constitutional foundations for the Special Administrative Region already existed (the Joint Declaration and the Basic Law) and the colony had plenty of existing laws that the new government could use to justify its actions in the first few months after the handover.
- From both a legal and logistical point of view, the Preparatory Committee could arrange for new elections to be held within three months after 1 July. Article 70 of the Basic Law says that if the chief executive dissolves the legislature for whatever reason, then it must be 'reconstituted by election' within three months. Meanwhile, if the Hong Kong government knew before 1 July that the Preparatory Committee wanted new elections soon after, then it could have begun preparations.
- The legislature would be dominated by pro-Beijing politicians.
- The legislature would pass many new laws or legislative amendments that would significantly limit the civil liberties of Hong Kong people and undermine their promised 'high degree of autonomy'.

Many of these fears are coming true. There are no democrats on the legislature (they refused to join because of the body's illegality and because they could never have gained more than a few token seats). And it is planning to repeal or amend 25 laws which the Preparatory Committee and Beijing believe to be in conflict with the Basic Law (many of these changes will affect civil liberties, as well as the structure of the future Legislative Council and the method of its election).

The membership of the Provisional Legislature (by political party) is:

- Democratic Alliance for the Betterment of Hong Kong (10 seats)
- Liberal Party (10 seats)
- Hong Kong Progressive Alliance (5 seats)
- Association for Democracy and People's Livelihood (4 seats)
- Liberal Democratic Federation (3 seats)
- Federation of Trade Unions (1 seat)
- Independents, small parties (27 seats)

(See Appendix 2 for a full description of each party.)

The extremely limited nature of the legislature's representativeness was reflected in the fact that it elevated from the political second division a number of politicians who had failed at the Legislative Council elections in 1995. They were: Peggy Lam, Elsie Tu (née Eliot), Lau Kong-wah, Wong Siu-yee, Tang Siu-tong, Raymond Ho, Ho Sai-chu and the entire senior leadership of the Democratic Alliance for Betterment of Hong Kong (Tsang Yok-sing, Cheng Kai-nam and Tam Yiu-chung). The legislature also helped to resurrect the legislative careers of several famous names from the 1980s: Rita Fan, Hui Yin-fat and Maria Tam.

The Provisional Legislature began preparing for its post-handover role in January 1997. It held meetings in Shenzhen before July, because the Hong Kong government refused to allow it to meet in Hong Kong. And it had to hold them on weekends so as not to clash with the existing Legislative Council (which 33 provisional councillors were still members of). It will cease to function in mid-1998, when a new two-year Legislative Council will take its place.

APPENDIX 2: POLITICAL PARTIES

MAJOR POLITICAL PARTIES, GROUPS AND COALITIONS IN HONG KONG, 1997

This appendix is arranged alphabetically. The organisations included are:
- 123 Democratic Alliance
- Association for Democracy and People's Livelihood (ADPL)
- Citizens Party (Minchuandang)
- Democratic Alliance for the Betterment of Hong Kong (DAB)
- Democratic Party
- Frontier
- Hong Kong Alliance in Support of the Patriotic Democratic
- Movement in China
- Hong Kong Progressive Alliance
- Liberal Democratic Federation
- Liberal Party

The criteria for inclusion are:
- Parties which won at least one seat in the Legislative Council elections of 1995 through a competitive election (some seats were uncontested).

And/or
- Political prominence.

Organisations not covered include:
- Major umbrella trade unions with a political presence, namely the pro-democracy Confederation of Trade Unions (CTU) and the pro-Beijing Federation of Trade Unions (FTU).
- Minor political parties that contested the 1995 elections but failed to win a seat (the pro-democracy United Ants and the pro-Beijing Civic Force) or which only acquired seats through uncontested functional constituency elections (the pro-Beijing New Hong Kong Alliance).

Recurring themes

Constraints created by Hong Kong's political vulnerability, the quasi-democratic nature of its legislature and its entrepreneurial economy have combined to produce many areas of overlap in the objectives of the colony's young political parties and a shared middle-of-the-road outlook on social issues.

Recurring themes found in party manifestos include:

- Support for China's resumption of sovereignty over Hong Kong and the full implementation of the Joint Declaration and Basic Law.
- Belief in 'one country, two systems', 'Hong Kong people ruling Hong Kong' and 'a high degree of autonomy'.
- Endorsement of Hong Kong's open and entrepreneurial economy.
- Emphasis on improving people's social and living conditions.
- Protecting Hong Kong's rights and freedoms.
- The further democratisation of the Legislative Council and the need for more open and participatory government. Yet, somewhat contradictorily:
- Acceptance of, or support for, the current executive-led system of government.

The parties are normally distinguished by labels such as pro-Beijing or anti-Beijing (or pro-China and anti-China), and pro-democracy or pro-business.

None of these contrasts is entirely satisfactory because they are either misleading or incomplete. For example, the label 'anti-China' is often applied to the Democratic Party. While this party is definitely opposed to the Communist Party's manner of ruling China–hence can be called 'anti-Beijing'—it is certainly not against the Chinese nation or is unpatriotic. Quite the opposite is true. Similarly, some pro-business groups express support (albeit of a mild sort) for democratic development; while all democratic parties basically endorse Hong Kong's current economic system. Yet the value of the labels is that they do point to differences among the parties in political ideology, emphasis, and the timing of reforms.

Factors which distinguish the parties from one another include:

- The extent to which they cooperate with China (are they part of the united front or not?).
- Their policy on the speed and nature of democratic reform.
- Their definition of democracy.
- Their degree of commitment to civil liberties.
- Their emphasis on social policy and the improvement of living conditions.

- Whether or not they accept the Basic Law as it is or want to see it amended as soon as possible.
- Their view on the relationship between the executive and the legislature (one party, the Citizens Party, thinks elected legislators should ultimately run the Hong Kong government–a radical view for what is still very much a colonial political system).

What's in a name?

The names chosen by political parties in Hong Kong may be confusing to readers outside the colony. Here are some general rules:

1. The word 'liberal' is only used by pro-business parties. It therefore means 'conservative'.
2. The word 'democratic' is so widely used that it needs to be read with care.
3. The word 'progressive' is used only by one pro-Beijing group, so should also be approached circumspectly.
4. The more unusual names—123 Democratic Alliance, Citizens Party, and The Frontier—all belong to genuine pro-democracy parties.

Usage

Common English versions of some party names differs slightly from their official translation. This is due to the non-standard English used for some of these translations.

For example, the official name of the Hong Kong Alliance in Support of the Patriotic Democratic Movement in China is the 'Hong Kong Alliance in Support of Patriotic Democratic Movements of China'.

This book uses the common versions, as they are the more widely known and easily read. However, a note is included in this glossary where a difference exists.

123 DEMOCRATIC ALLIANCE

(Should be read as 1, 2, 3... not one hundred and twenty-three.)

1. **Orientation:**   Pro-democracy, close links to Taiwan
    Part of China's united front?   No
    Pre-1997 Legislative Council strength: 1 seat
    Provisional Legislature strength: Nil
    Chairman: Yum Sing-ling
    Vice-chairman: Ng Wai-cho (resigned after joining the Taiwanese parliament)*
    When founded: March 1994
    History: Founders were Hong Kong Chinese who had studied in Taiwan
    Number of members: 200

* The party was about to elect a new vice-chairman as this book went to press (early May 1997).

2. Manifesto/platform: A reformist, nationalist agenda. The essence of the party's platform is found in its name. '1' refers to its support for the peaceful reunification (and democratisation) of China. '2' to its goal of promoting sincere exchanges between both sides of the Taiwan Strait (ie, China and Taiwan). And '3' to protecting and enhancing the mutual prosperity of the three places (Hong Kong, Taiwan, and China).

123 Democratic Alliance prides itself on being the only political party in Hong Kong that is concerned with issues affecting the whole of China. It believes most other parties are largely parochial.

On the issue of political reform, it supports the election of all 60 seats on the Legislative Council by universal suffrage.

3. **Address:**   Block D, 1/F, Lee Kwan Building
                    40 Argyle Street
                    Kowloon, Hong Kong
    Tel: 23911330
    Fax: 23800884
    Email: hk123da@interasia.com.hk
    Website: www.hk123da.org.hk

ASSOCIATION FOR DEMOCRACY AND PEOPLE'S LIVELIHOOD (ADPL)

1. **Orientation:**   Grassroots emphasis; pro-democracy (not aggressive)
    Part of China's united front?   Yes
    Pre-1997 Legislative Council strength: 4 seats
    Provisional Legislature strength: 4 seats
    Chairman: Frederick Fung
    Vice-chairmen: Law Cheung-kwok
                   Bruce Liu
                   Yim Chee-sung
    When founded: 1986
    History: Began as a political pressure group
    Number of members: 100

2. **Manifesto/platform:**   A reformist agenda focused on 'improving people's livelihood', 'propagating democracy', and upholding human rights. Supports Hong Kong's free-market economy, but believes the government should build an effective social security system and devote itself to improving living conditions, especially for the poorer members of society. Differentiates itself from the Democratic Party by this grassroots focus (whereas it sees the larger party as more oriented towards professionals and the 'middle class').

On political reform, supports the election of the chief executive and all 60 seats on the Legislative Council by universal suffrage. And believes the government should operate more openly. (Despite its commitment to democracy, though, the party joined the Preparatory Committee and the Provisional Legislature, and thus contributed to the demise of the pre-1997 democratically elected legislature. Other democrats are extremely critical of the party's contradictory stance, saying it is not sincere about its political beliefs. The ADPL, meanwhile, says it can do more for its grassroots constituency 'inside' the political process than outside it.)

Supports the 'peaceful and democratic reunification' of all China (including Taiwan as well as Hong Kong).

3. **Address:**   Room 1104, Sunbeam Commercial Building
                469–471 Nathan Road
                Kowloon, Hong Kong
    Tel: 27822699
    Fax: 27823134
    Email: None
    Website: Ready by October 1997

Citizens Party (Minchuandang)

(This party was being formed as this book went to press.)

1. **Orientation:**   Pro-democracy; emphasis on citizenship
    Part of China's united front?   No
    Pre-1997 Legislative Council strength: Nil (not yet formed)
    Provisional Legislature strength: Nil
    Chair: Christine Loh
    Vice-chair: To be elected in the latter half of 1997
    When founded: 4 May 1997*
    History: Loh was an independent legislator in the last Legislative
          Council before the handover
    Number of members: 14 founding members

*The date May 4th has tremendous significance in the history of China's early democratic movement. On that day in 1919 students protested in Beijing's Tiananmen Square against China's unfair treatment under the Treaty of Versailles (which concluded the first world war). The protests marked the beginning of a period of cultural and political awakening among Chinese intellectuals—which has since been known as the 'May 4th Movement'.

2. **Manifesto/platform:**   A reformist agenda. Emphasises 'people' and the rights of citizenship, particularly the right to participate in government decision making (which should be open and accountable). Hence, argues that Hong Kong's political system should allow for elected legislators to 'be responsible for policy direction'. Loh says her party 'aspires to govern'.

    Strong emphasis also on merging environmental imperatives into economic policy (though advocates no essential change to Hong Kong's economic structure). Believes in the need for sharper and more people-oriented social policies (education, housing, health, etc). Thinks health-care investment, for example, is too focussed on 'the current expensive, curative hospital-based model'; should be aimed more at preventive initiatives. Supports China's 'one country, two systems' principle and wants to promote dialogue with Chinese governmental and non-governmental institutions.

3. **Address:**   GPO Box 784, Hong Kong (temporary)
    Tel: 81007000 (temporary answering service)
    Fax: 28385969
    Email: cloh@hk.net.com
    Website: None yet. One is planned.

(An office and permanent contact details should be ready by July 1997.)

DEMOCRATIC ALLIANCE FOR THE BETTERMENT OF HONG KONG (DAB)

(Official translation: the 'Democratic Alliance for Betterment of Hong Kong'.)

1. **Orientation:** Steadfastly pro-Beijing; grassroots; mildly leftist
   Part of China's united front? Yes
   Pre-1997 Legislative Council strength: 7 seats (with the FTU)
   Provisional Legislature strength: 10 seats
   Chairman: Tsang Yok-sing
   Vice-chairman: Cheng Kai-nam
   When founded: July 1992
   History: Formed with the assistance of the New China News Agency, the public face of the Communist Party in Hong Kong
   Number of members: More than 1000

2. **Manifesto/platform:** A socially-oriented, mildly reformist agenda. Emphasises the need for a smooth transition through 1997 and urges China and Britain to abide by the Joint Declaration and Basic Law. Wants all legislators and the chief executive elected by universal suffrage by the year 2007 (hence supports only a gradual development of democracy).

Emphasises an economic agenda that is largely similar to Hong Kong's current one, although calls for a somewhat more activist and interventionist role from government in certain areas. For example, it should 'restrict the growth rates for prices and fees charged by various public bodies and utilities.' And it should 'provide incentives for the private sector to invest in our workforce' (in areas such as training). On social policy, talks about investing more in education, promoting gender equality in the workforce, ensuring that sales prices of public-housing flats not be dictated by market forces, and implementing a universal old-age pension scheme.

Note: The DAB began revising its platform a few months before the handover. The new platform should be ready soon afterwards.

3. **Address:** 12F, SUP Tower, 83 King's Road
   North Point, Hong Kong
   Tel: 25280136
   Fax: 25284339
   Email: info@dab.org.hk
   Website: www.dab.org.hk

THE DEMOCRATIC PARTY

1. **Orientation:** Strongly pro-democracy
    Part of China's united front? No
    Pre-1997 Legislative Council strength: 19 seats
    Provisional Legislature strength: Nil
    Chairman: Martin Lee*
    Vice-chairmen: Anthony Cheung, Yeung Sum
    When founded: October 1994
    History: Successor to the United Democrats of Hong Kong
    Number of members: 550

*Szeto Wah, a leading figure in the party, is an executive committee member. He is also chairman of the Hong Kong Alliance in Support of Patriotic Democratic Movements of China.

2. **Manifesto/platform:** A reformist agenda, but somewhat unfocused. Begins by stating the party's aim is to 'further unite the democratic forces in Hong Kong' and to pursue 'an open and democratic government' for Hong Kong. But then stresses that 'Hong Kong is an indivisible part of China' (wording which closely parallels the Basic Law and the Chinese state constitution) and, 'We support the return of Hong Kong's sovereignty to China.' (Yet how can Hong Kong enjoy 'democratic government' within the context of the current one-party political system in China?)

Likewise, although the party emphasises its support for direct elections (universal suffrage) for the chief executive, all 60 seats on the Legislative Council and the other tiers of 'representative government' in Hong Kong, it lays down no deadline or schedule as to when this should happen.

On economic policy, it basically supports the status quo. But believes that economic and social development should receive equal attention from the government. And supports a 'reasonable distribution of the fruits of economic growth' and a more flexible use of public finances to improve people's livelihood. Advocates that government should do more in a whole swathe of areas: urban planning, housing, transportation, education, worker training, social security, health care, and so on. Does not appear to have costed its demands.

3. **Address:** 4/F, Hanley House, 776-778 Nathan Road
    Kowloon, Hong Kong
    Tel: 23977033
    Fax: 23978998
    Email: dpweb@dphk.org
    Website: www.dphk.org

THE FRONTIER

1. **Orientation:**   Aggressively pro-democracy
    Part of China's united front?   No
    Pre-1997 Legislative Council strength: Nil (not yet formed)*
    Provisional Legislature strength: Nil
    Spokesperson: Emily Lau
    Convener: Cyd Ho
    When founded: August 1996
    History: Includes some members of the Democratic Party
    Number of members: 130 (+ 30 'friends')

*The Frontier does not consider itself a party, but a political group. It may not field candidates in future elections.

2. **Manifesto/platform:**   Hong Kong's most aggressive manifesto. Rejoices over the end of British rule, but bemoans the 'long shadow (cast) over the historic handover' by Britain and China's 'refusal to respect the wishes of the local people'. Laments that Hong Kong people will not 'finally become masters of their own destiny'. Believes that people have 'the right to (practise) civil disobedience and non-cooperation' when faced with laws which violate their human rights.

Demands the election of the chief executive and all 60 seats on the Legislative Council by universal suffrage. Emphasises the need to fight for human rights, the rule of law and, uniquely among Hong Kong's democrats, the right to *draft* 'our own constitution'. This is because, 'the process for drafting the Basic Law ... was not democratic. The Basic Law has never been subjected to any legitimization process to test its acceptance by the Hong Kong people, hence we do not endorse the drafting process.' (The Democratic Party, in contrast, calls only for the amendment of the Basic Law.)

This is a manifesto that is full of verve, but also sharply contradictory in areas. The Basic Law has not been 'legitimised', yet The Frontier believes in the constitution's key principles, namely 'one country, two systems', etc. The group implies its fundamental opposition to China's 'autocratic' government, yet demands the right to elect Hong Kong delegates to the National People's Congress, an organ of the same (autocratic) state. And so on.

3. **Address:**   Rm 301, Hong Kong House, 17-19 Wellington St
                 Central, Hong Kong
    Tel: 25249899
    Fax: 25245310
    Email: frontier@enmpc.org.hk
    Website: www.frontier.org.hk

HONG KONG ALLIANCE IN SUPPORT OF THE PATRIOTIC DEMOCRATIC MOVEMENT IN CHINA

(Official translation: the 'Hong Kong Alliance in Support of Patriotic Democratic Movements of China'.)

1. **Orientation:** Strongly pro-democracy, China-focused
   Part of China's united front? No
   Pre-1997 Legislative Council strength: Nil*
   Chairman: Szeto Wah
   Vice-chairman: Mak Hoi-wah
   When founded: 21 April 1989 (registered on 15 June 1989)
   History: Formed just a few days after the Tiananmen Square pro-democracy protests began in Beijing
   Number of members: More than 200 groups (no individual members)

*The Alliance does not contest elections and is not a political party as such. It is a coalition which organises rallies and events to promote its cause.

2. **Manifesto/platform:** Aims to promote 'any patriotic democratic movement and the cause of democratic reform' in China; and to 'support and assist students and autonomous student organisations in Beijing or elsewhere'. Will also make donations and subsidise people or organisations promoting the patriotic democratic movement in China.

The emphasis on 'patriotic' is important: though their actions reflect strong opposition to the Communist Party's one-party dictatorship, the members of the alliance maintain a deeply held emotional attachment to the Chinese nation (which they are trying to strengthen through their promotion of democracy). When Tung Chee-hwa was 'campaigning' for the post of chief executive in November 1996, he attacked the alliance's alter ego, the Democratic Party, for always 'objecting to anything Chinese', implying they were unpatriotic and anti-China. A wounded Szeto Wah retorted that Tung should explain what he meant, since the Democrats were not anti-China at all. (The Democratic Party and the alliance share almost the same senior leadership.)

3. **Address:** 9F, Good Hope Building, 618 Nathan Road
   Kowloon, Hong Kong
   Tel: 27826111
   Fax: 27702209/6083
   Email: alliance@alliance.org.hk
   Website: www.alliance.org.hk

THE HONG KONG PROGRESSIVE ALLIANCE

(The Hong Kong Progressive Alliance and The Liberal Democratic Federation announced a merger as this book was going to press.)

1. **Orientation:** Pro-business; strongly pro-Beijing
    Part of China's united front? Yes
    Pre-1997 Legislative Council strength: 2 seats
    Provisional Legislature strength: 5 seats
    Chairman: Ambrose Lau
    Vice-chairmen: Carson Wen
    Loh Daijur
    Yeung Chun-kam
    When founded: July 1994
    Number of members: 200

2. **Manifesto/platform:** A general and conservative agenda. Begins by emphasising the party's support for reunification and a harmonious relationship with China, and for the implementation of the Joint Declaration and Basic Law. Encourages people 'from all walks of life to participate in building a stable, prosperous, democratic and progressive society in Hong Kong'. Talks about cultivating 'civic consciousness' and 'participation in public affairs', and about 'the orderly progress towards a democratic political system'. But does not delve into any detailed discussion of democracy, such as the sort of system Hong Kong should have, the relationship between the Executive and Legislative Councils, or the timing of the 'orderly progress' the party pledges to work for. Unlike the Liberal Party's manifesto, for example, does not state any support for universal suffrage.

    On the economic system, essentially pledges to maintain the status quo. On social policy, says the party shall 'pay close attention to the people's livelihood', then lists things like education, medical services, housing and transport. But lacks any apparent original vision as to how Hong Kong should proceed in these areas. Overall, a strikingly bland and unspecific manifesto.

3. **Address:** 12F, Fung Lok Commercial Building
    157–163 Wing Lok Street
    Sheung Wan, Hong Kong
    Tel: 23773030
    Fax: 23772211
    Email: None
    Website: Ready by the end of May 1997

The Liberal Democratic Federation

(The Liberal Democratic Federation and The Hong Kong Progressive Alliance announced a merger as this book was going to press. The full name of this party is The Liberal Democratic Federation of Hong Kong; but as this is rarely used in the political arena, the shorter version is adopted in this book.)

1. **Orientation:**   Pro-business; strongly pro-Beijing
    Part of China's united front?   Yes
    Pre-1997 Legislative Council strength: 1 seat
    Provisional Legislature strength: 3 seats
    Chairman: Maria Tam
    Vice-chairmen: Chung Pui-lam (executive vice-chairman)
                        David Chu
                        Wong Siu-yee
                        Cheng Chun-ping
                        Tang Po-hong
    When founded: November 1990
    Number of members: 190

2. **Manifesto/platform:**   A very conservative agenda. Initially emphasises *promoting* prosperity and stability in Hong Kong, *implementing* the letter and spirit of the Joint Declaration and Basic Law, and *promoting and maintaining* mutual trust and cooperation between China and Hong Kong. But will only *participate in* the development of Hong Kong's democratic political system and, 'proceeding in a systematic manner', will help to coordinate the (often conflicting) demands of society and economic development. Again stresses the promotion of economic growth, as well as the joint progress of all social classes, and the harmonisation of differing points of view among them. Pledges to ensure the rights and liberties bestowed on Hong Kong by its own laws and international human rights conventions (though with its leading members on the Preparatory Committee and the Provisional Legislature, the party has not been paying much attention to this pledge).

3. **Address:**   2601 Workington Tower
                    78 Bonham Strand East
                    Sheung Wan, Hong Kong
    Tel: 28873661
    Fax: 28063048
    Email: None
    Website: None

THE LIBERAL PARTY

1. **Orientation:**   Pro-business; pro-Beijing (but not always uncritically so)
    Part of China's united front?   Yes
    Pre-1997 Legislative Council strength: 10 seats
    Provisional Legislature strength: 10 seats
    Chairman: Allen Lee
    Deputy chairmen: Ronald Arculli (Legislative Council business)
    Steven Poon (District Affairs)
    When founded: July 1993
    History: Successor to the Cooperative Resources Centre, a secretariat for some pro-business legislators
    Number of members: 500

2. **Manifesto/platform:**   A mostly conservative agenda. Its initial manifesto of 1993, however, is idealistic in part: talks a lot about 'upholding rights and freedoms', and the party's support for 'the rapid democratization of government'. Though its definition of 'rapid' is interesting: the party will 'strive for a wholly democratic government, including a democratically elected chief executive, in Hong Kong within 10 years after 1997'. (A 'democratic government' refers to a fully elected Legislative Council, not a Western-style parliamentary system in which the winning party governs. Indeed, the party expresses strong support for Hong Kong's traditional executive-led government.)

    A later, and shorter, party platform (1996) is even more pragmatic. Emphasises strict implementation of the Basic Law, social harmony, revitalising the economy, and improving people's livelihood. Thus the party slogan is 'Focus on the Economy and Concern for People's Livelihood'. Also states that the party would seek seats on the Provisional Legislature (which is rolling back Hong Kong's democratic development). The platform does not even include the words 'democracy' or 'democratic'. But a recent brochure does briefly refer to 'the systematic (meaning gradual) development of democracy' and Hong Kong's eventual achievement of 'a fully democratic government'. (Once again, this needs to be read in the same conservative context as is outlined above.) Interestingly, the party is the only member of the united front that says while communication with China must be maintained, the interests of Hong Kong should come first.

3. **Address:**   7F, Printing House, 6 Duddell Street
    Central, Hong Kong
    Tel: 28696833
    Fax: 25334288
    Email: liberal@liberal.org.hk
    Website: www.liberal.org.hk

ACKNOWLEDGMENTS

Like other authors, I have a lot of people to thank. And like other books, this acknowledgments page is part an expression of appreciation and part confession. Without further unnecessary chat, my unbounded gratitude goes to:

Helen, for your love, moral support and culinary treats—and for thinking up the title of this book (when I had run dry of ideas)!

John D Young (Yang Yilung), a good friend and an inspiration who encouraged me early on and provided critical comments on the drafts of several chapters (saving me in the process from taking a few potentially disastrous false steps). John died suddenly in a traffic accident in late 1996, thus robbing his friends of a kind soul and the public at large of his wisdom and intellect.

John Allen, my father in Sydney, for assiduously reading every word I wrote and loving all of them! Would every reader be so appreciative. And my mother, Heather, for being with my father.

Bill Barron, one of the most generous people I know, who gave me a rent-free work space for many more months than he should have. My belated apologies for those times when I really did get underfoot.

Gary Chapman (in Vancouver), for hounding me to 'get it right' and for the thousands of email messages with pieces of information and comments. One feels honoured when someone else takes such an interest in your work.

Jack Scott (also in Vancouver), for reading the entire manuscript along with Gary.

Dominic Ziegler and Oliver Jones, for casting sharp eyes over some long-winded early chapters.

Gracia Wong, librarian at the *South China Morning Post*, and Connie Mak, information resources administrator at the Economist Intelligence Unit in Hong Kong—a million thanks for allowing me to use your excellent libraries.

Joyce Nip and Susan Fong, for help with translations.

Joyce Nip, Paul Markillie and John Ure, for miscellaneous slabs of information.

The many people I interviewed or who helped in a myriad ways, such as supplying reports, press releases and contact numbers, confirming figures, and so on.

And, Rosemary Peers and Tiffany Hutton (in Sydney), for managing and editing this book with such good humour (can I ever make up for being such a difficult author?).

David Catterall and Margaret Tresidder (in Singapore), for being flexible and forgiving publishers. I couldn't have asked for more.

All mistakes in this book are, of course, my own.

NOTES

Numbers refer to page numbers in the text — where material spans several pages, the first page number is given.

(All translations from the Chinese language materials, except where noted, are my own.)

PROLOGUE: A CHANGING IDENTITY

xx   Bill Clinton on the Joint Declaration: 'Clinton warns Beijing on Hong Kong', *South China Morning Post,* 20 April 1997, p 1.

CHAPTER 1: THE PARTY ISN'T OVER (YET)

4   Army involvement in government and business: Willy Wo-lap Lam, *China After Deng Xiaoping,* PA Professional Consultants Ltd, Hong Kong, 1995, pp 196–201.

7   Guangdong's share of the national exports: *China Statistical Yearbook 1995,* China Statistical Publishing House, Beijing, 1995, p 551.

7   Change in sectoral shares of the economy: *China Statistical Yearbook 1995,* p 32.

7   Change in composition of industrial sector: *China Statistical Yearbook 1995,* p 377.

8   China's intake of food compared to other countries: Vaclav Smil, 'How rich is China?', in the journal *Current History,* September 1993, p 267.

8   Per-capita GNP in US dollar terms: 'How rich is China?', pp 265–6; The Economist Intelligence Unit, *China Country Report,* 3rd Quarter, 1996.

9   Vaclav Smil on purchasing power parity: 'How rich is China?', p 266.

10   Communism is the Party's ultimate goal: Preamble to the Constitution of the Communist Party of China, adopted by the 14th National Party Congress, 18 October 1992.

10   Quintessence of Mao's philosophy: Deng Xiaoping, *Selected Works, Volume 3* (1982–1992), Foreign Languages Press, Beijing, 1994 (English edition), footnote on p 373.

10   Resolution on Mao/seeking truth from facts: Stuart Schram, *Mao Zedong: A Preliminary Reassessment,* The Chinese University Press, Hong Kong, 1983, p 96.

11   Mao on Marxism with Chinese characteristics: *Mao Zedong: A Preliminary Reassessment,* p 35.

11   Mao on experimenting with land contracting: Barry Naughton, 'Deng Xiaoping: The Economist' in David Shambaugh (editor), *Deng Xiaoping, Portrait of a Chinese Statesman,* Clarendon Press, Oxford, 1995, p 88.

12   Mao on 'new bourgeois elements' and material incentives: *Mao Zedong: A Preliminary Reassessment,* pp 59–64.

12   Deng releases China from Maoist dogma: Kenneth Lieberthal, *Governing China: From Revolution Through Reform,* W W Norton & Co, New York, 1995, p 132.

12   Birth of four modernisations: 'Deng Xiaoping: The Economist', p 91.

13   Hua Guofeng on Dazhai and four modernisations: Jonathan D Spence, *The Search for Modern China,* W W Norton & Co, New York, 1991, pp 643–5.

20   China traditionally more decentralised than the Soviet Union: Susan Shirk, *The Political Logic of Economic Reform in China*, University of California Press, Berkeley and Los Angeles, 1993, p 29.

22   State enterprise 'technological innovation' plan: *Sunday Morning Post*, 'Money' section, August 25, 1996, p 4.

23   Mergers of state enterprises in Shanghai: *Far Eastern Economic Review*, May 23, 1996, p 56.

24   Definition of democratic centralism: *Governing China: From Revolution Through Reform*, pp 175–6.

24   Mao on democratic centralism: *Mao Zedong: A Preliminary Reassessment*, p 39.

27   John Burns on the *nomenklatura* system: 'China's *Nomenklatura* System', from the journal *Problems of Communism*, September–October 1987, p 36. (Information on the 1984 *nomenklatura* reforms is largely based on this paper.)

27   Lieberthal on the *nomenklatura* system: *Governing China: From Revolution Through Reform*, p 209.

28   China's 1987 *nomenklatura* reforms: John Burns, 'Chinese Civil Service Reform: The 13th Party Congress Proposals', from the journal *The China Quarterly*, 1989, pp 739–70.

29   The Party's unifying role: *Mao Zedong: A Preliminary Reassessment*, pp 40–1.

30   Total scope of *Nomenklatura* system in 1982: 'China's *Nomenklatura* System', p 46.

CHAPTER 2: PAPER TIGER

40   Hong Kong Transitions Project survey on the Basic Law: Michael DeGolyer, 'Politics, Politicians, and Political Parties' in Donald McMillen & Man Si-wai, *The Other Hong Kong Report 1994*, The Chinese University Press, Hong Kong, p 81.

41   Christine Loh on the Basic Law: *Hong Kong — 'A High Degree of Autonomy' and the Basic Law*, (a self-published pamphlet), September 1995, Hong Kong, p 2.

44   Xiao Weiyun on autonomy: Xiao Weiyun (editor), *Yiguo Liangzhi yu Xianggang Tebie Xingzhengqu Jibenfa* ('One country, two systems' and the Basic Law of the Hong Kong Special Administrative Region), Hong Kong Cultural and Educational Publishers, pp 99–101; also quoted in Loh, *Hong Kong — 'A High Degree of Autonomy'* (1995), p 27.

46   Martin Lee on autonomy: *The New Gazette*, September 1995, p 24.

48   British administration of Hong Kong under Chinese sovereignty: For a full account of Britain's tactics during the 1982–84 negotiations over Hong Kong, see Robert Cottrell, *The End of Hong Kong: The Secret Diplomacy of Imperial Retreat*, John Murray, London, 1993.

48   Deng's reprimand of Thatcher: Deng Xiaoping, 'Our Basic Position of the Question of Hong Kong' (September 24, 1982) in *Selected Works, Volume 3 (1982-1992)*, Foreign Languages Press, Beijing, 1994, p 23.

48   Deng on potentially disruptive forces in Hong Kong: 'Maintain Prosperity and Stability in Hong Kong', *Selected Works, Volume 3*, p 81.

48   Deng on the use of the army in Hong Kong: *Selected Works, Volume 3*, p 83.

49   Deng's talk to retired senior leaders in 1984: 'Speech at the Third Plenary Session of the Central Advisory Commission of the Communist Party of China', *Selected Works, Volume 3*, pp 92–3.

50   Different versions of the Basic Law: For a comprehensive comparison of the three drafts of the Basic Law, see Ming K. Chan & David J. Clark, *The Hong Kong Basic Law: Blueprint for 'Stability and Prosperity' under Chinese Sovereignty?*, Hong Kong University Press, Hong Kong, 1991.

54   Deng's definition of 'one country, two systems': 'One Country, Two Systems', *Selected Works, Volume 3*, p 68.

54   Deng's December 1984 talk with Thatcher: 'China Will Always Keep its Promises', *Selected Works, Volume 3*, p 107.

54   Deng's September 1982 talk with Thatcher: 'Our Basic Position on the Question of Hong Kong', *Selected Works, Volume 3*, p 24.

55   Deng's definition of socialism and capitalism: 'Excerpts from Talks Given in Wuchang, Shenzhen, Zhuhai and Shanghai', *Selected Works, Volume 3*, pp 361–2.

56   Deng on the indispensable precondition: 'China Will Always Keep its Promises', *Selected Works, Volume 3*, p 109.

56   'One country' is the precondition: *Weihu Xianggang Fanrong Wending de Falu Baozhang* (The Legal Guarantees for Safeguarding Hong Kong's Prosperity and Stability), *People's Daily*, 3 April 1997, p 9.

57   *Window* magazine on 'one country': May 31, 1996, pp 34–7.

62   Positive improvement in China's 1982 constitution: Albert H Y Chen, *An Introduction to the Legal System of the People's Republic of China*, Butterworths, Singapore, 1994, pp 51–2.

64   Zhang Junsheng on patriotic journalism: *Zai Xianggang Zhiye Shunlianju he Xianggang Baoye Gonghui lianhe jubande 'Xinwen Yantaohui' kaimulishang de jianghua* (Speech at the opening ceremony of the 'Press Symposium' jointly organised by the Hong Kong Vocational Training Council and the Newspaper Society of Hong Kong), 27 November, 1995.

64   Lu Ping on press freedom and advocacy: *Wen Wei Po*, 3 August 1996, section A, p 1.

65   Party tactics for controlling Hong Kong media: The Hong Kong Journalists Association and Article 19, 'Broken Promises: Freedom of Expression in Hong Kong' (1995 Annual Report), pp 23–32.

66   *People's Daily* on Hong Kong's political system: 'The Legal Guarantees for Safeguarding Hong Kong's Prosperity and Stability'.

CHAPTER 3: THE MAGIC WEAPON

68   Deng on the logic of the united front: Deng Xiaoping, 'The Entire Party Should Attach More Importance to United Front Work', in *Selected Works (1938–1965)*, English edition, Beijing, 1992, p 175.

70   Deng explaining why 'conditions were extremely bad': *Selected Works (1938–1965)*, pp 173–4.

71   Jiusan joke: James D. Seymour, *China's Satellite Parties*, M.E.Sharpe, Inc, New York, 1987, pp 20–1.

72   Foreign business forced to sell assets: Jonathan D. Spence, *The Search for Modern China*, W.W. Norton & Co, New York, 1991, p 534.

72   Spence quote on the 'Five Anti' campaign: *The Search for Modern China*, p 536.

73   Lieberthal on Maoist contradictions: Kenneth Lieberthal, *Governing China: From Revolution through Reform*, W.W. Norton & Co, New York, 1995, pp 72–3.

73   Mao attacks 'closed-doorism': *China's Satellite Parties*, p 9.

74   Deng chides cadres to do more united front work: *Selected Works (1938–1965)*, p 172.

74   Democratic League spokesman on the Communist Party's post-war intentions: *China's Satellite Parties*, p 15.

75   'New Era' united front will remain for a long time: *China's United Front*, Dongbei Teachers' University Press, Changchun, 1988, p 73; quoted in Li Kwok-sing, *A Glossary of Political Terms of the People's Republic of China*, The Chinese University Press, Hong Kong, 1995, pp 452–3. (Translated by Mary Lok.)

75   Deng on patriotism: Deng Xiaoping, *Selected Works, Volume 3 (1982–1992)*, Foreign Languages Press, Beijing, 1994, p 70.

76   Hong Kong's indirect involvement in the united front in late 1940s: *China's Satellite Parties*, pp 14, 19 & 23.

76   Establishment of Hong Kong and Macau Affairs Office kept secret: Robert Cottrell, *The End of Hong Kong: The Secret Diplomacy of Imperial Retreat*, John Murray, London, 1993, p 59.

77   Size of the Communist Party in Hong Kong: Own source.

77   Deng on patriots not needing to support socialism: *Selected Works, Volume 3 (1982–1992)*, pp 70–1.

78   Xu Jiatun on the united front in Hong Kong: *Xu Jiatun Xianggang Huiyilu* (Xu Jia-
       tun's Hong Kong Memoirs), Hong Kong United Daily, Hong Kong, 1993, Part 1,
       pp 119–23.

80   First batch of Hong Kong Affairs Advisers: 'Alarm over China plan on advisers', *South
       China Morning Post* (SCMP), 16 January 1992; 'Beijing's Recruiter', *SCMP,* 2 February
       1992; 'Powerbrokers get their invitations to the party', *SCMP,* 11 March 1992.

83   T.S Lo on dealing with China: Speech to a conference called 'Countdown to 1997',
       organised by the *Far Eastern Economic Review* magazine, 28 June 1996. The speech was
       excerpted in *Window* magazine, 28 June 1996, pp 8–10.

85   Lu Ping defence of S.Y Chung, and the latter's self-defence: *South China Morning Post,*
       7 December 1995, p 1.

85   Akers-Jones defends himself: 'How I can help Hong Kong communicate with China',
       South China Morning Post, 28 March 1993.

85   Akers Jones on provisional legislature: *Newsline,* ATV World (English), 21 July 1996.

86   Simon Li on the Provisional Legislature and public order laws: 'PWC moots stopgap
       "provisional legco"', *Eastern Express,* 6 September 1994; 'Li is laying down the wrong
       kind of law', *South China Morning Post,* 22 October 1994.

86   Simon Li on the Bill of Rights: 'Bill of Rights SAR's responsibility', *South China Morn-
       ing Post,* 26 October 1995, p 2.

87   Former Civil Servants' Association dinner: *South China Morning Post,* 20 September
       1995.

88   Allen Lee quote on Bill of Rights: *Far Eastern Economic Review,* 16 November 1995,
       p 36.

89   Allen Lee quote on democrats' trip to Beijing: *South China Morning Post,* 2 July 1996,
       p 4.

94   'Youth groups of various circles': *Wen Wei Po,* 11 July 1996, p A10.

95   Kowloon Eastern District Association of Various Circles: *Wen Wei Po,* 25 July 1996,
       p A10.

95   Kwun Tong Industry and Commerce Federation: *Wen Wei Po,* 27 July 1996, p A10.

98   Deng on splitting the enemy: *Selected Works (1938-1965),* p 175.

99   Albert Chan on Selection Committee: 'China said wooing HK Democrats over future
       chief', Reuters, 1 August 1996.

100   Qian Qichen on willingness to talk with democrats: *Hong Kong Standard,* 11 August
       1996, p 1.

101   Zhou Nan's comment on dialogue: *South China Morning Post,* 14 August 1996, p 1.

102   Frederick Fung on the 'olive branch': *Hong Kong Standard,* 11 August 1996, p 1. (First
       comment only. Other comments from an interview with the author.)

102   Leung Chun-ying on the duty of the democrats: *South China Morning Post,* 12 August
       1996, p 1.

105   Ronnie Chan's comments: made to the 'Hong Kong Into the 21st Century' confer-
       ence at the Hong Kong Convention and Exhibition Centre, 6 November 1995, organ-
       ised by the *Far Eastern Economic Review* magazine.

105   Hu Fa-kuang on labour legislation: *Window* magazine, 26 July 1996, p 16.

106   A 'complex' relationship: John P Burns, 'The Role of the New China News Agency
       and China's Policy Towards Hong Kong', in *Hong Kong and China in Transition,* Can-
       ada and Hong Kong Papers No 3, Joint Centre for Asia Pacific Studies, Toronto,
       1994, footnote on p 60.

106   Tsang Yok-sing's warning against favouritism: Radio Television Hong Kong, *Letter to
       Hong Kong,* reported in the *South China Morning Post,* 24 June 1996, p 4.

107   Ng Hong-mun on complaints handed to the New China News Agency: *South China
       Morning Post,* 17 March 1995.

108   DAB pledge on provisional legislature: *South China Morning Post,* 20 September 1995.

108   Lieberthal on united front tactics: *Governing China,* p 73.

110   Dorothy Liu on Zhou Nan: *Hong Kong Standard,* 4 April 1995.

110   Dorothy Liu on the Preparatory Committee: *South China Morning Post,* 29 December
       1995, p 1.

Additional background sources

*   One article which provided a very useful basis for this chapter, but was only briefly mentioned in the endnotes, was 'The Role of the New China News Agency and China's Policy Towards Hong Kong' by John P Burns.

*   One reference book which supplied helpful biographical information was *Xianggang Renminglu* (1995 Who's Who in Hong Kong), Cosmos Books, Hong Kong, 1994.

CHAPTER 4: CHANGING TRAINS

115   Wording of amendment to Letters Patent: pointed out by Norman J Miners, 'Constitution and Administration', Chapter 1 in Donald H McMillen & Man Si-wai, *The Other Hong Kong Report 1994*, The Chinese University Press, Hong Kong, 1994, p 1.

115   'Exploit the grey area': Lo Chi-kin, 'From "Through Train" to "Second Stove"', Chapter 2 of Joseph Y S Cheng & Sonny S H Lo, *From Colony to SAR: Hong Kong's Challenges Ahead*, The Chinese University Press, Hong Kong, 1995, p 27.

115   'Hideously complicated': Norman Miners, *The Government and Politics of Hong Kong*, 4th ed, Oxford University Press, Hong Kong, 1986, p 119.

116   National People's Congress decision on disbanding Hong Kong's three-tier system of 'representative' government: *Quanguo Renda Changweihui zuochu jueding* (Decision of the Standing Committee of the National People's Congress), 31 August 1994 (supplied to the author by the Secretariat of the Preparatory Committee, based in Hong Kong).

116   Preparatory Committee establishes the Provisional Legislature: *Quanguo Renmin Daibiaodahui, Xianggang Tebie Xingzhengqu Choubei Weiyuanhui guanyu sheli Xianggang Tebie Xingzhengqu Linshi Lifahui de jueding* (A decision of the Hong Kong SAR Preparatory Committee of the National People's Congress concerning the establishment of the Hong Kong SAR Provisional Legislature), 24 March 1996. (Reprinted in a pamphlet produced by the Secretariat of the Preparatory Committee.)

116   Preparatory Committee reaffirms the Provisional Legislature: *Xianggang Tebie Xingzhengqu Choubei Weiyuanhui guanyu Xianggang Tebie Xingzhengqu Diyiren Xingzheng Zhangguan, Linshi Lifahui zai 1997 nian 6 yue 30 riqian kaizhan gongzuo de jueding* (A decision of the Hong Kong SAR Preparatory Committee concerning the work of the Hong Kong SAR first Chief Executive and Provisional Legislature before 30 June 1997), *People's Daily*, 2 February 1997, p 2.

118   Lo Chi-kin on 'conservative package': *From Colony to SAR*, p 30.

119   Patten's personal stake in Hong Kong democracy: John Walden, 'Democratic brainchild neutered politically', letter to the *South China Morning Post*, 9 April 1997, p 18.

124   Qian Qichen on democracy: 'It's a first for democracy, says Qian', *South China Morning Post*, 16 November 1996, p 3.

125   Tsang Yok-sing on the mission of the Provisional Legislature: 'How to plug the SAR gap', *South China Morning Post*, 1 November 1994.

125   The first task of the Provisional Legislature: *Quanguo Renmin Daibiaodahui Xianggang Tebie Xingzhengqu Choubei Weiyuanhui guanyu sheli Xianggang Tebie Xingzhengqu Linshi Lifahui de jueding* (A decision of the Hong Kong SAR Preparatory Committee of the National People's Congress concerning the establishment of the Hong Kong SAR Provisional Legislature), 24 March 1996, Clause 5.1.

132   Preparatory Committee decides not to repeal New Territories' law: 'Rural chief walks out over inheritance rights', *South China Morning Post*, 2 February 1997, p 1.

134   Yash Ghai on the Provisional Legislature: Yash Ghai, 'Back to Basics: The Provisional Legislature and the Basic Law', *Hong Kong Law Journal*, Volume 25, Part 1, 1995, pp 2–6.

135   *Window* magazine on the Provisional Legislature: 12 April 1996, p 64.

136   *People's Daily* on the Provisional Legislature: 'China firm on legality of legislature', a report in the *South China Morning Post*, 10 May 1996.

136   Provisional Legislature not mentioned by name: *Quanguo Renda Changweihui zuochu jueding* (Decision of the Standing Committee of the National People's Congress), 31 August 1994.

139   Tsang Yok-sing on the Provisional Legislature option: 'How to plug the SAR gap'.

139   Lau Siu-kai's comment: 'Provisional legco (sic) a "necessary evil"', *Eastern Express*, 27 October 1994.

140   Association for Democracy and People's Livelihood on Provisional Legislature: *Manhip gaaikuet Chatnin 'Laapfaat Janhung' dik 'Linglui Jiktungche' Fongon* (The Association's Alternative Through-train Proposal for Solving the Legislative Vacuum in 1997). Issued as a press release in December 1994.

132   New China News Agency on the Bill of Rights: 'China broadside on Patten', *South China Morning Post*, 28 October 1995, p1.

141   Henry Litton attacks the Bill of Rights: *South China Morning Post*, 3 April 1990 & 14 May 1990, 'Analysis' section.

144   Sir Harry Gibbs on rights charters: quoted in Justice Michael Kirby, 'Human rights: The role of the judge', Chapter 10 in Johannes Chan & Yash Ghai (eds), *The Hong Kong Bill of Rights: A Comparative Approach*, Butterworths Asia, Singapore, 1993.

145   Statistics on trends in Bill of Rights' cases: Johannes Chan, 'The Hong Kong Bill of Rights 1991-1995: A Statistical Overview', in George Edwards and Johannes Chan (eds), *Hong Kong's Bill of Rights: Two Years Before 1997*, Faculty of Law, University of Hong Kong, 1995, pp 7–76.

146   Johannes Chan's criticism of the Court of Appeal: *Two Years Before 1997*, pp 19–20.

146   Justice Godfrey on the quality of judges: 'The Court of Final Appeal', a seminar organised by Asia Law & Practice (A Euromoney company), Island Shangrila Hotel, 28 October 1995.

147   T L Yang's official statement on the Bill of Rights Ordinance (BORO): 'Chief Justice's statement on BORO', Government Information Service, 17 November 1995.

147   Benjamin Liu on the Bill of Rights: 'The Past, the Present and the Future of the Hong Kong Bill of Rights Ordinance', *Ming Pao*, 16 November 1995; translated by Johannes Chan and published in *Two Years Before 1997*, Appendix D.

148   Scaremongering on Litton's agenda: 'Lofty task looms for Henry Litton', *South China Morning Post*, 3 February 1996.

150   Qian Qichen on 'previous laws basically unchanged': *Xianggang Tebie Xingzhengqu Chouweihui Baci Quanhui kaimu* (The 8th Plenary Session of the Hong Kong SAR Preparatory Committee Begins), *People's Daily*, 2 February 1997, p 1.

150   Shao Tianren on Bill of Rights: 'Rights bill "twisted"', *South China Morning Post*, 28 October 1995, p 2.

152   'Ordinance is profound': Johannes Chan & Yash Ghai, *The Hong Kong Bill of Rights: A Comparative Approach*, p 2.

152   'Ingenious solution': Yash Ghai, 'The Hong Kong Bill of Rights Ordinance and the Basic Law of the Hong Kong Special Administrative Region: Complementarities and Conflicts', *Journal of Chinese and Comparative Law*, Volume 1, Number 1, Centre for Chinese and Comparative Law, City University of Hong Kong, July 1995, p 38.

152   Ordinary status of Bill of Rights: statement issued by the Attorney General's Chambers in reply to the Chief Justice's statement, 23 November 1995, p 2.

CHAPTER 5: THE ELASTIC SOCIETY

159   SRH survey of political and economic confidence during 1996: Various stories in the *South China Morning Post*: 'Public confidence boost', 29 January; 'Economic confidence on the rise', 29 April; 'Consumers ready to open wallets', 30 July; 'Faith in economy growing again', 28 October.

160   Henry Tang on flexibility: 'Economic confidence on the rise'.

163   Emigration from the 1860s to 1939: Elizabeth Sinn, Chapters 1 & 2 in Ronald Skeldon, ed, *Emigration From Hong Kong*, The Chinese University Press, Hong Kong, 1995.

163   Illegal emigration to the United States, etc: Skeldon, *Emigration From Hong Kong*, p 55.

163   Emigration patterns from the 1950s to 1990s: For a fuller discussion see Chapter 3 of *Emigration From Hong Kong*.

164   Skeldon on waves of immigration from China: *Emigration From Hong Kong*, pp 51–2.

165   Surveys on Hong Kong identity in the 1980s: *Emigration From Hong Kong*, p167.

165 More recent surveys on Hong Kong identity and political affiliation: See Joan Leung Yin-hung, 'Political Parties and Voting Choice: The 1995 Legislative Council Elections in Hong Kong', a paper presented to the International Conference on Political Development in Taiwan and Hong Kong, Centre of Asian Studies, The University of Hong Kong, Hong Kong, 8–9 February 1996, p 29.

164 The 1991 survey on identity: Wong Siu-lun, 'Political Attitudes and Identity', chapter 7 of *Emigration From Hong Kong*, pp167-168.

167 Survey of registered voters in 1995: Joan Leung Yin-hung, 'Political Parties and Voting Choice', pp 27–8.

172 Louie Kin-sheun on the Liberal Party: 'Consolidation and Marginalization: Development of Political Parties in Hong Kong', a paper presented to the International Conference on Political Development in Taiwan and Hong Kong, Centre of Asian Studies, The University of Hong Kong, 8–9 February 1996, Hong Kong, p 4.

179 The symbolism of Christine Loh's meeting with the New China News Agency: 'Johbo dui Luk Gungwai "Fatyin Yatjaan"' ('Sudden eulogies' of Christine Loh in the leftist press), *Gausap Nindoi* (*The Nineties* magazine), August 1996, p 7.

180 Registered voters attitudes towards social policy in Hong Kong: Joan Leung Yin-hung, 'Political Parties and Voting Choice', pp 25–6 (Table 6).

181 Preliminary Working Committee takes an interest in housing: 'PWC members in visit to public housing flats', *South China Morning Post*, 11 May 1995; and 'More public housing for immigrants says PWC', *Hongkong Standard*, 7 July 1995.

182 Tung on livelihood vs liberty: 'Livelihood top HK concern, claims Tung', *South China Morning Post*, 1 March 1997, p 1.

183 Tung on competitiveness and livelihood: 'Tung sets up policy taskforces', *South China Morning Post*, 22 March 1997, p 1.

184 Deng on the 'subversive' Hong Kong Alliance: originally quoted in *Wide Angle*, a Chinese magazine, and requoted in the *South China Morning Post*, 9 February 1991, and Norman Miners, *The Government and Politics of Hong Kong* (5th edition), Oxford University Press, Hong Kong, 1995, p 199.

184 Qian Qichen on June 4 rally: 'Qian says Hong Kong faces curbing of political freedom', *Asian Wall Street Journal*, 16 October 1996.

185 Lu Ping on demonstrations in Hong Kong: 'Anti-Beijing protests to be banned, says Lu Ping', *South China Morning Post*, 5 June 1996, p 1.

CHAPTER 6: A BUSINESS DEAL

190 Deng Xiaoping on maintaining prosperity and stability in Hong Kong: 'China Will Always Keep its Promises', *Selected Works of Deng Xiaoping, Volume 3 (1982–1992)*, Foreign Languages Press, Beijing, 1994, p 108.

192 Contracted and utilised foreign investment, and Hong Kong's share: calculations based on various issues of *China Statistical Yearbook*, China Statistical Publishing House, Beijing; and of the *Almanac of China's Foreign Economic Relations and Trade*, China Economics Publishing House/Economic Information and Agency.

193 Hong Kong as a 'packager' of foreign investment for China: Peregrine Brokerage, *China: Worldly Ways*, a report published in May 1995, p 20.

193 *IFR* and Capital DATA Loanware figures on commercial loans: supplied to the author by the two companies.

198 Foreign investment in Shanghai: *Statistical Yearbook of Shanghai '96*, Shanghai Municipal Statistics Bureau, China Statistical Publishing House.

200 Deng Xiaoping on Li Hongzhang: 'Our Basic Position on the Question of Hong Kong', *Selected Works, Volume 3*, p 23.

201 Li Hongzhang founds China Merchants: Jonathan D Spence, *The Search for Modern China*, W W Norton & Co, New York, 1991, p 218.

203 Bank of China history and 75th anniversary data: Bank of China (Hong Kong Branch), *75 Years in Hong Kong*, a booklet published in 1992, various pages.

203   Yun-wing Sung on the Bank of China loan to Baoshan Steel: *The China-Hong Kong Connection; The Key to China's Open-door Policy,* Cambridge University Press, Cambridge, 1991, pp 97–8.

204   Size of mainland investment in Hong Kong: main sources include the Hong Kong Chinese Enterprises Association; and Ng Sek Hong & David G Lethbridge, *The Business Environment in Hong Kong,* (3rd ed), Oxford University Press, Hong Kong, 1995, Chapter 6.

204   *Far Eastern Economic Review* on mainland investment in Hong Kong: quoted in John P Burns, 'The Role of the New China News Agency and China's Policy Towards Hong Kong', in *Hong Kong and China in Transition,* Canada and Hong Kong Papers No 3, Joint Centre for Asia Pacific Studies, Toronto, 1994, p 59, footnote 61.

204   Kim Eng Securities on mainland investment in Hong Kong: *The Rise of the Red Chips: Tomorrow's Corporate Giants,* a special report published in April 1996, p 8.

206   Kim Eng Securities on undeclared profits: *The Rise of the Red Chips,* p 8.

207   Henry Fan quote: 'Citic earmarks HK$10 billion for key China deals', *South China Morning Post,* 27 March 1996, p 1.

207   Zhu Youlan quote: 'China Resources Spin-off', *South China Morning Post,* 27 June 1996, p 1.

207   Backdoor listings: main sources include *The Rise of the Red Chips,* pp 13–50; and 'Back on its Mettle: Shougang Concord International restructures', *Window* magazine, 21 June 1996, pp 48–9.

209   Kim Eng Securities on mainland listings on the Hong Kong stockmarket: *The Rise of the Red Chips,* p 8.

209   Y C Jao on banking failure: 'Monetary System and Banking Structure', Chapter 5 in Ng Sek-hong & David G Lethbridge (eds), *The Business Environment in Hong Kong,* 3rd ed, Oxford University Press, Hong Kong, 1995, p 120.

210   Hong Kong's exports to China plummet in early 1950s: Reginald Yin-wang Kwok & Alvin Y So (eds), *The Hong Kong-Guangdong Link: Partnership in Flux,* Hong Kong University Press, 1995, p 165.

211   Re-export trends in Hong Kong: *The Hong Kong-Guangdong Link,* p 168; and *Hong Kong 1996,* the Hong Kong Government yearbook, p 447.

211   The share of Chinese goods in Hong Kong's re-export trade: Supplied to the author by the Census and Statistics Department, Hong Kong Government.

CHAPTER 7: SCALING THE HEIGHTS

222   'One Centre, Two Flanking Sectors': quoted by Liu Qingwen, 'Hong Kong PRC-Invested Enterprises: Before and After 1997' in *The Hong Kong Chinese Enterprise,* a booklet published by the Hong Kong Chinese Enterprises Association, 1994, pp 39–44.

222   Li Lanqing promises no privileges for mainland firms in Hong Kong: 'Hong Kong PRC-Invested Enterprises: Before and After 1997'.

225   Rod Eddington complaint regarding CNAC: quoted in 'Only fittest will survive in airline industry, says Citic Pacific chief', *South China Morning Post,* 20 December 1995, p 3.

225   *South China Morning Post* confident about early Dragonair deal: 10 August 1995, p 1.

227   Cathay's 'coup': 'A Wing And a Prayer', *Far Eastern Economic Review,* 9 May 1996.

227   'On course to a brighter future': *South China Morning Post,* 30 April 1996, p 3.

230   Viktor Shvets on CNAC deal: 'Airline pact seen as neat solution', *South China Morning Post,* 30 April 1996, p 1.

232   Henry Fan 'attacks' Swire: 'CITIC hits back in battle for the skies', *South China Morning Post,* 20 December 1995, p 1.

235   David Li reveals Hang Seng Bank deal: 'HSBC denies 'offer' to Bank of China', *South China Morning Post,* 3 June 1996, p 3.

238   *Financial Times* interview with the Bank of China: 'Bank of China sees value of openness in Hong Kong', reprinted in *South China Morning Post,* 8 November 1995, Business Post, p 12.

239   Ng Leung-sing on mainland business in Hong Kong: 'Banker positive on China-funded firms', *South China Morning Post*, 3 January 1997, p 4.

239   Bank of China's share of total Hong Kong market: 'Bank of China sees value of openness in Hong Kong'.

240   HSBC honours the unlawful wartime cash issue: Maurice Collis, *Wayfoong: The Hong Kong and Shanghai Banking Corporation*, Faber and Faber, London, 1965, p 240.

240   Maurice Collis on China and the bank's future: *Wayfoong*, pp 252–3.

241   'Deals offer lessons ahead of 1997': *Financial Times*, 1 May 1996, p 18.

241   Academic speculation on Hongkong Telecom's future: *Telecommunications Policy* (Special Issue: Telecommunications and the Integration of China), Volume 18, Number 3, Butterworth-Heinemann, Oxford, 1994, pp 251 & 254.

242   China's total 1995 revenue from posts and telecoms: *China Telecommunications Construction*, June 1996, Vol 8, No 4, p 10.

249   Brian Smith on selling down Hongkong Telecom: 'HKT 'most certainly not up for sale', says chief', *South China Morning Post*, 15 May 1996, Business Post, p 1.

250   New China News Agency report on Qian Qichen: 'China praises Swire over historic airline deal', *South China Morning Post*, 10 July 1996, p 1.

CHAPTER 8: A LEAKY BORDER

257   The origin of the common law: based on Peter Wesley-Smith, *An Introduction to the Hong Kong Legal System* (2nd ed), Oxford University Press, Hong Kong, 1993, pp 32–33; and Anne Carver, *Hong Kong Business Law* (2nd ed), Longman, Hong Kong, 1994, Chapter 2.

257   Peter Wesley-Smith on the rule of law: *An Introduction to the Hong Kong Legal System*, pp 14–15.

257   The Tang Code: Thomas Chiu et al, *Legal Systems of the PRC*, Longman, Hong Kong, 1991, pp 6–7.

258   The advent of rights after 1979: *Legal Systems of the PRC*, pp 37–8.

259   The declining importance of duties: Albert H Y Chen, 'The Developing Theory of Law and Market Economy in Contemporary China', a paper presented to the Conference on Market Economy and Law, City University of Hong Kong, 13–14 October 1995, p 12.

259   China borrows legal ideas from the West: *Legal Systems of the PRC*, pp 37 & 39.

261   Preference for conciliation in China: *Legal Systems of the PRC*, pp 39–40.

261   Resolve disputes through conciliation: The Hong Kong Chinese Enterprises Association, 'List of Office Bearers of the Fourth Term of Office' (undated, circa 1995). This pamphlet contains a description of the association's terms of reference.

263   'Senior cadre' corruption statistics: Andrew Wedeman, 'Corruption and politics' in Maurice Brosseau, Suzanne Pepper & Tsang Shu-ki, *China Review 1996*, The Chinese University Press, Hong Kong, 1996, pp 66–70.

264   'New high plateau': Independent Commission Against Corruption, Annual Report, 1995, p 28.

264   Figures for 1993–95 corruption reports: ICAC Annual Reports, 1994 (pp 20–1) and 1995 (pp 28–9).

265   Survey on public attitudes towards corruption: Supplied to the author by the Hong Kong Ethics Development Centre, a body established by the Community Relations Department of the ICAC.

265   De Speville on corruption priorities: ICAC Annual Report, 1994, p 10.

270   'Rules of Games' quote: taken from 'Hong Kong PRC-Invested Enterprises: Before and After 1997', *The Hong Kong Chinese Enterprise* (booklet), published by the Hong Kong Chinese Enterprises Association, Autumn 1994, p 43.

275   The advantages of competition in power generation: Christine Loh, 'Steps to Lower Electricity Charges', LegCo Panel on Economic Services, 17 February 1997.

276   Obstacles to participation of small developers in property market: Consumer Council, *Competition Policy: The Key to Hong Kong's Future Economic Success*, November 1996, p 28.

276   Examples of restrictive trade practices in Hong Kong: *Competition Policy,* pp 83–5.
278   Kleinwort Benson's estimates of the China earnings of Hong Kong companies in
       1996–2000: 'Cross-border Investors Profit from Patience', *Window,* 24 May 1996,
       p 51.

EPILOGUE: WORKING WITHIN THE SYSTEM

281   Richard Hughes on China and democracy: Richard Hughes, *Borrowed Time, Borrowed
       Place: Hong Kong and its many faces,* Andre Deutsch, 1968, p 10.

INDEX

MANAGING
IN CHINA
An Executive Survival Guide

Managing in China - An Executive Survival Guide is based on dozens of interviews with expats from all over the world who are living and working in China. It is mostly anecdotal in nature but addresses many of the important issues that face expats in hardship posts.

An Executive Survival Guide is divided into 3 main sections :

1. Surviving at work
   - Recruiting & managing staff
   - Managing customers
   - Managing suppliers
   - Managing your Chinese partner
   - Dealing with infrastructure and the political system
   - Managing your boss

2. Surviving at home
   - Finding somewhere to live
   - Getting settled quickly
   - Domestic comfort
   - Health
   - Family concerns
   - Using local services

3. Surviving socially
   - Making friends
   - Exploring your locality
   - Understanding Chinese culture

Basically a manual of advice, hints and tips for expatriates, based on other people's practical experience, **An Executive Survival Guide** will complement the technical information in the **Business Guide** series.

Recommended retail price **SGD$24.95**
ISBN **981 00 8086 7**
Available from bookstores
Fax orders to (+65) 3380073
Email orders to chris.anthony@rapa.com.2